WEBS OF KINSHIP

New Directions in Native American Studies

Colin G. Calloway and K. Tsianina Lomawaima, General Editors

WEBS OF KINSHIP

Family in Northern Cheyenne Nationhood

CHRISTINA GISH HILL

UNIVERSITY OF OKLAHOMA PRESS : NORMAN

Library of Congress Cataloging-in-Publication Data

Names: Hill, Christina Gish, 1976– author.
Title: Webs of Kinship : Family in Northern Cheyenne Nationhood /
    Christina Gish Hill.
Description: Norman, OK : University of Oklahoma Press, [2016] | Series:
New Directions in Native American Studies ; volume 16 | Includes
    bibliographical references and index.
Identifiers: LCCN 2016036151 | ISBN 978-0-8061-5601-9 (hardcover :
    alk. paper)
Subjects: LCSH: Cheyenne Indians—History. | Cheyenne Indians—
    Kinship. | Cheyenne Indians—Government relations. | Cheyenne
    Indians—Migrations. | Forced migrations—Great Plains.
Classification: LCC E99.C53 .H48 2016 | DDC 978.004/97353—dc23
LC record available at https://lccn.loc.gov/2016036151

Webs of Kinship: Family in Northern Cheyenne Nationhood is Volume 16 in the
New Directions in Native American Studies series.

CONTENTS

List of Illustrations   vii

Acknowledgments   ix

Introduction: Potatoes and Mountain Dew   3

1. Our Ancestors Were There:
   Family, History, and Native Nationhood   16

2. I Was Rich in My Relatives:
   Kinship and the Cheyenne Nation   46

3. We Are Still One Nation:
   Family in Migration and Diaspora   83

4. We Never Surrendered: Two Moons's People
   and an Alliance with General Nelson Miles   113

5. We Could Not Forget Our Native Country:
   Dull Knife and Little Wolf's People and the
   Long Journey Home   155

6. We Are Not All Fools:
   Little Chief's People and the Language of Kin   202

7. It Belonged to Us: Northern Cheyenne
   Homesteading as an Assertion of Autonomy   236

8. Make Us Strong on This Reservation: The Northern
   Cheyennes' Struggle to Remain in Their Homeland   265

Conclusion: For the Unborn   288

Appendix: The 1874 Agreement with the
    Northern Cheyennes   307

Notes   309

Bibliography   349

Index   369

Illustrations

FIGURES

Two Moons   117

Two Moons's tipi and family   143

Two Moons's children, Fort Keogh, Montana   150

Little Wolf   180

Bobtail Horse and Dull Knife   196

Little Chief   206

Black Wolf   245

Col. Nelson Appleton Miles in council with
   Cheyenne chiefs, Lame Deer, Montana   276

Indian camp at Lame Deer, Montana   292

MAPS

Treaty-designated territories of the northern plains   xiii

Northern Cheyenne diaspora   xiv

ACKNOWLEDGMENTS

I wish to thank the many people and institutions whose support made this book possible. This book, like every narrative, has been shaped by each of the relationships detailed below in profound ways, but any inaccuracies within it are solely my responsibility. During the long process of researching and writing, I have received much-needed financial support. Thank you to the University of Minnesota's American Studies program and Graduate Research Partnership Program, which both awarded me funding for research. The American Philosophical Society furthered my research with a Phillips Fund for Native American Research grant. I was also honored to receive the Newberry Library's Short-Term Fellowship that allowed me to work as a fellow in the library's extensive collection and gain guidance from other researchers working there at the time, including C. Joseph Genetin-Pilawa, Loretta Fowler, and Father Peter J. Powell. I am indebted to the entire staff of the Newberry, but especially Brian Hosmer, Laurie Arnold, and John Aubrey. Iowa State University supported further research as I worked to turn the dissertation into a book with a departmental summer research grant and the College of Liberal Arts and Sciences Early Achievement in Research award. The American Association of University Women allowed me to complete my manuscript by awarding me a Short-Term Research Publication Grant. These generous grants have made traveling to the Northern Cheyenne reservation and to archives possible.

I must also thank the many archivists whose in-depth knowledge of the collections they care for was invaluable to my work. I was at a loss when I first encountered the vast materials at the National Archives, but with the help of Mary Frances Ronan, I found letters and reports detailing many significant moments in Cheyenne history. She also helped me find one of the treasures of my archival work—the cache of letters sent from Little Chief to the president of the United States asking to be allowed to return from the South to Montana and later from Pine Ridge to Montana. A grateful thank you to Jodie Foley at the Montana State Historical Society and Tom Mooney at the Nebraska State Historical Society for sharing their detailed knowledge with me. John Doerner, the archivist at the White Swan Library at the Little Bighorn Battlefield National Monument, was an incredible resource, providing me not only with new sources but also with a sense of the landscape that was important to the Northern Cheyennes. A heartfelt thank you to the late Tom Buecker at the Fort Robinson Museum Library, who not only showed me the incredible resources he had collected for the fort's archive, but also gave me a tour of the site, showing me the original location of the Red Cloud Agency and walking me through the reconstructed barracks. His knowledge added depth to my understanding of Cheyenne history, and his warm enthusiasm for my project encouraged me to keep at it. Each of these archivists shaped my research in valuable ways. This book would not be as rich without their help.

My journey to complete this book has been shaped by many relationships. I am profoundly indebted to my first mentors in anthropology at the University of Chicago, Terry Straus and Ray Fogelson. Terry taught me how to produce ethical scholarship, and I strive to practice this every day. Ray always stood by my work, supporting me as a scholar. I was first able to imagine myself as an academic because of them. When I arrived at the University of Minnesota to complete my graduate work, I found myself lucky to be immersed in a supportive community of scholars. My dissertation committee stood by me as I fumbled with my initial attempts at research and writing. Thanks to Jennifer Pierce for her helpful insights, Brenda Child for her warm encouragement, Jean O'Brien for her tireless support, and Riv-Ellen Prell for her constant faith in the project and in me as an academic. Thanks to my Dakota professor, Neil "Chantemaza" McKay, for cultural insight gleaned through language, hours of conversation, and friendship. My fellow graduate students created a supportive community that furthered my success in uncountable ways. I am especially thankful to Jill Doerfler, Heidi Kiiwetinepinesiik Stark, Matthew Martinez, Keith Richotte, Jenny Tone-Pah-Hote, Scott Shoemaker, and Boyd Cothran for their support, insight, thoughtful commentary, endless humor, and friendship.

And finally, I am profoundly indebted to my advisor Patricia Albers for tirelessly reading drafts, making me feel like family, and taking me to task when debating my early articulations of the connection between kinship, sovereignty, and nationhood. As my mentor, Pat set a powerful example for how I should conduct myself as a Euro-American academic engaged with American Indian communities. I would not be the scholar I am without her diligence, faith, and generosity. I am also honored to be shaped by relationships with excellent scholars at the universities where I have taught, especially Claire Potter, Joel Pfister, Richard Slotkin, and J. Kēhaulani Kauanui at Wesleyan University; Danielle Moretti-Langholtz and Andrew Fisher at the College of William and Mary; and the American Indian Studies and Anthropology programs at Iowa State University. Thank you for the warm welcome and insightful conversations.

This book has also benefitted from the critical readings of many colleagues. Thank you to Robert Urbatsch, Mariana Medina, and particularly Nell Gabiam. Nell has provided feedback on every chapter as well as collegial support as I went through the publication process. I am lucky to share a department with her. Thank you to Larry Nesper and Brian Hosmer, who also gave me commentary on the entire manuscript. I am especially grateful for Brian's support and advice during my publication process. Thank you to Jacki Rand for a lunch conversation that helped illuminate my arguments surrounding diaspora. I would also like to thank my editor, Alessandra Jacobi Tamulevich, my copyeditor, Lori Rider, and my manuscript editor, Sarah Smith, who made the publishing process as quick and seamless as possible. A special thanks to Erin Greb, whose beautiful maps enhance this text. I am also grateful to all those who helped me find such unique photos for the book under such a tight deadline.

My debt to those I have spent time with at Northern Cheyenne is profound. I have difficulty putting my gratitude into words, so please know I am fully aware that this acknowledgment is in no way satisfactory. Thank you for welcoming me into your lives, families, and homes, feeding me, talking with me, and listening to me. I am honored to know you all and to be treated with such kindness and generosity. What you have taught me about what it means to be a relative has shaped me as a scholar and a person, improving both profoundly in ways I probably don't even recognize.

Last but not least, I am eternally grateful to my family—by blood, marriage, and choice. Thank you to those of you who call me sister, aunt, and cousin. I am honored you have chosen me and so thankful for your place in my life. I am especially grateful to Jade and her beautiful family for embracing me and my family. My life is richer in countless ways as a result. Thank you to my parents, John and Fay, who have supported this journey in ways too numerous to relate here. They raised a scholar, encouraging my intense curiosity from the cradle. Their enthusiasm for my vision helped me through some of the most challenging obstacles to publishing this book. My heart is also full of gratitude to Alon for believing in me from the start and for seeing the light at the end of the tunnel even when I couldn't. His unconditional love has allowed me to find the wings I didn't know I had. And finally, thank you to Benny, who arrived at exactly the right moment. His story has taught me that it's not as foolish as it might seem to believe the impossible. Impossible stories can provide one of the most powerful forces we know—hope.

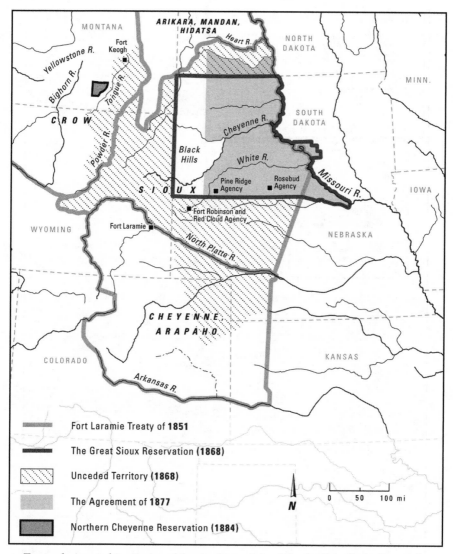

Treaty-designated territories of the northern plains. Map by Erin Greb. Copyright © 2017 University of Oklahoma Press.

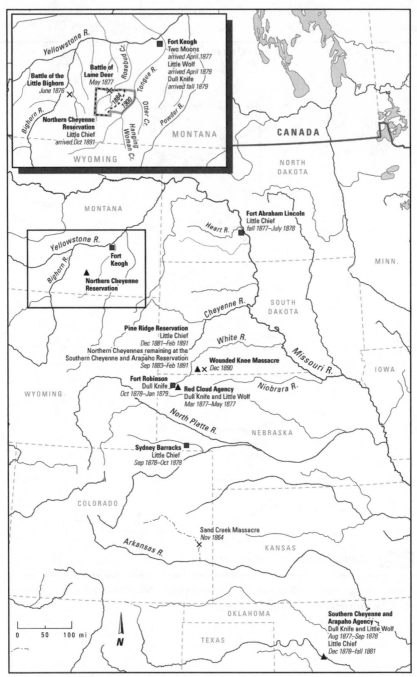

Northern Cheyenne diaspora. The dotted line around the Northern Cheyenne
Reservation indicates its borders in 1894, and the shaded gray line marks
the expansion in 1900. Map by Erin Greb. Copyright © 2017 University of
Oklahoma Press.

WEBS OF KINSHIP

INTRODUCTION

Potatoes and Mountain Dew

The summer of 2006 had been too hot to spend much time outside, but when the sun sets in Montana, everything cools down quickly so that even the hottest days fade into pleasant nights. One August evening, Ms. DG and I used the break in the heat as an opportunity to relax after dinner on folding chairs in the driveway of her apartment in Billings. We enjoyed multiple cups of coffee and watched her grandchildren ride their bikes back and forth. The sky slowly faded from rosy yellow to deep blue, and the stars began to shyly wink. In the comfort of that evening, I remembered my anxiety during my first meeting with her several years earlier.

One of my mentors, a professor who had worked with Ms. DG, had put me in contact with her. We had emailed back and forth, but I had not been able to get her to agree to work with me before I went to the reservation. I was naïve then about the importance of meeting face-to-face. I did not realize the extent of the favor I was asking. So I headed to Montana in the spring of 2004, not knowing whether she or anyone else would even consider speaking with me about Cheyenne history. When I got to Billings, I settled into a hotel room and called Ms. DG. She asked me to come to her workplace. When I met her, she suggested we head outside into the warm air for a smoke break. I still smoked then and was quick to offer her a cigarette as we settled on the concrete retaining wall under a shady tree in front of the building. I knew that Ms. DG played important roles in the political, cultural, and religious workings of her nation and was highly respected—and still is—for her knowledge of Cheyenne

3

history, but I did not realize at the time how lucky I was to meet with her. As we smoked, I started to tell her about how I imagined my project.

I told her that I was interested in the formation of the Northern Cheyenne reservation and that I wanted to trace the bands that came together there. I wanted to tell the story of how they won the reservation from the federal government on land that had never been recognized as theirs, at a time when other Native peoples were losing millions upon millions of acres. After talking for what felt like a really long time while she politely listened, I gathered the courage to ask her face to face whether she would be willing to work with me. She still did not say yes; instead, she asked if I had a tent. I was a little surprised, but I told her of course, in the trunk of my car. In what seems to be the tradition, my anthropology professors had been quite mysterious about exactly what we were meant to do in "the field," but I had known enough to bring a tent. Once she knew I was equipped, Ms. DG extended an invitation to camp with her family at the powwow that coming week. I still did not have a yes, but it was much better than a no.

I also knew that I should not arrive at the camp empty-handed, so I asked what I could bring. She answered by telling me about the first time that my mentor camped with her family many years earlier. Apparently my mentor had asked the same question, and Ms. DG, who wasn't sure exactly what her mother might need, suggested potatoes and Mountain Dew, but my mentor brought more potatoes and Mountain Dew than they knew what to do with, cases of soda and bags upon bags of potatoes. We both laughed and I relaxed on learning that my mentor had made mistakes in her day, too. Looking back, I think Ms. DG was teaching me several things at once with her story. She had humbled herself by implying that she had little knowledge of what was needed in a camp kitchen, and she indicated that whatever I saw fit to bring would be fine. She also welcomed me by reminding me that, even though I had not been aware of it, I was embedded in a larger web of personal relationships that had history and resilience. I could not process all of that in the moment—I only thought that I still wasn't sure what to bring. Slowly, I was beginning to realize that it was going to be much more difficult than I thought to move from archival research to learning from the Cheyennes themselves. Not until much later would I begin to understand the power of the large web of personal relationships that connected me to people I had yet to meet.

The powwow was my introduction to Ms. DG's extended family. It gave me my first opportunities to cook and work with her family at their campsite and to introduce my project. The family got to size me up as I negotiated unfamiliar cultural expectations. By spending time with Ms. DG's family and working alongside them, I was able to demonstrate that I was serious about learning from them. As I met more community members, I identified people who were interested in telling me about Northern Cheyenne history. Although I conducted formal interviews with members of several families, much of what I learned was told to me as I lived with and performed daily tasks alongside Ms. DG's family or at formal events such as powwows, ceremonies, and other large gatherings where I was introduced to extended family and other community members.

I spent as much time as I could on the Northern Cheyenne reservation from the spring of 2004 until the fall of 2008, arriving as soon as I finished teaching in the spring and leaving as late as I could in the fall. I was familiar with the critiques launched against non-Native researchers working in Native communities, and I had had many conversations with Native professors and graduate students about the colonial nature of much of the research conducted by outsiders. Fully aware of my position as a middle-class, Euro-American woman, I proceeded with caution, working to build trust, paying attention to protocol, and developing respectful relationships with those with whom I discussed Cheyenne history. I never went to anyone's house empty-handed, and I made myself as useful as I could. Most of my interviews were open ended; I often posed a question or two and allowed the conversation to take its course, which meant that my research evolved slowly but naturally.

I discovered that conversations flow more easily without a tape recorder. Elders valued my ability to listen and remember what they said, so we were able to have fuller discussions. In fact, most people I worked with commented at either the first or second meeting that they were glad I did not have a tape recorder or even a pencil and paper. For me, these initial interviews were meant to get to know people without the awkwardness of recording conversations, but I was so praised for this that I made the conscious decision not to record my interviews. Instead I listened as carefully as I could and used mnemonic devices to remember details. I made extensive field notes as soon as possible after conversations. At subsequent visits, I brought lists of questions to make sure that I hadn't misremembered. As a result, I have not quoted any conversation word for word. I have, however, given what I have written to each conversant and asked for corrections to ensure that when I have used their ideas, what was written reflects what they wanted to say. Some conversants wished to be recognized, but others wanted to retain anonymity, so I have encrypted these conversants' names and represented them using initials. I have used "Ms." and "Mr." to indicate the gender of the speaker, but I have attempted to exclude any other identifying information.

I had come to the community with the idea that I would research the bands that came together in Montana to form the reservation, but many Northern Cheyenne people shaped my project and encouraged me to think about the impact of family relationships on history and to more fully explore the early reservation period. I had planned to end my narrative in 1884 with the establishment of the reservation, but several Cheyennes I worked with strongly encouraged me to discuss the homesteading of reservation lands and the expansion of reservation boundaries in 1900. I knew very little about this history because it is rarely mentioned in the secondary scholarship on the Northern Cheyennes, but in the archives I discovered a powerful story that strengthened my original purpose. Furthermore, I was able to explore a history of importance to the Northern Cheyennes themselves. They talked to me about the oral histories they had heard about the expansion, they encouraged me to find government documents from this period, and their narratives guided me as I sifted through materials in the archives. They provided names of places and people and instructions for finding materials written about them. Without their direction, I would not have been able to uncover such a trove of rich documents on the early reservation period.

I gained some of my most important insights from impromptu stories like the one Ms. DG told me the day we met. In fact, during that cool, clear Montana night on lawn chairs in the driveway, I had no idea that what she was about to tell me would completely reshape the way I thought about the Cheyenne history I had been researching. We had been talking about all kinds of things, from her new cigarette-rolling machine to the multiple ways Cheyenne people have interpreted and used their own historical narratives. After a lull in the conversation, Ms. DG broke the silence by telling me that the histories that have been written about the Cheyennes by outsiders had gotten the story all wrong. I was not taken aback that a Cheyenne woman who was well versed in her family's history and in Cheyenne nationalist histories would be critical of what had been written about her people. Nevertheless, as a non-Cheyenne, I got a little nervous that she might be launching a critique of my own work, carefully veiled out of respect for me as a friend.

I asked her what she meant, hoping that she would tell me about specific narratives that outsider writers had represented inaccurately and reference texts that I knew she had read. Although I was nervous about how her comments might change the direction of my research, I was also excited to hear details that contradicted or enhanced the histories I had pored over for such a long time. I had tried to come to the reservation with a sense of humility and an openness to learn. I had spent years with excellent teachers in college and graduate school who taught me to read critically and interpret archival documents. Most of them were either Native themselves or had spent years living and working in Native communities. At the same time, I assumed that as a young, non-Native woman without much life experience or time on reservations, I would be positioned as a student at Northern Cheyenne. Actually, I discovered that I started out with less knowledge than children. Often the youngest members of the family would explain to me that I shouldn't touch this or walk over there while that was going on. I would immediately obey, but by the time Ms. DG and I were enjoying the sunset in Billings, I felt more confident about my ability to understand what people were trying to teach me. Of course, comprehending Cheyenne perspectives of history and how they are shaped by a Cheyenne worldview takes a lifetime, not just in a Cheyenne community but in a Cheyenne family, and I knew I still had a lot to learn.

Ms. DG responded to my question by explaining that non-Native authors usually focused on one man who had done extraordinary things—like Dull Knife or Little Wolf. These texts described Cheyenne history as the outcome of the actions of a few exemplary individuals. The authors assumed that these men—and it was always men—used their courage or intelligence or strategic abilities or military prowess to determine the historical trajectory of the entire people. She told me that this was simply not true. Certainly Cheyenne leaders and warriors were brave, and they led the people with intelligence and strategy, but they did not determine the course of Cheyenne history as individuals. I was impressed with this critique, but it was not new to me. Social historians have for some time taken issue with the idea that specific great men determined the course of historical events.

The alternative Ms. DG proposed, however, opened my eyes to a motivation for social and political action I had not yet considered. For her, the narrative of great men represented a profound disconnect between the individualistic way that Cheyenne history had been portrayed by scholars and the centrality of social life in the way Cheyenne people themselves presented it. Yet she was not suggesting a move to examine the impact that categories such as race, class, power, or gender had on historical action. Nor was she encouraging me to understand history by considering the impact events had on the average Cheyenne, or even Cheyennes' participation in the sweeping story of global history. Instead of any of these other social categories, Ms. DG emphasized family. She argued that non-Native scholars missed the centrality of kinship relations as a motivating factor in Cheyenne history.

Those famous Cheyenne men always thought of their relatives first, not themselves, she told me. She explained that the leaders never acted out of personal interest. When they made the decisions that are emphasized in Euro-American histories, they were thinking first of their families. She was not arguing that warriors and leaders fought and made decisions for the good of their wives, children, and grandparents, as Euro-Americans have often claimed about their political and military leaders. She was saying that Cheyenne leaders made decisions with their entire extended family in mind—not just those living today, but those who came before and those yet to be born.

In Cheyenne political thought, establishing, perpetuating, and strengthening networks of personal relationships based on kin was the
driving motivation behind not just cultural or social action but political
and economic action as well. I came to discover that these kinship
relationships were the channels that Cheyennes accessed in order
to act on economic or political decisions. As a result, each person,
including leaders, acted first to maintain the web of kinship that tied
them to each other, to their ancestors and descendants, to their cultural and political identity, and to the land and its resources. Cheyenne
life depended on this web. The decisions of leaders did not simply
account for family; they were shaped by its mechanisms. Any political
action sought to strengthen internal and external social relationships,
not to dominate land or people. Ms. DG inspired me to theorize kinship as a primary political mechanism within the Cheyenne nation,
and so I made kinship the theme of my study of Cheyenne removal
and the establishment of the reservation. She reminded me that Dull
Knife had a family. He still does today.

Dull Knife is famous in the history of the American West. In his
Cheyenne language, he was called Morning Star, but Euro-Americans
and Lakotas called him Dull Knife, the name he is most known by
today.[1] His picture hangs on the walls of countless roadside diners
throughout Nebraska and South Dakota. He has been immortalized
not only in scholarly histories but in novels and films as well. Many
tourists believe he was at the Battle of the Little Bighorn in 1876. He was
not, but his camp suffered severe retribution from Colonel Ranald S.
Mackenzie and his troops, forcing them to take refuge with Crazy
Horse's camp. After Little Bighorn, federal officials exerted more effort
to contain all Cheyenne people on the southern reservation. When
Dull Knife's group finally came to Fort Robinson in 1877, they were
forcibly removed from the Great Sioux Reservation in Dakota Territory
to the Southern Cheyenne agency in Indian Territory. He captured
the American imagination when he, along with Little Wolf and more
than three hundred men, women, and children, fled the reservation
to return north.[2] Their goal was to return home and reunite with relatives in their beloved valley along the Powder River.

The Northern Cheyennes hunted, gathered, and traded from the
Powder River region in southeastern Montana onto the plains of

Nebraska and traveled an even larger swath of land for economic, social, and political purposes. Their Southern Cheyenne relatives preferred the plains of Colorado and Kansas for their home. Families in both groups traveled this entire region to hunt, visit relatives, trade, put up Sun Dances, and join in military action. While their southern kin had signed treaties for land south of the Platte River, Northern Cheyenne bands had signed treaties that acknowledged their joint ownership, along with the Lakotas and Northern Arapahos, of the Black Hills complex. They had never signed a treaty acknowledging their ownership of the Powder River, their favorite hunting and camping grounds, but the Cheyennes knew that this land was theirs. Dull Knife and Little Wolf paid no attention to such U.S. legal barriers when they fled Indian Territory. They were more concerned with the military might, more than 2,000 men strong, biting at their heels as they ran. Dull Knife and the others were not just fleeing to return to their homeland; they were also fighting to reunite their families. Those who were removed were not only separated from their landscape but also from their families, including Lakota and Arapaho relatives as well as other Cheyenne family members—brothers, sisters, parents, and grandparents—who had escaped the long walk south. Americans were instantly fascinated by this story as they watched it unfold in their newspapers in 1879. They have not stopped telling it since.

Dull Knife's story fascinates Americans because it is heart-wrenchingly tragic and the end (at least in the popular version) is so satisfying. So many people died on the journey, and even women and children were massacred at Fort Robinson, but the United States ultimately granted the Cheyennes the land they sacrificed so much for. The Cheyenne characters represented so often in novels and movies play the role of "the Indian" in the hegemonic American nationalist narrative perfectly. They begin the story as bloodthirsty savages who threaten to disrupt U.S. national unity but, through struggle and suffering, shift to the role of noble savages who fall before the inevitability of coming civilization. While they succeeded in returning to their homeland, they were no longer able to roam the plains, living free among the buffalo. The hegemonic power of settler society subdues the savages and ultimately assimilates them. In this narrative, the United States plays the role of the repentant benefactor who abuses his might to control his most unruly children but ultimately redeems himself by granting the Cheyennes their deepest wish, while simultaneously bringing them the light of civilization. American listeners can feel sympathetic toward the romantic noble savage without pausing to question the motives of their nation.

It is easy to see where the novels and movies came from, but this is not the story Cheyenne people tell themselves, and anyone who listens closely will be left with many unsettling questions. Why is there a northern and a southern reservation if the Cheyennes are one people? Why did the United States establish a Northern Cheyenne reservation at the same time they were taking millions of acres of land away from other Native peoples through the Allotment Act and its corollaries?[3] Does it seem likely that Congress or the president set land aside for Native peoples simply because of a sympathetic response to a massacre committed by U.S. troops? Such a telling of Dull Knife's role in the American nationalist narrative ends in an emotionally satisfying way, but it is doubtful that this is where the motivation lay.

While many historians have devoted entire books to the Cheyenne exodus from Indian Territory, they often spend most of their pages on the actions and concerns of Dull Knife and Little Wolf and the other warriors. Usually, such histories argue that Northern Cheyenne military persistence in returning home either wore out government officials or inspired them to take pity on the Northern Cheyennes.[4] These narratives emphasize Cheyenne military action and the political negotiations between prominent headmen and U.S. government officials, often ending either with massacre or loss of identity through assimilation. As they write about attack after attack, focusing on the Cheyenne men who faced the soldiers from behind the barrel of a gun, they provide far fewer details of the stories of their wives and children, elders with grandchildren, and mothers with infants who were hiding within a stone's throw of the battle.[5] While the thousands of soldiers who relentlessly pursued this band had the freedom to keep their wives, parents, and children safely at home, the Northern Cheyennes did not. If they were going to return home and build their lives, they had to do it as families. The young warriors did not have the privilege of sending for their wives once they had cleared the path home. If they were going to return, they all had to go together.

When Dull Knife and Little Wolf fled Indian Territory, families in tow, they were responding to the imposition of Euro-American colonial control. The Northern Cheyennes forced onto the southern reservation may seem to have had little choice beyond the binary of assimilation to reservation life or a violent, military response. This book argues that instead, they were making a choice to return home to reunite with family members. This choice was based on Cheyenne political formations that foregrounded kinship with both people and the landscape, what I call the Native nation. These formations helped the Cheyennes, who were faced with excruciating choices, move beyond the binary of assimilation or violence. Chapter 1 explores the idea of the Native nation as an Indigenous assertion of political autonomy different from European and Euro-American conceptions of sovereignty. To illustrate the workings of the Cheyenne Native nation, in chapter 2, I explore the Cheyenne kinship system, demonstrating that the Cheyennes strategically activated kin relationships to take political, social, and economic action within their own nation and in their relationships with other Plains peoples before developing a political relationship with the U.S. government.

In chapter 3, I discuss the sacred relationships the Northern Cheyennes cultivated with their landscape, expressed through kin-based reciprocity. Then the chapter describes the disruption to these relationships created by the influx of Euro-Americans and eventually by forced migration and removal. I demonstrate that when the Cheyennes began to interact with representatives of the United States and began to negotiate their political relationship with this nation-state, these interactions were also guided by the strategic use of kinship. Furthermore, I illuminate the power of kin relationships to sustain Cheyenne social organization, not only allowing the people to maintain reciprocal relationships through upheaval but even providing them with a mechanism to continue to exercise political autonomy.

To fully illustrate the strategic use of kinship as political action, even during diaspora, in chapters 4, 5, and 6, I explore the history of three groups of Northern Cheyennes: Two Moons's people, Dull Knife and Little Wolf's people, and Little Chief's people. Each group negotiated as a political unit with representatives of the United States under different circumstances, yet each group also asserted its autonomous sense of Cheyenne nationhood through activating kinship ties and through using the language of kinship obligations. Kinship emerges as an important factor for these groups in treaty negotiations, choosing an agency, and military action. These histories demonstrate that the Cheyennes continued to assert political agency over their lives and their land through kin-based social relations even in their negotiations with the United States.

I conclude by exploring how the Northern Cheyennes continued to assert a sense of political autonomy through activating social relations and employing the language of kin during their fight to secure a permanent land base in southeastern Montana at the turn of the nineteenth century. In chapters 7 and 8, I discuss Cheyenne efforts to safeguard this land base when it was threatened by the aftermath of allotment and to sustain their current relationship with the landscape for future generations. The conclusion traces the efforts by the Northern Cheyennes to safeguard their reservation during the twentieth century. It discusses the use of kinship, particularly as a powerful metaphor, to rally the people to political action. It argues that the Northern Cheyenne people continue to the present moment to utilize kinship to understand themselves as a people—not just culturally but also politically. The stories of Cheyenne families must be included in the telling of this history not only to illustrate what was at stake for the Cheyenne people but also how the mechanisms of kinship shaped their journey home.

Thomas King muses, "The truth about stories is that that's all we are."[6] In saying so, he is sharing a profound insight. Our whole world is shaped by stories, from our own lives to the places we call home to the land itself, and our stories evolve over time. My personal story has changed as I sought new places, new knowledge, new people, and new jobs. Of course all our stories begin long before we are born, but we don't start learning them until we arrive here. From the moment we can listen, we learn who we are and what our place in the world is from the stories we hear. All of us come from stories. We know who we are because we know our ancestors, and we can only know them through stories. The stories we tell about our origins not only ground us in our past but also shape the beliefs and values that we draw on to construct our futures. As King rightly points out, those who originated from a woman who fell from the sky see themselves very differently from those whose ancestors were molded from the earth and placed in a lush garden.[7] And those whose story begins with a big bang see themselves differently still.

Stories are wonderful because they can both create and destroy. They depend on the teller and the listener for their effect, and a lot can happen as they travel from mouths to ears and from eyes to minds. For example, the stories we tell about our nations can fill us with pride and a sense of entitlement. This depends, however, on our role in the story, and our roles are shaped by the tellers and interpreted by the listeners. If our ancestors were not the ones who founded the nation, but instead were the ones who were conquered, enslaved, disenfranchised, and interred, then these national stories often act to reinscribe a hierarchy of power relations that place us on the bottom rungs. A new storyteller can make a nationalist narrative into something completely subversive. She can take an activist and turn him into a weakling or a traitor or even an emblem of the very thing he was fighting against. It all depends on who is telling the story, who is listening, and why they came together in the first place.

As I write this book, much of the dominant American society is telling stories about Native people that emphasize human suffering, the inevitability of loss, and eventual extinction, either physical or cultural. These stories are powerful in their ability to dismantle and erase Native histories and living communities. On the other hand, the stories the Cheyenne people are currently telling about themselves emphasize survival over destruction, connectedness over fracture, and commitment to land and community over dispossession. These stories helped this Plains nation survive through violence, internment, and diaspora. The stories have had the power to hold people together, individually and communally, fighting erasure and loss and breathing life into the community.

In the following pages, I'm going to tell you a story. Well, actually I'm going to tell you many, many stories. Please do not misunderstand me; I do not have the ability to tell you the stories that kept the Northern Cheyenne people strong. I have heard some of those stories. Perhaps there are bits and pieces of those stories here, but probably little more. I am not the first to tell many of the stories you will read.

Some were told to me while I listened, some were told to anthropologists decades ago and written down, and some were scribbled in letters to loved ones or inscribed in government documents. A few are my own stories, describing my process of trying to understand the bigger story I attempt to tell here. The stories we tell about ourselves and our histories shape the direction of our lives, but so do the stories we tell about others—our children, our families, our communities, those who came before us, and those who live beside us. We must be careful of the stories that we tell because, as Leslie Marmon Silko's witches learned, once they have been released, they can never be taken back.[8] These witches saw firsthand that stories can do horrible damage in the world; they create hate, war, and hunger. Yet they can also reveal beauty, encourage strength, and foster compassion. My humble wish is that the stories I am telling here will do the latter. My hope is that these stories will open my listeners up to a new perspective about American Indian history, and perhaps the United States as well. Now that they are in the world, I ask that you use them well.

CHAPTER ONE

OUR ANCESTORS WERE THERE

Family, History, and Native Nationhood

My first summer at Northern Cheyenne, I quickly realized that before anyone would talk with me, they needed to learn about me as a person. Would I listen? Was I respectful? Did I approach learning with humility? I was welcomed because a family member had introduced me. Even though I had this connection to the network of kin, I was still an outsider. I spent most of that summer learning what the community expected of researchers, such as the proper way of introducing myself, asking for knowledge in a respectful manner, listening politely, and observing preferences for tape recording or note-taking. I learned a lot by doing, but I learned even more through stories. As on every other reservation in the United States, researchers—historians, anthropologists, and sociologists—have descended on the Northern Cheyennes. They have plenty of experience fielding steady streams of questions with microphones in their faces. I heard story after story about this or that bumbling researcher who failed to be respectful or listen or who simply knew next to nothing about Native people.

Over time, many of the warnings veiled by humorous stories sank in and began to guide my behavior. I kept returning to one story because it not only taught me how to behave when seeking to learn from Cheyenne elders, but it also revealed something profound about the connection between family, Cheyenne history, and identity. During one of our many evening chats over coffee in her little kitchen, Ms. DG told me about a young man who was eager to ask her about Cheyenne history. She never told me whether he was a scholar or a journalist, but I imagined him as a documentary filmmaker. She also never told me why she agreed to the interview, but she did. Apparently he came to her house with all kinds of equipment and spent close to an hour setting it up. He positioned a chair for her ringed by bright lights to illuminate her face. He finally sat down and asked her to do the same. He pushed one of those big fuzzy microphones in her face and said, "So tell me about the Battle of the Little Bighorn."

When she told me this, we both laughed. "Of course," I said. "Everybody wants to know about the Battle of the Little Bighorn. That's all anyone ever writes about!" But I had misunderstood the point of the story. She told me kindly that what I said was true, but that she had a bigger issue—she could not talk to him about that battle. "You can't?" I asked, not masking my surprise because she seemed to know everything about Cheyenne history. She explained that she had told him that she was not the person he wanted. He had to pack up all of the equipment that he spent so much time setting up. She laughed heartily at that, but I was still confused. She paused, noticing that I still failed to understand the actual joke. You see, she gently told me, her family was not at the Battle of the Little Bighorn. She could talk about the fight led by Ranald Mackenzie against Dull Knife's village, she explained; her ancestors were there. But not the Battle of the Little Bighorn. Of course she could tell him anything that other Cheyennes knew about it or that anyone could read in books, but she could not tell him the whole story. She explained that while the Battle of the Little Bighorn has become part of the nationalist history for the Cheyenne people, the details of such histories are archived within the families whose ancestors experienced the events. Family is not simply an important part of each individual's cultural identity; it is the main path for learning social and cultural values, as well as the primary repository for Cheyenne history.

Archiving histories within families complicates the process of constructing a Cheyenne national narrative. Cheyenne tellings of the past are not often presented as part of a unified national narrative; instead, many elders weave webs of diverse narratives that parallel the webs of kinship. Cheyenne history is polyphonic because different families archive different pieces of it.[1] Some families preserve the history of the massacre at Sand Creek, some of Dull Knife and Little Wolf, some of the scouts that made an alliance with General Miles. No one can possess the "complete" corpus of knowledge about Cheyenne history because it emerges from the experience of ancestors. Although the Northern Cheyennes today use their histories to present a unified nationalist narrative, writing tribal histories and memorializing important persons in the names of buildings, the detailed, personal, and experiential component of these histories is retained in families.[2]

Like in many Indigenous communities, a Cheyenne person is expected to gain cultural knowledge—including family histories—over time in small pieces. As Clifford points out, a researcher from the outside cannot expect to gather the entirety of such knowledge and can only access fragments through "an open-ended series of contingent, power-laden encounters."[3] Within any culture, differential knowledge exists in multiple locations, affecting the results of ethnographic research. During my time on the Northern Cheyenne reservation, I gathered narratives from families who experienced different moments in Cheyenne history, but I know I have barely begun to access the knowledge that Cheyenne families collectively preserve. Furthermore, these are not my histories to claim, so it is doubtful that I heard them as a family member who had a more intimate relationship with those narratives would. I had to piece together my perceptions of Cheyenne history—by not only weaving together multiple narratives but also carefully considering how Cheyenne people today perceive the motivations of their ancestors, how they might filter them for someone like me, and why these histories are both an important part of creating the current community and of positioning that community within the dominant society.

Native oral histories archived within the community reveal the flexible constructions of Native national identity. These narratives were—and still are—transmitted along kin networks and can only approximate a description of Cheyenne history in its entirety when woven together into a collection. Historical narratives in a Native nation have loosely woven families together into a larger sociopolitical group by creating connection through shared histories, while allowing for divergent histories within families and bands. Such divergent histories did not contradict the Native nation in the way they contradict the hegemonic narratives of the nation-state. Recognizing that a Native nation's history exists as multiple narratives traced through and passed down by kinship suggests that political actions operated using a similar logic. This web of shared and divergent histories provided the flexibility to assert national autonomy while also recognizing the shifting status of both the individuals within it and the group over time.[4]

Ms. DG's critique of the body of historical scholarship about the Cheyenne people rests on her observation that kinship's centrality to the operation of the Cheyenne nation has yet to be recognized, resulting in histories that emphasize the motivations of famous men. By seriously considering her critique, I have come to view family as both a motivation for and a mechanism of Cheyenne historical action. Furthermore, using the lens she proposes to reexamine the most tumultuous moments of Northern Cheyenne removal, I have been able to demonstrate that the people not only maintained kinship ties across vast distances but also used these ties strategically to gain resources, to escape the U.S. military, and to establish alliances that in turn aided their efforts to remain a nation in their northern homeland.

By listening to Cheyenne elders focus their histories on family, I came to understand that the actions taken by the Northern Cheyennes in their efforts to remain in their homeland were embedded in a system of social relations based on kinship ties as opposed to objective sociopolitical markers. Historically, the Cheyenne nation did not need to maintain rigid cultural or territorial boundaries or require its members to submit to sovereign institutions in order to exist as a political body. Instead, as a Native nation, it depended on the maintenance of kin-based relationships that could be strategically activated for political, economic, religious, or social actions when needed. Every person understood his or her place within the Cheyenne nation in terms of privileges and obligations to other members created through relationships defined by family. While kinship acted as the mechanism through which members could take political action, the nation was also motivated by creating and sustaining social relationships, not by asserting sovereignty over its members or the land. Although kinship organized Native peoples at many levels, including the family, the clan, or the band, the Cheyenne used kin ties to construct a sociopolitical body that connected people across these smaller kin-based social units, tying people together by blood, by marriage, or by differing levels of adoptions.

Native oral histories often reveal the primacy of kinship to political and economic action, demonstrating that Native nations asserted their distinctiveness by maintaining networks of familial relationships instead of defending external boundaries supported by hegemonic nationalist narratives. Kin relations were a part of the fluid processes that affected the group's cohesion, as well as its response to external forces such as territorial or trade disputes. These networks of kin remained central as Native nations encountered Europeans and Americans and wrestled with the onslaught of colonialism.

It may seem unlikely that kinship could have the power to affect political change when a group fled a reservation for their northern homeland, outnumbered, accompanied by women and children, and with the U.S. military in hot pursuit. How could family affect more than the immediate decisions of fighting or fleeing? In Cheyenne narratives, those who fled with Dull Knife and Little Wolf did so believing that it was best for their families to maintain the kin networks that connected them to their homeland. These leaders did not impose their decisions on the people; all were free to choose to participate. Many who fled were desperate to escape the intolerable conditions on the southern reservation but also to reunite with their relatives. Cheyenne narrators describe this flight as the best option for families who had been torn apart by removal, and for children and elders, the foundations of Cheyenne family life, who were sick and dying in a strange land. Kinship played a central role in motivating the political action behind the fight to return home and in shaping the mechanisms that made it possible. Kinship also became a tool the Northern Cheyennes could use to gain leverage in their negotiations with U.S. officials over land.

When Dull Knife and Little Wolf made the decision to return north and each extended family decided whether to join or stay, this choice was discussed as a family. Sometimes individual members chose different paths, but each decision was affected in part by what was best for the family as a whole. When Ms. DG reminded me that Dull Knife had a family, she was reminding me not only that every member of the family was involved in the decision to flee, but that these family members were also thinking of their relatives who needed them in the north, and perhaps more importantly, who were yet to come. In a conversation with Alan Boye about fatherhood, one of Dull Knife's descendants stated, "If fatherhood doesn't go beyond your own off-spring then you're just selfishly protecting what you think belongs to you. Dull Knife understood the danger in that kind of fatherhood. In a way, he was a father for all of the children, even down to children of this day."[5] This philosophy played out in the decisions that he made. The people who left wanted to escape the suffering they experienced in Indian Territory, but they also wanted to secure a homeland for their great-grandchildren in the place that they loved. At all costs, they needed to protect the two greatest foundations for their future—the landscape and the unborn.

Listening for family in Native histories reveals not only the flexibility that Native people had in taking political action but also that they acted according to a set of motivations and priorities connected to the primacy of family that have not been fully recognized in Euro-American scholarship. Many scholars have addressed the importance of family for extending economic opportunities and establishing political alliances, most often between Natives and non-Natives.[6] Yet, as Donald Fixico argues, these histories still often rely on "factual interpretation of historical events and human deeds recorded in written documents," while Native histories "stress a sociocultural kinship of relationships."[7] Using Northern Cheyenne history as a case study, this book argues that because kinship ordered social, political, and economic life and determined a people's relationship to the landscape and its resources among Native peoples, kinship acted as a central mechanism through which these nations expressed political autonomy, internally, in negotiation with other Native peoples, and even in response to European and American colonial encroachment.

For several decades, scholars have sought to incorporate Native perspectives using Indigenous philosophy as a means to reflect theoretically on historical and cultural processes both within and beyond Native communities.[8] In order to develop a truly Indigenous theory, however, scholars need to be able to navigate the distinctions between Western and Indigenous perspectives.[9] Since Linda Smith launched her seminal critique *Decolonizing Methodologies*, there has been much discussion of decolonizing as a way to illuminate such distinctions. Smith points out that dominant cultural institutions have denied the historical formations of the social, political, and economic difficulties Native communities struggle with and that such a denial also erases Indigenous peoples' claims to their history, humanity, and even to hope.[10] It is vital, therefore, to disentangle Native political formations from Western ones in order to reveal Indigenous motivations in their encounters with European and American empires.

One way to begin the decolonizing process is to listen carefully to Indigenous histories—not simply the events of the narrative but how the narrative is told. Geoffrey White has argued, "if representations of history (or more generally, the past) mediate social relations and identities, then they become tools for shaping those identities."[11] The way people tell their history reveals its purpose. By telling histories from the perspectives of the different families that make up the web of Cheyenne relationships, the tellers acknowledge the centrality of kinship not only to Cheyenne identity but also to historical action.

Just as Indigenous histories reveal the different perspectives that shape Native sociopolitical organization, hegemonic nationalist histories illuminate the assumptions that undergird the formations of specific nation-states. Unlike the polyphonic nature of Cheyenne history, the nationalist U.S. history found in textbooks, children's media, and mainstream film has often been narrated as homogenizing and progressive, uniting certain sections of the population to the exclusion of others.[12] Of course, American Indian people have played important roles in U.S. narratives since the earliest imaginings of the nation, yet these histories supported U.S. hegemony by telling the story from only one perspective.[13] Until the late twentieth century, American Indians were mainly granted stereotypical roles, appearing as warriors and chiefs responding to American encroachment, as princesses aiding the movement of settlers, or as victims of progress.

Frederick Hoxie has demonstrated that until very recently the description of Native histories within American history remained "contained by the all-encompassing, intersecting narratives of modernity and the 'rise' of the nation."[14] In the past few decades, theorists have begun to question these overly clear distinctions between people with history and people without history so common in popular narratives of American Indian peoples.[15] Johannes Fabian has argued that scholars had constructed a hierarchy based on time that represented "the other" as atemporal and ahistorical.[16] In most U.S. nationalist narratives, Native people have not been portrayed as agents in their own histories. They simply remained as they always had been until a European or American power acted on them.[17]

Ned Blackhawk and Jacki Thompson Rand have pointed out that even American history that has included Native perspectives has still neglected to recognize the internal colonialism perpetrated by the United States on American Indian people as a part of nation-building.[18] Blackhawk has noted that Native people "are not simply *peoples with a history*" whose experiences of violence and dispossession can be reshaped and inserted into the dominant narratives of U.S. history.[19] When Native histories are used in this way, the Native role becomes reactive and only requires focus on the actions of a few highly visible individuals, such as political or military leaders. In order to understand Indigenous motivations during colonial encounters, scholars must dismantle the legacies of colonialism present not only in their sources but also in the predominant discourses.

Nation-state histories create a hegemonic nationalist identity by constructing specific social roles as the basis for belonging that serve to shunt some people to the edges. Narratives of bloodthirsty Indians construct settlers as victims in order to justify conquest first through extinction and then assimilation. Violence is not only explained away as self-defense but also portrayed as a natural part of the exercise of authority that tames chaos to make one group the sovereign and the other its subject.[20] Narratives of noble savages helping Euro-American settlers construct Native peoples as collaborators in settlement justifying theft of land, expulsion, and ultimately absorption and erasure. These portrayals of Native roles in popular history have helped establish a nationalist identity for Americans, as united against a common enemy by creating a sense of pride in accomplishment at settling a hostile landscape and as the rightful heirs of the landscape through a claim of moral, spiritual, and biological supremacy.

To justify European conquest, Indigenous peoples the world over had to be constructed as natural subjects, lacking the ability to assert sovereignty. Thomas Hobbes amplified this perception by asserting that human beings enter society in a state of nature.[21] He proposed that this state is prior to the civil state and that by definition order can only exist after humanity has submitted itself to the rule of common measure, thereby ending the chaos of a world where each individual strives for his own desires.[22] Notions of the orderly interior and chaotic exterior, as well as the naturalness of the relationship of ruler to subject, certainly colored European and Euro-American writings about Native people. These theoretical constructions encouraged scholars initially to view Native peoples as existing in a state of nature, incapable of submitting themselves to a sovereign. As a result, these writers often recognized the shared cultural heritage of Native peoples but not their distinct collective political organization.

Early scholars of American Indian culture often employed these constructions when describing Native groups. Lewis Henry Morgan, one of the first anthropologists to explore the sociopolitical mechanisms of American Indian peoples, recognized the centrality of kinship to shaping American Indian communities in his seminal research, yet he used this fact to place Native peoples on the lower rungs of the evolutionary scale. He argued that peoples who assigned status, protected property rights, and secured personal safety using kin-based relationships existed in a state of savagery or barbarism.[23] He declared that civilization emerged when the protection of the law or the state replaced the influence of kin connections.[24] Morgan's evolutionary assumptions drew on the understanding of his time that Indigenous peoples existed as loosely organized conglomerations of kin whose sense of responsibility did not extend past the self and the family.

Foucault has demonstrated that the justification of colonialism as a way to save its inhabitants from an assumed chaotic "state of nature" occurring in the so-called New World shaped the emergence of nationalist sovereignty in Europe as well. He has argued that in colonial models, sovereignty shifts from rule by a victor in a reversible battle to the result of a human will to overcome the state of nature.[25] This construction allowed enlightenment thinkers to present sovereignty as a question of rights rather than domination. Under these conditions, non-European peoples were not simply understood as dominated peoples, excluded from the ranks of those allowed to exercise sovereignty. Instead, all humanity was constructed as part of one ontological universe—all subject to the same abstract rules—and then divided into those who have the right to exercise sovereignty and those who need others to do it for them.[26] Colonialism imposed this system on all peoples, giving them only two ontological positions—that of a people able to subdue others with their sovereign power or that of subjects without the ability to assert sovereignty. For Europeans, this hierarchy ordered all social organization, and the only access to power came through subjugation.

The nation-state operates within the same ontological universe of colonialism but does not emerge until the eighteenth century. Originating in Europe from Enlightenment critiques of older socio-political formations, the nation-state used mechanisms such as news-papers, compulsory public education, and public institutions including museums and libraries to impose the concept of a uniform citizenry contained by a clearly demarcated sociopolitical and geographic boundary.[27] These nationalist constructions morphed into a means of neatly categorizing humanity horizontally across space as belonging within particular territories and vertically into classes of peoples more or less fit for participating in citizenship. This lack of fluidity established incredible power for those who claimed the right to set the bounda-ries, creating a similar social hierarchy within and among nations.

As part of the Enlightenment ideology that critiqued power based in religion and family, fledgling nationalists constructed territorial boundaries based on contractual obligation in opposition to kingdoms and empires based on divine or familial obligations. Membership was marked by the contracts of citizenship. Territory was carved out through purchase or treaty. Kinship ties no longer sustained political alliances; instead, documents articulated the relationships between political powers. Political power became located in institutions, laws, and con-tracts instead of in individual or familial claims asserted through either a sheer show of force or claims to divinity or both. European nation-states utilized their newfound power not only to set boundaries and categorize their citizenry but also to literally contain peoples, through colonial practices abroad and by enforcing policy using jails, schools, factories, and the military at home.

European nationalist ideologies came to naturalize the concept of bounded, uniform human groups as the proper way to order human social organization. The categories used in nation-states to order human-ity became commonsensical for their citizens, creating a lens through

which all social formations have come to be viewed as easily demarcated groups based on language, laws, and customs.[28] This definition
of "nation" became the model for understanding group political autonomy, and scholarship often assumed that, while Indigenous peoples
lacked national institutions, the construction of their sociopolitical
formations mirrored those of the ideal nation-state in the sense that
they had static territorial boundaries, ethnically homogenous membership, and internally uniform cultural traits.[29] Viewing Indigenous
peoples as the proto-nation-like entities that most Euro-Americans
have called "tribes" provided both scholars and colonial government
officials with a set of categories that facilitated their efforts to contain,
define, and control Native peoples.

The categorization of Native peoples as "tribes" and not "nations"
reached prominence in the nineteenth century and was based on the
idea of a tribe as a bounded ethnic unit without true political autonomy.
As Eric Wolf has demonstrated, a bounded understanding of human
social organization emerged with the rise of the social sciences. As
part of this epistemological shift, scholars came to endow "nations,
societies, or cultures with the qualities of internally homogenous and
externally distinctive and bounded objects," making it "easy to sort
the world."[30] By the turn of the twentieth century, the concept of
nation-state so thoroughly governed scholarly thought on human
organization that a totalizing explanation for human groupings developed from it.

This period also was marked by an intensified focus on asserting
U.S. nationalism at home and abroad, creating a strong drive for a
homogenization of American nationalist identity. American Indian
peoples found themselves subject to intense assimilation pressures
while at the same time represented as exotic but bounded, homogenous entities. Susan Sharrock demonstrated that, prior to the 1970s,
most scholars imagined tribes as composed of members "of one ethnic
identity who spoke a common language and shared a common lifeway
in contiguous territories."[31] Morton H. Fried noted that ethnographers
had tended toward representing tribes as "a reality transcending
time" that had a history of integrity and homogeneity.[32] As Sharrock
and Fried demonstrated, the tribe was imagined as a limited social
community that emerged from a relationship with a particular, bounded

landscape, producing a unified cultural and spatial ethnicity, although it did not necessarily produce rational citizens. Such representations paralleled constructions of the nation-state as eternal, emerging from a condition of purity, and made up of a diverse population unified in national purpose and recast as homogenous. These state-centric assumptions about Native sociopolitical organization imposed a definition of "tribe" onto Native nations without acknowledging any of the political power granted to the nation.

The Cheyennes have not escaped these definitions. Into the early twentieth century, scholars such as George Bird Grinnell, Fred Eggan, E. Adamson Hoebel, and Karl N. Llewellyn assumed that the Cheyennes had a fixed membership, and that tribal membership and Cheyenne descendancy were one and the same thing.[33] They represented Cheyenne people as having a homogenous tribal identity unified by shared language, religion, customs, and territory bounded by geographical borders. Yet these scholars were central to countering the social evolutionary theory that kin-based social organization is inferior to the state's political system, an important endeavor in its own right. In their haste to right this wrong, however, they often overemphasized the unity and homogeneity of the Cheyenne people.[34]

American perceptions of "the American Indian tribe" reflected a certain ambiguity about acknowledging the political status of Native nations, present in both U.S. policy and scholarship about American Indian peoples. Throughout the history of the United States, officials representing the government have treated Native people as both members of their own politically autonomous tribal nations capable of self-rule and as irrational, chaotic noncitizens prone to factionalism who should be incorporated as wards into the American nation.[35] Depending on the agenda of the moment, the ambiguity of these two constructions has allowed both scholars and officials to portray Native groups either as bounded entities with a uniform membership, culture, territory, and occasionally with political agency similar to the state, or as chaotic, boundless, irrational entities lacking national formation.[36] Both constructions represent American Indian peoples through the lens of the nation-state, defining them either as parallel to the nation-state for purposes of containment or as contradictory to the nation-state for purposes of control. A bounded tribal nation can be categorized and therefore contained and controlled. A boundless entity must be forced to submit to mitigate the threat its chaos poses to the stability of the state. Therefore, both constructions legitimate the state's domination of Native peoples.

Despite their European colonial origins or perhaps because of them, state-centric constructions of the tribal nation based on objective criteria, such as language, religion, or territory, have had incredible staying power. Some Native people have become just as wedded to the concept of "tribal nation" as Europeans and Americans, but for different reasons. For Native peoples, the ambiguity of the term "tribe" and the comparisons made between it and the nation-state could be used to both maintain distinctness in the face of assimilationist pressures and to justify self-governance. Representing one's group as the unified cultural entity called a tribe has given Native nations some validity in the national and global political arena. Tribe has been a political marker that Europeans and Americans can understand, even if it has lowered Native peoples in their hierarchy. Therefore, Native people have used the nationalist constructions embedded in the term "tribe" strategically to establish a recognizable political identity when negotiating with the United States.

Since contact Native nations have gradually adopted political formations that resemble European concepts of nationalism, including some of the trappings of the state—discourses, institutions, policies, and practices—in their efforts to gain the United States's recognition of their sovereign status.[37] Scott Richard Lyons has noted that because the nation-state is such a dominant political construction, all nations must make political claims using the universal language and conceptual apparatus of the state. When articulating their own political autonomy, Native people have had to speak "in a discursive context that, thanks to colonization, is never of pure origin."[38] To erase the implications of chaos and factionalism inherent to the term "tribe," Native peoples have emphasized the bounded and homogenous aspects of the concept at the expense of the past fluidity of the Native nation.

The ways in which Native people construct and exercise political autonomy today has been shaped by five hundred years of colonization and specifically by U.S. assimilationist policies over the past hundred years. Native political assertions must be situated within the historical and cultural relationships in which they are articulated.[39] During Euro-American colonization, Native people used the terms "tribe" and "nation" to carve out the political space they needed in the dominant discourse so that they could be heard. While Native people incorporated Euro-American ideas into their political forms, because of its fluid nature the Native nation remained, allowing for contingent meanings without disintegration. Regardless of the problems with the concepts of tribe, nation, and sovereignty in Euro-American social science and political constructions, Native people have taken these terms, shaped them, and modeled them to fit their own political needs.

Around the turn of the twenty-first century, American Indian studies scholars began to challenge the prejudices of Euro-American nationalist constructs and attempted to demonstrate that Native peoples exist as sovereign entities based on factors other than those put forth by the state.[40] There has also been an effort in current scholarship to demonstrate that Native people manipulated Euro-American ideas and practices to maintain a sense of sovereign identity in the face of colonial oppression designed to reshape and subsume Indigenous constructions.[41] Sami Lakomäki cautions, however, that current revisionist approaches often assume Native national formations to be the products of European colonial expansion.[42] He and several other scholars have begun to explore forms of political expression that privilege Native articulations, recognizing that previous scholarly constructions of Indigenous sovereignty have emerged in comparison to state formations, focusing on external mechanisms of social change.[43] Scholars have also begun to recognize the distinction between the fluid political constructions of the nation that have existed historically and its more specific political form, the state.[44]

Although Native people often did not have rigidly structured political organizations, they clearly held autonomous political powers that Europeans could recognize from the moment of contact. Early chroniclers seem unfazed by the fluidity of Native political organization. They acknowledged Indigenous categories of leadership and negotiated international political activity with an awareness of Native constructions. Perhaps these Europeans could more easily recognize the political within these fluid social worlds because their own political institutions were in flux. In fourteenth- and fifteenth-century Europe, principalities struggled to secure land, church leaders and noble families fought each other for control, and alliances shifted to suit the needs of the moment. For these Europeans, sovereignty had not yet been divested from personal authority. Although they might have denigrated Native political organizations as not sanctioned by the Christian God, they still could recognize these kin-based organizations as political. This suggests that Indigenous sovereignty is inherent and therefore does not depend on the recognition of the state.

While the political constructions of Native nationhood in American legal and cultural discourses have changed over time, the recognition of American Indian political bodies as nations has held up throughout the history of the United States, even when under attack. The fledgling United States constructed its relationship with Native groups as between nations, establishing treaties with them, and in turn encoded this into the policies and laws of the new government.[45] In fact, the potential of Native political organization so impressed Benjamin Franklin that he looked to the Iroquois Confederacy as a model for the new government he helped develop.[46] Native nations have extraconstitutional status today because they were defined in the Constitution as distinctive polities separate from the United States and the states of the union.[47] The United States reaffirmed this status by negotiating with Native governments through nation-to-nation relationships articulated in treaties. Native nations made their own legal and political decisions, regulating themselves entirely, until Congress passed the Seven Major Crimes Act in 1885 that gave the federal government the right to try to punish members of Native nations that committed serious crimes, such as murder.[48] Further, although federal and local government officials have often broken treaties, these documents have never been fully discarded as markers of Native sovereign status. While Native peoples are often represented as conquered peoples, the United States did not deal with them as such until rather late in the nineteenth century.

Although the United States still recognizes the limited sovereignty of the Native nations within its borders today, the political autonomy of these nations has never depended on this recognition. Because these nations were politically and militarily powerful when the United States was established, it was to the advantage of the new nation-state to recognize them as sovereigns. For Native peoples, however, their autonomy existed before the drafting of the Constitution and the founding of the United States, and it continues to exist today outside of the state or the Constitution.[49] Native sociopolitical bodies have always been autonomous entities because an inherent sense of political autonomy always exists in self-governing groups.[50]

Recognizing the inherent autonomy of Indigenous political formations without the state, however, has only been a first step. Scholars have also worked to delineate the mechanisms through which Native nations articulated political autonomy before incorporating state-centric formations. Vine Deloria and Clifford Lytle proposed the concept of "the People" as separate from nationhood, stating, "The idea of the People is primarily a religious concept" that has its beginning in time immemorial.[51] Frequently the People lived together but did not see themselves as a distinct group until they were instructed through a holy man or other figures of cosmic importance and were given ceremonies and rituals. Native nations often point to this as a moment of origin when the People were brought together into a nation and were given rules to live by, emphasizing both the religious and the sociopolitical elements embedded in the idea of the People.[52] The Cheyennes view the time when Sweet Medicine arrived to teach political organization and religious ceremonies as the genesis of their nation. Prior to this point, according to oral histories, although the Cheyennes existed, they did not exist as a nation with a distinct sociopolitical order.[53]

Drawing on Deloria and Lytle, I use the term "people" to refer to a group that is held together by cultural connectedness. While the term can refer to a nation, because all nations are made up of one or many peoples, it also refers to a group less formally. During the upheaval of colonialism, the mechanisms necessary for Native nations to operate remained, but members were not always able to access them, so they sometimes operated as peoples. Yet, during this same period, they could occasionally shift between a people and a nation because of the flexibility of kinship as a political conduit.

Tom Holm, J. Diane Pearson, and Ben Chavis have taken the concept of The People further, reimagining Native group identity. In developing the idea of peoplehood, the authors attempted to move beyond the rather ambiguous term "ethnicity" and to transcend the notions of "state," "nation," and "tribe." They defined the concept of peoplehood in terms of four factors: language, sacred history, religion, and land, contending that each factor combines to form the matrix that supports a group's distinctive identity. They asserted that "A people, united by a common language and having a particular ceremonial cycle, a unique sacred history, and knowledge of a territory, necessarily possesses inherent sovereignty. Nations may come and go, but peoples maintain identity even when undergoing profound cultural change." For the authors, the sovereignty of a peoplehood does not depend on the state. Instead it exists beyond and can continue without the state, and sometimes in spite of the bounded constructions imposed by the state. They have argued that Indigenous peoplehoods were and are culturally distinct, self-perpetuating, sociopolitical entities, and therefore sovereign, proposing that the concept of peoplehood explains a group's resiliency in the face of profound changes imposed by colonialism.[54] This is a compelling argument, as long as the language, sacred history, religion, and landscape of one peoplehood can be neatly distinguished from those of another.

For Native people on the plains, however, such distinctions were seldom possible. Historically, Plains groups rarely asserted political autonomy by delineating and then protecting static geopolitical boundaries. Furthermore, group identity for Plains peoples was defined within a shifting political, economic, and cultural matrix rather than fixed categories such as language, religion, territory, or other cultural traits. The nineteenth-century Cheyennes complicate attempts to neatly categorize the identities of Plains nations because they shared territory, treaties, and relatives with the Lakotas and Arapahos, and their language is very similar to Arapaho. They shared sacred landscapes and even some religious narratives with both of these groups, and with the Kiowas and Kiowa-Apaches.[55] Cheyenne national identity has never been static. Some bands of Cheyennes aligned themselves more closely with the Lakotas, some aligned with the Arapahos, and some were allies with the Kiowas. Some bands moved onto the southern plains, and others headed north from the Missouri River. While these widespread bands shared language, religion, and political organization, individual Cheyenne people debated their nation's course of action and the future of their community.[56] Defining Native group identities by objective criteria such as language, religion, cultural traits, or even a bounded territory denies these groups the intellectual autonomy to creatively negotiate group identity and to exist as a people on completely different terms.

On examination of the political and economic actions of American Indian peoples historically, it becomes clear that peoplehood cannot account for the shifting, flexible, and hybrid nature of the expression of political autonomy by Native nations. Anthropologists have been critical of such bounded representations of Plains peoples for some time.[57] Scott Richard Lyons heavily critiques what he calls "the problematic peoplehood paradigm" as essentialist and therefore unable to account for the diversity of today's Native communities.[58] Alexandra Harmon, Karen Blu, and Loretta Fowler have all demonstrated that group identity is defined within a shifting political, economic, and cultural matrix rather than fixed categories such as language, religion, territory, or other cultural traits.[59] These scholars argued that Native people have the agency to control, shape, and reshape who they are in relation to changing contexts while maintaining their own fluid collective identities. More recent scholarship has recognized that assuming that Native sociopolitical organization and interaction mirror the rigid categorical constructions of the state ignores the complexity of Native historical action in a way that benefits the hegemonic narrative of the United States.[60]

Because the categories of language, religion, history, and territory have become so naturalized during the emergence of the nation-state as markers of distinct group identity, however, they have contributed to problematic constructions of Plains history. For example, if Plains peoples are divided into nationlike tribes with unified memberships and bounded territories, then a successful military campaign against a tribe would result in the capture of their territory and control over the population. Conversion to Christianity and language loss invalidate sovereignty based on the maintenance of Indigenous language, history, and religion. If tribes had been originally bounded like nations, considering the extreme disruption they experienced through military conquest, coerced conversion to Christianity, and forced assimilation, it would be easy to construct them as conquered and controlled by colonial violence.

Recently, the use of sovereignty as a framework for describing Indigenous communities has encountered equally suggestive critiques.[61] Over the second half of the twentieth century, sovereignty was imagined as the ability to establish some sort of national independence; therefore, oppressed peoples have often marked their suffering in relation to their ability to effectively exercise sovereignty over their own communities. Powerful critiques emerged, however, as scholars began to realize that the history of state formation in the Western hemisphere has been intimately connected with the colonial endeavor there, particularly certain constructions of sovereignty based in the Christian church and structured by a social hierarchy that separates the sovereign from the subject.[62] According to Alvaro Reyes and Mara Kaufman, such constructions of sovereignty allowed for the creation of a topography of subjects and sovereigns by distinguishing the norm as inside the boundaries and chaos as outside. The conditions for creating this topography were only apparent after the establishment of contact with peoples previously unknown to Europe—in the Americas. Reyes and Kaufman argue that Juan Ginés de Sepúlveda, the official chronicler for the Spanish king in the mid-1500s, established the building blocks of the modern notion of sovereignty when he proposed the necessity of a dominant and subordinate faction in all relations to justify conquest of the Americas.[63]

The European nationalist construction of sovereignty has been so problematic that Taiaiake Alfred has proposed that Native peoples discard the idea all together. He has suggested it is useless to Indigenous political efforts because it cannot be separated from its European roots in the Christian church and in monarchy.[64] For Alfred, Western notions of sovereignty should not be applied to Indigenous groups because they utterly fail to describe past political organization, nor do they serve these communities in efforts to gain autonomy today. His critique emerges, in part, as a response to several hundred years of Euro-Americans imposing state-centric constructions on Native peoples despite their inappropriateness for ordering Indigenous lifeways.

The ideology also leaves non-Western peoples with little alternative other than to demand inclusion within the nation-state paradigm, simply to gain recognition of their humanity and to deny that they exist only in a "state of nature." These efforts to assume sovereignty, however, ultimately demand that groups abandon pieces of their worldview because sovereignty is by definition in conflict with it.[65] When the United States asserted its sovereign status over Native peoples and declared them subject to the state, many histories represent Native groups as acquiescing to this role by eventually assimilating or rejecting these new boundaries through both military and political action. K. Tsianina Lomawaima has argued that Native peoples have often found themselves stuck in this binary when dealing with a nation-state that seeks to maintain the individual status of Indian people as wards and the tribal status as domestic dependent nations. She has encouraged scholars to move creatively beyond the binary, asking, "How might we think of sovereignty in a less self-centered, reactive way?"[66] These scholars are searching for something beyond this polemic of Native peoples as either chaotic, ravaged by colonial violence, and stripped of their ability to govern, or bounded, sovereign peoplehoods reduced to essentialist definitions of the nation with their rights to self-determination intact.

Instead of relegating Native political assertions to those easily recognizable within Euro-American forms, this book seeks to illuminate older political formations embedded in family networks that Cheyenne peoples used not only to advance their political agenda concerning land during the colonial period, but to attempt to shape Euro-American responses as well. Kathleen DuVal has revealed the European recognition of this type of political autonomy, arguing that before 1820 in the heart of North America, Native people were more often able to shape the style and content of intercultural relationships than non-Native newcomers. DuVal has coined the term "Native Ground" to describe the power of Native control and the fact that non-Natives only gained political power in these regions through diplomacy and alliances with Native peoples.[67] Anne Hyde has described the same circumstances on the plains, arguing that before the 1860s, political encounters were dominated by the expectations of kinship.[68] For both DuVal and Hyde, the Native Ground breaks down as non-Natives flood the regions and are able to demand increasing political power without relying on alliances with the Native inhabitants.

They argue that the Native Ground as a place where Euro-Americans had to follow Indigenous rules eventually dissipated with the influx of Euro-American military men and settlers, often ushered out with extreme violence.

Recognizing that colonial violence dramatically reshaped American Indian communities has been one way that scholars have used to destabilize the bounded, ahistorical, and apolitical analysis of American Indian history.[69] The physical violence inflicted by the military and by some settlers; the economic violence of theft of land and destruction of resources; and the psychological and cultural violence of remapping, renaming, census taking, boundary enforcement, missionizing, and educating necessitated new and creative responses from American Indian people. Certainly American Indian people struggled to maintain their Native nations under extremely oppressive colonial forces; however, as Rand suggests, it is important to recognize the destructive results of colonialism as well as the creative and productive responses to oppression that have emerged.[70] During colonial encounters, both the colonizers and the colonized worked to create the new sets of conditions that would come to shape their lives, although in unequal relations. Scholars have also begun to warn against the assumption that dispossession was the inevitable outcome of violent encounters between Europeans and Native people.[71] They have revealed that in some regions, Native people held the upper hand, creating prosperous collaborations with newcomers for centuries after contact. They have also noted that Natives sometimes take on the roles of conquerors or settlers and that sometimes settlers are as subject to the violence of colonialism as Natives.[72]

While it is true that the influx of Euro-American settlers created extreme chaos for Native peoples, I argue that even after the 1860s on the plains, Native people did not acquiesce to the impositions of the settler state. Although they no longer dominated the Native Ground, Plains people continued to depend on diplomacy and alliances grounded in the rules of kin to order their lives and their relations with other Native nations and even with the United States. DuVal and Hyde have both argued that these rules involved accepting places within systems of real and fictive kin that imposed obligations and privileges on each person.[73] Hyde calls this relational outlook a basic cultural tenet for Plains nations. This outlook created the mechanisms that not only defined membership within a Native nation but drove its workings as well. Native people did not give up this cultural tenet simply because they had lost the upper hand. In fact, the Northern Cheyennes continued to use it to determine their political course to the best of their ability given the circumstances. Furthermore, this relational outlook survived colonial impositions and allowed Native nations to continue to assert some political autonomy, even though it was limited by both violence and colonial power.

A profound impact of colonial violence is the imposition of neatly bounded social categories designed to ease the visibility and therefore the control over Native people. By emphasizing violence, scholars risk reifying these social categories, particularly the portrayals of Native nations as eternal, bounded tribal entities or as chaotic, loosely formed conglomerations that lack self-determination. But neither of these categories accurately reflects Native political action prior to or during their dealings with colonial encroachment.[74] Illuminating kinship as a component of Indigenous theory using the case study of Cheyenne history, and thereby granting the processes of political cohesion to families, disrupts these polemic portrayals of Plains Indian history and reflects a more Indigenous political perspective.

In an effort to navigate the rapidly changing circumstances of the nineteenth century, Cheyenne people utilized both the implementation of violence and the articulation of kin ties to assert political agency. While violence kept encroaching settlers and the U.S. military at bay for short periods of time, the political mechanisms embedded in kin systems allowed the Cheyennes to shape their political and economic relationships with newcomers according to their own cultural perspectives as opposed to simply responding to colonial impositions. Although they were not able to use kin networks to completely deflect colonial impositions, the Cheyennes never allowed these networks to unravel but instead maintained them because they were a more effective tool for long-term survival than violence. Therefore, the Cheyennes were still able to draw on these kin-based networks during removal and diaspora to take political action and even secure access to land. At certain moments in history, Cheyenne people garnered more success at undermining colonial hegemony through accessing and activating multiple kin-based relationships to take action than by responding to colonial violence with violence.

Yet simply including kinship in a discussion of Cheyenne history is not enough. Several scholars working with the Cheyennes throughout the twentieth century have researched Cheyenne kin relationships and their impact on social relations.[75] For example, George Bird Grinnell and E. Adamson Hoebel both delineated Cheyenne kinship terms and the social behavior that these relationships entail; however, they failed to explore the way these relationships shaped political and economic action either within or beyond the nation. Fred Eggan did address the relationship between social relations and economic action within the Cheyenne kinship system, but his interpretation was highly deterministic. Living kinship is not neatly structured; it changes over time and its functions shift, providing the ability to respond to changing political and economic circumstances. What's more, kinship rarely functions in one way. The function does not determine the outcome, nor does the structure determine the function. Eggan's descriptions of what kinship feels like for those embedded in it, how people employ it, and the cultural expectations surrounding it ring true, but his dependence on the concepts of structure and function created an overly simplified, ahistorical explanation.[76] When American Indian history is embedded within the context of social relations, however, a narrative emerges that can point to the mechanisms through which Native nations continued to assert a sense of political autonomy that could withstand U.S. colonialism.

In order to emphasize kinship as central to both Cheyenne political organization and articulations, I use the term "Native nation" to describe Cheyenne political formations as distinct from European understandings of the nation-state. Native nationhood is not just an assertion of the binding nature of a communal Indigenous identity defined by kin, nor simply the ability to establish a national independence, but the kin-based mechanisms that a group used to assert its distinctiveness and to make autonomous political decisions. Native nationhood articulated not only what it meant to call someone Cheyenne or Lakota, Wintu or Hopi, Hochunk or Choctaw, but also the privileges and obligations associated with that designator.

Although ease of use necessitates an English term, "nation" is not a perfect descriptor. However, its history is much more fluid than that of "tribe" or "sovereignty" because it has never had a specific connection with the Christian God or with the emergence of the state. Over time the term "nation" has been used to refer to cultural political organization ranging widely from rigid nation-state formations to loose pre-state conglomerations of like-minded peoples who share cultural attributes. I take advantage of this loosely defined term to describe both flexible, kin-based, pre-reservation Native sociopolitical formations and state-based formations. I distinguish between these two forms, using "Native nation" for the first and "nation-state" for the second, but I include "nation" in each to imply shared political organization. After all, there are many nations of people today existing as entities with a legal status that distinguishes them from the states they dwell within.[77] These nations often share a cultural heritage, but they are not simply ethnic groups. They have their own political systems that exist often beyond the state and sometimes at odds with it.

In the current global system, dominated by nation-state constructions, Indigenous peoples often combine nationalist ideologies with Native nationhood. I use the term "national" in reference to Cheyenne history to indicate both the sovereign status of the Cheyenne people today as recognized by the United States and the nationalist level at which some Cheyenne historical narratives currently operate. Both the Northern and Southern Cheyennes use many of the histories related in this book to assert a unified, sovereign cultural and political status in relation to the United States. I imagine these forms not as separate spheres or evolutionary phases but as fully realized social formations existing along a spectrum. For example, most tribal governments in the United States today draw on both forms simultaneously to construct their political sphere.

Vine Deloria and Clifford Lytle illuminate this spectrum by distinguishing between nationhood and self-government, arguing that nationhood "implies a process of decision making that is free and uninhibited within the community" and isolated from outside factors while it considers its options. Self-government "implies a recognition by the superior political power that some measure of local decision making is necessary," but it also implies that the superior power, usually the state, must always monitor the process.[78] Although Native nations have accepted self-government to a certain extent during the twentieth century, they have also retained the Indigenous sense of nationhood as Deloria and Lytle used the term. This nationhood, as Deloria and Lytle defined it, emerged before the state and therefore drew on ideologies different from those of the nation-state. This type of nation*hood* is not the same thing as national*ism*—far from it. Native nationhood is kin-centric and strives for consensus, while nationalism is state-centric and strives for sovereignty.

Aware of the history of the term "sovereignty," some nations have attempted to exercise their own forms of political power independent of the state-centric constructions that undergird the term. Zapatista communities in Mexico have challenged the idea that there is a "fundamental irresolvable antagonism between two practices of power, one that can be taken (sovereign power) and the practical exercise of another power, present in Zapatista communities, which challenges both sovereign power and its contemporary derivative in governance."[79] The Zapatistas have called this practical exercise of power "autonomy," but only in the past few decades have they begun to exercise this form of power in response to oppression and neglect from the state. Essentially, they have created an internal system of governance completely independent from the state and devoid of its hierarchies. Although this form of governance is new to this community, it draws on political autonomy already present in Indigenous nations.

Indigenous peoples have been exercising this type of autonomous political power throughout their historical colonial encounters as well. Indigenous autonomy was not an attempt to assert sovereignty over others by taking power but instead the exercise of autonomous power that was already present. This type of political assertion, while clearly different in form and purpose from that of the state, has always been articulated through diverse mechanisms and dependent on the practices of different cultural groups. Native people did not use the institutional mechanisms of the state (for example, legal contracts, citizenship, or geopolitical borders) to assert a sovereign identity. Nor did they use ruder forms of these mechanisms, such as maintaining cultural hegemony. They asserted political autonomy using entirely

different frameworks centered on reciprocity and relationships organized by kin.

The writings of Leslie Marmon Silko inspired me to use the metaphor of a spider's web to imagine the organization of Native nations.
Like Pueblo storytelling, Native nations have a clear center, with threads
radiating out from it and crisscrossing each other.[80] The structure of
the web emerges as it is made, and it can be remade when it is torn
by the wind or a struggling fly. Native nations have the same flexibility to remake themselves without losing their center. This center is
different for each group and depends on the origins of a particular
people. Furthermore, the circular nature of the web seems to more
accurately reflect the reciprocal nature of the relationships that create
its threads.

I distinguish a Native nation from other political formations in two
primary ways. First, a Native nation is organized as a web of social
relationships defined by reciprocity and not by the imposition of hierarchical power. While some people may acquire greater respect, granting them more power to influence national decisions, this power is
conditional and often depends on upholding responsibilities to their
kin network. Second, kinship creates both the organizational patterns
of the Native nation and the mechanisms through which a person can
take economic, political, religious, or social action. While the political systems of Native nations operated through specific political or
religious assemblies, such as chiefs' councils or military societies,
access to positions within such systems and even the relationships
between their members were defined and articulated, at least in part,
by kin relations.

The political autonomy of a Native nation, therefore, must be seen
as shaped not simply by a uniform membership, distinctive language, sacred history, religion, or landscape but by a matrix of reciprocal
relationships with a language, history, religion, and landscape that
are developed and maintained through kinship. Eric Wolf argued
that kin-based groups institutionalize political power through "the
management of consensus among clusters of participants." I expand
this idea to argue that kinship is the key to understanding how Native
nations demarcated themselves and exercised autonomy. They established or regulated political power not through national contracts

but through the processes of establishing and maintaining consensus within the group. Members took social, political, or economic action by accessing the specific kin ties that would aid them in their endeavors. As Wolf noted, these aggregates of kin would disperse again when the conditions changed, and when new conditions arose, new arrangements would form. As a consequence, Wolf stated, "the extension and retraction of kin ties create open and shifting boundaries of such societies."[81] While Wolf's argument could imply that such societies lacked the ability to exercise power as a collective, I propose that Cheyenne history demonstrates the reverse. While the Native nation had shifting boundaries, it also had a center where language, religion, history, and land were woven together into a web of kin that in turn articulated an ethnic identity. As we will see, however, Native nations do not strive to maintain unity; in fact, they are quite tolerant of factionalism. Instead, they seek connectedness.

While some scholarship on Native history has acknowledged the importance of kin systems to Indigenous political assertions, more research is needed to trace exactly how kinship has worked as a political mechanism through which Native nations asserted autonomy.[82] Scholarship on current transnationalism and diaspora recognizes the utilization of kin networks in times of disruption, but kinship has a much more powerful role in Native nationhood than only helping peoples maintain cultural identity during periods of massive upheaval.[83] It was used by Native nations as a political formation to exercise Indigenous political agendas long before contact with Europeans and has continued through the dramatic changes of colonization.

Kinship remained a useful mechanism through which Native people could assert political autonomy during colonialism because Europeans and Euro-American could recognize kin networks as a tool for political action. Before the emergence of the nation-state, both Native and European peoples asserted political power using mechanisms of kin. While the political philosophy behind their systems of rule differed, this shared organizational style made Indigenous political power recognizable to early European settlers in the Americas. Originally, the main difference between European and Native political organization was not kin-centric versus contract-centric systems, but political authority imagined as sovereignty versus authority understood as autonomy. Europeans shifted the concept of sovereignty, conceived of as a set of inalienable rights granted by God, from royal families to the state, imagining the relationships between rulers and ruled as hierarchical. Subjects and later citizens could own land or goods, but the monarch and later the state retained authority over all property and all subjects.[84] Although the people have negotiated with the powerful throughout history over the limits of this authority, its hierarchical nature has never been undermined, even in democratic nation states. Vine Deloria helped illuminate this distinction when he argued that Europeans depend on creed, dogma, and doctrines to interpret their world while Native peoples depend on experience—experience grounded in relationships.[85]

Native nations have emphasized asserting autonomy, conceived of as a set of relationships regulated using systems of kinship, and maintained through respect and reciprocity, that defined access to resources as well as political, economic, and religious power. Vine Deloria noted that while these were not relationships of conquest or imperialism over people, animals, or the land, some were antagonistic from the start.[86] Human beings hunt and eat certain animals, and peoples defend specific territories and resources from other groups. Yet all these interactions were delineated by types of relationships and the responsibilities allocated to each entity in the kinship web. Doctrines did not rule these interactions. The reciprocal act of maintaining the relationship, even if it was antagonistic, determined the outcome. Reciprocity, and the respect inherent in it, was at the heart of the relationships Native people formed with animals, the landscape, other people, and even other nations. Alfred argued that both European and Indigenous nations can accomplish peace, "but for peace the European demands assimilation to a belief or a country, while the indigenous demands nothing except respect."[87] In this statement, he described a central difference between sovereignty and autonomy.

Unlike sovereignty, autonomy does not demand unity. Because Native nations were defined by relationships, as opposed to a set of rights, they had open and shifting boundaries. Each Native nation, and sometimes parts of it such as bands or clans, made decisions that not everyone followed. If members disagreed with the direction their nation was taking, they could leave, join a different nation, or break off and form a new division, but the Native nation remained. Certainly, there were Native nations that dissolved under external pressures, like European encroachment and colonization. A group may not have had the same external boundaries as before, but cultural elements were transferred to the surviving members' new nations. Some political forms were transferred as well. While kinship reckoning and the specific duties and privileges of each relative might change, networks of kin themselves are profoundly resilient. In fact, political formations based on kin can be much more resilient than the state during times of upheaval, because individual people can make different decisions based on their specific circumstances without disruption to the group as a whole. If one family shifts its national affiliation to survive, the Native nation remains intact. Its edges might shift, but the center remains. My telling of the Northern Cheyennes' struggle to return to their homeland illustrates the resiliency of the Native nation. This history will illuminate the centrality of what Ms. DG called family and what I call kinship to the cultural, economic, and political action taken by the Cheyenne nation before removal, and will demonstrate that these mechanisms continued to undergird Cheyenne actions when dealing with U.S. colonial policy as well.

Illuminating the centrality of kinship to how Indigenous people operated politically refocuses sovereignty as the frame for pre-reservation political action revealing that Native nations did not assert sovereignty over their people or their land, but instead maintained relationships with them to exercise autonomy. They took political and economic action by establishing relationships not only with members of their own group, and with allies or enemies, but also with animals and plants. The flexibility of establishing and maintaining networks of kinship both within and beyond a group gives this political mechanism staying power. People on the plains continued to use it not only after colonial encroachment but also after the establishment of their reservations. State-style mechanisms of political power vie for dominance on reservations today, but even so, kinship continues to shape American Indian political activities. Listening to Cheyenne histories and becoming aware of the constructions of nationalist ones reveals that Cheyenne people used kinship to assert political autonomy in ways completely different from state-style sovereignty and based in totally different worldviews—they had distinctly Native nations.

CHAPTER TWO

I Was Rich in My Relatives

Kinship and the Cheyenne Nation

I still visit the people I first worked with at Northern Cheyenne. I consider my fellow historians and collaborators and their families to be good friends. My visits are short now, often only a week during the summer. By this time we have shared deaths, births, divorces, and other personal struggles. They might have known years ago that when they opened their homes to me, I would keep coming around. They have friends who visit from across the United States and around the world. I am honored to be one of them. I did not know, however, that I would be sending presents and sitting in hospitals, celebrating graduations, and getting advice from them. My mentor had become part of their family over the years, and I am honored to be treated with similar warmth.

A couple of summers ago, I was sitting with Ms. DG at her kitchen table when she told me she had been thinking more and more about kinship as she watched her grandchildren grow up. "You talk about it a lot in your book, too," she told me. Before I defended my dissertation, I had given her a copy, which she kindly read. As we sat together, looking out at the bluffs on the reservation, she reminded me again that historians so often misrepresent Cheyenne history. She told me that her ancestors were not just fighting for their own freedom. They fought for their children, their children's children, and all those children who had not yet been born. Cheyenne leaders, she told me, always considered those who were yet to come. She got up from the table and walked into the narrow kitchen. She took a cup out of the cupboard and poured herself some freshly brewed coffee. As she placed the pot back in the coffeemaker, she turned to me and said, "Dull Knife had a family, you know."

I stared at her, setting my cup down a little too loudly. I stopped short because I had been considering this as the title of my book. A couple of years earlier, in conversation with a colleague, we had come up with it, but I had not openly discussed the idea. She could not possibly have known. All I could say was, "That's right. He did," and stand up to refresh my own coffee to mask my surprise as she returned to the table. Thinking about this moment on the long drive home, I wondered if perhaps something about Cheyenne worldviews had sunk in, despite all my struggles to understand.

Spending time with Cheyenne families had taught me more about kinship than I had realized. I had witnessed the respect that family members had for one another. Generosity is a constant lesson among siblings. Euro-American parents tend to distribute treats equally among their children, but I have seen Cheyenne parents and grandparents give little presents to the oldest child and instruct him to share with his siblings. Families share with any visitor, always offering them something to eat or drink. They give away food and gifts, such as blankets and dishes, at public events such as powwows to honor their family members. One honors his or her family by being generous and respectful, both within the extended kindred—family relationships established by blood, marriage, or adoption—and beyond it.[1] One of the Cheyennes' greatest resources has always been family. Several people told me that they are often asked by non-Cheyennes what it was like to grow up in such poverty. Each of them told me, separately, "I never realized I was poor. I never felt poor because I had my family. I was rich in my relatives." Not only did they have the financial safety net of extended family; they also had the emotional support of many parental figures, grandparents, siblings, and cousins who all were taught to respect and fulfill their obligations to each other and the family from birth.

Ideally, each Cheyenne person is raised to know that his or her behavior could affect the family either positively or negatively. Cheyennes pay attention to the needs of the family, especially the elderly members and the children. They are raised to appreciate that their actions have a ripple effect on their family and their entire community far into the future, as all our actions do.[2] Cheyenne children are taught that a thoughtless or selfish act might hurt their siblings or parents, while a generous or respectful act would benefit the family as well as themselves. Each person's behavior affects the group, and even living entities beyond the group, sometimes with lasting impacts.

Instead of ordering people through an imagined solidarity shaped by allegiance to the state, Native nations ordered their members through obligations to each other defined by their kin relationships. Fixico has described kinship as "the bonding element that holds together the entities of the Indian world."[3] Ella Deloria has detailed the way the bond works, depicting Dakota people as caught up in "a fast net of interpersonal responsibility."[4] DeMallie has argued that the net of kinship embraced all significant social action, organizing the way people interacted and providing the driving force for daily life.[5] People understood their obligations and duties to their band, kindred, and society in terms of their kin relationships, prioritizing these relationships in the decision-making process. Therefore, kinship was essential to the process of constructing and maintaining the internal order of the nation.

A Native nation approximated a sense of collective identity by maintaining a web of kin-based relationships that could be strategically activated in order to take political and economic action and assert access to resources and territory. DeMallie has argued that the result of utilizing a kin network to organize social actions had two dimensions. First, each person was marked through kinship terminology in mutually recognized relationships to other members of the kin group. Second, these relationships consisted of specific behavioral expectations that organized daily life. Using kin terms when speaking to someone implied consent to the reciprocal duties and privileges represented by the term.[6] Each person depended on his or her web of kin relationships for social, economic, ceremonial, and political support. They activated the appropriate relationships by using their social knowledge of which relatives were obliged to take on which tasks.

Every child was and still is born into a network of kin that delineated the responsibilities he would assume as he aged. Because Cheyenne kin is collaterally extended, each person has rather close ties with a large number of other Cheyennes. A Cheyenne person considers all of his or her mother's sisters to be mothers and all of his or her father's brothers to be fathers. The children of each mother and father are considered siblings, creating a tight bond among a large group of biological siblings and cousins. Both sets of grandparents nurtured the growing child. Aunts (the father's sisters) prepared cradleboards and moccasins for their newborn nieces and nephews. If the child were a girl, they would take on the responsibility of correcting her when she had been wayward. Uncles (the mother's brothers) would do the same for boys, perhaps helping him join his military society when he was older. Each child's set of siblings would be colleagues for life. A girl's sisters would help her with her work, share child-rearing, and stand by her in any difficulty, and brothers would be equally united. Each person also created close ties with his or her brothers- and sisters-in-law, sharing responsibilities toward their mutual extended family and maintaining a joking relationship, often quite playful in nature.[7] Family members sought to bestow privilege on their relatives, honoring them in the public sphere, helping them to pledge ceremonies or giving away in their names. These actions cemented a relationship of respect and responsibility between aunt and niece, uncle and nephew, brother and sister, and parent and child.

The relationships between relatives of the same generation held high importance for the Cheyennes. Such relationships were formal-ized into a set of sisters or brothers, including all the daughters of a set of sisters or the sons of a set of brothers. This grouping is such an important part of Cheyenne life that there is a word for it: *nisson*. The members had reciprocal obligations to each other throughout their entire lives. Even though men often moved to their wives' camps once married, they retained their ties with their nisson, even over vast dis-tances. The female nisson formed a set of maternal figures for their collective children as well.[8] The daughters of a set of sisters called each of their mother's sisters "mother." Ideally, the Cheyennes strove to keep a group of sisters geographically close together so that they could express these relationships in daily interaction.

Ms. DG expressed to me her deep grief at losing her last mother. She told me that it had always been a great comfort to her, especially when her biological mother died, to have several mothers in her life. Anthropologists call these relationships classificatory, but a nisson cared for all of its children as mothers to each. Jeffrey Anderson has noted that the "ongoing social construction of kinship has more to do with shared social space and time than with inherited substance or property."[9] A female relative who lived close to her sister and participated in the daily life of the family would likely be called "mother" by her sister's children, while a female relative who lived far away might be distanced in kinship terminology. While blood and marriage mattered in the demarcation of kin, each person's actions could also define his or her kinship status. In this way, making and remaking relatives could have a pragmatic role within the social order by creating reciprocal obligations between people who were not necessarily biologically related. For example, Native peoples in North America have been making relatives with non-Natives for quite some time, in part to instill an appropriate sense of obligation on Euro-Americans entering their communities as traders, government officials, medical professionals, educators, and researchers.[10]

Because extended families form the main units for organizing collective events among the Cheyennes, kinship has been central to participation in wider political and ceremonial life.[11] A Cheyenne person cannot pledge the Sun Dance by him- or herself; families must support them by preparing giveaway items and meals. A young woman does not become a powwow princess by herself. Her family members help produce her regalia, they collect and make giveaway items, they travel with her to regional powwows, and they maintain a camp during the event. The hat keeper, who cares for the Sacred Buffalo Hat, a bundle that protects the health of the earth and the people, does not keep this powerful object by himself. His ability to care for the bundle is determined by his family's identity: he must be Suhtaio, a designation that reflects their association with either the Suhtaios or the Tsistsistas, the two groups who came together generations ago to form the main body of the Cheyenne people. His entire family, particularly his wife and children, support his efforts. Their behavior influences the well-being of the entire nation. When the hat keeper's family is clean, responsible, and generous, the people adopt these traits as well. Chiefs' families also affect the activities of a chief. As his relatives, they are responsible for carrying out the expected generosity of a chief and for carrying some of the burdens.

Their actions can transform the nation, just as the hat keeper's can. Kinship relationships among the people connected individuals through privileges and responsibilities, reaching beyond relatives by blood or marriage to each member of the nation.

Kinship ordered both the internal organization of a Native nation and its position as an autonomous political entity in external relationships with other nations. Most Native people were also embedded in a wide web of relationships with members of different nations. Kin ties that stretched across ethnic boundaries did not splinter Native nations. Instead, they regulated political, economic, and social relationships between these nations. Because these webs cut across ethnicity, Native nations could rely on them when determining access to land and resources or when confronted with political or social conflict. Importantly, geopolitical structures on the plains did not rely on the maintenance of cultural distinctness or geographic borders; instead, they used social ties that the people themselves defined. Albers and Kay have argued that while "American Indian populations maintained distinct ethnic identities, unique culture patterns, and even differentiated sociopolitical structures, they did so while embedded in geographically far-ranging and ethnically-mixed systems."[12] Albers noted that for Plains people, "ethnicity in the generic and highly abstract sense of a 'tribal' name did not always function as a marker of geopolitical boundaries." In other words, names such as Tsistsistas or Cheyenne that were used to mark the entire sociopolitical body of the nation did not necessarily mark a stable, unified political entity, a homogenous cultural group, a nation with a bounded territory, or even a uniform biological group. Instead, groups organized around pluralistic patterns of land use and alliance making, using social ties to determine access to territory, labor, and resources.[13] These ties were constructed and articulated through kinship.

Ultimately, even relatedness was not a definitive marker of Cheyenne identity. Cheyenne people had relatives, especially ones who had joined non-Cheyenne communities, who were not necessarily considered Cheyennes. While members of the nation were certainly connected through kin, language, religion, social organizations, and cultural expectations, it would be inaccurate to assume these shared elements created the kind of national unity ascribed to a nation-state.

The level of flexibility created by the open and shifting boundaries of a kin-centric nation discouraged this type of unity. By activating family with affiliations to other nations, members, camps, and occasionally bands could come and go from the Cheyenne nation. Individuals and even groups had the freedom to shift their alliances if they disagreed with the direction their camp, band, or nation was taking. Moore has argued that while some members of the core bands had strong, definitive places within their bands, other members were more marginally related to the core and could be considered members of other bands by tracing other lines of descent. Therefore, reorganization of Cheyenne society could be accomplished by moving these periphery members from one band to another. Sometimes movements between bands could cause deeper rifts in the nation. Throughout history Cheyenne camps have split away from the nation. Moore noted that although traumatic events are always given as the impetus for a band or camp breaking away, small groups could smooth over the difficulties, while large groups often stopped talking and moved apart.[14]

Of course, Cheyenne people, like all peoples, have sometimes behaved in antisocial ways. Every community has members whose behavior skirts socially acceptable norms. Some individuals are more or less generous or quick to anger. Among the Northern Cheyennes, the trauma of forced removal and the struggle to return home led to moments of social disorder among Dull Knife and Little Wolf's people. For example, during the return north, young men made decisions about raiding Euro-American settlements that did not align with the wishes of their leaders.[15] In another example, one traumatized man physically attacked his family, leading his daughter to kill him in self-defense. Stands In Timber related another instance on the journey north, in which a man named Black Coyote killed Red Robe. Red Robe's father, a chief, first grabbed his gun, then he paused, changed his mind, and filled his pipe instead, stating that a true chief must never get angry.[16] These incidents occurred under extreme stress, but even during this period, order mostly prevailed, indicating the strength of Cheyenne social and kinship systems. Kinship systems among Plains people had also shifted to accommodate entrance into a market economy driven by European and Euro-American interests. Hide trading and horse raiding led to changing understandings around family organization.[17]

The influx of the market economy created new expectations around women's labor, while an increase in military violence shifted the focus from the female nisson to the male military society. How people responded to changing circumstances, including misfortune, was certainly shaped by these expectations. Yet the underlying principles surrounding kinship ties remained.

Kinship systems not only endured as a central regulator of social relations across time; they also held the Cheyenne people together across vast distances as they migrated onto the plains. Even though they are identified as a Plains nation today, according to both Cheyenne oral histories and anthropologists, the people who would become the Cheyenne nation originated somewhere north of the Great Lakes.[18] George Bent, the son of an American trader and a Cheyenne woman, declared that Cheyenne elders had told him that they were once a part of the Cree people and separated from them long ago, moving to the south and west.[19] Grinnell also noted that the Cheyennes considered the Crees to be relatives and declared that the Cree name for the Cheyennes was *Kaneaheawastsik,* meaning "they talk a little Cree."[20] Like the Crees, the Cheyennes speak an Algonquian language, and at one time they were probably both part of the same group.[21] Bent stated that the earliest Cheyennes migrated from the north "in canoes and at last came to a land of great marshes filled with tall grass and reeds."[22] According to Bent, the Cheyennes settled in the area of Minnesota.

During this period, the Cheyennes and the Siouan speakers of the region who would become the Dakotas and Lakotas became allies. Moore explained that these Siouan speakers used the term *Shahiyedan* to refer to a people "who spoke a foreign language but were not regarded as enemies."[23] Literally the word translates to *sha* meaning "red," *eya* meaning "to speak," and *dan* meaning "little," often used as a term of endearment.[24] Both Moore and Grinnell stated that this term referred to foreign speakers, but Grinnell noted that many Lakota stated that they used the term "red" because when they first met the Cheyenne, the people painted themselves red.[25] Nevertheless, the term clearly indicated a friendly relationship. This Siouan word was picked up by European and American travelers who transformed it into "Cheyenne," now used to refer to both the Tsistsistas and the Suhtaios.

As the French fur trade began to affect their homeland, many Cheyennes decided to migrate rather than allowing themselves to be caught
up in the fierce competition for guns and furs. They traveled south
into what would become Dakota Territory, settling for a time along
the Missouri River, farming and living in semi-sedentary earth lodge
villages, but eventually venturing westward to the Black Hills.[26] Over
time, the Northern Cheyennes developed stronger alliances on the
northern plains, and the Southern Cheyennes developed alliances
on the southern plains. It was during this period that the Northern
peoples asserted their presence in the lands around the Powder River
valley and established their hunting and camping grounds there.
Nevertheless, the Cheyennes still understood themselves to be one
Native nation and continued to travel across the plains to visit kin,
practice ceremonies, hunt, and fight together.

Membership in the Cheyenne nation was marked by a shared language and a shared sacred history embodied in certain central narratives. In terms of religion, all Cheyennes relied on the power of their
medicine bundles—the Sacred Arrows and the Sacred Buffalo Hat—
to protect the well-being of the people. These two bundles were and
still are the primary bundles maintained by the Cheyenne nation.
Sweet Medicine is the prophet of the Tsistsistas, who brought the
Sacred Arrows to the people. He was an orphaned boy who set out
on a journey as a young man to help his people. When he left, his
people were starving and did not know how to live in a good way.
Sweet Medicine made his way to Bear Butte in the Black Hills, and
there in a cave in the mountain, a man and a woman instructed him
to bring military societies to the people to live in a good way, giving
him the Sacred Arrows.[27] The Sacred Arrows bundle protects the people against their enemies and brings success in warfare and hunting,
and this bundle currently resides with the Southern Cheyennes.[28]

Erect Horns is considered the prophet of the Suhtaios. Erect Horns
also journeyed to a sacred mountain, Black Mountain. He went there
with a woman to receive holy power so that the people could live
well. He could then teach the people how to conduct themselves
through ceremony, including the Sun Dance. He came out from the
mountain with the Sacred Buffalo Hat and brought it to the Suhtaio
people. The Sacred Buffalo Hat safeguards the fertility of the people

and the earth, and protects the people from hunger and illness.[29] Today this bundle resides with the Northern Cheyennes. The Tsist-sistas and Suhtaios existed before the prophets came to them, but these prophets remade the people with their teachings. Keeping these bundles also connects the Cheyennes with a particular land-scape, by maintaining a relationship with the specific places that were connected to their sacred historical narratives and to their religious ceremonies.

While the Cheyennes shared an identity based on the cultural markers of language, sacred history, religion, and landscape, none of these four markers was sufficient to identify a separate Cheyenne political or even cultural identity. For example, many Lakota people also spoke Cheyenne fluently; some Lakotas participated in Chey-enne religious rituals; the territories of the Lakotas and Cheyennes overlapped (e.g., they shared the Black Hills); and both pointed to Bear Butte as a center of religious power and even shared some of the same religious narratives, such as the stories of the Great Race and the Children and the Bear.[30] Cheyennes and non-Cheyennes could share elements of the four markers, but each marker would retain distinct cultural meaning for each group. Elements from nations with distinct histories could also be incorporated into the Cheyenne nation without fear of erasing Cheyenneness. Relationships with other Plains nations suggest that Cheyenne nationhood historically could not be delineated using only the markers of language, sacred history, reli-gion, and landscape. Instead, these markers acted in concert and, when shared, became part of a larger matrix that encompassed Cheyenne identity. All these variables formed a loose configuration that could be called on at specific times to express collective identity when it was needed.

Furthermore, each of these markers only became culturally mean-ingful when a person accessed them through kin relationships. Kinship formed the channels through which people learned, interpreted, and utilized language, sacred history, religion, and the characteristics of their known landscape. People could speak the Cheyenne language, know the history, and even participate in religious ceremonies, but without relatives, they would not be Cheyennes.[31] If a person was intermarried or adopted in, he or she pointed to these newly formed kin relationships as evidence of membership. Just marriage or adoption into a Cheyenne family was not enough to grant membership, however; the person needed to adopt these other cultural elements as well. Cheyennes shared all of these elements as a part of their collective identity, but they made these elements Cheyenne by passing them on, regulating them, and ordering them through kin relations.

Ultimately, Cheyenne communal identity was based in a heartfelt relatedness among people that was expressed in many ways, including kinship, language, sacred histories, religion, and a connection to a landscape. These elements could come together in different combinations. Their importance as markers and their meanings all shifted over time and from one context to another. Cheyenne identity was flexible and could accommodate diverse definitions without any preordained rigidity. Group symbols, language, histories, religion, kin ties, and relationship to land all could be invoked to put forth a Cheyenne identity, but none defined or bounded this identity, and none of these bounded or defined the Cheyenne nation, either.

The flexibility of kinship found at the core of Cheyenne nationhood gave the people the ability to resist a rigid definition, which in turn provided them with the power to remain autonomous during the dramatic cultural changes of the nineteenth century. Officials in the Indian Office and the military attempted to define the Cheyenne nation as a concrete entity in order to contain and control its people. One technique used by the nineteenth-century nation-state to subdue Native nations was to attack Indigenous kinship practices. State officials often depicted American Indian families as depraved to justify conquest and assimilation.[32] Through reservation policies, education practices, and missionization, the state attempted to force Native people to conform to heteronormative, bounded nuclear family units. For example, John Stands In Timber described how common polygamy was among the Cheyennes in the nineteenth century. He noted that around 1920, reservation officials forced families to choose one wife because they would only record one husband and one wife on their census rolls, but he reported that while each man recorded only one wife, most families continued to live as a polygamous unit.[33]

Native families rarely fit into the state's neatly defined categories. Polygamous and extended families were very common; one family often combined several generations, as well as the nuclear families of several siblings, and sometimes families with multiple wives. Most Native nations also embraced flexible understandings of gender, allowing for categories beyond simply male and female and incorporating such persons into their families.[34] Cheyenne kinship depended more on expressing reciprocal relationships using culturally appropriate expectations than on playing out a specific familial role defined by a rigid gender construction and kin structure. When faced with the imposition of fixed boundaries by U.S. officials, the Cheyennes activated their varied and fluid kin networks to elude these efforts.

Members of the Cheyenne nation recognized a collective identity, but like Cheyenne families, it eluded definition when approached concretely, confounding American attempts to categorize Cheyenne people. By maintaining webs of kin, the Cheyennes retained the open and shifting boundaries of their nation and in turn used the flexible quality of their identity to their advantage when faced with the rigid imposition of the state's policies.

Collective identity for the Cheyennes was not as simple as marking all people who participated in the nation as Tsistsistas. Every person's identity was layered, manifested by memberships on various levels. Each Cheyenne person was considered Tsistsistas or Suhtaio. It is believed that the Suhtaios were once a separate band.[35] According to Cheyenne oral history, the Tsistsistas and the Suhtaios met on the Missouri River and began traveling together.[36] The two groups had camped on opposite sides of the river, and the older people warned the young men in both camps to leave the other camp alone. But the young men did not listen and started to fight. As the people came running out of their lodges yelling to their young men not to fight, they realized that they could understand each other's language.[37] Then the chiefs met and made peace between the two groups.[38] From that point on, the people depended on both the Sacred Arrows bundle of the Tsistsistas and the Sacred Buffalo Hat of the Suhtaios. The Northern Cheyennes say that the Tsistsistas met the Suhtaios after Sweet Medicine traveled to Bear Butte to receive the Sacred Arrows, demonstrating that Cheyenne journeys onto the plains have not simply been linear and progressive.[39] Those on the Missouri knew about the Black Hills, some of them perhaps even before they had seen the hills because the Cheyennes were making trips far out into the plains and then returning to their villages farther east. By 1820 the Suhtaios had been interacting with the Cheyennes for some time and had become merely a distinctive group within the larger nation.[40]

Most likely, intermarriage occurred between the Tsistsistas and the Suhtaios before 1820, considering the importance placed on exogamy and the frequency of interband marriage among Cheyennes and inter- ethnic marriage between Cheyennes and members of other Native nations. Over time, Cheyennes began to intermarry with Suhtaios to such an extent that today every band has ancestors from both groups, but every Cheyenne man or woman can still trace ancestry to one group or the other. This identity was and is still important today, because the two most sacred bundles of the Cheyennes that influence the health and welfare of the people remain in the care of these divi- sions. The Sacred Buffalo Hat belongs with and is cared for by the Suhtaios, and the Sacred Arrows belong with and are cared for by the Tsistsistas. The divisions of Tsistsistas and Suhtaios proscribe Cheyenne identity at a level above the bands and the societies but below the nation. This distinction has been an important level of identity that has bifurcated the people as a whole but has never divided them in two.

In addition to identifying as either Tsistsistas or Suhtaio, affiliation with a kindred, a camp, a band, and a society also shaped a person's social relations and cultural identity. Some of these affiliations were quite fluid and could mark people who saw themselves as part of a group in the moment the affiliation was invoked. A person identi- fied first with their kindred, and usually members of one kindred formed a camp. A person could decide to change camps but could only choose from camps with relatives to welcome him or her. During the upheavals of the 1860s and 1870s on the plains, families shifted camps frequently depending at any given moment on the decisions of leaders and whether they were willing to risk encounters with U.S. troops.

Camps were made up of like-minded people, sometimes from several kindreds, who lived and worked together, but band identity was determined at birth and could not be changed by choice. Members of one camp might come mainly from one band, while members of a different camp might come from several bands. Nevertheless, each person was identified in speech by his or her band affiliation, not his or her camp.[41] Each camp tended to be organized around a nisson, or group of sisters and female cousins, who brought their husbands into their family's camp.[42] These intergenerational groups of related women formed the core of Cheyenne bands and in fact are still at the heart of kinship dynamics among many Plains peoples today.

Band identity was meaningful in that it marked a person's place in the tribal circle and told others something about that person's family and history. George Bird Grinnell stated that band identity was passed through the mother's line, noting that a woman was a member of the band she was born into and remained a member of that band her entire life. A man was a member of his mother's band, and even if he joined his wife's band at marriage, he retained his own band identity throughout his life. His children would be born members of his wife's band. This way, if a man left his family, his children would be raised by their mother and her kin.[43] According to Grinnell, a person might also acquire a band identity from a father or husband. For example, if a woman from another nation married a Cheyenne man, she would not be granted a distinct band identity, and her children would take their father's band identity. A woman captured from an enemy nation belonged to the band of the man who took her as his wife.[44] If a woman died leaving a very young baby, the father might take the child to his relatives to raise, in which case the baby would take the father's band identity.[45] Although ideally band identity passed through the female line, occasionally different rules applied, forming a complex picture of social organization at the band level.

It is important to note that a family for the Cheyennes includes all of one's consanguinals or blood relatives, affinals or relatives by marriage, and fictive kin or ties by adoption, creating an expansive network. As such, the members of one family often lived in multiple camps, depending on marriages and other personal proclivities. The members of each band also dispersed into smaller camps for everyday living. People did not necessarily camp with fellow band members during the year but instead spread across the plains in different camping locations. The nation did come together in the summer for the Sun Dance and for communal buffalo hunts. Both band and society identities were important during these national gatherings. Societies were central to maintaining order within the large camps gathered for the buffalo hunts. When the Cheyennes came together as a nation for the Sun Dance, the camp circle was organized by both bands and military societies. Each band camped in a specific location around the circle.[46]

The Cheyennes also had another set of kin ties based in society membership that cut across both kindreds and bands. Men partici- pated in two types of societies that connected people from different kindreds and bands, the four military societies and the chief's society. Different scholars have reported slight variations in the names of the four Cheyenne military societies, but the Northern Cheyennes today use the designations of Kit Foxes; Bow Strings; Elk Scrapers, Elk Horn Scrapers, or sometimes just Elks; and Crazy Dogs, Dog Men, or Dog Soldiers.[47] John Moore listed the four societies as Kit Foxes, Elks or Hoof Rattlers, Bow Strings, and Dog Soldiers.[48] Stands In Timber stated that Sweet Medicine organized the Swift Fox, Elk, Bow String, and Red Shield societies and that the Dog Men (Dog Soldiers) or Crazy Dogs came later.[49] Women had a society of their own, the quill workers' society. Membership in this society was based on a woman's artistic accomplishment and did earn her certain social privileges.[50] Northern Cheyennes also talked about a chief's society, which seems to have emanated from the Council of Forty-Four.[51] The Council of Forty-Four consisted of the chiefs from each band who gathered to discuss the major political decisions of the nation.[52] Nearly all men participated in one of the military societies when they were younger, and a society man could potentially become a chief later in his life. Any man could be elected to the Council of Forty-Four but had to give up his affilia- tion with his military society.[53]

The military societies consisted of young fighting men and func- tioned as both social and political organizations. The societies gave young men military comrades and were organized to honor war deeds, to socialize, to carry out the orders of the chiefs, and to police and guard the camp. Although these societies were not organized like an army, a militia, or even a war party, they helped people organize for war. A young man did not need his military society to help him pull together a war party; he could simply recruit other warriors. Furthermore, according to Grinnell, a military society could start off to war, but other young men often joined them who did not belong to the society.[54] Young men joined societies not to have a group of comrades to fight with, but for individual interests and to help them to gain honors and make themselves known to the wider community. The military societies were not meant to further the interests of the kindred.[55] They were meant to further individual interests associated with honor and prestige gained in warfare, to provide internal order for camps, and to further the political interests of the Cheyenne nation in times of war.

Because society membership was not related to the kindred, a young man could join any society he wished. A young man often joined the military society of his father or brother, but he was not required to.[56] Regardless, a young man could not accomplish society membership on his own. Pledges depended on their extended family as they went through the pledge process, to show generosity and to honor the society men in their name. Eggan demonstrated that society members established kin relations with each other by using terms such as "grandfather," "grandson," and "brother."[57] These terms implied specific ties that carried particular responsibilities, and these bonds of reciprocity were just as strong as those of extended families.

Many of the societies also selected young unmarried women to participate in society ceremonies and other activities.[58] The society men called these young women "sister" and their role was a high honor. These women were not allowed to marry while they served as a society sister, and they could never marry a man of the society they were a part of.[59] If a woman wished to marry, she had to get the consent of her society brothers, just as she would have had to from her biological brothers. The role of sister came with incredible power because these women could chastise society men and correct their behavior.[60] A society sister depended on the support of her extended family to fulfill her responsibilities toward her society. These roles are still central to sociopolitical organization in the Cheyenne nation today. Not only do societies organize social life and make political decisions; they have religious roles as well, such as making decisions regarding preparations for the Sun Dance.

Although some bands were closely associated with certain military societies, each society had members in essentially all the bands and camps. When a man married and joined a new camp because of the pressure toward matrilocal exogamy, there would always be members of his own military society living in this new camp. Military societies cut across both band affiliations and kindreds, forming powerful and permanent bonds between Cheyenne men and connecting them beyond their camp, beyond their kindred, and beyond their band.[61] In all these ways, kinship terminology and kin relationships were extended beyond the kindred, making nonrelatives into relatives. Therefore, every Cheyenne person was embedded in wide networks of kin relationships, including their kindred, their band, and their society. Each of these relationships required the fulfillment of certain responsibilities to relatives, based on blood, marriage, and fictive ties.

The Council of Forty-Four was made up of forty-four chiefs who, although they were associated with the bands, were elected to represent the Cheyenne people as a whole, so a camp could have any number of chiefs.[62] Some camps had no chief; instead, the head of the most prominent family made decisions for the camp. In an interview for the American Indian Tribal Histories Project, Butch Sooktis stated, "The chief is supposed to ensure that there is peace among the people."[63] In interethnic relations, the chiefs could either opt for peace between the Cheyennes and other Plains nations or take no action, and if no action was taken, the military societies could take over the discussion from the chiefs and declare war. As Moore stated, "The chief's council could not declare war; they could only declare peace."[64] Chiefs were first and foremost peacemakers, so they had to comport themselves as such. A chief embodied modesty and compassion, demonstrated his proficiency as a leader, and followed high ethical standards.[65] A chief had to be generous, giving away what he had particularly to those in need, and he had to be even-tempered, moderating his anger toward those who wronged him.[66] The chiefs complemented the military societies, working with them to resolve disputes and keep order among the people.

Although members of the military societies and the chief's society gained personal prestige and influence, these societies were concerned with the interests of the entire nation. For example, when the chiefs decided to move camp, they called the heads of the military societies together and told them the time of departure and the new camping location. Then the military societies would police the breaking down of the camp and ride with the moving column to protect it from attack.[67] Moore argued that "societies, not bands, were the most powerful expressions of political life" and demonstrated that military societies and the Council of Forty-Four both had political roles that affected the entire nation.[68] Bands acted for the interests of their individual members, deciding where to camp and where to hunt. While they were much more stable than camps, bands could be formed, reformed, and dispersed over extended periods of time. They were not permanent political units; the societies were. Military societies were chartered by the Sweet Medicine origin story, and although membership shifted, they did not have the flexibility to form and reform easily. According to some oral histories, Sweet Medicine brought the Council of Forty-Four and the military societies to the Cheyennes at the same time.[69] The council was to act as a governmental body, and the military societies were to act as the police and military protection.[70] In an interview for the American Indian Tribal Histories Project, Rubie Sooktis stated, "The Council of Forty-Four does not have a document that says this is a government recognized by the federal government. Their recognition comes from a sacred beginning."[71] These societies transcended the kindreds and the bands. All these units acting together connected the Cheyenne people in a sociopolitical body.

The societies brought the Cheyenne people together every summer. They met and took care of business when all the bands joined in one camp circle. Eggan related that "with the formation of the camp circle a whole series of dormant institutions came to life."[72] The Council of Forty-Four met during this time to discuss the affairs of the nation. Communal rituals of importance to the entire nation such as the Sun Dance would take place. The military societies acted as police to carry out the council's decisions and keep order. The men of each military society came together from different camps and kindreds to hold ceremonies, to do the business of their society, and to band together for the summer military actions of the entire nation. Moore demonstrated that when the camp circle was activated, it was organized not only by bands but also by military societies. He noted that when the people came together in the summer, each society would build an arbor used for initiations just before the Sun Dance. These arbors formed a square outside the circle made by the bands. According to Moore, the societies also organized the order of the inner circle of bands because each band camped near the military society to which it was most closely connected.[73]

Moore stated that a council chief and a society headman would look at the same camp and see different organizational patterns, and he argued that this represents an ingrained cultural ambiguity.[74] This ambiguity did not manifest as uncertainty or indecisiveness but may be more accurately represented as a duality, a balance of two ways of being that were both represented within the camp circle and had equal standing.[75] There were two models of good behavior among the Cheyennes, the active model of the warrior and the wise model of the chief. Every person had the potential to develop these qualities, usually over the course of his or her life.[76] Energy preceded wisdom in personal development. A young warrior had a lot of energy and would fulfill his potential for good through energetic activity and strength. As he aged, his potential for good shifted from energy to wisdom. At this point in a man's life, he could become a chief and take on the activities and bearings expected of this role. These different ways of manifesting positive behavior in men of different ages suggests a cause for the tension between the military societies and the chiefs.

Cheyenne political organization revolved around two institutions that worked together but had different sets of expectations and agendas. As they experienced dramatic changes in their cultural landscape with the influx of European market economies and Euro-American settlers, the military societies sometimes disregarded the chiefs' efforts to work for peace. Anne Straus, following Peter Powell's lead, has suggested that the dialectic between the warrior model and the peace chief model has shaped Cheyenne history.[77] This was particularly true in the nineteenth century, when military societies began to diverge from the chief's authority. Some societies even formed separate bands at this time.[78] The chiefs and military societies had more difficulty maintaining a balance during this period; the tensions that emerged shaped Cheyenne history.

The ambiguity of Cheyenne political organization as revealed in the tension between these societies also demonstrates the incredible flexibility inherent in kin-based national formations. While society men had kin responsibilities to their society brothers, uncles, grandfathers, and sisters, they also had kin responsibilities to their relatives and their bands. Society brothers supported each other in the pursuit of military honors, the defense of their camps, and the implementation of Cheyenne laws at the camp and band levels. They had a duty to each other, to the kindred and band they were born into, and to the family into which they married. While all these competing affiliations must have created the kind of ambiguity Straus and Powell describe, they also created a web of kin connecting relatives by blood, marriage, and society affinity that wove itself across the entirety of the Cheyenne nation. While a person might find himself having to decide whether to support society brothers or kindred, these conflicts did not sever the responsibilities each person held to multiple entities. In this way, every person stood at the center of a vast network of ties that he or she could draw on to accomplish social, economic, religious, or political actions. Activating these expansive relationships allowed a person access to multiple social resources and helped maintain relationships between people physically separated by great distances. Because Cheyenne people engaged in social, economic, and political activities along channels of kin, a wider web of kin opened more opportunities for the individual. The more flexible the kin system, the more opportunities it afforded its members.

Such flexible constructions of social organization raise questions about the meaning of membership in the Cheyenne nation. Any Cheyenne person would be Tsistsistas or Suhtaio, would have a band identity, would affiliate themselves with a certain camp, and might also be a member of the chief's society, a warrior society, or the quill workers' society. These groups marked a collective identity, but

not a bounded and unified ethnicity. These names were used to identify membership in a flexible way; they did not confine people to a
specific membership. Someone who identified as Cheyenne participated in a certain community, lived his or her life in a certain manner,
and recognized others who were like-minded. Within this community
there were several levels of communal identity: kindred, band, and
society. Each of these identities was fluid, and their delineations could
change over a lifetime.

At any given moment, a Cheyenne camp circle would also include
people not considered Cheyenne. Non-Cheyennes visited and camped
for ceremonies, trade, and multiple other purposes. Furthermore, for
American Indian people on the plains, a person's identity at the level
of the nation could shift during his or her lifetime. Over time, a non-
Cheyenne person could become Cheyenne, recognized as a member
by people both within and outside of the nation. Cheyenneness was
therefore a state of being, not based on birth and not based on a
political contract–like citizenship. Identity was simultaneously an
internal awareness of self and an external relationship exhibited by
others, both Cheyenne and non-Cheyenne, who acknowledged a
person as Cheyenne.

Eventually non-Cheyennes living in a Cheyenne camp could gain
the full status of Cheyenne membership. This created kinship ties
between Plains people who claimed different ethnic affiliations. Moore
demonstrated this point, stating "Adoptees and captives of all stripes,
after a period of residence, became citizens of the nation. According
to modern elders, there was no onus of 'mixed blood' in those years.
Although captives and adoptees were sometimes denied certain ritual
roles because of their inability to speak Cheyenne, their Cheyenne-
speaking children were full citizens. The basis of citizenship was not
'racial' or biological but was established by birth in a Cheyenne band.
In aboriginal times a captive or adoptee was accepted merely by consensus of the camp."[79] Moore claimed the Cheyennes had clear-cut
distinctions between citizens and noncitizens. According to him, non-
Cheyennes incorporated into the nation gained full citizenship at a
specific point, most often delineated by cultural markers such as
language acquisition. Their previous affiliation remained in collective
memory, but it did not taint their status as Cheyenne.

Those with non-Cheyenne affiliation could become politically useful if the nation needed to open political or economic negotiations with the foreign nation from which an intermarried or adopted person originated. While some people certainly took longer than others depending on their age, gender, and specific circumstances, it is evident that those who were brought into the Cheyenne nation were fully incorporated at some point. Depending on the circumstances, even a member of an enemy nation could gain full membership. The term "membership" more accurately describes this process; the body of the Cheyenne nation did not contractually obligate citizens but instead absorbed new members. Cheyennes today will say, in the same breath, that their great-grandmother or grandfather was Pawnee, Crow, or Lakota, and that they are full-blood Cheyenne.[80] For them, these two statements are not contradictory.

The Cheyennes' ability to incorporate and assimilate outsiders rested on certain dimensions of kin organization. Establishing beneficial interethnic relationships by making new relatives succeeded because of shared understandings between Plains nations that outsiders were incorporated through intermarriage and adoption, and that kin relations engendered obligations. Interethnic kin relationships acted as the channels through which interactions between Plains nations took place.[81] Plains peoples agreed that intermarriage or adoption could open doors to build beneficial relationships with other nations. They established kinship across ethnic lines to help secure allies, trade relationships, or access to hunting grounds.

The Lakota and Arapaho kin systems closely resembled the Cheyennes in kin categories and in the reciprocal obligations expected in most relationships.[82] A Cheyenne who married among Arapahos or Lakotas would already know how to respond correctly to the expectations and obligations of his or her new family. On the other hand, the peoples of the Missouri River had a different type of kin organization, so an adopted or intermarried Cheyenne would have to learn the normative expectations of a different kin system. Establishing interethnic relations demanded certain cultural negotiations that varied in complexity depending on the differences between the groups. Yet each party drew on shared understandings of kin roles and requisite expectations to build the relationship. Although the specifics of these responsibilities were played out in distinctive ways in different communities, reciprocal obligations always tied relatives together, creating bridges between communities who established kin connections.

The Cheyennes used kinship to advance their interests throughout their history by not only expanding their web of social support but also by strengthening ties with allies and creating new ties with enemies through intermarriage and adoption. Cheyennes valued these connections and encouraged their establishment. Historically creating connections with non-Cheyenne peoples was not a rare occurrence. In fact, Cheyennes placed a high value on exogamous marriages. Moore declared, "the Cheyenne nation was predicated not on preserving the biological separateness of the population, but on extending and hybridizing the nation with other groups."[83]

By establishing kin relationships with non-Cheyennes, Cheyenne peoples were able to migrate from Minnesota to the Missouri River and onto the plains. By 1800 the Cheyennes had established alliances stretching along their entire migration route from the Black Hills to Minnesota. Using these alliances to establish a solid trade route connecting the Kiowas, Plains Apaches, and Arapahos to the Mandans, Hidatsas, and Arikaras, the Cheyennes came to dominate the region between the Black Hills and the Missouri River. On their journey west, the Cheyennes stopped on the Missouri, establishing relationships that connected them to peoples living in Minnesota and farther out on the plains. During his youth, George Bent heard stories from Lightning Woman and Twin Woman about life on the Missouri. They talked about planting corn and beans, fishing in the wide river, and hunting buffalo on the plains to the west.[84]

On reaching the Missouri, the Cheyennes allied themselves with the Arikaras and the Mandans who lived there already, building an earth lodge village in between the Arikara Village and the Mandan Village along the river. The Cheyennes traded with these groups for agricultural goods at first, and later for guns and other European products. They brought buffalo meat, hides, wild plants, particularly wild turnips, and later horses to trade.[85] They also intermarried with the Mandans, Arikaras, and Hidatsas during this period.[86] Sometimes the Mandans and the Arikaras warred against each other, and at these times the Cheyennes allied themselves with the Arikaras.[87] According to Jablow, as they moved onto the plains the Cheyennes became allied with the Kiowas and the Arapahos, introducing these groups to trade with the Missouri River nations.[88] Furthermore, as the Dakotas and Lakotas neared the Missouri River, the Cheyennes began trading with their old allies, supplying them with horses and buffalo robes.[89] Although they had moved far from Minnesota, they had not ruptured their old alliances.

All these alliances were facilitated through kin channels, establishing trade relationships through both intermarriage and adoption. Participants who consented to interethnic marriages or adoptions for the purposes of trade or alliance understood they also might be asked to take on the role of conduit between the nations. These relationships were established strategically often for political or economic purposes and sealed with the power of reciprocal obligations that a kinship tie demanded. For the nation-state, incorporation of people of other national affiliations can be disruptive to the national unity, but incorporation of outsiders at different levels did not threaten Cheyenne national stability.[90] Having multiple, widespread allies gave the Cheyennes connections to new landscapes, far-ranging political support, and access to diverse resources, demonstrating the strategic use of kin relationships by Plains peoples in pursuing their social, political, and economic well-being.[91]

In the early nineteenth century, the bands of Cheyennes living along the Missouri developed valuable trade relations. Parent-child adoptions took place between the Cheyenne and the Missouri River nations to create a relationship connecting groups that had access to different goods.[92] Siouan speakers disrupted these relationships when they moved into the area and began making it difficult for other groups to trade with the Hidatsas. In 1806 the Cheyennes decided to secure their trading situation with the Hidatsas, so they returned a prisoner to them and gave one of their own young men to the Hidatsa chief, Le Borgne, to adopt as a son.[93] In this case, a captive became a conduit to open negotiations between two groups, and the adoption was meant to cement the established relationship. During this negotiation, the Cheyennes and the Hidatsas exchanged many meaningful and valuable gifts that were not just symbolic. The people placed an extremely high value on the act of giving and on the objects themselves.[94] The Cheyennes secured their trade relationship with the Hidatsas by establishing kin ties across the two groups in a ritualized manner through the Adoption Pipe ceremony that included both adoption and gift exchange. Although the adoption took place, the efforts of the Cheyennes and Hidatsas failed to secure the lasting peace that would ensure continued trade. This historical example, however, demonstrates that Missouri River nations used father-son adoption strategically to establish trade relationships with Plains nations.[95] When successful, this adoption created obligations between the two groups that both parties were compelled to fulfill beyond the ritual of the moment.

These types of adoptions usually occurred between men, but women occasionally participated in adoptions as well.[96] More often, however, women acted as conduits for trade through intermarriage with non-Cheyenne men. As wives, women facilitated contact and encouraged trade between peoples. Chiefs' families especially encouraged groups of sisters to bring husbands from outside in matches that would facilitate trade.[97] William Bent's marriage to Owl Woman is an important example.

According to George Bent, his father, William Bent, his father's brother, Charles, and a friend, Ceran St. Vrain, set out from the Missouri to the upper Arkansas River sometime between 1824 and 1832 to establish a post and begin trapping beaver in the area. Yellow Wolf, the headman of the Hevhaitaneo band (Hair Rope People), approached Bent and encouraged him to build a fort farther down the Arkansas River in order to trade with the Cheyennes. Yellow Wolf agreed that his band would move south to be nearby, which occurred sometime between 1828 and 1835.[98] The Oivimana (Scabby) band also moved south, but the Wotapios were already in this area.[99] The Bent brothers and St. Vrain established relationships with Cheyenne and Arapaho bands over time, benefiting from their knowledge of the country and setting up a lucrative trade for all involved.

This friendly trade relationship was ultimately sealed through marriage. William Bent married a Cheyenne woman named Owl Woman in 1835, exemplifying the Native Plains practice of cementing trade relationships through intermarriage. She was the daughter of a prominent Cheyenne man, White Thunder, keeper of the Sacred Arrows.[100] As was common for daughters of prominent men, she married to seal an interethnic relationship that would benefit her band, fostering an advantageous trade relationship between Bent and Owl Woman's people. Women such as Owl Woman were expected to become human conduits when they married, facilitating contact between cultures and peoples. The role of conduit had the most power to affect new relationships in ethnically mixed marriages. This marriage gave the Cheyennes relatives at Bent's Fort, meaning they would always be welcome there. The Cheyennes associated with Owl Woman's father moved with them toward the fort. Although the region had ample game and resources, having relatives at this particular fort secured trade with these newcomers for useful European goods. Bent was able to secure a ready partner for trade, as well as a valuable ally in a world new to him.

Sometimes extensive intermarriage led bands to merge into new groups.[101] Albers and Kay argued that interethnic marriages were an institutionalized feature of mergers, necessary to establishing the connections that made the joint use of territory possible.[102] Often when a camp of Cheyennes met with a camp from another nation, the young men and women would court those from outside their own nation.[103] When these young people married, they established beneficial kin relations across two nations. For example, the Cheyennes intermarried with Mandans, Arikaras, Kiowas, Arapahos, Teton Sioux, and later with Americans. Large-scale intermarriage created hybrid bands, such as the Masikotas, Wotapios (Cheyenne/Kiowa), and the Dog Soldier bands (Cheyenne/Lakota), that played key roles in Cheyenne history.[104] Establishing kin relationships with the peoples they encountered as they traveled west created a network they could draw on as they entered new territory, helping the Cheyennes learn about their new environment and how to best utilize the resources it provided.

As Cheyenne bands moved into the Black Hills, they also began to form new interethnic relationships with other nations already in the area. By the 1770s the Cheyennes and Suhtaios had began traveling to the Black Hills annually to hunt buffalo. The Kiowas, Plains Apaches, Comanches, Arapahos, and Crows already occupied the area.[105] The Arapahos were one of the first nations to give the Cheyennes horses.

According to Bent, the Cheyennes and the Arapahos became friends the first time they met and never had a serious disagreement that disrupted their alliance.[106] The Cheyennes traveled with the Arapahos to trade on the Missouri River and by the first decade of the nineteenth century were hunting with them.[107] The Cheyennes also developed friendly trading relationships with the Kiowas and Kiowa-Apaches, but eventually the strength of the Arapaho alliance with the Cheyennes pushed these nations to the edges of the region; later the alliance aided the Cheyennes in their wars with the Crows.[108]

Once the Cheyennes established themselves in the Black Hills, it became the center of their territory and, with the inclusion of Bear Butte, an important locus for spiritual activity. Powell noted that when discussing claims to landscape, the old men spoke of the Cheyenne connection to the Black Hills. They said that the Cheyennes controlled the region until about 1850.[109] The period spent living near the Black Hills sparked a renaissance in Cheyenne cultural, social, and political life. Bent stated that the movement into the area of the Black Hills created dramatic material change for the Cheyennes, such as acquiring horses, learning to make tipis, and depending mainly on buffalo to subsist.[110] The Cheyennes who moved into the region of the Black Hills also gave up a semi-sedentary lifestyle, including using the earth lodge village as a home base. They turned to a mobile lifestyle that depended mainly on hunting, neglecting horticulture as their primary subsistence method. The Cheyennes made this shift in lifestyle gradually because they began hunting buffalo on the plains before they left their earth lodges on the Missouri. Over time, however, mobility became essential to the Cheyenne way of life.

John Moore has argued that the Cheyenne nation was founded in the Black Hills.[111] The prophet Sweet Medicine brought his charter for unifying the people from Bear Butte.[112] This charter forbade warfare among the bands by defining it as murder, defined the relationship between the military societies and the social whole, defined the bands as sacred, placed these sacred bands within the tribal circle, and in some versions, established the Council of Forty-Four.[113] Each of Sweet Medicine's directives was central in establishing and regulating the political life of the Cheyenne people. Sweet Medicine's charter gives the impression this unification of Cheyenne bands was a seamless and swift process, which obscures the complexities of interethnic relationships that often pulled bands in multiple directions, even after the charter was established. Although the charter gave the nation a distinct political order, the process of bringing bands together under the umbrella of a Cheyenne social and cultural identity was continuous and shifting throughout the nineteenth century. Although the Black Hills remained the spiritual heart of the Cheyenne nation and an important part of their geographic universe, some groups of Cheyennes continued to migrate, moving south out of the area. The Cheyenne people have always returned to this area, particularly for ceremonies that must take place here. Their relationship remains strong today.

By 1780 the Cheyennes were positioned in the Black Hills to be able to welcome their Lakota friends who had not yet arrived.[114] After a smallpox epidemic in 1781 decimated the peoples living along the Missouri River, the Lakotas, who had often encountered hostility to their presence in the area, were able to move across the Missouri without impediment and camp on the streams that flowed near the Black Hills.[115] Stands In Timber related that when the first Lakotas came into the area, they went straight to the Sacred Hat Tipi for sanctuary, causing the Cheyennes to receive the next group of Lakotas peacefully.[116] As beneficiaries of the rich resources and lucrative trade around the Black Hills, the Cheyennes took pity on the poorer newcomers, giving them horses, meat, and buffalo robes.[117]

As the Lakotas moved west, they infringed on the territory of the Kiowas, and the Cheyennes became caught in the middle of a new conflict. The Cheyennes had recently allied with the Kiowas, depending on them for horses, useful for life on the plains and valuable in trade with the Arikaras and Mandans. While the Cheyennes and Lakotas had been allies generations earlier near the Great Lakes, skirmishes now erupted between the two nations. Patricia Albers has demonstrated that most of this fighting probably occurred between the Lakotas and the Wotapios, who were intermarried and closely allied with the Kiowas.[118] Although the Wotapios had Lakota origins and were descended from intermarriages with the Lakotas, once the Cheyennes moved into the area of the Black Hills, their relationship with Lakota peoples became uneven. In the early part of the nineteenth century, many Wotapios moved south of the Platte River away from the main body of the Cheyennes and joined forces with the Kiowas and some Arapaho bands.[119] Despite the move, the band remained distinct from the Kiowas and the Arapahos and stayed part of the Cheyenne national body.[120]

Ultimately, the Cheyennes and Lakotas would renew their strong military alliance, intermarrying and sharing territory. Moore argued that the Cheyennes joined forces with the Teton band of the Lakotas because "the Pawnee were a military problem for the Cheyenne in the Black Hills, so they allowed the Teton joint occupancy . . . of the Black Hills and aided them in attacks on the Pawnee."[121] Bent also mentioned this alliance, stating that soon after the Lakotas arrived, they joined forces and drove the Kiowas, Comanches, and Apaches out of the Black Hills region and then attempted to drive away the Crows.[122] The Cheyennes and Lakotas continued to fight with the Crows over this region until the 1860s when the Crows abandoned these hunting grounds.[123] The alliance between the Lakotas and the Cheyennes had been suspended by distance for a time, but because the Lakotas had intermarried with the Cheyennes, these kin ties could be reactivated through channels that were remembered and maintained. This alliance would last far into the reservation era, becoming vital to the Northern Cheyennes' struggle to remain in their homeland.

In the last decades of the eighteenth century, the Cheyennes began to establish the territories and alliances that would be important as they negotiated their relationship with the United States. The Omisis, Tsistsistas proper, and Suhtaio bands established a presence north of the Black Hills and the Wotapios began moving south of the Black Hills and intermarrying with the Kiowas, providing the first evidence that the Cheyennes would distinguish themselves more and more along north-south territorial lines as the nineteenth century passed.[124] Because Cheyennes had relatives among the Wotapios, it became easier for more groups to migrate south. By the beginning of the nineteenth century, Cheyenne bands had spread out around the Black Hills in patterns that would affect their eventual split into northern and southern bands.[125] As the Cheyennes drifted into a wider circle, the Arapahos established northern and southern bands as well, maintaining the alliance bolstered by intermarriage that would remain strong throughout the nineteenth century. Because Cheyenne bands lived from the north of the Black Hills all the way to the Arkansas by 1820, they could utilize their network of kin to access a large swath of the northern central plains. By the 1850s some Cheyenne bands had remained north of the Black Hills, while other bands camped mainly between the Platte and the Arkansas Rivers.

Due to later events in the Cheyennes' relationship with the United States, such as treaty negotiations and the establishment of reservation boundaries, historians have often portrayed the division between the northern and southern bands as quite pronounced, representing the Cheyennes as a unified nation that became divided around 1830.[126] Considering the impacts of kin networks on Cheyenne actions, however, reveals that the division of the Cheyennes into northern and southern peoples did not happen in a moment of conflict. It happened slowly over time, as bands of Cheyennes made decisions based on economics and social relationships.

Many scholars of Cheyenne history have argued that the split of the Cheyennes into northern and southern divisions was the result of Bent's Fort, stating that some Cheyennes moved south to be a part of the trade taking place at the fort.[127] Bent's Fort surely encouraged the Cheyennes who had been traveling from the Black Hills and the Missouri River to remain more permanently south of the Platte, but other forces were working long before 1830 to instigate these migrations. These two groups were embedded in interethnic alliance patterns that pulled them in different directions. Despite this, the people were not divided into two sociopolitical bodies. The Cheyennes still visited, traded, intermarried, helped each other as military allies, and shared the Sacred Buffalo Hat and the Sacred Arrows.

Patricia Albers illustrated the complexity of intertribal relations during this period using a story told by George Bent and also recorded by Grinnell. It is clear that some Cheyennes traded with the Kiowas, Comanches, and Apaches during 1825, but around this time, larger bodies of Cheyennes began to travel south toward the Arkansas, and hostilities intensified. Around 1826 a band of Cheyennes were camped with some Arapahos and Atsinas along the South Platte in Colorado when a group of Crows arrived and set up a camp nearby. When the

Crows feasted their Arapaho and Atsina friends, they requested that the Cheyennes return a child who had been captured a few years earlier. The Cheyennes refused and the Crows threatened to start a fight, depending on their Arapaho and Atsina friends for support. Their friends, however, decided to side with the Cheyennes instead, and a battle ensued between the Cheyennes, Arapahos, and Atsinas on one side against the Crows and their allies, the Kiowas, on the other side.[128]

While the Arapahos were able to act as go-betweens, keeping a balance between their Cheyenne and Kiowa allies for the purposes of trade, these three groups maintained peace. When put in a position where they could no longer remain neutral, however, the Arapahos chose to fight beside the Cheyennes. Such tensions solidified alliance relationships. Yet the fact that both the Crows and the Cheyennes could claim the Arapahos as an ally demonstrates the complexity of these interethnic relations. This battle supposedly instigated the collapse of friendly relations between the Cheyennes and Arapahos on one side and the Kiowas, Plains Apaches, and Comanches on the other. This full-scale warfare between the Cheyennes and the Kiowas was too intense for the Wotapios to remain neutral; they ultimately sided with the Cheyennes, but the Kiowas and the Cheyennes did make peace again in 1840.[129]

Social relations connected people at war because they created overlapping kin networks through captivity. Albers described war as a "condition of total competition" that was based on raiding—enemies took horses and also captured women and children. Under the conditions of war, groups fought over territory and resources affecting a nation's economic and political position on the plains. After the influx of European trade, certain regions became valuable, not just for ecological features or resources but also for the economic advantage their geographic position provided in relation to trade routes.[130]

Warring nations exchanged women and children through the practice of captivity. Stands In Timber noted that Cheyenne warriors did not kill women and children if they could help it; they captured them.[131] Captured women and children were eventually incorporated through marriage and adoption, creating kin ties even between enemy groups. Unlike the kin ties established by allied groups, interethnic kin ties created by war were not meant to establish relations between nations. Whether captives returned to their community of origin depended on the specific political circumstances of each captive. Captured children were adopted into families quite quickly and rarely returned, but adult captives who had resided in a camp for only a short period sometimes became objects of exchange during peace negotiations with enemies.[132] Eventually the Cheyennes fully incorporated both captured women and children and considered them Cheyenne once they had been adopted or married and particularly once they spoke the language. While such a practice was expected with Plains women captives, Euro-American women captives were less frequently incorporated and more often held for negotiation and ransom. Such practices aligned more closely with Euro-American expectations surrounding warfare.

Incorporated captives did not maintain ties with their communities of origin, but these connections did become useful when enemy groups required a peaceful encounter. For example, two groups at war sometimes attended the same trade gatherings and even traded directly with one another. Sometimes a nation depended on an allied nation to help attend a trade gathering with an enemy. For example, the Arapahos were able to trade with their enemies the Arikaras by using the Cheyennes as go-betweens. Such an encounter was a delicate undertaking. Although tensions between enemies were often high, individuals could even visit relatives across enemy lines. These visits were often conducted through kinship channels created by intermarriage with captive women.[133] Captive women and children incorporated into a kindred of an enemy nation often had the power to open a channel between these enemies.

Intermarried and adopted captives occasionally activated their kin ties in enemy nations for trade, for political negotiation, and ultimately for peace or alliance. Patricia Albers describes this process: "Captives were incorporated into the kinship networks of their captors. In this light, the practice of abduction takes on new meaning, for not only did it contain grounds for conflict, but it also embodied (quite literally) the terms of reconciliation. In other words, the capture of women and children was both a quintessential element of war, and a fundamental opportunity for peace. It maintained, yet rearranged, the social nexus through which tribes were able to rework their relation-ships."[134] Because captives had kin among the enemy group and often could still speak their natal language if captured as adults, they could facilitate peace by drawing on their old kin ties to establish new relationships.

Adult captives usually gained their new status in an enemy com-munity quite slowly. Full membership in the Cheyenne nation certainly rested on knowledge of the language, religious traditions, and shared history of the nation, but a person could not become Cheyenne without Cheyenne relatives, regardless of how well he spoke the language or how fully she participated in ceremonies. Lack of relations definitely marked a person as non-Cheyenne.[135] On the other hand, relatedness could grant a culturally competent non-Cheyenne person full member-ship in the nation, even during the reservation period. For example, Teddy Wooden Thigh, a Cheyenne elder in the 1970s respected for speaking the Cheyenne language and retaining knowledge of Chey-enne history and traditions, was racially white. According to Anne Straus, who knew Mr. Wooden Thigh personally, he had been aban-doned as a baby at the St. Labre Mission and adopted by the Wooden Thigh family in accordance with long-standing tradition. He was also an enrolled tribal member, even though he did not meet blood quantum requirements.[136]

Whereas citizenship within the nation-state depends first on a willingness to enter into a legal contractual relationship with the state, membership within a Native nation depends instead on willingness to accept a familial relationship within a kindred and to adopt the status of a relative. While the privileges and obligations of citizen-ship are delineated by the doctrines of the state with no requirement of kin, the duties and benefits of membership are delineated by related-ness and expressed through channels of kin. Furthermore, forging kinship ties that linked ethnic groups on the plains provided an impor-tant vehicle for diplomatic interactions between nations. John Moore has argued, "It is misleading, I think, to claim that the strength of the Cheyenne nation lay in its tight political integration, its homogeneity, and its maintenance of ethnic boundaries. I believe it is much more accurate to say that the political and military strength of the Cheyennes lay in their dispersal across broad reaches of the central plains, their economic and productive specializations, and their special trade relationships and intermarriages with neighboring groups."[137] Remaking Cheyenne bands and camps through intermarriage and the incorporation of outsiders did not diffuse the nation but instead made it more able to negotiate and defend its position on the plains. In the past, the incorporation of members of outside ethnic groups facilitated trade, created alliances, and helped bring peace. By incorporating individuals in the kinship system, the Cheyennes could reinforce close relationships with outside groups for political and economic purposes.

While some might assume that kin-centric societies are prone to an extreme factionalism disruptive to higher levels of integration, Jeffrey Anderson has argued that such divisional interests should not be understood as negative, but instead as a constructive adaptation to a way of life marked by change.[138] Members of a Native nation may disagree on the specifics of religion, territory, history, trade, or politics, but they remain connected by obligations of kin. Often those obligations tie them to religious practices, trade alliances, or political roles. The open boundaries of kin-centric nations create flux—too much to establish consistent unity. Yet while kin ties are very flexible, they are also very strong. Establishing new alliances and breaking old ones is possible, but doing so involves reformulating familial relationships. While Native nations placed little value on unity, they instead sought to maintain connectedness expressed in terms of kin obligations.

Because Native nations created connectedness by maintaining channels of kin through which members could access cultural institutions, they have had a flexibility that has allowed them to maintain a national identity even in times of dramatic social, cultural, and political change. Fixico has noted that kin relationships draw people inward, binding them together even during periods of factionalism.[139] By contrast, the rigidity of the nation-state makes it susceptible to destruction. When factionalism erupts and old institutions are overthrown and remade by a new power, a new state is formed. A Native nation, on the other hand, continues regardless of the nation-states that rise and fall around it. Moore has argued that the flexibility of the Cheyenne kin system, with its diffuse authority spread across peace chiefs and military societies, explains the ease with which the Cheyennes were able to shift from a matrifocal emphasis on trade to a patrifocal emphasis on war in the 1860s.[140]

The ability to shape and reshape kin ties to form strategic relationships had always been a part of Cheyenne social organization, but the new challenges of the nineteenth century encouraged significant reshaping of camps and bands.[141] In 1836 the Cheyennes banished the Dog Soldier Porcupine Bear because he had murdered another member of the nation, and this encouraged the formation of permanent military bands.[142] Usually a tribal member banished for murder would have followed the main camps for several years and humbly rejoined the nation with loss of membership privileges.[143] Porcupine Bear, on the other hand, was able to set up his own camp because his friends and family quickly joined him in exile. These groups then distinguished themselves as brave warriors two years later in the fighting against the Kiowas.[144]

Eventually this band encouraged the formation of a separate Dog Soldier band among the Cheyennes that began to intermarry intensively with Lakota warriors. In shifting their social organization to privilege military societies instead of trade, these bands also shifted their kinship dynamics away from a matrifocal emphasis toward organizing around a group of society brothers.[145] By 1861 these Dog Soldier bands were often making decisions about their political and military actions that differed from those made by peace-oriented bands. By the reservation period, however, they had been incorporated back into the larger political body of their respective nations, and both the Cheyennes and Lakotas returned to placing women at the center of their kinship systems.

The Cheyennes established a wide-ranging and flexible web of social support built on kinship. The people were able to journey onto the plains, spread across them, and still remain a nation. They were able to create multiple alliances with outsiders—even enemies—and remain a nation. Cheyenne people often used kinship relationships to gain access to new resources, landscapes, and political and military support through alliances created by intermarriage and adoption. Colonialism, reservation life, and forced assimilation did adversely affect Plains families. As reservation boundaries eventually solidified and individuals had to enroll to receive annuities, families descended from intermarriages had to choose a tribal identity. A family that ended up at Pine Ridge, who now has the last name Dull Knife and claims descendancy from the famous leader, exemplifies this type of decision-making. Because they chose to remain at Pine Ridge, they consider themselves Lakota.[146] Yet the family still recognizes their Cheyenne ancestors today, indicating that these imposed tribal affiliations never erased more multifaceted identities. Cheyenne people continued to activate relationships with Lakota, Arapaho, and even Crow relatives well into the reservation period.[147] While many current families appear to have collapsed these complex identities into one by enrolling their children as Lakota or Cheyenne, their interethnic heritages are recorded and related in family oral histories.[148] Families still have wide-ranging kin networks, among Americans of all races and even citizens of other nation-states, such as Canada, Germany, or Denmark. Furthermore, they often draw on these interethnic networks for economic and social support, just as they did in the past.

Because kinship has ordered not only social and ceremonial life but political and economic life as well, it has been an important factor in shaping the history of Plains peoples. Cheyenne people made decisions and took action based on the expectations of and duties within their kindreds. These relationships affected who people chose to marry, asked to join a war party, turned to for access to hunting and gathering grounds, or depended on for shelter. Each of these personal decisions, made in relation to kinship ties, affected one's personal history and had the potential to affect the history of the Cheyenne nation. Wider kinship networks that ordered the bands, societies, and relationships between Plains nations also had a powerful role in shaping Cheyenne history. These wider kinship ties affected whom the Cheyennes traded with, whom they went to war against, whom they allied with, and even the territory they inhabited. The Cheyennes sealed economic relationships, negotiated for peace, and proposed political alliances all through channels created by kinship ties. Because kinship ties opened some courses of action and closed off others, shaping the exercise of Cheyenne autonomy, they affected Cheyenne history as much as the events the people experienced. This remained true even after European and American newcomers arrived, attempting to wrest control of the plains. It is exactly the flexible nature of kinship that provides a Native nation with the resiliency to sustain not only cultural identity but also some semblance of political autonomy, despite the onslaught of colonialism and the attempts by the nation-state to impose its boundaries.

CHAPTER THREE

WE ARE STILL ONE NATION
Family in Migration and Diaspora

One sunny afternoon, as Elva Stands In Timber and I were sitting at her tiny kitchen table, sharing the chicken strips and fries I had brought from the Charging Horse Casino, my gaze wandered to the trees outside her window. I could see several children playing with a brown puppy. It was a clear, warm day, and I absentmindedly wondered when I would have the opportunity to go camping again. As I ate the fried chicken and sipped iced tea, I thought about the times I had gone with Cheyenne families and about the coolers full of food and five-gallon tanks of water we hauled. Camping near one of the springs on the reservation was so convenient because we did not have to drive all the way to town to fill our jugs.

Picking up another piece of chicken, I asked Ms. Stands In Timber, "How did people choose their camping locations in the old days?" She told me that it was not like today, when we can carry everything to a site and take our cars to get more water if we need to. She talked about the importance of wood and water close by and how people had favorite camping sites that they would return to again and again. "But you had to move on at some point," she told me, "you know, after the place gets too dirty." I must have given her a quizzical look because she explained, "Because people have been using the bathroom." I laughed. "Sure, of course!" "Moving to a new spot gives the place time enough to repair itself," she told me. At some level, this is obvious. I suppose as a sedentary dweller who relies on city water, trash collection, and sewage systems to take care of my waste, I had not thought much about how dirty a campsite might get after weeks of occupation.

The Cheyenne people I have camped with are always very careful. They dig deep postholes to bury leftover food after meals. They take all dirty water away from camp and pour it out close to the ground. They keep trash bags tied up high and are even careful with cigarette butts, putting them in coffee cans. They leave a campsite, even one that lacks facilities, with little evidence that they were there, at least to my untrained eye. This kind of care is not simply an ecological ideology but a central element of survival for mobile peoples. The well-being of the people depends on maintaining a respectful relationship with the land. Historically, the Cheyennes have articulated this relationship using kinship terminology, providing guidelines for reciprocal behavior between people and the animals, plants, water, and rocks that shared the same space. This reciprocity entailed ceremonies to show respect to the land and its inhabitants, as well as practical measures taken while hunting and gathering to give back to the environment. Establishing reciprocal kin ties between the people and these other entities turns land, an object that can be alienated, into a landscape, a space defined by relationships.

These relationships were also determined by seasonal cycles. Cheyenne camps separated from each other during the winter and came together in a large camp circle in the summer for major ceremonies and tribal hunts.[1] When these camps all united in the summer and formed into bands, they required vast grazing lands for their horses, plentiful water, and a buffalo herd nearby to supply meat for such large numbers. Large groups could not be sustained for long periods of time, so as the winter came, the people separated into camps to pass the colder months. It was easier to supply meat, water, and grazing land for these smaller groups.[2] Eggan stated that the Cheyennes told him that they once tried to stay together over the winter in the early nineteenth century and almost starved to death, so they never tried it again.[3] In order to sustain themselves with hunting, gathering, and trading, small camps needed to be mobile and able to spread out over large areas of territory.

Ms. Stands In Timber demonstrated the intimate ways that kinship linked the Cheyenne people to the landscape during a discussion of her grandmother's wisdom. Her grandmother told her that as a Cheyenne person, she should always live in a good way because the earth is our grandmother and we came from her: she knows us completely and sees everything we do, and one day we will go back to her. The grandmother hears our stories, which is why people smoothed the ground in a particular way before beginning a narrative, an action that was meant to indicate that the teller would only relate the truth as he or she knew it.[4] For the Cheyennes, the connection to the landscape through kinship ties is so strong that going back to the ground from where you first came is like going home and returning to your grandmother.

A landscape is a home filled with relatives in a very explicit way. These relationships existed before each person was born and will be there after the person passes on. The places on the land and the non-human entities that inhabit them know the people and remember them. In turn, the people know the landscape and all the nonhuman relatives, plants, animals, and specific places such as rock formations and rivers within it. Ceremonies must take place on precise spots on the landscape. They have little meaning held elsewhere. Ms. Stands In Timber told me that the old people never said, "This is our land." They always said, "This is our home." The Cheyennes' relationship with their landscape has always been more than economic or political. It is emotional in a way that resembles a familial connection. There has been a respect and love that emerges not only from dependence on the landscape but also from the awareness that this relationship is reciprocal. The landscape depends on people as well.[5]

The idea that Cheyenne people could be tied to land in such an intimate way has been counterintuitive to many Euro-Americans. After all, the Cheyennes were nomadic. In European thought, nomadism inspires visions of homeless wanderers, always traveling to new places, with no real connections to the lands they travel through. The idea of place as it has often been articulated during the twentieth century has come to associate ethnic groups or nations with land in political, legal, and economic terms. In this system of thought, people articulate their relationship to place through land ownership, political boundaries, and production such as agriculture, industry, or resource extraction. Even recreational use of the land is often profit-driven today. Land is understood as a resource for people to use and not as a landscape, a living entity with which people enter into a reciprocal relationship.

The Cheyennes had been on the move for generations, but they maintained relationships with their entire landscape. Even their earliest origins in the Great Lakes region of Minnesota is still remembered through oral histories. In fact, Ms. DG told me that her grandmother described Minnesota so vividly that when she first traveled to the state, she felt as if she had been there before. She related a sense of coming home, even though neither she nor her grandmother had ever been there before, because oral history had recorded Cheyenne relationships with this landscape in loving detail. Such powerful relationships with landscape, as articulated by Native people, have often been couched in sacred language. The reverent articulations of these sacred relationships expressed through kin-based reciprocity has allowed mobile peoples to move through space while sustaining deeply meaningful connections with the landscape.[6]

Early origin narratives reveal that the Cheyennes commemorate their relationships with multiple landscapes, including ones they no longer regularly inhabit. Such stories recognize mobility as a vital part of Cheyenne history, indicated by the fact that as the Cheyenne people migrated, they had several awakenings, renewals, or perhaps origins.[7] These awakenings happened at different points—when the Creator made people from the earth, they came out of caves, they received buffalo and no longer were poor, and they received the teachings of their prophets and learned how to live in a good, moral way. The Creator first formed Cheyenne people into human beings, and later they were remade into the Tsistsistas and Suhtaio peoples by their prophets, Sweet Medicine and Erect Horns. The people recorded their history before they came together as an organized nation, pointing to the specific times and places that they learned how to create social order. Their experiences at each of these places remade the people as they migrated across the landscape, becoming the Plains nation known today as the Cheyennes. Because of their importance in the history of the people, each place has been inscribed in Cheyenne narratives.

When preparing the listener to hear these histories, the narrator for the American Indian Tribal Histories Project noted, "The origin of the Cheyenne people is complex. The complexity is the result of the

coming together of two groups of people who spoke a similar language."[8] Because the merging of the Suhtaios and the Tsistsistas formed
the sociopolitical body of the Cheyenne nation, the earliest histories
and origins probably describe the experiences of both of these groups.
Some narratives vary because they emerged from the different peoples who came together to form the nation, and perhaps others vary
because they speak about different moments in history. Henrietta Mann
noted that because Cheyenne history is oral and passed down over
generations, there could be different versions of these early creation
stories; some versions could have been lost while other versions could
be compilations of several earlier stories.[9] Beginning a telling of Cheyenne history with their origin stories acknowledges that these are the
narratives that the people tell about their own beginnings.[10] Nevertheless, no single narrative should be granted the status of *the* Cheyenne
origin story by scholars.

George Bird Grinnell recorded several Cheyenne origin narratives
at the turn of the twentieth century. Despite the time that has passed,
the narratives that Cheyenne people tell today still reflect many of the
same elements in the stories that he recorded.[11] Grinnell described a
creation narrative in which a Being was floating on the surface of a
great body of water and this Being asked the water birds to bring
mud from the bottom; finally a little duck brought some earth, and this
Being made the land from it. From here Grinnell related a narrative
in which the creator made a man and a woman. He also recorded a
narrative told to him by Ben Clark, a Euro-American man married to
a Cheyenne woman, who often acted as an interpreter during negotiations with the U.S. military or government officials. Clark explained
that people first came from under the earth to live on the earth's surface. He also presented a very old and sacred narrative that described
a time when the people had buffalo to eat but then lost their ability
to hunt buffalo.[12]

In *Cheyenne Memories*, John Stands In Timber recounted what seems
at first a very different origin narrative. He stated that he recorded
these narratives in 1905 from two elderly women, Yellow Haired
Woman and White Necklace. Stands In Timber stated that he was told
that the Creator made people from mud and taught the people how
to find food. He declared, "All this took place in another country,

where great waters were all around them." In this country the people had only small animals to eat and were frequently hungry, but after some time two brothers found a larger and better environment with plenty of game and encouraged the people to move toward it. The animals here were very fierce and the people lived in caves for a long time to protect themselves. John Stands In Timber described this time as difficult and chaotic. He stated that it was during this time that the people "became more able to take care of themselves," but "they were not an organized people."[13] Stands In Timber stated that Sweet Medicine, the Tsistsistas prophet, brought the people order at a later time. He also discussed the story of the Great Race, an early narrative in which people raced around the Black Hills against the buffalo to determine who would be the predator and who would be the prey.[14] In the story, with the help of the magpie, people won the privilege to hunt and kill buffalo and the freedom to no longer fear these animals. Both Stands In Timber and Grinnell talked about a large body of water, about living for a period in caves or under the earth, and about having difficulty hunting buffalo.

In an interview for the American Indian Tribal Histories Project, Henrietta Mann began her telling of Cheyenne origins with the creation of four sacred beings by the Creator, Ma'heo'o. During interviews for the same project, Mann and Silas Big Left Hand both talked about how the water birds dove to the bottom of the water that covered the earth to bring up mud so that the Creator could make the land. These elders then discussed the time after the world was created, declaring that the Creator created a male spirit and a female spirit. Next the Creator created a Cheyenne man and woman.[15] John Moore provided a detailed version of the narrative of the first man and first woman, discussing how the couple learned to reproduce and to hunt, build fires, make things, and live in the world in general.[16] He attributed this story to the Aorta band, stating that it is their origin story. He then demonstrated that the bands could have shared their narratives when they came together, forming the fabric of the earliest histories of the Cheyennes as they are told today.

Scholars and Cheyenne historians agree that Cheyenne oral histories point to the Great Lakes as their earliest known landscape, their home before they lived on the plains. Silas Big Left Hand stated that he learned from his family and the elders that the Tsistsistas came from the Great Lakes region, that it was a heavily wooded place, and the people lived as fisherman, eating fish and turtles.[17] According to oral tradition, the Suhtaios also originated from the Great Lakes region.[18] They point to a place they call "the marshlands" along the current border between Canada and Minnesota. Big Left Hand stated that the people were very poor in the beginning.[19] Both Bent and Stands In Timber related that the people discovered the Red Pipestone Quarry while they lived in Minnesota.[20] It is unclear whether both the Tsistsistas and the Suhtaios knew about and utilized the Pipestone Quarry at this time, but they likely did because many people in the area who were allied with the Cheyennes used it. Today Cheyenne people talk about Pipestone, relating that Cheyennes still return there to get the red rock for making pipes.[21] The Suhtaios state that Black Mountain, the place Erect Horns received the Sacred Buffalo Hat, is near Pipestone. Both the Suhtaios and Tsistsistas point to the Great Lakes region as their earliest known landscape, but according to oral tradition, these two groups did not come together again until they moved away from the area.

In Western scholarship, migrating peoples have often been represented as dislocated. Home is understood as rooted. Territory is seen as bounded by geographical markers. For Indigenous people, however, territory is bounded by relationships. Hokulani K. Aikau described this sense of home for Native Hawaiians as a reciprocal obligation to care for the places where their ancestors are buried so that the living can be nourished by the bounty of the environment and the spiritual power that resides there. Privileges to land get articulated through burial and the presence of ancestors, but the presence is not enough. The relationship with the graves, and therefore the landscape, establishes Hawaiian territory. Aikau points out that Native Hawaiians continue to ground their claims to territory in burial practices and familial ties, even in diaspora—even on the mainland of the United States.[22] Mobility does not sever an Indigenous person's tie with a particular landscape while the relationships remain. Gerald Vizenor coined the term "transmotion" to articulate these types of connections to landscape that emerge from a population's movement. He describes transmotion as "that sense of nation motion and an active presence."

Native relationships with territory get articulated and rearticulated during motion, establishing an active presence. For Vizenor, transmotion is "a reciprocal use of nature, not a monotheistic, territorial sovereignty."[23] He argues that this type of relationship is *sui generis* sovereignty. It emerges from these relationships and thus exists in a category of its own.

Different Native nations have articulated their relationship with a territory using different mechanisms, but kinship generally has been a central part of the process.[24] For mobile peoples, articulating a relationship to the landscape through kin ties established a way to demonstrate an autonomous presence in a particular space without the violence associated with establishing sovereignty over the land and the peoples already living there. The people moved into different landscapes and encountered different Native nations throughout their history, creating kin ties to establish military and trade alliances along the way. The makeup of the Cheyenne nation changed over time, as some Cheyennes joined other nations and peoples of other nations were incorporated among the Cheyennes. New peoples brought new resources, new knowledge, and sometimes new ceremonies. Even the processes by which the Cheyennes marked and incorporated kin varied slightly over time.[25] Regardless, kinship established the reciprocal relationships the Cheyennes needed to determine a legitimate presence on a particular landscape.

Native people formed familial relationships with both human and nonhuman entities when they entered a new landscape in order to gain the privileges of resource acquisition, of ceremonial and medicinal knowledge tied to a particular landscape, and of the ability to gain power from specific locations where it was concentrated, leading to a sense of belonging in that place. Certainly, alliances with other tribal nations aided these processes, but so did establishing ties with nonhuman relatives. Donald Fixico has related that Native peoples developed relationships with the natural environment using the logic of kin, stressing reciprocity and noting that receiving is as important as giving.[26] These plants, animals, and places provided both materials and knowledge to newcomers learning about a different landscape. People, in turn, had the responsibility to use resources sparingly with respect and to give back to their nonhuman relatives through ceremony.

It might be as simple as saying a prayer for a tree that provided choke-cherries or as elaborate as sponsoring a Sun Dance to rejuvenate the entire earth.

The kin-based ties that Cheyenne people formed with nonhuman individuals are remembered in narrative today, many of which speak of plants and animals as deserving of reciprocal respect. Some clearly articulate how the relatedness of some animals to people has been central to the very survival of the nation. For example, because the magpie is more closely related to people as a two-legged being, she was on their team during the Great Race of the two-legged against the four-legged. This race came at a time when buffalos hunted humans, causing them much suffering. The human could not last against the strength of the buffalo, but the magpie used her skill to help them win.[27] Humans owe their very existence as plains hunters to magpies, and therefore the Cheyennes give her a great deal of respect. Ms. Stands In Timber told me that when she was young, the old people would always say "haho," or "thank you" to a magpie when they saw one.[28] Furthermore, the memory of the activities of these ancestors is marked in the very soil of the Cheyenne landscape. Their blood stains the land. People say this is why the racetrack around the Black Hills has red soil: it was stained by the blood of the runners during the Great Race.[29]

Cheyenne people also have ancestors who have literally been incorporated into the landscape, both during ancient times and his-torically. For example, the Cheyennes have relatives in the sky as stars and on the ground as rock formations. According to Cheyenne narra-tives, Bear Butte was once a little boy who was trying to sleep but his siblings kept pestering him until he got so angry that he turned into a bear. He chased the other children until they climbed onto a tree stump or perhaps a large boulder. The bear kept following while the children prayed to be saved. The tree grew larger to take the children out of harm's reach, but the bear grew larger, too. Finally, the tree could grow no larger and the children were pulled safely into the night sky to become stars we still see today. The tree stands today at Devil's Tower; the lines in the tower were made by the bear's claws as he jumped to attack the children. The bear himself, exhausted from the strain, traveled east across the plains and finally fell asleep on the northeastern edge of the racetrack. You can see him today at Bear

Butte.[30] These profoundly spiritual places, Devil's Tower and Bear Butte, are not only places of power. They are relatives of the Cheyenne people, denoting an intimacy with the landscape that wraps the religious and familial together with a distinct sense of nationhood. Remember this is the spot where Sweet Medicine gained his teachings that established the Cheyennes as a people.

Certain bodies of water are connected to the ancestors as well. Some Cheyenne families still commemorate their connection to the Missouri River through ceremony. They view the river as part of their origin, saying that they came from it. Certainly the Missouri was important during their migration onto the plains, but it is not just a historical place worthy of remembrance. There is a deeper spiritual connection that is commemorated through ceremony and requires spiritual observance whenever a member of these families crosses this river. Another example of kinship with water is a lake that some Cheyennes travel to for ceremonial purposes. It is said that Cheyenne people who understood how horrible life would be after Euro-Americans colonized the plains simply walked into the water and still live in the old way on the lakebed. Cheyenne people still bring offerings and prayers to both these bodies of water, knowing that their ancestors will hear them.

These places reveal that the Cheyennes developed lasting reciprocal relationships with the landscape as they moved through it. They demonstrate an active presence, not simply one based on mobility or even on resource exploitation, but something deeper. The Cheyennes clearly maintained their relationships, articulated and activated as reciprocal kin-based relationships, with a wide landscape over long periods of time through oral narrative and ceremony. These relationships established and maintained what Craig Howe called the nation's "known geographic universe," defined as "that spatial domain of its members' historical experiences."[31] Native nations not only exercised their political and economic autonomy through kin relationships with their ancestors who lived in particular landscapes; they also expressed their relationship to particular landscapes by establishing familial ties with the animals and plants of the region. As they moved onto the plains, they incorporated corn, beans, squash, buffalo, and later horses into their sphere of respected relatives, using a ceremony designed to establish kin ties with the plants and animals in a new landscape.

Schlesier relates this ceremony in his ethnography of the Cheyennes. On first reading about it, I had doubts about its validity. Because Schlesier is the only ethnographer of the Cheyennes who describes this ceremony, I suspected he might have misheard a description or misinterpreted a participatory experience. A few summers ago, however, one of my friends at Northern Cheyenne had asked me to camp with his family during a ceremony. We were all sitting around one morning, eating scrambled eggs hot off the propane stove, when the conversation turned to the land and taking care of it. People had been talking a lot about the decision to develop coal. This had been a hot topic on the reservation for decades, and it flared up every so often as another company would come forward promising jobs and tribal income. One of the men leaned to me and said something like, "You know, we're all related, plants, animals, and people. We have to be careful about what we do."

As usual, I assumed I knew what this person was talking about. Lakota people also have the idea of "All Our Relations" that you occasionally see co-opted by New Age practitioners and ecological activists. Donald Fixico has argued that American Indian people view the world from the perspective that all things are related. He has suggested that these beliefs encourage Native peoples to strive for equilibrium not only within their own nations but with other nations as well, including plant and animal nations.[32] This man surprised me, however, when he said, "We have a ceremony that makes relatives out of the plants and animals." "You do?" I said, perking up. Could this be what Schlesier had talked about? He told me that yes, they do. It was a ceremony used when the people moved into a new territory. He described it as a way to introduce themselves to the current inhabitants and develop a positive relationship with them. I couldn't help ask what it is like. He told me he didn't know because he had never seen anyone perform it. There hadn't been a reason to in a long time.[33] Through this ceremony, the Cheyennes entered into a kin-based relationship with the beings in the landscape that demanded reciprocal obligations. These relationships established with the plants and animals would then mark the limits of their territory and grant the Cheyennes permission to use the landscape to live.

The logic of this ritual mirrors the logic of kinship as the network through which sociopolitical and economic action took place between Native nations. Kin ties with non-Cheyennes gave people the privilege of military support and the access to joint resources. Cheyenne people simply expanded these privileges and responsibilities articulated in kin relationships to the nonhuman world by making the familial ties institutional through ceremony. Once these kin ties were solidified, the people could assert their privilege to access and their responsibility to protect a given landscape.

Cheyenne people did not just establish reciprocal familial relationships with the plants and animals of the places they entered; they articulated these relationships on a daily basis once a place became home. For example, before berry picking, older generations at Northern Cheyenne would always put down tobacco and explain to the plant that they were not there to hurt it. Resources were neither owned nor exploited. They were respectfully utilized with an understanding of the plant or animal as a partner in the process. Native nations were not sovereign *over* other people or the land. Political autonomy was not enacted as sovereign dominance but as a reciprocal relationship. By maintaining this type of relationship, a nation secured the privilege to act in the political or economic sphere in relation to other peoples or a particular landscape. Native people did acquire access to new territory and resources through military exploits, but more commonly they did so by establishing new relationships through intermarriage and adoption, making relatives not only of people but also of animals, plants, and even particular places on the landscape.

Many distinct American Indian groups used territories and resources jointly. Although they sometimes shared use only for short periods, they often based this shared access on stable relationships lasting for generations.[34] Although the peoples of the northern plains did not hold property with inalienable and private rights, they did have an understanding that each group was associated with a certain territory. The Cheyennes placed markers on the landscape indicating that they were connected with a specific place. For example, they would leave rocks piled in certain ways to mark a trail or specific location, and they would often leave tipi poles in their favorite camping locations.[35]

Groups also regulated usufruct, regulating the use of the resources of certain landscapes by assigning gathering responsibilities to certain groups. On the northern plains, there were no lines marking where one group's territory ended and another's began, but in the words of Albers and Kay, "there were social relationships which stipulated how groups would separately or jointly occupy a given landscape." Extensive kinship ties, often widespread in allied bands, connected two groups who jointly utilized a territory in a peaceful fashion.[36] Allied peoples had a general understanding of the limits of their territory as indicated by markers on the landscape, such as rivers and mountain chains.[37] Groups at war usually remained geographically separate, but groups at peace often shared the same landscape.

The mobility of the Cheyenne people never prevented them from establishing and maintaining an intentional relationship with the landscape. Scott Richard Lyons notes that migration produces difference by creating new identities, new practices, new narratives, and new ceremonies, but the old never dies—the new is simply added on.[38] The plains, the Black Hills, the Missouri River, the Powder River basin, and all the important places in their homeland belong to the Cheyennes like a sister or a husband or a child belongs to his or her family. Just like a family, the exact specifications of the interactions might change over time, but the relationship remains as long as it is fed through reciprocity and continued through stories. In the same way that one person can be an aunt, a sister, a wife, and a mother and each relationship is different, a landscape can be related to many peoples. A Native nation's relationship with one territory did not necessarily prohibit other nations from entering into a relationship, but they were required to establish their relatedness. By establishing kinship with other peoples of the area and with the nonhuman inhabitants of a place, Native nations of the plains maintained their specific relationship to the landscape. No institutional power determined the rights of a person or a nation; instead, the people's place within a shifting web of social relations determined the ability of access of both individuals and larger sociopolitical bodies.[39]

Just because the Cheyennes had shifting relationships with the land, however, does not mean that they did not claim and control a specific territory. Certainly, by the 1850s the Cheyennes and Lakotas claimed control over the Black Hills region, stretching as far north as the Powder River. Nevertheless, regulating access to a landscape is not enough to articulate a relationship with a homeland. As colonialism clearly demonstrates, the ability to control a territory does not make the place one's home. By viewing a connection to the environment as constructed through kin relationships that are shifting but grounded, Native nations dispute settler-colonial understandings of territory as bounded by geographical markers and acquired through legal contracts controlled by impersonal governments. This disruption, however, can lead to questions about the concept of homeland. If Native peoples migrate and their relationships with place shifts over time, how can they point to one spot on the landscape as a homeland? The Cheyennes narrate their migration as a people from Minnesota, but their point of origin is Bear Butte. How can the construction of homeland accommodate such shifting relationships with the landscape?

A homeland can have multiple locations because it is constituted through spiritual historical relationships with particular places and maintained through nurturing the memory of the place and a reciprocal obligation with it. Homeland is the place where a Native nation has established an active presence that connects the people to their identity as a cultural group. This presence remains active even when people have moved away from that landscape as long as it is remembered and nurtured through narrative and ceremony. Homeland evolves over time and is often built up across multiple locations. Just like every town where U.S. presidents spent part of their childhoods claims to be their hometown, Bear Butte, the Missouri River, and Minnesota are all homelands for the Cheyennes. Colorado, the Platte River, and even Indian Territory have developed reciprocal relationships with the nation. Each place is part of their construction of homeland, although their presence in some parts of this landscape is more immediate today than it was in the past. The people have been becoming Cheyenne in all of these places, and this journey lives in memory, narrative, and ceremony. Therefore, homeland for the Cheyennes encompasses all the places that gave birth to and molded the Native nation. They are the places where their ancestors resided, and the kinship ties formed in those localities live on. The Cheyennes continue to articulate their relationship with these places in terms of kin and maintain reciprocity with them through narrative, ceremony,

and travel. Homeland is not just a place for Native people. It is a reciprocal relationship sustained through obligations and privileges and
remembered in their history and religion.

Although Europeans living at the time of contact understood
governance systems that depended on establishing kin relationships,
they did not construct their relationship with the land as based on
reciprocity or view the landscape as populated with nonhuman relatives. By 1492 Europeans had already developed sovereign relationships over the land. A ruling family asserted its control over a given
territory and the inhabitants of it, human and nonhuman, forcing
compliance of these subjects and policing their boundaries with violence. When Europeans first arrived in the unfamiliar landscape of
the Americas, Native nations were able to incorporate them into their
kin-based system of accessing territory. Fur traders, such as the Bent
brothers, often intermarried with Native women so that they could
gain access to resources and ensure safe passage.[40] Over time, European and American encroachment shifted the political and economic
practices of Plains peoples, as Native populations participated in the
global capitalist economy both as laborers in the fur and hide trades
and consumers of goods from Europe and around the world. Pressures
on resources—including human resources such as labor—increased
with the demands on production from a global market. By the mid-
nineteenth century, scarcity of materials became an issue for Plains
people as encroachment from other displaced Native peoples and
from Americans hungry for furs, gold, and ultimately land ate away
at limited resources.

Plains nations often responded with diplomacy while they were the
dominant powers in the region, but eventually the speed and violence
of encroachment and the lack of willingness to participate in Native
networks of relatedness in order to access resources required a militaristic response from Native nations.[41] By the nineteenth century,
Americans had begun attempting to take the plains in any way possible. They even used public relations to attack Plains peoples by label-
ing them as wandering aimlessly and failing to use the land to its full
capacity. Plains nations were also constructed as prone to commit random acts of violence, because they were seen as not only biologically
incapable of prolonged rational thought but also as lacking political

unity or lasting control over any given territory. U.S. government officials drew on such representations of Native people to justify their authority over setting territorial boundaries in treaties, and ultimately over encroachment and land seizure.

During the mid-nineteenth century, anxiety steadily increased in the United States concerning the establishment of sovereignty over the entire territory from the Atlantic to the Pacific and over a diverse population of newly encountered Indigenous peoples, new immigrants arriving in the United States on both coasts, and new citizens in territories captured from Mexico. These groups all existed on the edges of the state, not only geographically but also culturally and politically. To those in power, their fluid boundaries threatened the integrity of the state. Because the nation-state strives for uniformity within its borders, the United States began to use the apparatus of the state to control all peoples that lived inside its boundaries. One main mechanism used to subdue Native nations was to curtail free movement and to spatially contain the people. Colonial and imperial powers, including the United States, have trapped and incorporated Indigenous peoples through demarcating space and enforcing boundaries, creating censuses and maps to legitimize the way they imagined their dominion.[42] Maps put space under surveillance, and censuses did the same to people.[43] Representatives of the United States used all these tactics to impose the order of the state onto Native people before the imposition of the reservation system, and they continued to regulate Indigenous movements and spaces once it was in place by providing agents, schools, missions, farmers, and doctors.

At the height of U.S. nationalist assertions, policy makers were attempting to break up Native nations and incorporate their members into the state. During this period, the government began to conceive of Native communities less as distinctly autonomous nations and more as domestic ethnic and racialized communities.[44] The ambiguous construction of the Cheyennes as both politically autonomous and in need of physical containment is apparent in the first treaties to delineate a bounded Cheyenne land base. Scholars of American Indian history have most often explored negotiation and enforcement of treaties as the dominant land retention efforts employed by Native peoples.

Stuart Banner has called for scholars to explore other forms, arguing that most of the scholarship on American Indian land loss has assumed "that conquest and sale are mutually exclusive alternatives that exhaust the possible methods of land transfer."[45] The Northern Cheyennes' struggles to remain in their homeland reveal another mechanism Native people employed: kinship.

By 1851, the steady stream of Americans traveling west had become a turbulent river and tensions increased between the travelers and the Native people whose territory they ransacked as they crossed. The United States did not have the means to police these trails so they decided to clear them of Native inhabitants by establishing treaties with the nations of the region instead. The Fort Laramie Treaty of 1851 was meant to contain each Plains nation within an assigned territory, to grant the United States' rights to build roads and military posts within Native landscapes, and to provide payment for the damage done to the peoples' means of subsistence by passing settlers. A huge council was called at Fort Laramie and the Lakota, Cheyenne, Arapaho, Crow, Assiniboine, Gros Ventre, Mandan, and Arikara delegations all arrived to negotiate. The treaty that emerged set the boundary lines of each nation's territory.[46]

The Cheyennes and Arapahos were assigned a region jointly that encompassed land south of the Platte River. The Lakotas were assigned a region that stretched to the Missouri River in the east and encompassed the Black Hills in the west. The treaty assigned the Powder River region, which the Lakotas and Northern Cheyennes recognized as their own, to the Crows and assigned hunting grounds below the Platte claimed by the Lakotas and Cheyennes to the Kiowas.[47] The treaty did not recognize Cheyenne connections to any territory north of the Platte, including the Black Hills; however, in article 5, it stated that no American Indian nation abandoned any rights of claim it may have had to other lands, nor abandoned the ability to hunt, fish, or pass through any of these territories, partially recognizing Native peoples' rights to their own fluid understandings of territory.[48] Even so, this document certainly did not reflect the connection to the landscape that each nation had established through interethnic social relations. Nevertheless, spatial boundaries had been set, and it became easier for U.S. government officials to imagine Plains Indian nations as bounded ethnically and confined spatially, and to act as if they were.

Only ten years later, in 1861, the United States presented a new treaty to the Cheyennes and Arapahos. The camps living south of the Platte River had become more restless about white encroachment. Some chiefs wished to have a permanent piece of land set aside for their people, and William Bent pushed for treaty negotiations to make this happen.[49] According to article 1 of this treaty, these bands agreed to give up the lands assigned to them in the Fort Laramie Treaty of 1851 and to accept a reservation along the Arkansas.[50] This treaty reduced lands, federally recognized as belonging to the Cheyennes, to a very small island far from the Black Hills and Powder River region where many Cheyenne people still lived, traveled, and hunted. The treaty of 1861 was negotiated at Fort Wise along the Arkansas River with only some of the Cheyennes and Arapahos that lived and hunted in this region, and it encouraged a deeper division between northern and southern bands.[51] The Cheyennes living north of the Platte and the southern Dog Soldier bands refused to sign.[52]

Yet these treaties did not reshape Cheyenne constructions of their homeland, nor did they contain Cheyenne people within the boundaries they set. During the first half of the 1860s most Cheyennes living in the region along the Arkansas were peaceful. Young warriors did carry out a few raids, the people did not confine themselves to a reservation, and there were occasional skirmishes with troops, but overall the people lived quietly. In November 1864 the Cheyenne chief, Black Kettle, and the Arapaho chief, Left Hand, had camped with their people along Sand Creek to hunt where army officers had assured them that they would be safe.[53] For many reasons, Americans in the area were anxious about Native populations, and these anxieties culminated in the infamous massacre of Black Kettle's people at this peaceful camp along the creek.[54]

The Sand Creek massacre had far-reaching consequences for the Cheyenne people. Cheyenne bands and their allies responded by reorganizing themselves socially and coming together to fight the United States, bringing both northern and southern bands that had formerly been oriented toward peace together with Dog Soldier bands. Runners hurried north to bring the news of the massacre to the Southern Cheyenne Dog Men who ranged between the Platte and Republican Rivers and allied with the Lakotas and Northern Arapahos.[55] News of the violence encouraged Southern Cheyenne warriors and families to head north to camps of their kin's people. The Northern Cheyennes, with Spotted Tail's and Pawnee Killer's band of Lakotas, and a few allied Northern Arapaho families also decided to go to war, coming together in a camp on Cherry Creek, a tributary of the Republican River.[56] There were still more Cheyennes living in the Black Hills and Powder River countries, and the group on Cherry Creek decided to send runners still farther north to get the support of these kinsmen, as well as their Northern Arapaho and Lakota allies.[57]

The Cheyennes and Lakotas, with a few Arapaho warriors, took swift military action in retaliation, fighting the U.S. military throughout the plains during the second half of the 1860s. By March 1865 Southern and Northern Cheyenne bands were camping together along the Powder River.[58] When the Southern Cheyennes came north, they brought the Sacred Arrows with them. Apparently some of the young men of the north had never seen the Arrows, and some of the young men of the south had never seen the Sacred Buffalo Hat. Regardless of previous geographic division, Cheyenne bands were able to unite in a time of crisis to maintain their territory, the sanctity of their nation, and the safety of their people. They were still united by the Sacred Arrows and Buffalo Hat. They were also united by kinship ties that had been remembered and maintained.

Although the military did try to subdue these bands, they failed to contain them. In an attempt to regain control, the federal government proposed a treaty in 1865. Only a very few Southern Cheyennes and Arapahos signed this treaty, in which the United States convinced them to relinquish their lands in Colorado and accept a reservation that lay partly in Kansas and partly in the Indian Territory.[59] At the treaty negotiations, Black Kettle stated that it was unwise to cede or accept land when only eighty lodges of Cheyennes were present and the other two hundred lodges usually associated with the Arkansas River and Dog Soldier bands were north of the Platte River.[60] Because so few people agreed to this treaty, there was little chance it would end the hostilities on the plains. Those living, camping, and fighting with the Lakotas in the north essentially paid no attention to it at all.

The continuing hostilities both north and south of the Platte convinced the federal government that they had to take action. On June 20, 1867, Congress created the U.S. Indian Peace Commission, intending that a special group of civilians and military officials who had competence in Indian affairs would negotiate treaties meant to deal with Native people's complaints and make the plains safe for Americans.[61] In the fall of 1867 the commission negotiated the Medicine Lodge Treaty with the Cheyennes, Arapahos, Kiowas, Apaches, and Comanches on Medicine Lodge Creek in Kansas. This treaty established another Cheyenne reservation that was bounded by the Cimarron and Arkansas Rivers.[62] Not all Southern Cheyennes acquiesced to this new treaty or the new territory, but many did. The Northern Cheyennes as a whole did not participate, further dividing the nation from the perspective of many government officials.

The Peace Commission also attempted to calm the hostilities on the northern plains through treaty making. Lakota, Northern Cheyenne, Northern Arapaho, and Crow peoples all made treaties with this commission at Fort Laramie in 1868. According to John Stands In Timber, the Native nations at this meeting paid more attention to developing alliances with other Native nations and less to the U.S. treaty negotiation. The northern and southern bands had the opportunity to visit relatives. The Pawnees, Utes, and Cheyennes all came together to negotiate peace and bind it by establishing individual friendships across these nations and exchanging horses, shirts, and other goods.[63] These nations used the opportunity to come together to negotiate peace and joint access to territory by establishing reciprocal relationships. The contracts of the state still meant little in comparison.

The Fort Laramie Treaty of 1868 established the Great Sioux Reservation for the Lakotas. The reservation was bounded on the east by the Missouri, the north by what is today the North Dakota state line, the west by the Wyoming state line, and the south by the Nebraska state line. This treaty also established an unceded Indian territory that would be shared by the Lakotas, Cheyennes, and Arapahos, encompassing territory north of the Platte River and east of the Bighorn

Mountains and south of the Yellowstone and Missouri Rivers. The Northern Arapahos were explicitly listed as party to the Fort Laramie Treaty with the Lakota bands, but strangely the Cheyennes were not.[64] The Northern Cheyennes and Arapahos signed a separate document during these negotiations. In this document, they agreed to relinquish the right to all their territory in the north, but they retained the right to hunt while sufficient game existed. The Cheyennes and Arapahos who signed this treaty also agreed to accept as their permanent home either a portion of the Southern Cheyenne and Arapaho Reservation established by the Medicine Lodge Treaty or a portion of the Great Sioux Reservation.[65]

According to Stands In Timber, the Cheyenne people never fully understood the implications of either 1868 treaty. The interpreters had not provided a solid translation, and all the people understood was that Americans wanted to build roads through their territory and help them protect their land. They had no idea that the treaty could begin to push the Cheyenne people south away from their beloved homeland.[66] At the same time, this was the first treaty with the Cheyennes that recognized any connection to the landscape above the Platte, although it did not grant the land only to the Cheyennes. It did recognize that the Northern Cheyennes and Arapahos were allied with the Lakotas to such a degree that each nation should have had access to this landscape. Despite this, it ironically gave prominence to the Lakotas—the latest arrivals—as the primary occupants of the area. The Cheyenne and Arapaho claim to this region was treated as secondary.

Things were peaceful in the north for a little while after the Fort Laramie Treaty of 1868. During the following decade, the federal government began the process of establishing agencies where Northern Plains people could pick up the annuities guaranteed under their treaties. These agencies could also act as centers for assimilating Plains peoples, educating their children, teaching them Christianity, and convincing them to farm. Because of their ambiguous status in the 1868 treaties, the Northern Cheyennes and Northern Arapahos did not have separate agencies where they could receive annuities. Most received annuities at the agencies that served Red Cloud and his Ogalala followers, but some became affiliated with Spotted Tail and his Sicangus.[67] This was a time of radically changing circumstances for these northern bands, and socially they realigned themselves in an attempt to remain in their homeland despite such dramatic changes. The flexibility of Cheyenne kinship allowed families to adapt to this new situation, shifting band affiliation when needed. Some bands and families attempted to accommodate their lives to the presence of the new agencies and tried to establish permanent homes near them. Others tried to maintain their independence far from the agencies. Many of the Northern Cheyennes opted to join the Lakotas who spent most of the year far from the agencies, living and hunting in the landscape they favored. The membership of camps reflected the choices that each family made given the limitations created by American encroachment.

Regardless, the United States refused to formally recognize Northern Cheyenne rights to the territory set aside as the Great Sioux Reservation in the Fort Laramie Treaty of 1868. The government did not or would not recognize that the Northern Cheyennes were more intimately connected to the Black Hills region and allied more closely with the Arapaho and the Lakota than with their Southern Cheyenne relatives and the territory along the Arkansas. The language of the two treaties represented the Cheyennes as visitors to the Black Hills—visitors who belonged farther south where the United States had acknowledged territory for them. The treaty with the Lakotas declared that the reservation is only for the occupation of the nations named in it, specifically excluding the Cheyennes, but allowing any American Indian nation or individual that the Lakotas requested to live among them with the consent of the United States.[68]

Treaties have long been understood as one of the markers of federal recognition of Native political sovereignty. On the other end of the spectrum, they have been viewed as coercive documents used to manipulate Native people into signing away rights to land and agreeing to assimilationist programs at agencies and on reservations. Many volumes have been written on how a given Native nation understood the consequences of the treaty-making process. Certainly any encounter between Euro-Americans and Natives was culturally negotiated, both sides bringing their own values and expectations to the meeting.[69] Lyons has eloquently argued that the x marks made by Native people on treaties can be understood to represent a hope for the future.[70] He argues that often these signers recognized that treaties would lead them down a path to modernity. Far from being the unwitting savages who were duped into selling their land for shiny mirrors and pretty beads, Lyons presents those who made their x marks as politically sophisticated leaders who realized that their world was changing quickly and attempted to take the action that they believed would most benefit their community.

This surely was true for the Cheyennes who signed each of these treaties. They most likely felt that maintaining the social relationships established by meeting, discussing, and exchanging gifts with allied Native nations and the United States had more weight than an "X" on a piece of paper. Americans, on the other hand, were classically bad at nurturing these types of relationships. The goal of the U.S. treaty commissions on the plains was not to establish sustained reciprocal relationships with the current inhabitants of the landscape in order to foster joint access to land and resources. They strove instead to contain and control Native populations.

The U.S. failure to formally recognize Northern Cheyenne rights to the Black Hills and the Powder River region set the stage for the multiple and lengthy struggles of the people to remain in the heart of their homeland detailed in this text. The leaders who signed the Northern Cheyenne and Northern Arapaho Treaty had been told that the federal negotiators acknowledged Cheyenne and Arapaho claims to the Black Hills, as well as the country beyond the Hills from the north branch of the Platte all the way north to the Yellowstone. Technically, this was true. The treaty recognized that the Cheyennes wished to access this territory, but required permission from the Lakota to do so. According to Peter Powell, however, Little Wolf was told by the commissioners that a great swath of land north of the Platte River and stretching west to the Bighorns and east to the Missouri would belong to the Cheyennes and the Arapahos.[71] It is easy to believe the Northern Cheyennes were convinced that the United States understood their connection to this landscape and that the treaty declaring their right to live on the Great Sioux Reservation cemented this recognition because the treaty recognized a significant marker of their relationship with this landscape—the alliance between the Cheyennes, the Arapahos, and the Lakotas.

The commissioners, however, failed to realize that the Cheyennes believed they, and not the Lakotas, held the primary relationship with much of the territory set aside by the Great Sioux Reservation. From a Cheyenne perspective, they lived and hunted in the Black Hills and the rich hunting grounds to the west, with their friends the Arapahos, long before the Lakotas arrived. The Cheyennes had allowed the Lakotas to enter the country and had allied with them against enemies, but the Lakotas certainly did not have a stronger claim to the region than the Cheyennes. The United States, however, privileged one nation over the other with complete disregard for Native understandings of land tenure and social relations. For U.S. officials, the containment of all Cheyennes on one reservation was the most pressing issue, and most of them lived south of the Platte.

Of the chiefs of the Council of Forty-Four, only Little Wolf, Dull Knife, Big Wolf, and Short Hair signed the 1868 Fort Laramie Treaty. The other northern chiefs disagreed with this treaty, and when Little Wolf returned from Fort Laramie to the main Cheyenne camp, they were angry with him. Little Wolf tried to convince them that it was a good treaty, but to no avail. Most northern people rejected the 1868 treaty as a binding agreement because it had not been approved by the Council of Forty-Four.[72] Stands In Timber stated that the chiefs made decisions according to the will of the people and in consultation with other chiefs, so no one man could approve major tribal commitments such as treaties or surrenders.[73] This decentralized political power was in fact an advantage for the Northern Cheyennes because every family could potentially make its own decision instead of following one chief in whom the power of the nation was invested. Representatives of the U.S. government had to convince a community and not just one man. They did not make this attempt, however, for the 1868 Fort Laramie Treaty.

Even today, many Northern Cheyennes state that they had no treaties with the U.S. government. While Cheyenne leaders clearly put pen to paper several times, none of these treaties recognized the landscape that the Northern Cheyennes understood as theirs. After the first treaty they signed with the United States in 1825, each treaty was one that the nation entered into with their allies, not alone.[74] None of these treaties recognized the status of the Northern Cheyennes as a people more closely connected to the northern landscape than their Southern relatives or with a political autonomy separate from their Lakota and Arapaho relatives. Later treaties established the Northern Cheyennes' rights to settle on the Southern Cheyenne and Arapaho Reservation in Indian Territory and the Great Sioux Reservation in Dakota Territory. The 1868 treaty even stated that the Northern Cheyennes could attach themselves to Crow Agency if they wished.[75] Regardless, these documents did not recognize Cheyenne understandings of their relationship to the landscape, nor was the 1868 treaty submitted to the Cheyenne political process. When Cheyenne people today say they have no treaties with the United States, this recognizes the inadequacy of the treaties they have to reflect their autonomous sense of nationhood and their relationship with their homeland.

Such a blatant disregard for Cheyenne constructions of territory and resource use placed Cheyenne people in the difficult position of either acquiescing to the boundaries set by the state in order to maintain peace or challenging the state by remaining mobile. While some families chose to stay close to the agencies during this tumultuous and violent period, these choices did not save Cheyenne people from the whims of the government. After the Battle of the Little Bighorn in 1876, government officials were determined to remove any and all Cheyennes from the northern plains using whatever means necessary. While the agencies were within the territory the Cheyennes utilized historically, they were not in favored camping locations. The treaty process had pushed the Northern Cheyennes away from their seasonal campsites, laying the political groundwork for a Cheyenne diaspora. By whittling away at their land base and establishing a reservation in Indian Territory, far from their northern homeland, the Cheyennes ultimately had no land to call their own in the eyes of the state save the southern agency.[76] Many Northern Cheyennes clearly had no desire to leave their homeland around the Black Hills for Indian Territory, but as the plains became more desirable to Euro-Americans seeking passage to land and minerals farther west, the United States worked harder to contain all Plains peoples associated with this territory. These efforts, both political and militaristic, and at times genocidal, gave Cheyenne families little choice but to engage with government officials at established agencies.

Yossi Shain and Martin Sherman have argued that diasporic formations, like those of the Cheyennes, are endemic to a world order dominated by nation-states.[77] The term "diaspora" designates a segment of people forced from their homeland who preserve elements of their language, religion, and sociocultural practices despite the dislocation. The work of memory and commemoration is central for unifying diasporic peoples, as is an emphasis on returning to the homeland, either physically and permanently or temporarily and metaphorically.[78] In theory, the nation-state should eliminate ethnically motivated strife because these groups can either migrate to their own states or become absorbed as multicultural citizens in their state of residency. Because the state strives for unity, however, those who aspire to maintain their cultural distinctness are often treated with extreme coercion.

In the United States any group not willing to fully assimilate to Euro-American middle-class expectations has suffered greatly under the policies of the state. For many Native people, this meant genocide, removal, and forced assimilation. After the Battle of the Little Bighorn, the Cheyennes, Lakotas, and Arapahos who refused to come into the agencies threatened to undermine the work of military and government officials to populate the plains with assimilated citizens. Interestingly, the Northern Cheyennes bore much of the punishment handed out once these bands had settled at the agencies. Military officials had used removal to Indian Territory as a threat to control the Northern Plains groups. As a way to frighten everyone into submission, these officials decided to separate the relatively small group of Cheyennes from their Lakota and Arapaho relatives and force them south. By coercing a smaller and therefore easier-to-manage group into removal, local officials believed they could gain control over all those Plains people who continued to resist them.

This divide-and-conquer practice used by U.S. officials in the Indian Office and the military made many Native people diasporic peoples. Many reservations are located far from original homelands. Often people were forced onto them under threat of starvation or violence. The Northern Cheyennes lived in diaspora in Indian Territory, remembering their homeland, preserving their way of life to the best of their ability, and always hoping to return. Confinement to a reservation can be a diasporic experience, even if the place lies within a traditional homeland. Living on a reservation in the nineteenth century meant having to leave many parts of your homeland outside of its boundaries and not knowing when you might see those places again. It meant not being able to perform ceremonies because they made no sense away from the landscape where they needed to be performed. It meant continuing to fight for a chance to return to these places, even if for a short time, and continuing to preserve these places in memory so that your children or grandchildren would know them if they were ever able to return.

James N. Leiker and Ramon Powers use the term "exodus" to describe the Northern Cheyennes' struggle to return home that followed removal. They describe this history as "a movement of ethnic refugees from an area of forced concentration toward a spiritual homeland."[79] By attempting to return, Cheyenne people asserted their cultural and political autonomy, refusing to accept both the cultural definitions and the physical boundaries that U.S. officials tried to impose on them. This was not simply resistance; the Cheyenne diaspora also involved a mixture of Lyons's x marks and older ways of asserting autonomy. No return would have been possible without kinship.

Khachig Tölölyan points out that maintaining kin ties across vast distances is often a central component of the effort to return for diasporic peoples.[80] The stories of those Cheyennes struggling to return demonstrate the centrality of kinship to their efforts to maintain connectedness across the distance and ultimately to live in their northern homeland. These narratives also reveal that the network of kin as the basis for Native sociopolitical organization was and is flexible enough to resist the state and to sustain the Native nation through diaspora. In fact, the easy ability of camps and bands to fracture and separate under difficult circumstances helped generate a diversity of strategies, creating the flexibility Cheyenne people needed to pursue their goals of returning home. This history demonstrates that such fragmenting mechanisms actually aided the maintenance of a Cheyenne nation connected along networks of kin. In the case of the Northern Cheyennes, the strategic use of kinship helped them not only return home but also establish a land base within their homeland.

From their earliest history to their first interactions with Europeans and Americans, kinship created the network that kept them connected as a people to their entire homeland. Throughout this period, different bands of Cheyennes established interethnic alliances with different Native nations, connecting them to new lands. Unlike the nation-state that relied on rigid social, cultural, and physical boundaries, the Cheyenne nation was woven together by kin relations. Therefore, the process of migration did not threaten the exercise of Cheyenne political autonomy.

Kinship allowed the people to build relationships with human and nonhuman entities along their migrations to secure their presence in these new landscapes. As Americans entered the region and attempted to impose a new understanding of territory on Plains peoples through treaties, Cheyennes continued to utilize networks of kin to access land. They had to negotiate with a people who saw the world in terms of the nation-state—a social construction very different from that of the kin-based nation. While establishing treaties with Plains nations, representatives of the United States used state-based policy to delineate both Native and American rights in the territory. For the most part, representatives of the United States were guided in their interactions with Native people on the plains by a naturalized concept that all humanity was divided into nations, basically resembling their own.

In the 1860s and 1870s, U.S. relations with Plains nations became more and more marked by contradiction and ambiguity. Federal policy vacillated from removal to containment to assimilation, but each new policy was steeped in nation-state understandings of political relations between the United States and Indian people. It was during this period that Plains people began to learn how the institutions of the state were imposed and also to sense the contradictions in the process of imposition. All the while, local agents and military officials realized that Plains nations did not conform to the nation-state style boundaries they attempted to impose, and occasionally these officials proposed boundaries that more closely reflected local realities.

The Fort Laramie Treaty of 1868 poses an interesting example. This treaty reflected the interests of Cheyenne people by acknowledging their rights to the territory contained in the Great Sioux Reservation.

The local officials who negotiated the treaty emphasized this point, surely realizing that it would be of essential importance to the Cheyennes. The treaty also stated that these Northern Cheyennes would accept either the Great Sioux Reservation or the Southern Cheyenne and Arapaho Reservation as their permanent home. Federal officials continued to assert that the Northern Cheyennes belonged on the southern reservation, contradicting the intentions of some of the local officials to allow the Cheyennes to remain in the north. In the two decades following the Fort Laramie Treaty, the vacillating Indian policy and the contradictions between federal policy and the understandings of local officials often led to problems for local agents in dealing with Native populations. In some of these contradictory moments, the Northern Cheyennes succeeded in convincing American officials to acknowledge their kin-based rights. At other times, their actions had severe consequences for the people. Regardless, Northern Cheyennes continued to activate kin relationships in order to take social, political, and economic action that had meaning according to Cheyenne understandings of autonomy even if these actions confused and angered officials representing the United States. In this way, Northern Cheyennes continued to base their collective social identity on kinship, even while federal and local officials attempted to impose the boundaries of the nation-state. Local officials still understood the world as naturally divided into nations, but they also realized it could be easier to contain Plains people if their boundaries more closely reflected the divisions the people made among themselves. Their local knowledge of Native people, however, often led them to proposals that contradicted policy at the federal level.

Despite the dramatic changes taking place on the plains caused by the ever-increasing American presence, the Cheyenne people continued to depend on kinship to negotiate and order their social, ceremonial, political, and economic life, as well as their relationship to land. They historically used the language of kin to adapt and survive, and they chose to continue this strategy in their negotiations with representatives of the United States as well, including treaty negotiations. Although treaties created boundary lines on the landscape meant to fix the territorial and ethnic boundaries of each Native nation, the members of these nations often did not accept these boundaries.

They continued to travel across the plains, determining their access to the territory based on the kin they had there. They continued to camp in groups that contained multiple ethnic affiliations, determining membership on kinship not ethnicity. Lakota and Cheyenne Dog Men camped and lived together, traveling through territory that they shared. Southern Cheyenne bands traveled north to join Northern bands regardless of the fact that they had passed out of their treaty-designated territory. Northern Cheyennes took rations at Red Cloud Agency with Northern Arapahos and Lakotas, because this agency was located within the territory these three groups had shared for generations.

As life on the plains began to change dramatically with the increased American presence, Cheyenne people continued to draw on this flexible kin system to help them trade for new goods, retain access to hunting grounds and territory, defend against the new enemy of the U.S. military, and even to establish peace with these American newcomers. Throughout the nineteenth century, the disruption caused by the American presence, first to trade and then to access to territory, certainly did affect Cheyenne social organization. Even during diaspora, however, the Cheyennes kept their kin-based political and social system and deployed it in strategic ways, just as they had in the past, to maintain a Cheyenne identity, to order political and economic relationships with non-Cheyennes, to maintain their presence in their homeland, and most importantly to assert political autonomy when faced with the imposition of state-based political, geographic, and cultural borders.[81] By recognizing kinship as an important element in the exercise of Native political autonomy, it becomes clear that the state has not had the level of power to control landscapes or to absorb outsiders that it has been granted. This perspective emphasizes persistence over the dichotomy of resistance versus assimilation, negotiation over surrender, and the flexibility of family over the rigidity of the state.

CHAPTER FOUR

WE NEVER SURRENDERED

Two Moons's People and an
Alliance with General Nelson Miles

My friends kept mentioning Elva Stands In Timber. After that first summer of introductions, I began having detailed conversations about Cheyenne history with members of the family that had generously welcomed me. Elva Stands In Timber is a good person to talk to, I was told. She knows a lot about Cheyenne history, people said. She likes visitors, they told me. Her nephew offered to introduce me, but we were never able to find the right time. Eventually I decided to simply show up at her doorstep with a bag of plums and a smile and hope she would offer me a seat at her kitchen table. As I got to know her, I learned that she would willingly sit across the little linoleum and chrome table from most people who stopped by to chat, including health professionals, random family members, and even missionaries. She once showed me a pamphlet that some Catholic visitors had given her that was written in Lakota. "Do you want this?" she said. "You can have it if you do. I don't know why they gave it to me. Why did they think I would be able to read it?" She paused and smiled kindly before adding, "But they were really nice people anyway."

That initial afternoon, I introduced myself as a student interested in Cheyenne history and gave her the plums. Her eyes lit up when I said "plums," but my first lesson from her was that while plums from the store were very nice, wild plums gathered from the trees on the reservation were better. Ms. Stands In Timber offered me the seat across the kitchen table from her. I told her that I particularly wanted to learn about how the reservation was established. "Well, what do you want to know about?" she asked me as we munched on the plums. I was

113

taken aback because no one I had spoken with had been so business-like. I had to think for a moment. What did I want to know about? And from her—about her family?

Not really sure of her family's history, I decided on a topic about which I still had very little material. "Well, I've been wondering about the Cheyennes who surrendered to General Miles at Fort Keogh. What do you know about that?" I asked.

"Oh, we never surrendered," she said, quickly. I'm sure the surprise on my face was obvious—mouth gaping, maybe a little plum on my chin. I listened very carefully to what she had to say after that, all the while trying to figure out in my head how she could possibly think that the Northern Cheyennes had never surrendered. What else would you call it?

According to the books I had read, the U.S. military relentlessly pursued the Cheyennes and Lakotas after the Battle of the Little Big-horn in 1876, where Lt. Col. George Armstrong Custer infamously lost his life along with all the men in his cavalry unit. Previous to this battle, the military had attempted to attain their goal of restricting all Plains peoples to the agencies through force, but they failed. The United States established these agencies, often on land ceded to Native peoples through treaties, as a way to regulate their activities and movements by creating territorial boundaries, distributing rations, and taking censuses. Although most Northern Plains peoples had spent some time at these agencies, as hostilities escalated over the invasion of their homeland—particularly the Black Hills—many Plains peoples left their agencies to fight, to join their families, or to hunt and live on the plains. Although the Fort Laramie Treaty of 1868 pro-hibited Americans from entering the territory without permission, hostilities between these Plains nations and the United States slowly increased as more non-Native people encroached on the territory, compelled mainly by the discovery of gold deposits in the region. After the battle, the U.S. army committed to ridding the plains of all roving peoples. In their letters, government officials called these Chey-enne, Arapaho, and Lakota camps "hostiles," indicating the antago-nistic relationship they had toward unconfined Plains people. History books mainly described these peoples as starving and exhausted, forced into agencies at the end of a bayonet and made to relinquish their horses and weapons. The writers called these events "surrenders," and I never questioned the nomenclature.

Elva Stands In Timber was a knowledgeable elder. Nevertheless, I initially told myself that her statement must be hyperbole. Perhaps she simply wanted to present the Cheyennes in the best light to an outsider. As "revisionist history," this idea held a certain political saliency. If the Northern Cheyennes never surrendered, they remained a free people, not controlled by the United States. Very appealing. Soon I discovered Ms. Stands In Timber was not the only Cheyenne who held this view. Every book I had read used the term "surrender" to describe the moments when Cheyenne camps came into agencies and forts. Military documents from the time did as well. I had the habit of using the term in my conversations, but every time I asked about this or that surrender, I was corrected. Over and over I heard, "Oh, we never surrendered." It was simply too compelling to dismiss the idea. The more I heard it, the more I started to question those books and documents. After all, U.S. officials were as compelled to call these events a surrender as the Cheyennes were to say they were not.

Jeffrey Ostler has presented a fresh perspective on this history, stating, "The army was never able to score a major victory. In fact, the Indians' ability to avoid military defeat forced [General Nelson A.] Miles and [General George] Crook to rely on diplomacy. Although the militants were unable to avoid surrendering, they did win important concessions."[1] By focusing on diplomacy instead of surrender, he has illuminated the leverage Plains peoples used to negotiate terms for peace and have a say in future political decisions. Questioning the hegemonic assumption that the U.S. military could easily overpower Plains nations also provides a new lens through which to examine Cheyenne history. In fact, peace became particularly elusive for Generals Crook and Miles after the major victory won by Plains nations at the Battle of the Little Bighorn. The U.S. military continued their campaign but with little lasting success. The brigades destroyed a few villages, including a devastating attack by General Mackenzie on Dull Knife's village camped along the Powder River.[2] These generals could not force these camps to surrender, however; when one group suffered, their relatives living in another camp provided for them. Their wide-ranging kin networks allowed these

Lakota, Arapaho, and Cheyenne families to continually elude the soldiers, frustrating the military's attempts to bring all Plains people to their designated agencies.

The realization that their military losses actually forced the United States to enter into negotiations with Plains peoples sheds new light on one historical narrative of surrender—that of Two Moons. After the Battle of the Little Bighorn, Two Moons and a small group of Northern Cheyennes chose to come to Fort Keogh, not a reservation or an agency but a military cantonment on the Yellowstone River near the present-day town of Miles City, Montana. The history of this group raises several questions about the assumptions scholars have made about the end of the Indian Wars on the plains. Nationalist histories often assume that prisoners of war are at the mercy of the state, and because the Northern Cheyennes at Fort Keogh were officially classed as prisoners, histories told from a Euro-American perspective have either struggled to explain or simply ignored the fate of Two Moons and his followers. These histories tend to focus on the federal government's determination to remove all Cheyennes. As Cheyenne oral history asserts, however, what emerged between General Miles and the Northern Cheyennes who came to his post at Fort Keogh was not actually a surrender. A careful examination of Plains interethnic relations reveals that the relationship that developed between Miles and Two Moons and his followers was one of alliance and not of defeated and victorious enemies.

Considering the Cheyennes' use of kinship as a political strategy in its dealings with government officials illuminates the efforts of local agents such as Miles, explaining why he took actions that contradicted U.S. Indian policy. It also explains how some Northern Cheyennes were able to remain in the north despite the pressure to relocate to the south. The alliance formed between him and Two Moons's camp proved to be so strong that Miles fought to retain some Northern Cheyennes at Fort Keogh even when federal policy dictated their removal to Indian Territory. His dedication to aiding the Northern Cheyennes in their struggle to remain in the Tongue River valley would last through the 1884 formation of the Northern Cheyenne reservation. By coming to Fort Keogh and forging a peace with Miles, the Northern Cheyennes did not simply relegate their lives to white

Cheyenne Chief Two Moons by
Laton A. Huffman. From the
collection of Gene and Bev Allen,
Helena, Montana.

policy makers. Instead, this alliance gave the Northern Cheyennes the
power to demand that Miles fulfill certain obligations and provided
the leverage the people needed to convince the U.S. president to
establish a reservation in the heart of their homeland in Montana
through executive order. By advancing and enforcing the reciprocal
obligations the alliance implied, the Cheyennes living at Fort Keogh
not only remained in their homeland but were also able to help bring
the rest of their kin home. The history of this group illustrates that the
Cheyennes continued to use kinship strategically to take political action
in relation to the actions of the United States even after 1876.

In the decades before the Battle of the Little Bighorn, the United
States had adopted a restrained approach to its relations with Ameri-
can Indians. Although many Americans desired the containment of
Native people on reservations, they did not support violent mili-
tary force to subdue Indian peoples. The general sentiment was that
Americans and American Indians could live separately and peacefully.
Containment and assimilation, aided by the establishment of reser-
vations, instead of removal or extermination, were believed to be

humanitarian methods to deal with the American Indian people that lived within the geopolitical boundaries of the United States. Americans had seen the devastating effects of earlier removal policies, and both sides of the Indian policy question began to support efforts they considered less violent.[3] Humanitarians believed Natives could live quietly on reservations where they would have enough time to assimilate, and expansionists realized that designating bounded lands as "Indian country" would open the West more quickly for settlement.

In the case of the Northern Cheyennes, officials debated about the location of a Cheyenne reservation. Officials in Washington, D.C., believed the Southern Cheyenne reservation was the obvious choice. Although the Northern Cheyennes had treaties that recognized their relationship to the northern lands of the Great Sioux Reservation, each of these treaties also pointed to the southern reservation as a location for permanent settlement. In November 1873 a delegation of Northern Cheyennes and Arapahos visited Washington to discuss removal to Indian Territory. Even at this early date, federal officials had decided the Northern Cheyennes and Arapahos should be removed to the south. This delegation strongly opposed removal, but federal officials were determined to convince them to agree.[4]

Whirlwind, a chief of the Southern Cheyennes, remembered this trip to Washington in an 1880 interview. He stated that the Southern Cheyenne leaders had come to meet the Northern leaders and to invite them to live on their reservation. He said to them, "We are the biggest part of the tribe, you are the smallest; we have plenty of buffalo and other game to hunt; we would very much like to have you come down here with us."[5] By bringing the Southern and Northern leaders together, the United States attempted to put pressure on the Northern Cheyennes to make their permanent home in Indian Territory. From what Whirlwind remembered, the Southern Cheyennes extended their hospitality and encouraged the Northern Cheyennes to join them.

Regardless of the efforts of the government and the hospitality of the Southern Cheyennes, the Northern leaders responded cautiously. Dull Knife and Little Wolf did most of the talking for the Northern camps. Their delegation finally told the government officials, "Wait until we can go back and see our people, and find out what they think about it; then maybe we will decide to go down."[6] By November 1874 four

Cheyennes including Little Wolf and Standing Elk and five Arapahos including Black Coal had been convinced to sign a document that the officials called a "treaty," stating simply that the Northern Cheyennes and Arapahos agreed to go to the southern reservation at any time as long as they were allowed to remain at Red Cloud and receive rations and annuity goods until that time.[7] Despite the signed document, there is little evidence that the Northern Cheyennes consented to a removal or believed that they had committed themselves to a permanent reservation in Indian Territory.

When showed this document, Ms. DG declared that she had never heard of any treaty like this and that Dull Knife and Little Wolf could not have had any idea that this document would be construed by the government as acceptance of a permanent reservation in Indian Territory. They would have understood it as an agreement to visit the south but not to live there. The documents support her assessment because the Cheyennes were encouraged many times to visit the Southern Cheyenne reservation, and if they did not like it, they were allowed to return home. Furthermore, the treaty itself did not indicate that going to the Southern reservation was permanent. Most likely they thought they were agreeing to visit the south to negotiate but not to stay. Yet when they came into the agencies after the Battle of the Little Bighorn, federal officials not only dedicated themselves to removing them but also used this 1874 document to pose the argument that the Northern Cheyennes had wanted this removal all along.

Despite the determination of Washington, many agents in the field supported Cheyenne and Arapaho opposition to removal. These agents interacted with Northern Cheyenne people on a regular basis and at least understood that even though the Northern Cheyennes were still Cheyennes and had a cultural connection with the Southern Cheyennes, they saw the north as their home. Both J. W. Daniels, the agent at Red Cloud, and Samuel D. Hinman, a member of the Sioux Commission, attempted to relate the importance of allowing these Cheyennes to remain in the north. In 1873 J. W. Daniels argued that the Northern Cheyennes and Arapahos should have their own northern reservation distinct from the Lakotas. He noted that nearly all of the Northern Cheyennes had spent most of the year at Red Cloud Agency and argued that sending the Cheyennes and Arapahos to Indian

Territory was impractical—but keeping them together with the Lakotas was also ill advised because of their military alliance.[8] While he
couched his reasoning in economic terms, he apparently empathized
with the Northern Cheyenne people's desire to remain in the north.
Ironically, Daniels's suggestion that the Northern Cheyennes were
dangerous when allowed to live and interact with the Lakotas would
be an argument used many more times in the coming decades to support removal.

In 1874 several Cheyenne and Arapaho headmen met with members of the Sioux Commission who had come to investigate the boundaries of the reservation. Samuel D. Hinman, a member of the commission
present at this meeting, discussed the headmen's statements concerning removal: "They do not wish to go, and will not go, except forced
by the use of troops. They have never lived south, and their friends
there are at war and unsettled. This is their home and the Sioux their
friends. They desire to remain here and be consolidated with the Sioux.
This the Sioux agree to. In this way they will be even lost as a tribe,
and they will be no extra expense to the government. I think their
ground well taken, and that we have no right to remove them against
their will." Hinman's sentiments became the official recommendation
of the Sioux Commission, emphasizing the benefit to the government;
consolidating these peoples reduced their responsibilities. He concluded that the agent should be instructed to consider the Cheyennes
and Arapahos as part of the Lakotas and that they should be issued
rations and annuities at the northern agencies.[9] The commission recognized not only the Cheyennes' and Arapahos' relationship to their
homeland but also their close relationship with the Lakotas.

While the general ideology of ethnic nationality held by most Americans at the time categorized the Northern and Southern Cheyennes
as one tribal nation, Hinman and other officials working directly with
Native peoples often had more complex understandings of Indigenous social organization. Occasionally they recognized the importance
of intertribal alliances and the flexibility of national boundaries. As
people assigned to overseeing the day-to-day operation of agencies,
these officials frequently composed more practical and less ideological agendas using knowledge they had gained through their interactions with Native peoples. Hinman revealed both perspectives when

he argued that although the Cheyennes would be "lost as a tribe," they were at home in the north with their friends, the Lakotas. The attitude that the Cheyennes should be allowed to remain in the north did not prevail, however, and larger forces pushed these local voices to the side in favor of the wishes of the federal government. Even before Custer's dramatic defeat, removal from their homeland in the north to the Southern Cheyenne and Arapaho Agency was the biggest threat to their sense of Native nationhood the Northern Cheyennes faced from federal policy.

Although federal officials were concerned over the fate of the Northern Cheyennes, their most pressing problems lay elsewhere. By 1873 the United States was headed into a severe economic depression. Farmers lost their land, workers lost their jobs, and most of the previously discovered gold fields held few new opportunities.[10] Even though the Fort Laramie Treaty of 1868 forbade Americans to enter the Great Sioux Reservation, guaranteeing this land for the Lakotas and their allies, the government was under pressure to open new lands to renew the struggling economy, and it was rumored that the Black Hills were full of gold. These circumstances set the stage for the illegal invasion of the reservation, first by government expeditions and then by miners and fortune seekers, breaking the tenuous peace between the Cheyennes, the Arapahos, the Lakotas, and the United States.

In 1874 a military expedition under the command of Gen. George Armstrong Custer entered the Hills with a mission of exploration. This expedition confirmed the rumors that the region contained gold. According to the press, Custer declared that there was gold in the grass roots. Eastern newspapers painted a picture of a land where nuggets covered the gurgling streambeds and gold flakes lay just under the grassy meadows. Immigrants swarmed to the Great Sioux Reservation. Although the military was responsible for keeping Americans out of the Hills and occasionally removed some parties, they were unable or unwilling to stop the mad rush.[11] By 1875 the military had essentially abandoned efforts to keep Americans out of the region. It has, in fact, been documented by the discovery of three confidential letters in the National Archives that President Grant ordered the military to turn a blind eye to the invasion of the Black Hills.[12] This order enjoyed support from both the Departments of War and the

Interior. Since the 1868 treaty, there had been minor skirmishes between bands of Cheyennes, Arapahos, and Lakotas on one side and the military and other Americans on the other. The invasion of the Black Hills in violation of the treaty, however, opened a wound that demanded nothing less than a full-blown military response from these allies.

By the early 1870s the economic downturn and sharpening class conflict in the United States, as well as increased warfare throughout the plains, encouraged the northeastern middle classes to retreat from liberalism and reassert rights of private property, the priority of national development, and the necessity of stricter social control. According to this new political ideology, those who asserted rights thwarting these goals threatened to destroy the stability of the nation. Jeffrey Ostler has suggested that Grant knew that withdrawing troops from the Black Hills would allow the possibility of Lakota and Cheyenne attacks on miners that in turn would justify a final conquest of Northern Plains peoples.[13] Not only did American officials turn from liberalism; they turned toward a renewed effort to completely conquer Native people and assert colonial rule. The powder keg of the Black Hills invasion exploded into the Great Sioux Wars. This, in turn, resulted in the Battle of the Little Bighorn.

On December 3, 1875, the Secretary of the Interior ordered all "hostile Sioux Indians residing outside of their reservations" to arrive at their agencies by the end of January 1876.[14] Any Cheyennes, Arapahos, or Lakotas found away from the agencies after this date would be considered "hostile," and the military would be allowed to use force against them. David Wilkins has argued that this declaration was meant to spur the Lakotas into a full-fledged military response, authorizing the army to use any means necessary to control these peoples, even though they were engaged in the treaty-stipulated activities of hunting and camping on treaty-recognized lands.[15] Nevertheless, some families decided to concede to the wishes of the United States, at least for the time being, and come into the agencies.

In her interview with Thomas Marquis, Iron Teeth, a Cheyenne woman who lived through these events, described the Fort Laramie Treaty as a peace agreement and not as a land cession, indicating that the Cheyennes and Lakotas believed at the time that they had not surrendered their territory to the United States and that their relationship with the landscape had not been compromised. Furthermore, she stated that the United States recognized that this land belonged to both the Cheyennes and the Lakotas, demonstrating that the Cheyennes understood that the United States had acknowledged their connection to the land making up the Great Sioux Reservation. Iron Teeth also related that the Cheyennes and Lakotas were angry over the attempts to drive them from their home, and that the most angry people left for the hunting grounds between the Powder and the Bighorn Rivers. She and her husband took their family to Red Cloud Agency, believing it was best to do what the United States ordered at that particular point in time.[16] Although most Cheyennes and Lakotas were incensed over the invasion, the people realigned themselves socially. The flexibility of Cheyenne kinship allowed each family to choose whether to join the camps prepared to fight in the northwest or whether to come into the agencies.

The Cheyennes, Arapahos, and Lakotas who traveled to the Powder River region were certainly assembling warriors. The War Department mobilized as well, sending General Terry toward the Yellowstone and Missouri Rivers and General Crook to the headwaters of the Powder, Tongue, Rosebud, and Bighorn Rivers. On June 17, 1876, General Crook met a camp of Cheyennes and Lakotas on the bend of the Rosebud River near the current boundaries of the present-day Northern Cheyenne reservation. Although few men were lost on either side, the Cheyennes accomplished a resounding victory over Crook's men.[17] The Cheyennes who fought named the battle "The Battle Where the Girl Saved Her Brother" for an act of bravery on the part of Buffalo Calf Road Woman, the sister of Chief Comes In Sight.[18] From this battle, these Cheyenne and Lakota warriors and their families rode to meet the other camps of Cheyennes, Arapahos, and Lakotas coming together on the Little Bighorn River. Only eight short days later, at the hands of the warriors of these camps, General Custer would suffer one of the most famous and most devastating military losses in American history.

After the battle on the Rosebud, the Cheyennes that had camped there decided to move westward toward the Little Bighorn River in pursuit of a herd of buffalo that they spotted. Several Cheyenne and Lakota camp circles set up their tipis along the river in the afternoon and, according to Wooden Leg, had dances in the evening and traveled to different camps to visit.[19] The Cheyenne and Lakota scouts had been watching for soldiers and knew that they were in the area. Both Cheyenne and Lakota leaders gathered to decide how they would prepare for the soldiers, so the camps all knew to be ready for an attack.[20] On June 25, 1876, when Custer and his men rode down on this large encampment on the Little Bighorn, the warriors were on alert. The newspapers of the day reported that Custer, a highly celebrated man in his own time, was killed along with every last man under his command. Americans were thrown into turmoil over their loss: Plains warriors had massacred a military hero just as the United States was about to celebrate the centennial anniversary of its Independence Day.

The Battle of the Little Bighorn quickly became an excuse for the United States to attack any people who had left the agencies. This victory over the U.S. military had dramatically amplified the American public's fear of American Indians off their reservations. Speaking of the Little Bighorn battle, General Miles stated: "It seemed to magnify in the public mind the power and terrors of the Sioux Nation, and immediate orders were sent to different parts of the country directing that detachments of troops be ordered to the seat of war."[21] The shock of the dramatic defeat sent Americans into an uproar, calling for revenge and supporting a surge in military forces on the plains.[22] Although some Cheyennes camping in the Powder River region did not participate in this battle, U.S. military officials did not attempt to determine which camps, instead striving to control and contain all people outside of the agencies. For example, Dull Knife's camp, which suffered so much in the Mackenzie attack, was not involved in the battle at all.

The Battle of the Little Bighorn also bolstered federal officials' long-held plans to gain access to the Black Hills. In September 1875 a commission headed by Senator William Allison had arrived at Red Cloud Agency to negotiate the sale or lease of the Hills, in order to open them to mining.[23] The Lakotas present allowed no concessions to the commissioners, who had to return to Washington without an agreement, but Grant and his administration continued to make plans to wrest the Black Hills from the Lakotas and Cheyennes. The shock and outrage of the American people at the Battle of the Little Bighorn provided them with enough impetus to act without regard to prior agreements. On September 7, 1876, the Manypenny Commission arrived at Red Cloud Agency to extort a cession from those gathered. Congress had decided to give the Cheyennes, Arapahos, and Lakotas an ultimatum. They declared that the people would receive no more rations until they relinquished the lands the United States wanted, mainly the gold-laden Black Hills, which had already been invaded by miners and fortune seekers.[24] By threatening starvation, the commissioners wrested a handful of signatures from the American Indians at the several agencies they visited, including some Cheyennes and Arapahos at Red Cloud Agency, but they never received the signatures of three-fourths of the adult male population as the 1868 treaty required.[25]

Although some Cheyennes and Arapahos signed this agreement, it did not explicitly recognize their rights, separate from those of the Lakotas, to the new reservation that had been formed or to the land they had relinquished. In fact, this agreement was an attrition of the principles both sides understood as important in their relationships with other nations. Although Congress ratified this agreement in February 1877, it was illegal in relation to previous Lakota, Cheyenne, and Arapaho treaties and did not align with Northern Plains nations' understandings of the peace previously negotiated. The United States still purported to be their friend, sealed through gift exchange, but would no longer allow them access to territory that they should share as social equals. But this agreement and the simultaneous military campaign did not simply destroy Cheyenne claims to the region. Because of the power kinship has to order Native social organization, and because it grants the nation the flexibility to survive as a people, the Cheyennes not only survived diaspora but also found new ways to assert their political autonomy despite the continuous efforts by the United States to completely erode it.

The escalating war on the plains also gave U.S. federal officials impetus for one more action they had been pursuing for several years. Now they could finally justify the removal of the Northern Cheyennes to Indian Territory. In the past, local agents in the north had encouraged the government to allow the Northern Cheyennes to remain where they were. Although this conflicted with the government's desire for creating homogenous tribal designations that could be easily contained and controlled, in the interest of maintaining calm, they did not attempt a removal. By 1876, however, as the agents struggled to keep the Cheyennes and Lakotas at the agencies and the military struggled to round up those who had left, federal officials had shifted their stance. As war exploded on the plains, both federal and local officials became more desperate for containment. The solution they sought was to separate the Cheyennes from the Lakotas.

J. S. Hastings, the Indian agent at Red Cloud agency in 1876, wrote to the commissioner of Indian affairs, stating, "The Cheyennes have been more troublesome particularly after the first fight between General Crook and the Indians last winter. They have caused me more trouble and anxiety in their management than the Sioux and the Arapaho combined. I would here suggest that the Sioux of this agency could be more easily and pleasantly managed if the Cheyennes and Arapahoes were separated from them."[26] Around this time, officials began to suggest that the Northern Cheyennes had a more warlike nature than other Plains peoples and were causing most of the trouble on the northern plains. In fact, in 1877 the commissioner himself stated that during the previous year's warfare, "the Cheyennes took prompt and active part in hostilities, while the Arapahoes, almost without exception, remained loyal to the government."[27] The suggestion to separate the Northern Cheyennes from other Plains people to obtain peace fed the government's desire to send these Cheyennes south, containing all Cheyenne people on one reservation.

According to federal officials of the time, the solution to what was considered "the Indian problem" was control through incorporation. The only way this control could be established by 1877 on the northern plains was through surrender. Philip Deloria astutely recognized that "only when defeated Indian opponents were rounded up and successfully contained on reservations could one imagine the state of nation-to-nation war that had characterized the eighteenth and nineteenth centuries no longer existing."[28] The United States had ended treaty making with American Indian nations in 1871, working toward an end to their nation-to-nation relationships with Native nations within their boundaries. The government planned to bring Native people under the umbrella of the state eventually by incorporating them completely into American society. The state would exact this assimilation through the imposition of state-recognized categories on American Indian people, determining their territorial boundaries, ethnic identity, political leaders, political decisions, the content of their children's education, and even the spiritual material of their soul. Crook was not simply charged with ending a war with a foreign nation over territory but exercising colonial control over its people and ultimately incorporating them into a new nation.

Containment on reservations began the long process of transforming American Indian people from colonial subjects to members of the American state. The United States used census rolls that assigned standardized and often English names, church records, ration distribution records, and other agency records as a way to obtain power over Native people. The institutions of the church, the school, and the government agency created state-based boundaries through maintaining surveillance, restraining and defining ethnicity, space, personality, knowledge, and even sentiment. As Philip Deloria pointed out, these institutions were designed to incorporate Native people into the polity of the American state—"albeit without citizenship or significant rights." Defining Native people in terms the state recognized became central to its exercise of power. Reservations provided the mechanisms through which the United States could impose these definitions on Native people. The agency and the reservation represented what Deloria has called "a colonial dream of fixity, control, visibility, productivity, and, most importantly, docility."[29] Docility was the first priority of the federal government in their efforts to contain the Cheyennes.

The threats made at the agencies did not persuade those in the Powder River region to return. While the Manypenny Commission intimidated the people at the agencies to sign their agreement and cede the Black Hills, the people in the Powder River region enjoyed the fall, hunting and setting up their tipis in their favorite locations. The U.S. military, on the other hand, geared up for a winter campaign to flush these camps out of the region and into the agencies. To support the military's efforts, the War Department established two new

posts on the northern plains. They built the Tongue River Canton-
ment, which would become Fort Keogh and was commanded by
General Miles, and Cantonment Reno on the Powder River near the
Bighorn Mountains, commanded by General Crook.[30] By late fall,
General Crook had sent out a military expedition under Gen. Ranald S.
Mackenzie to look for camps of Plains Indians.[31] The first and perhaps
the strongest blow in what the military saw as punishment for George
Custer's defeat was their attack on Dull Knife's village on November 25, 1876. Dull Knife and many other Cheyenne families had made
their winter camp in the vicinity of the Powder River, but soon they
heard from their scouts that soldiers were headed toward them.[32]
They did not flee but prepared to fight. The battle lasted for almost a
day, and in the end the Cheyennes were driven out. The soldiers
then burned everything they owned, including their tipis and their
winter food supply.[33]

Ms. DG stated that around 2002, she had traveled to the site of this
battle and could still see where the earth had been charred in rings
where the tipis had stood. These fires must have burned so hot, fueled
by meat, furs, and hides, that the landscape is still marred. Many
military officials believed that Dull Knife's people had participated
in the Battle of the Little Bighorn, but they had not.[34] Yet there were
families who had participated in the battle camping with Dull Knife
at this site. This is more evidence that Crook and other military officials
ignored the fact that Cheyenne people had the freedom to ally themselves with whomever they chose and shift these alliances as needs
changed. The people did not always act in the unified manner of the
state, but military officials categorized all families away from the agencies as "hostiles" and all Northern Cheyennes as troublemakers.

Despite the swift and brutal efforts of the United States to bring
Plains peoples in line with the understandings and the goals of the
nation-state, the military could not defeat or contain these camps.[35]
Although Mackenzie clearly had the advantage over the Cheyennes
of Dull Knife's village after the November battle, he did not succeed
in driving the people to the agency. Regardless of their destitute condition, the Cheyennes could always turn to other kin. After the battle,
most families struggled across the countryside with what they had
saved and were spotted by the Cheyenne warrior Wooden Leg and

several other young warriors who had been roaming the area. Together, they found Crazy Horse's village and took refuge with their relatives, who fed and clothed them, even giving away horses and robes for new lodges.[36] Because they had a wide safety net of relatives outside of their own camps that they could count on in times of need, the Cheyennes could continue to assert their own political autonomy despite the state's plan to contain their people.

As the destruction of Dull Knife's camp illustrates, military officials redoubled their efforts to force all Plains peoples onto their reservations after the Battle of the Little Bighorn. The hegemonic narrative of American history tells us that they succeeded; eventually all the Cheyennes, Lakotas, and Arapahos living on the plains surrendered at reservations by military force. One account by a current historian, Edward Lazarus, is representative of the language of conquest many historians have used to describe the events that transpired after the battle:

> Up in the Powder River country, the army was getting its revenge. Through the short fall and long winter, Crook, Terry, and General Nelson Miles chased Sitting Bull, Crazy Horse, and the other hostile leaders, tracking them across the deep snow, burning their camps, destroying their food stores and shooting down the stragglers. Outnumbered and outgunned, by February they had run out of food, ammunition, and places to hide. Sitting Bull took the remnants of his band to Canada. Crazy Horse, Big Foot and Touch-the-Clouds, the last holdouts from reservation life, began to turn themselves in at the agencies.[37]

American history has considered the Cheyennes and Lakotas to be defeated tribes, forced to surrender. By insisting that these tribes lost the Sioux Wars, however, this telling of history has justified the colonization of Plains people, including the seizure of thousands of acres of land by the United States. According to this historical narrative, they lost not only land but also the all-important stereotypic marker of the Plains Indian: freedom. Without their freedom, many have lamented, Plains people ceased to be truly Indian. A current historian, John H. Monnett, stated, "That terrible winter marked the beginning of the end of independent lifeways in their northern homelands."[38] Another current historian, Orlan Svingen, described the surrender of the Northern Cheyennes, stating, "Never again could they make independent decisions about summer or winter camp locations, nor were they free to visit friends or relatives at nearby agencies. All future decisions would now depend on white approval."[39] Of course, the changes reservation life brought for Plains peoples should not be ignored. Cheyenne movements across the plains became less frequent and extensive. To declare, however, that Plains Indians no longer traveled away from their reservations and that all decisions were based on Euro-American authority is simply inaccurate.[40]

The aftermath of the Battle of the Little Bighorn is much more complex. The Plains nations' victory changed the circumstances of many Cheyenne families, but not simply to a life of suffering under the pursuit of the military, as hegemonic histories would have us believe. For example, the victory initially drew many people away from the agencies. When families that previously had chosen to stay at the agencies and avoid the hostilities heard about Custer's defeat, people left to join their relatives in the rich hunting grounds of the Powder River region. Iron Teeth recalled that before the battle, she and her husband had taken their family to Red Cloud Agency, or White River Agency as they called it, because this was where the military ordered the Cheyennes to go. She noted that her husband was angry "because of our having been driven from our Black Hills home country," but they thought it was best to come in to the agency.[41] She continued, "Later, in the middle of that summer, we heard that all of the soldiers had been killed in a great battle at the Little Big Horn [sic]. When we were told of the great victory by the Indians, my husband said we should now go into the Montana lands, to join our people there. With many others, we left Dakota and found the Cheyennes. The tribe traveled together during much of the remainder of that summer, hunting along the Powder, Tongue, and Rosebud Rivers."[42] After the victory at the Battle of the Little Bighorn, many people who had come into the agencies left them again to join their family and friends and to camp in their favorite hunting grounds. The camps in the Powder River region grew with the security the victory had brought the people. These large and widely dispersed camps were almost impossible for the military to defeat because they had the security of kin networks ranging across Cheyenne, Arapaho, and Lakota bands, including those living at the agencies.[43]

General Miles was committed to the government's goal to hold all Plains Indians at the agencies, and as he became more aware that military force would not succeed, he searched for other solutions. He did not enter the region with this intention, at first embarking on persistent military campaigns, believing they would end the hostilities. In his memoirs, written two decades later, Miles described his first intention, stating, "It was my purpose when I found I had been designated to remain in that country [the Powder River region] not to occupy it peaceably in conjunction with the large bodies of Indians that were then in the field, and which practically included the entire hostile force of the five Indian tribes, namely: the Uncpapas under Sitting Bull, the Ogallalas under Crazy Horse, the Northern Cheyennes under Two Moons, and the Minneconjoux and Sans Arcs under their trusted leaders."[44] American history remembers General Miles in this light. He oversaw many brutal campaigns to subdue Plains peoples. Miles was an ambitious man who had impressed his commanding officers during the Civil War and used his posts on the plains to continue to build his career. To further climb in the ranks, Miles competed with Crook to secure an end to the violence on the northern plains, hoping to gain credit by bringing the people into his fort.[45]

It is important to note that in historical scholarship on American Indian history, General Miles has rarely been portrayed as sympathetic to Native interests. This possibly stems from his dramatic reaction to the Ghost Dance movement. According to Jeffrey Ostler, Miles first responded to the movement by insisting that it would eventually subside. He argued that poor federal policy and incompetent local agents had caused it. Once the military began to take action, however, Miles dramatically changed his tone. He began to publicly declare that lack of swift and brutal military action would lead to a mass outbreak on the plains, endangering the lives of thousands of Americans. Ostler argued that Miles again was acting out of personal interest, in the hopes of maintaining a strong military presence on the plains. Exploring Miles's reasoning for his actions during this period reveals that his motivations reflected his personal ambition, but also his many years of experience with Native peoples.[46]

Despite their relentless military campaigns in the dead of a bitter winter, neither Miles nor Crook succeeded in forcing a surrender from the Cheyenne and Lakota camps. Although both officers originally intended to force all Plains peoples into the agencies, they realized that military action was an ineffective, costly option, so they decided instead to attempt to open diplomatic channels with the Cheyennes and Lakotas. There is evidence that General Miles believed that in order to succeed, he needed to consider the Native perspective concerning their struggle with the United States. In 1879 he proposed, "Could we but perceive the true character of the Indians, and learn their dispositions, not covered by the cloak of necessity, policy, and interest, we should find that they regard us as a body of false and cruel invaders of their country, while we are too apt to consider them as a treacherous and bloodthirsty race, that should be destroyed by any and all means, yet, if we consider the cause of this feeling, we might more readily understand the result."[47] By the time he wrote this article, Miles had recognized a Native claim to the land and presumably understood that the loss of resources Plains people experienced so suddenly resulted in the bloodshed he had witnessed. He also knew that the ongoing hostilities would allow Native people to continue to escape the process of assimilation. Although Miles attempted to understand Native perspectives, he still believed that the best course of action was "civilizing" Indian people by encouraging them to shed any vestiges of their way of life and adopt Euro-American culture in all forms.

In 1880, when asked by the Select Committee on the Removal of the Northern Cheyenne about the civilizing process, Miles stated, "You have got to approach that matter gradually. From barbarism to civilization is a gradual process."[48] Like many Americans of his day, Miles viewed Native people as living in a state of savagery. He accepted the common belief, articulated by Lewis Henry Morgan, that human groups evolved progressively through the stages of savagery to barbarism to civilization.[49] Most Euro-Americans assumed that civilization as exhibited by northern European cultures was the highest stage and therefore a desired goal for any group, whether the members realized it or not. While some Euro-Americans questioned whether Indigenous peoples could even attain this conception of civilization, Miles perceived the U.S. government's civilizing agenda as the best solution to the strained relationship with Plains Indians. Extraordinarily, he also believed that considering Native perspectives, views, and desires was essential to the success of the civilizing agenda. These personal perspectives surely led Miles to consider an Indigenous Plains understanding of the protocol surrounding peacemaking with enemies, not only to end the bloodshed but also to begin the assimilation process.

For Miles, the opportunity for culturally appropriate negotiation emerged through a Cheyenne woman named Sweet Woman.[50] In January 1877 a large group of Lakotas and Cheyennes who had been camping together at Hanging Woman Creek decided to separate. The Lakota camp moved up the creek, and as usual a few Cheyenne families joined them. The main body of the Cheyennes traveled up the Tongue River. Miles's soldiers were also camping in this area. Twin Woman, one of Sweet Woman's traveling companions, had already been living away from the main group near the Belle Fourche River with Tangle Hair and his followers. After the large group on Hanging Woman Creek separated, a man named Big Horse who had been scouting for the Cheyennes along the Tongue River came to the camp near the Belle Fourche River to visit. Twin Woman and some other women heard Big Horse was returning to the main camp on the Tongue River, so they asked him if they could join him because they missed their relatives in the main camp. A Cheyenne woman named Crooked Nose, Wooden Leg's sister, joined this little party at some point. When the main camp on Hanging Woman Creek separated, Crooked Nose had left with the Lakotas, heading up the creek. Perhaps Twin Woman's party passed through this camp on their way back. Nevertheless, she joined their party, also wishing to return to her family in the main Cheyenne camp.

When they reached the Tongue River, near present-day Birney, Montana, the party consisted of Big Horse, Twin Woman, Crooked Nose, Sweet Woman, perhaps a teenage boy and up to five children. Here, no more than a day's travel from the main camp, they encountered Miles's soldiers. The men of the little party were either away scouting the area or getting fresh meat, and the women and children were surrounded and captured by Miles's men.[51] Big Horse arrived in time to see the group being taken and rode to alert the camp on the Tongue River. Immediately, warriors rode out and fought the soldiers to bring their relatives back, but they could not get to the captives.[52] After the battle, the twenty-five men with the strongest horses followed the soldiers in hopes of recapturing the women, but they were never able to get close enough to free them. They followed them all the way to Fort Keogh, where they watched as the women were taken inside.[53] Accounts differ on the exact events surrounding the capture of these Cheyenne women, but all agree that only women and children were captured, including Sweet Woman and Twin Woman.[54]

These captured Cheyenne women provided General Miles with a unique opportunity to use culturally mediated negotiation to bring in the Plains Indians who continued to live away from the agencies. Miles must have realized the opportunity because he asked Sweet Woman, the oldest of the group, to counsel him on his best course of action. She told him that the chiefs might be willing to make an agreement, if approached correctly. Sweet Woman tutored Miles in the ways of Plains Indian diplomacy; she told him to send gifts of tobacco as well as sugar, coffee, bacon, and beans.

Elva Stands In Timber, the first person to insist to me that the Cheyennes had never surrendered, was a descendant of members of the group who came to Fort Keogh. During my quest to understand what she meant, she related to me the following story of Sweet Woman. She stated that Miles did not know how to bring in the Indians because he could not manage to get close to them. There was a woman living at Fort Keogh named Sweet Woman who was a good friend of General Miles. He asked her for help, wanting to know how he could get close to the camp of Cheyennes who had not come in to any agency. She told him to bring them gifts including tobacco. Sweet Woman agreed to travel to their camp with an interpreter, John Broughier, to listen to what they had to say.[55] He and his men piled their horses high with gifts such as meat, beans, blankets, tobacco, and whatever other things that the people gave at the time. Ms. Stands In Timber said that then they rode to meet Two Moons and his followers.[56]

In Ms. Stands In Timber's account, Sweet Woman was essential to the success of this diplomatic endeavor as the one who taught Miles

what was culturally appropriate so that he might successfully negotiate with the Cheyenne and Lakota camps. As a Cheyenne woman,
she also could move easily in the camp in a way Miles could not.
The people of the camp would have already known her and would
not have turned her away. Furthermore, Ms. Stands In Timber depicted
Miles and Sweet Woman as friends instead of identifying Sweet Woman
as a prisoner. One might assume that she was revising Sweet Woman's
position from the perspective that hindsight provides because the
Cheyennes eventually considered General Miles a dear friend. I suggest, however, that Ms. Stands In Timber's use of the term "friend"
has deeper implications. Considering Sweet Woman to be a friend
of Miles recognizes her position as a captive woman who has become
incorporated into the community at the fort, giving her legitimacy
as a cultural go-between who could negotiate between Miles and the
Cheyenne camps. John Stands In Timber spoke of the women who
were held at Fort Keogh, stating, "The family was treated good that
winter. My grandmother talked about it."[57] While these women and
children were officially prisoners, they were not jailed.

As a captive, Sweet Woman took an active role in galvanizing negotiations for peace and developing a beneficial relationship with General
Miles. Ostler suggested that "because she was tired of seeing her
people suffer and die, Sweet Woman took her captivity as an opportunity to mediate negotiations for peace between Miles and her own
people."[58] He understood Sweet Woman's captivity as an opportunity
for her as an individual to act in the best interest of her community,
but he did not explore Plains Indian concepts of captivity as a legitimate social role that established channels of kin through which one
could negotiate between enemy groups. Plains Indians have a long
history of depending on captive women as a way to negotiate with
enemies for access to their land and resources and even to create
new alliances.[59]

Connection to enemies depended on kin ties most often created by
captive women. Arranging trade among enemies was the responsibility of go-betweens who had kinship connections with the hostile
party.[60] Sweet Woman, at almost fifty years old, would have known
the potential of captives to become diplomats, as she had surely seen
others act in that capacity many times. Most likely she not only saw

it as an opportunity to use her preexisting social ties to facilitate cease-fire negotiations with General Miles but perhaps also believed that her socially defined role among her people as a captive woman might lend the negotiations a weight that could lead to a lasting peace to the benefit of both parties.

Realizing that Sweet Woman was probably his best chance to convince the Cheyennes and Lakotas to come to his fort and not Red Cloud Agency, Miles enlisted her help.[61] By the time Sweet Woman and Broughier found their camps, the Lakotas and Cheyennes had come together and then moved on to the Bighorn River. John Stands In Timber related that before they left Fort Keogh, Sweet Medicine told Broughier to enter the Sacred Hat Tipi once he arrived at the camp, because then not only could no one could hurt him, but they would also be required to listen to Miles's terms. The Cheyennes revered the Sacred Hat Tipi as the place where an enemy would be safe even in the midst of battle. When they arrived, Broughier took the first chance he had to slip inside the tipi.[62] At this point, Sweet Woman could distribute the gifts, and they could speak about General Miles's terms for peace. There is little evidence to collaborate Stands In Timber's account of the Sacred Hat Tipi. Still, whether Broughier used this sanctuary or not, its presence in Stands In Timber's telling powerfully demonstrates that Sweet Woman's mission was recognized as one of peace and reconciliation because the Sacred Hat Tipi facilitated peaceful relations with other Plains enemies.

Wooden Leg, who was in this camp on the Bighorn River when Sweet Woman arrived, recounted that she told the people that the captives were safe and that General Miles had invited all of them to his fort where they would be given plenty of food and would remain unharmed by the military.[63] Again, in Wooden Leg's telling of the event, he implies that the Cheyennes in the camp read Miles's actions as a diplomatic effort to negotiate for peace. Miles offers not only a cessation of hostilities but also an invitation to Fort Keogh to share his food. These certainly were not actions to force a surrender. In fact, from a Cheyenne perspective, these actions implied more than simply an invitation to peace; they would have contained the possibility for alliance, just as they had with other Plains enemies in the past. Gifts, tobacco, the use of the Sacred Hat Tipi, and Sweet Woman as a cultural mediator demonstrate that, from a Cheyenne perspective, the interchange that took place was a diplomatic negotiation.

The people, who were understandably suspicious of the United States, disagreed on the best course of action. The chiefs first discussed the matter but failed to reach a consensus, so they passed the decision to the headmen of the warrior societies, who deliberated for days and still disagreed on the best course of action. Finally, they chose to move closer to Fort Keogh in order to send a small party to discuss their options with Miles; they would decide when the party returned. Once they reached the Tongue River, Two Moons left with a group of those considering coming into Fort Keogh to see the conditions at the fort for themselves.[64] P. H. Sheridan, a lieutenant general working for the War Department, recounted Miles's report of Two Moons's arrival to William Tecumseh Sherman, the secretary of war at the time, stating, "Twenty nine Ogallalas and Cheyennes including seven chiefs came to his [Miles's] camp at Tongue River on February 19th to know the terms of surrender."[65] This group included Sweet Woman, Two Moons, Broughier, White Bull (also called Ice), as well as Old Wolf, Crazy Head, Little Chief, Brave Wolf, White Wolf, Sleeping Rabbit, Iron Shirt, Crazy Mule, Black Bear, Little Creek, White Thunder, and a Lakota man named Hump.[66]

Once they arrived at Fort Keogh, Miles met with the Northern Cheyenne headmen in his cabin to work out an agreement. Miles told them that if they gave up their arms and their horses and placed themselves under his care, he would treat them well. John Stands In Timber related that Miles told the headmen that he wanted peace and that he would let them choose a place for their own reservation if they came to the fort.[67] Elva Stands In Timber described the Northern Cheyenne response, stating they had accepted his gifts, so they shook hands and agreed to move to the fort, explicitly connecting the gifts with the agreement.[68] Two Moons told Miles that he would go back to his people and return to the fort with them, but Miles was afraid that they would change their minds when they reached their camp, so he asked for volunteers to remain. When no one else came forward, White Bull (Ice) agreed to stay. Miles immediately asked him to become a scout and he agreed. Only one day after the people had arrived at Fort Keogh, White Bull was sworn in as an army scout and given a uniform. Enlisting him had several advantages for Miles. Once the other Cheyennes saw that White Bull was being treated well as a scout, other men offered to stay as well, including Little Chief, and two Lakota men, Hump and Horse Road.[69] Furthermore, because Fort Keogh was a military cantonment and not an agency, the only way to justify providing the Cheyennes with rations was to put them on the army payroll.

In P. H. Sheridan's report to Sherman, he stated, "They [Two Moons and those with him] were informed [of Miles's terms for peace] and on the 23rd started back promising in apparently good faith to bring in their people."[70] By this time, the large camp of Cheyennes and Lakotas had moved to the Powder River. Two Moons, Crazy Head, Old Wolf, and several other Cheyennes returned to the camp with Miles's offer and with a report of life at Fort Keogh. They told the people that the captives had been well treated, that one of their men had become a scout, and that Miles had promised them access to land in the Powder River region. However convincing this might have been, another alternative had appeared, making the decision even more difficult. A group of Lakotas with Spotted Tail had arrived from Red Cloud Agency to urge the Cheyennes and Lakotas to come there to surrender. It is likely that General Crook, who sent this delegation, authorized Spotted Tail to tell those at the camp that he would also work to secure them an agency in the north.[71] Apparently, Miles and Crook used the same promise of a northern agency; Crook even used a similar tactic by sending Lakota negotiators with gifts to offer his terms for peace. In Eli S. Ricker's interview with George Sword, Sword stated that he left Fort Robinson on January 1, 1877, under General Crook's orders to obtain peace, bringing with him bags of tobacco to offer to each of the chiefs. Sword stated that Spotted Tail traveled north after him to ensure the people would come in.[72]

With this new option open to them, the two competing promises surely heightened the debate among the headmen. Wooden Leg told Thomas Marquis about these visits to their camp, stating, "They came only to tell us we ought to surrender at the agency. They said all of the Indians there were being fed well, were being treated well in every way. Nobody was being punished in any manner for past conduct in warfare against the soldiers. To my father and to most of the Cheyennes this sounded more attractive than the invitation to go to the Elk River Fort [Fort Keogh]. Our people were better acquainted with conditions at the agency. Besides, the Ogallalas had the same agency with us, so these people also would be there."[73] Most of the Northern Cheyennes found Crook's terms for peace more compelling than Miles's terms. The families who chose to travel to Red Cloud Agency and make peace there were choosing the known over the unknown because they had camped and taken rations there before. They also had relatives who were already living at the agency. Yet some Cheyennes still believed that they would be more content at Fort Keogh with General Miles. Some had relatives among the captive women. Stands In Timber claimed that Little Chief was in love with one of these women and went in for this reason.[74] Ultimately the camp was not able to reach a consensus, and the chiefs decided to allow each family to act on its own.

While most Cheyennes and Lakotas traveled to Red Cloud Agency near Fort Robinson, some decided to remain on the plains traveling and hunting in small groups, and others, who had relatives among the Arapahos in Wind River, Wyoming, or among the Southern Cheyennes in Indian Territory, decided to return to their families. In the end, only a small number of Cheyennes left for Fort Keogh, and these were mostly Two Moons's and White Bull's relatives.[75] On March 23, 1877, General Sherman in Washington, D.C., received a telegram from P. H. Sheridan detailing that "One hundred and thirty-three hostile Cheyennes and one hundred and thirty Sioux surrendered at Red Cloud on the 13th and 14th. The total number surrendered at that point since last report is three hundred and sixty-nine. The Indians report that other parties are on their way in, delayed by snow and mud."[76] Miles also wrote about the people who came in to the White River agencies (Red Cloud and Spotted Tail Agencies): "From the first of March to the 21st over 2,200 Indians surrendered in small groups at Camps Sheridan and Robinson. More were reported on the way to give themselves up. On May 6th, Crazy Horse with 889 people surrendered to General Crook at Camp Robinson."[77] Many headmen of the Cheyennes decided to come to Fort Robinson, including Dull Knife, Little Wolf, Standing Elk, Spotted Elk, Tangle Hair, Wild Hog, and American Horse.[78] The Sacred Hat keeper, Charcoal

Bear, who took care of the sacred bundle that kept the entire nation safe from harm, also chose to travel to Red Cloud Agency. This surely affected the decisions of many other families. Most Cheyennes chose to travel to Red Cloud Agency because they had already experienced the conditions there, they had relatives there, and some of their most powerful leaders chose to make peace there as well.

Before his relationship with General Miles, Two Moons was not considered a chief by the Cheyenne people. Although those who traveled with him surely saw Two Moons in a new light, his people did not grant him the status needed to make decisions; officials at Fort Keogh placed this on him. John Stands In Timber himself noted Two Moons as one of the chiefs only made famous by white people, although he was very brave and had a fine record. He took a decisive role in the choice to travel to Fort Keogh, but he had no power to coerce others, only the charismatic power to encourage them to join him. Those who traveled with Two Moons to Fort Keogh certainly felt they had made their decision freely, without coercion, and based on responsibility to their kin and to their newly established relationship with General Miles.[79] Miles, for his part, did not seem threatened by Northern Cheyenne political fluidity; he instead realized that embracing their diplomatic systems would ultimately win him success.

While each family had the freedom to make its own decision, traveling with powerful leaders and their sacred bundle would provide protection that Fort Keogh could not offer. The Cheyennes who traveled to Red Cloud Agency included Black Wolf, Old Bear, Black Eagle, Medicine Bear, White Dirt (Clay), Broken Jaw, Wolf Medicine, Plenty Bears, Tall White Man, Beaver Claw, Red Owl, Snow (White) Bird, Strong Left Hand (Arm), Tangle Hair (Big Head), and Black Bear. Several Southern Cheyennes, who had come north to help their relatives fight, also came to Red Cloud Agency and ultimately returned south to live permanently when Dull Knife and Little Wolf were removed to Indian Territory. The Southern Cheyennes included Turkey Legs, Yellow Calfskin Shirt (Broken Dish), Leaving (Living) Bear, Brave Bear, and Yellow Nose.[80]

Another group of Southern Cheyennes headed straight back to Indian Territory, including the Sacred Arrow keeper, Black Hairy Dog;

White Buffalo; and eighteen families who had traveled north.[81] John Stands In Timber also stated that a group who were Arapahos or were married into the Arapaho nation, including Little Shield, Black Coal, and Little Raven, decided to travel west and join the other Arapahos who had already settled at Wind River.[82]

Wooden Leg told Thomas Marquis that he joined another group who decided not to travel to any agency because this group sought the freedom they felt was rightfully theirs. The group was led by Last Bull with his wife and two daughters, and it included Many Colored Braids with his wife, two daughters, and a son; Little Horse with his wife, two daughters, and a son; Black Coyote with his wife and son; Dog Growing Up with his wife and son; and many young, single warriors including Fire Wolf, Yellow Eagle, Spotted Wolf, Chief Going Up Hill, White Bird, Buffalo Paunch, Big Nose, Meat, Medicine Wolf, Horse Road, Little Shield, Yellow Horse, and Yellow Hair, Wooden Leg's brother. This group remained on the plains for several months, hunting and living in the way they were accustomed. Eventually they traveled to Red Cloud Agency. Another group of fourteen or fifteen Northern Cheyenne men led by White Hawk decided to join the Minneconjoux Sioux on Lame Deer Creek who were camping with the Lakota headman, Lame Deer.[83] Six or seven of these young warriors had wives and children with them.

While more than 2,200 Cheyennes and Lakotas eventually traveled to the White River agencies to the south, Miles reported that only 303 Cheyenne men, women, and children surrendered to him on April 22, 1877, at Fort Keogh.[84] Two Moons had related Miles's promise that the Cheyennes would be safe, but only those who had seen this for themselves or whose relatives remained at the fort seemed to be assured. Those who returned to Fort Keogh with Two Moons included Black Moccasin (Limber Lance), Crazy Head, Wrapped Hair, Ridge Bear, Sits Beside His Medicine, Weasel Bear, Iron Shirt, Little Creek, Crazy Mule, Stands Different (John Stands In Timber's father), Left Handed Shooter, Brave Wolf, White Wolf, Fast Whirlwind, Sits In the Night, White Elk, Howling Wolf, Chief Bear, Walks On Crutches (Wooden Leg's father), and Old Wolf (Cut Foot).[85] Box Elder, Spotted Wolf, Elk River, and Bear Woman also came to Fort Keogh a few days later.[86]

These moments when different bands separated and selected different agencies have often been portrayed as a permanent loss of unity for a bounded ethnic group.[87] The flexibility of the Cheyenne and Lakota kinship system, however, could maintain the connections that supported the nation while divided geographically. For example, the Cheyennes maintained a connection despite the division between the Southern and the Northern people. Southern Cheyennes traveled north after the Sand Creek massacre to take refuge with Northern relatives, and they also traveled north to support their kin in their military battles with the United States in the 1870s.[88] People would often decide whom they would follow based on familial connections, military society connections, or other kinds of allegiances, but this would not preclude them from maintaining other social connections with distant bands. When a large camp had to separate, the reality that each family acted independently would not have disrupted the nation as a whole because the Cheyennes were used to separating and reconvening later. It seems unlikely that the people who chose Fort Keogh over Red Cloud Agency felt that any separation of this kind was permanent. No similar spatial division of bands had been permanent in the past. They could not have known that these relatives would soon be forced into diaspora, risking their lives to return home, fighting to be reunited with their relatives remaining in the north.

When Two Moons and those who came with him arrived at Fort Keogh, they moved into an area about one and a half miles away from the military cantonment. They surrendered their firearms and horses and were designated prisoners of war in the official military documents.[89] The Cheyennes, however, did not think of themselves as prisoners. In fact, they were given guns and horses again almost immediately after their arrival when they enlisted as U.S. military scouts. Furthermore, the soldiers at the fort did not treat the Cheyennes like prisoners and eventually came to see these men as part of normal military life. The Cheyennes had their own camp; the women cooked for their families, and people were given tents or allowed to set up their own tipis. The Select Committee's Report on the Removal of the Northern Cheyenne stated that Miles spoke of those who surrendered as prisoners of war, but that "this was only a nominal capture, and the Indians were treated as prisoners of war because

Two Moons's tipi and family by Laton A. Huffman. From the collection of Gene and Bev Allen, Helena, Montana.

the army could not hold or provide for them in any other character."[90] Even Miles did not consider the Cheyennes at Fort Keogh prisoners; he considered it a "capture" in name only.

When Miles met with the Northern Cheyenne leaders, he told them that becoming scouts in the U.S. army would not rob them of their rights, and he would even help them relocate onto a reservation of their choice. Clearly these Cheyennes were not prisoners of war, but the designations in the official documents made their status unclear. For some men at the fort, the swift transition from enemy to scout raised suspicions. One of the U.S. soldiers who fought with the Cheyenne scouts recalled his experience: "My first real scouting was done with a party of them [Northern Cheyennes], Little Chief, Brave Wolf, Black Wolf, White Bear and White Bull Hump and they were of the 7th cavalry. The army had an idea that they had only surrendered a short while before and could not be trusted."[91] It quickly became apparent, however, that the Cheyenne scouts could be trusted. They were quite successful at finding groups that had evaded the army. Some might view this willingness to take up arms for the U.S. military as fickle, dishonorable, and opportunistic, but such a reading fails to consider Indigenous constructions of political action and alliance. Although the Cheyennes acted as a nation in some political and cultural decisions, at times different bands found it beneficial to establish extranational alliances. This was allowed unless these alliances conflicted with the interests of the nation. During the tumultuous 1870s, when each family had to decide its course for itself, what was best for the nation was not always in the fore of people's minds.

Many scholars have concluded that the Northern Cheyennes surrendered to Miles because the hostile Cheyennes and Lakotas had suffered such a great loss of food and resources as a result of constant military pressure.[92] Although the government documents of the time described the act of Plains Indians coming to the agencies as a surrender, by examining the interaction between Miles and the Lakota and Cheyenne camp on the Powder River through the lens of Northern Cheyenne social relations, a different picture emerges. It becomes evident that U.S. military action did not govern the Cheyennes' and Lakotas' decisions to come to the agencies, because those in the Powder River camp were so confident that some chose not to come to any agency at all. Furthermore, had this been a surrender in the Euro-American understanding, no warrior would have been free to choose a different course of action. Actually, Miles had abandoned his attempts to force a military surrender, as did Crook when he sent Spotted Tail with gifts. Instead, both resorted to negotiation, not as Europeans or Euro-Americans negotiated, but instead following the norms of Plains

Indian negotiation and alliance forging. The enemy, the United States, had brought gifts using go-betweens who lived with the enemy, but who had kin ties in the Cheyenne and Lakota camp. This action would have been understood as an attempt to establish peace, not force surrender.

For Miles to convince the Cheyennes and Lakotas of his sincerity, his power as a leader, and the legitimacy of his terms, he had to demonstrate his generosity. For them to even consider his terms, Miles was required to present gifts, making the receiver responsible for deliberating on the request. Returning the gift would have indicated that the receiver declined the proposed agreement, but acceptance forged a new relationship, one based on cooperation and reciprocity. From a Cheyenne perspective, Miles was not simply asking the people to come to Fort Keogh; he was asking them to enter a new relationship—an alliance with him. Trusting a new military official would have been a difficult decision. It is not surprising that so few chose to accept his offer.

Additionally, it is likely that Two Moons and the men with him did not view themselves as fighting for the U.S. government. They instead forged an alliance with General Miles, which would help them secure access to their territory even during invasion by the United States. The agreement had all the markers of an alliance. Miles sought peace, offering gifts and negotiating through a captive woman. He invited these families to join his camp, provided them with food, guns, and horses, and asked them to fight alongside him. These families lived in their own tipis close to the fort and could even leave the fort to hunt. These Cheyennes had forged a new military alliance and were true to it.[93] This relationship assumed an obligation to Miles and the Americans at Fort Keogh, but not to the United States as a whole. Cheyenne nationhood did not assume such abstract allegiances; it was based on tangible social relations. For these scouts, this alliance with Miles followed older Plains constructions of military cooperation.

Among the Cheyennes, a leader has a sincere responsibility to the people. He was required to act as a highly moral man and to make himself poor in service to the people. Hoebel quoted a Cheyenne who told him, "Whatever you ask of a chief, he gives it to you. If someone wants to borrow something of a chief, he gives it to that person outright."[94] Northern Cheyennes today talk about a chief who saw a very poor man walking while he was riding a horse, so this chief got off his horse and gave it to the man.[95] Generosity was paramount among the Northern Cheyennes, especially for leaders. Whether Miles realized it or not, he demonstrated to the Northern Cheyennes that in the alliance he proposed he could embody moral Cheyenne leadership.[96] He appeared to take the role of a headman, as he was already a leader of his own people. He also indicated through his actions that he would consider the Cheyenne worldview and social order, as well as accepting the leadership of the headmen among the Cheyennes with whom he would continue to negotiate.

Most readers who are familiar with Miles's track record will rightly take pause at his willingness to support Northern Cheyenne claims to their homeland. Why would a man who treated so many Native peoples so inhumanely show such sympathy for this particular group? It is unlikely that he ever understood this relationship to be an alliance in the way that the Cheyennes did. He probably suspected that these scouts would advance his career if they remained loyal, so he encouraged this loyalty and they fought by his side, and ultimately, these scouts helped Miles rise much higher than he would otherwise have. Yet these successes still fail to explain his tireless efforts to help the Cheyennes remain in their homeland.[97]

When I asked Elva Stands In Timber about these issues, she described the power of the long relationship that the people at Fort Keogh had with General Miles. Nevertheless, this alliance was not without political complications for the new scouts. During their first battle, these men would meet their relatives on the battlefield at Lame Deer Creek.[98] When General Miles asked them to fight against the headman, Lame Deer, and his Minneconjoux Lakota band, the scouts were well aware they would face Cheyenne and Lakota family across the battlefield. Although they hesitated to fight against their relatives, after gathering together to carefully consider their actions, they ultimately helped Miles subdue these Minneconjoux and Cheyenne warriors.[99] Given the tumultuous times, they were forced to choose which social ties they would emphasize. Yet fighting alongside Miles did not require them to completely neglect their friends and family on the other side of the lines. Often, as scouts, Cheyenne men could manipulate these military encounters to improve the outcome for their relatives, striving to spare lives and bring about a peaceful resolution.[100]

Elva Stands in Timber stated that Miles's dedication to the Northern Cheyennes' efforts to remain in their homeland began with a moment at the Lame Deer battle when Ice (White Bull) saved the general's life. Some Lakotas were surrendering and had laid their guns on the ground, but one, possibly Lame Deer himself, had left his cocked. Ice had warned Miles by pointing this out with his eyes, so when the warrior went for his gun, Miles was able to jump out of the way. She related that this was exactly what happened; when the warrior went for his gun, Miles ducked away, dodging the bullet. Once the battle was over, Miles thanked all the scouts for their help. He told them he would give them whatever they asked for out of gratitude. The scouts of the other Plains nations said they wanted all the captured horses, so Miles gave them all away. When he asked Ice what he wanted, he said, "Promise me you will let us live on this land and not make us leave." She told me that Miles gave his word and that is what made him work so hard for the land for the Northern Cheyennes.[101]

As this narrative demonstrates, the Northern Cheyennes would not have simply expected shared military responsibility and resources from an alliance with Miles; they would have also expected shared land. When Plains people made alliances, they gained access to new lands.[102] The Cheyennes surely thought of the Powder River region as their land, but they had also witnessed the loss of the Black Hills to the United States. Two Moons believed that coming together with General Miles was a way to safeguard their relationship to their land.[103] They had secured their connection to the Black Hills only a few decades earlier by allying themselves with the Lakotas, and perhaps they hoped the same strategy of alliance formation would work with General Miles.

Even if Miles did not consider the relationship an alliance, his views on Plains Indians and land meshed with the desires of the Northern Cheyennes. Miles stated himself that "The Indians, as far as possible, should be localized on the public domain, in sections of the country to which they are by nature adapted." He believed the Northern Cheyennes should settle in their own country, but he also believed that they should learn to become self-sufficient in the manner the United

States expected, as permanent residents of small tracts of land.[104] He encouraged them to claim their land by taking homesteads, not through the creation of a reservation where they would be at the continual mercy of the United States. In order to further his career, Miles needed this relationship with the Northern Cheyennes, but he also owed these scouts his life and apparently was a man of his word. Furthermore, Miles did not need to impose the boundaries of the state to maintain control over the Northern Cheyennes at Fort Keogh—the alliance was sufficient. He did not take a general census, distribute rations, or confine the Northern Cheyennes to barracks at Fort Keogh. They signed enlistment papers, received army rations, and traveled to hunt when they had free time. They were treated like other soldiers with families.

Working for the U.S. military, these scouts were involved in many of the incidents that are famous today as the bellwethers of the end of the American Indian way of life on the plains.[105] When Chief Joseph's band of Nez Perces had continued to elude the army, Miles's Northern Cheyenne scouts found them and helped pacify them. These scouts also helped capture Sitting Bull and his people in Canada and bring them to the United States.[106] The U.S. government, and particularly General Miles, must have considered enlisting Cheyenne scouts an overwhelming success.

In every way, the Northern Cheyennes at Fort Keogh appeared to be giving up their old way of life, by becoming not only scouts but also farmers. This provided ample evidence to ease the concerns of government officials that the Plains Indians whom they believed to be wild, roving hostiles would not take to civilization. This group of Northern Cheyennes, who had defeated Gen. George Armstrong Custer and the Seventh Cavalry a year earlier, now had joined the U.S. military and become successful at farming, which the government deemed the highest mark of civilization. A report of the produce grown near Fort Keogh by "captured and surrendered Northern Cheyenne Indians" between 1878 and 1881 demonstrated their success. It lists the many fruits and vegetables they raised, including more than a thousand bushels of potatoes, as well as bushels of turnips, onions, parsnips, carrots, corn, oats, and beans. They also raised cabbage, pumpkins, and many varieties of squash, as well as melons, cucumbers, peas, radishes, tomatoes, and beets. The Northern Cheyennes planted, tended, and gathered these crops and built two large root houses to store their produce. They used this harvest to supplement their army rations and hunting expeditions. They also were able to sell some of their produce and use the proceeds to purchase food and clothing.[107]

Those military officers above Miles noticed this success with the Northern Cheyennes living at Fort Keogh. In the summer of 1877, only a few months after the scouts and their families had settled at the fort, General Sherman, the commander of the U.S. army, traveled to Fort Keogh. While at the post, he addressed a letter to George W. McCrary, secretary of war, in Washington, D.C.: "I now regard the Sioux Indian problem, as a war question, as solved by the operations of General Miles last winter, and by the establishment of the two new posts on the Yellowstone, now assured this summer. Boats come and go now where a year ago none would venture except with strong guards. Wood-yarns are being established to facilitate navigation, and the great mass of the hostiles have been forced to go to the agencies for food and protection or have fled across the border into British territory."[108] The U.S. government lauded General Miles as instrumental in securing the surrender of the Northern Cheyennes, as well as Lame Deer, Chief Joseph, and even the great Sitting Bull. Not only had he made the northern plains safe for the passage of Euro-American civilians, as noted by Sherman; he had taken steps to start the Northern Cheyennes on a path toward "civilization," as government officials understood it at the time, through encouraging them to join the military, settle on the land, and farm. What federal officials saw as the surrender of these hostiles undoubtedly encouraged those in Washington to believe that they had created a successful Indian policy. These officials watched the Northern Cheyennes scout and farm and believed that they were melding slowly but successfully into American society.

While these Cheyenne families did adapt to a new way of living, they did not represent assimilation in the way these government officials assumed. Countless Cheyennes today insist that their ancestors never surrendered, and finally I had some idea as to why this is true. Instead of surrendering, they made a sacrifice to safeguard their people and build a better life for themselves and their nation, and in order

Two Moons's children, Fort
Keogh, Montana, 1879, by
Laton A. Huffman. Buffalo
Bill Center of the West,
Cody, Wyoming.

to do so, they were required to make the kind of x marks that Lyons
describes.[109] One warm afternoon, relaxing on lawn chairs under the
trees in her yard, Ms. DG helped me understand what an incredible
sacrifice this had been for her ancestors. We were chatting about Dull
Knife and Little Wolf and their struggle to return home. She paused
and I stared off at the perpetually blue sky, waiting for her to finish
her thought.

"You know," she told me, "those families wouldn't have had any
place to come home to if those scouts at Fort Keogh hadn't made the
sacrifices they did."

"What do you mean?" I asked her. I had been thinking of the decision to become scouts as one without much agency. In my mind, these
families had surrendered at a military camp and had the unenviable
choice between living as prisoners or living as scouts. I never thought
that becoming scouts might be a strategic decision made based on
the hope for building a stronger, safer future. That warm afternoon,
in the shade of that old willow, Ms. DG taught me that fighting is
only one way to retain your culture, your identity, and even your

nationhood. Sometimes your best choice to survive as a people is to make that x mark.

One of the most challenging aspects of the Northern Cheyennes' alliance with General Miles must have been fighting against longtime allies. While the Cheyenne scouts had no connection to the Nez Perce families they tracked, they were also asked to track groups of Lakota and Cheyenne people, some of which even contained relatives. It is highly likely that Cheyenne scouts felt little sense of responsibility toward Native people with whom they had no connection, but understanding their willingness to scout with U.S. troops against Lakota and Cheyenne bands deserves some consideration. Both Lame Deer's band and Sitting Bull's people living in Canada had been allied with the Cheyennes and included relatives. To scout against these groups must have been a painful choice, but those who made it were under incredible pressure. They had seen the might of the U.S. military and understood what a powerful threat it posed to their way of life. Like other Native peoples who chose to make an x mark, these Cheyenne scouts had a narrow range of options available to them and took the path they believed was ultimately best for their families, hoping it would also be best for their people.

Being caught between enemies, however, was not a new experience in Cheyenne history. In the past, members of the Cheyenne nation had made similar choices between two groups at war, for example, when those with Kiowa and Cheyenne relatives had to decide which side they would support. The flexibility of Plains social organization allowed space for such choices, resisting imposing rigid, singular identities on members. As long as a person had relatives within a group, they could move between groups, even groups in conflict. Such movement required cautious negotiation, but it was possible. These Cheyenne scouts were not considered traitors to their own people because it was always possible to renegotiate and renew alliances. For this reason, these scouts were able to activate relationships across enemy lines and often did so in an attempt to save lives.

Ms. DG stated that these Northern Cheyenne scouts wrestled with a difficult decision and ultimately made a great sacrifice. She emphasized that they gave up their old ways and started "living like white people." They also fought for the U.S. military, at times against their own friends. They stopped moving across the plains and stayed in one place. She declared that these sacrifices eventually allowed the Cheyennes to obtain a reservation in Montana. She also indicated that their relationship with General Miles helped them win their land. She stated that the Northern Cheyennes at Fort Keogh had a very close relationship with the general; he was their good friend in whom they placed a lot of trust. She talked about writings she had seen by him, noting that he upheld that relationship and the obligations that came with it, fighting hard to win the Northern Cheyennes a reservation of their own. For Ms. DG, these scouts who gave up so much to stay in their homeland also deserved credit for founding the reservation. She did not characterize their actions as assimilationist or as traitorous to her people but instead spoke of these sacrifices with respect and recognition of their ultimate power.[110] These scouts chose to engage in a difficult balance, navigating life in the military while still recognizing their alliance with the main body of the Cheyenne and Lakota nations. Certainly, they adjusted to the Euro-American way of life before their relatives who traveled to other agencies did, but ultimately this sacrifice preserved the people's connectedness, identity, and autonomy through preserving the landscape.

John Stands In Timber attributed the Northern Cheyenne reservation to Two Moons's people and his scouts as well, stating, "That was how they got this land, and it shows that Two Moons was right. When Standing Elk and the other chiefs were arguing and not wanting to go in to Fort Keogh, he told them: 'We have had enough troubles. More soldiers come to us each time. The white people are moving in like ants and covering the whole country. If you go on fighting we may lose our land and be prisoners, but if we surrender we might get to keep some of it.' And things turned out that way."[111] John Stands In Timber did not equate surrendering with becoming prisoners. He suggested that they stopped fighting to save their landscape—just as establishing peace with a Native enemy nation would have in the past. Elva Stands In Timber pushed this point, stating that Two Moons and the people who came into Fort Keogh never surrendered; she even said that the Cheyennes never surrendered to the United States.[112] On considering the deep implications of her assertion, it becomes clear that the Cheyennes remained in Montana through utilizing the kin relationships and social organization on which they had relied since before Euro-Americans came to the plains. In fact, the Cheyennes were not the only Plains people to utilize ties with military officers, created by scouting, to secure access to their homelands. Many Plains peoples used similar tactics based in older diplomatic mechanisms; some such as the Northern Arapahos and Crows were even able to secure their position in their homelands in this way.[113]

Establishing this alliance with General Miles brought with it several advantages for Two Moons and those who joined him. When the young Cheyenne men enlisted as scouts, all the Cheyennes at the fort could receive rations from the military instead of the Indian Department, a major advantage because the corruption in the Indian Department often impoverished the supplies before they reached the people. They could also establish a legitimate presence in the Powder River region where they wished to remain; their residence was sanctioned not as wards of the state but as its agents. They lived comfortably near Fort Keogh; they had plenty to eat and were allowed to leave the fort to hunt. Most Plains peoples were required to get permission to leave their agencies, but the Northern Cheyennes at Fort Keogh could come and go as they pleased.

Two Moons and those people who followed him were using their own strategy of creating alliances with enemies to expand their social network and to maintain access to their landscape. Miles had promised these Northern Cheyennes a reservation in a location of their choosing. If the scouts created a military alliance with Miles as they had with other Plains peoples in the past, he would have an obligation to keep his word and to share the territory with these families. These are the same tactics the Cheyennes had been using for centuries to maintain access to a landscape, so in fact this act upheld their autonomy because it was in line with Cheyenne constructions of political organization based in personal relationships and reciprocal obligations. Through Plains diplomacy that led to the formation of an alliance with General Miles, Two Moons's people successfully remained in their homeland near their beloved Powder River.

Two Moons's people had forged an alliance with General Miles, and through him, the U.S. government had a responsibility to them. Miles upheld his part of the alliance for personal reasons by fighting alongside the Northern Cheyennes and by providing them with resources, but he also respected their independence as a people. Because this alliance followed the cultural expectations of the Northern Cheyennes at its inception, they had reason to assume it would continue to follow their expectations, and they made this clear to Miles. Because both sides respected this relationship, albeit for different reasons, the Northern Cheyennes at Fort Keogh found themselves in the position to help their relatives return to their homeland. Although different families had separated and chosen different agencies, they never severed their wider network of kin ties during diaspora. These ties connected the Cheyenne people from Montana to Dakota Territory to Indian Territory, lighting a trail for those who needed to come home.

CHAPTER FIVE

WE COULD NOT FORGET OUR NATIVE COUNTRY

Dull Knife and Little Wolf's People
and the Long Journey Home

Today there is little left of Fort Keogh. The USDA has placed a range research station there, running cattle among the skeletons of the few remaining buildings. A plaque on a rock in Miles City, Montana, is the only commemoration of Fort Keogh's existence. The site of the Sand Creek massacre is now honored by a marker, a repatriation burial site, and an interpretive center, yet these memorials were erected only after a difficult campaign by both the Northern and Southern Cheyennes.[1] The Northern Cheyennes also struggled to gain a memorial acknowledging their harrowing experiences at Fort Robinson. Fort Robinson State Park has recently made quite an effort to educate the public about this massacre. Now a tourist can walk through the reconstructed barracks where the Cheyennes were held prisoner and read information about the massacre. Signs are posted along the White River and along the scenic road in the bluffs describing the progression of the massacre as the people fled. These recognitions were hard won for the Cheyennes. Apparently the park service was reluctant to remind its visitors bent on camping and picnicking of the horrors that took place at their campsites.

During my research, I knew I had to visit the archive at Fort Robinson State Park, but to actually spend time at that location was quite disorienting for me. I did not camp there or rent a room in the hotel, though it would have been convenient. Instead I drove into the park each day from my hotel in town. I sat in the library most of the first day, compiling old newspaper articles and journal entries, but late one afternoon, as I passed the marker commemorating Crazy Horse's murder, walking to the old guardhouse, and then on toward the reconstructed barracks, an oppressive sense of the suffering that had taken place there overwhelmed me. I felt short of breath. The warm summer sun contrasted with the bitter winter night on which the massacre occurred. Hearing the laughter of children ironically called to my mind the little children who had fled from the barracks in the arms of their mothers, on the backs of their grandfathers, and on the hips of their siblings. As I walked the path toward the creek that most Cheyennes took on that terrible night, I saw where the laughter came from. Young children were chasing each other while their father barbecued and their mother set the picnic table with paper plates and plastic forks. The plaque that commemorated the flight and death of those other children and their families more than a hundred years earlier stood close by. I have no idea if that family had looked at any of the signs or exhibits, but it struck me suddenly that not everyone wants to remember or commemorate. Some people do not even want to know.

Still, both the Sand Creek massacre and the Fort Robinson massacre loom large in the history of the American West. Any Plains military history buff knows these events in detail. They might not appeal to picnicking tourists, but they fit perfectly into the hegemonic nationalist narrative. These tragic events often act to underpin the vanishing Indian stereotype. This narrative mourns the victims of these massacres as the last of a noble race that died resisting Euro-American contact, encroachment, and assimilation. Following this logic, the descendants of those Native peoples living today are not "real Indians," simply another ethnic group blended into the melting pot of the United States. This narrative allows Americans to feel sadness and remorse over the destruction of Native peoples during the nineteenth century without recognizing any responsibility for continuing to ravage Indigenous lands in the name of resources and to appropriate Native imagery and religion in the name of profit or personal enlightenment. All the while, Americans can comfortably turn a blind eye to the impoverished living conditions and limited opportunities found on many reservations by explaining them away as a product of a failed work ethic or moral decay and not of a historic process of colonialism.

Given this discourse, it is not difficult to understand why the current Cheyenne nationalist narrative emphasizes the tragedy and the perseverance of the Fort Robinson massacre. Schoolchildren learn the narrative at a young age and see proud acknowledgments of the bravery of these bands all over the reservation. The tribal government building is named after Little Wolf. The tribal college is named after Dull Knife. Its new sign, visible from Highway 212, even includes a striking image of him. These heroes work differently in Northern Cheyenne nation-building narratives than in Euro-American ones. Instead of marking disappearance, they denote a refusal to acquiesce to colonialism and the maintenance of a nation against overwhelming odds.

Gerald Vizenor has called for the importance of emphasizing survivance over victimhood as a way for Native people to undermine the vanishing Indian stereotype and to assert continued autonomy over their lives and cultures.[2] Too much emphasis on the massacre at Fort Robinson can work to reinscribe Cheyenne people as victims helpless in the face of Euro-American violence. Ms. DG has also expressed her concern over emphasizing tragedy in Cheyenne historical narratives. She has wondered why Cheyenne children are taught so much about this history and not as much about sacred places such as the Black Hills or traditional knowledge such as the meaning behind beading patterns. She seems to imply that maintaining the nation depends more on retaining cultural knowledge than constructing a hegemonic nationalist narrative.

The Fort Robinson massacre can be seen either as the tragic collapse of one Plains tribe or as one of the bloodiest moments in the ultimately successful fight to retain Cheyenne autonomy. During the same moments that Two Moons's people were strategizing to secure their presence in their homeland, Dull Knife and Little Wolf's people were forced into diaspora. These men joined the majority of the Northern Cheyenne people when they came into Red Cloud Agency after the Battle of the Little Bighorn, compelled both by General George Crook's terms for peace and the security of an agency that they knew. Like Two Moons's people, the people with Dull Knife and Little Wolf assessed their difficult circumstances and acted on them utilizing kincentric expectations. Many members of this group made their decision to come into Red Cloud Agency because they had Lakota and Cheyenne relatives already living there. Furthermore, this location was familiar to the northern bands, and the Sacred Hat keeper chose to return there. While it was not necessary for each person to remain close to this sacred bundle, the keeper's family's actions protected the Hat, which in turn protected the people, so most families followed suit. Many probably also concluded that General Crook's terms for peace secured their ability to remain in their northern territory. After all, he had come to them with this promise, sealed by tobacco, seeking an end to the hostilities. There was no reason to risk a new relationship with General Miles when the people could reestablish an older, presumably more secure one with the officials at the agency.

This was a logical assumption, considering Crook's method of negotiation and the fact that the Northern Cheyennes signed most of the same treaties the Lakotas did; however, the history of Dull Knife and Little Wolf's people illustrates that by the 1870s, U.S. representatives no longer needed to respect the rules of diplomacy expected by Plains nations. This history also demonstrates that the use of kinship as a political strategy was not always enough to convince American officials to support Cheyenne claims to their homeland and to their sense of autonomous nationhood. Once the Cheyennes arrived at the agency, Crook completely ignored the agreements he made, as well as their claims to the northern country and their kinship ties with the Lakotas living there. Unlike Miles, he had no need for enlisting more Indian scouts, nor did he develop an emotional connection with the people who came to the agency. Although these bands probably believed that Crook would respect the kin-centric political strategy embedded in the workings of Plains diplomacy, he had no incentive to keep his promises. They could not have known this when making their decision, but they had little power to stop their removal from Red Cloud Agency to Indian Territory.

The history of Dull Knife and Little Wolf's people also illustrates the contradictory responses of American government officials to federal Indian policy. The comparison of Generals Crook and Miles demonstrates that individual actors responded to military duties on the plains in multiple and varying ways, particularly in relation to American Indian peoples. Because the nation-state constructs its identity by maintaining specific social and physical boundaries, those outside the state must be contained or assimilated. Miles believed the Northern Cheyennes could be assimilated, whereas Crook believed they must be contained. Both generals enacted policy steeped in nation-state ideology, but they did so in contradictory ways.[3] Two Moons's agenda to remain in the northern country overlapped with Miles's agenda, constructed by his duty to the state to attain Indian scouts, demonstrate military success on the plains, and ultimately assimilate Plains peoples into American lifestyles. Dull Knife and Little Wolf's agenda to remain with their kin in the north was at odds with Crook's agenda, also constructed by his duty to the state to contain the Northern Cheyennes. Crook accomplished containment by removing them to Indian Territory in order to attain control over the Native people remaining at Red Cloud Agency.

With the aid of Lakota kin on the Great Sioux Reservation and Northern Cheyenne kin at Fort Keogh, Dull Knife and Little Wolf were eventually able to escape the southern reservation and return home, but only after taking great physical risks and suffering much loss of life. The history of Dull Knife and Little Wolf's people demonstrates that sometimes the ambiguous and vacillating federal policy of the United States, the contradictory actions of its representatives, and the misunderstandings of Native constructions of kin and land had dire consequences for American Indian peoples. It also reveals that in the midst of diaspora, family could be the most important means of escape. Without family who took in the refugees, there would have been no hope of returning home. Kinship kept the people together when they literally had nothing else. These relationships extended beyond human relatives. According to oral histories, the group heading north gained help from their nonhuman kin as well. Pawnee Woman, one of Dull Knife's two wives, was one of the few remaining people who could converse with wolves. During the trip north, wolves visited her often, and on their final visit they told her that the place they were headed was a bad place.[4] Sadly, she died on the journey, never even making it to Fort Robinson. She is just one example of how the people depended on their network of kin to stay connected as a Native nation even during forced removal.

Dull Knife and Little Wolf listened to the same offers Two Moons heard, but they chose to negotiate with Crook instead of Miles. Ultimately, General Crook, like Miles, resigned himself to negotiating when he realized that a military campaign would certainly be long and costly and could ultimately fail.[5] Like General Miles, who sent Sweet Woman to these camps, Crook found Lakota men at Red Cloud Agency who were willing to travel north with gifts and tobacco. At Lt. William P. Clark's encouragement, both Spotted Tail and Red Cloud headed toward the camps of their friends and relatives with terms for peace from Crook. Clark also talked to Red Cloud about Crazy Horse, saying, "It was your men who studied out this scheme to get him in."[6] This statement suggests that Crook had turned to Native leaders for advice about encouraging these camps to return to the agencies, and these leaders had suggested negotiation. Just as Miles depended on Sweet Woman's knowledge of the culturally appropriate way to negotiate peace with Two Moons, Crook and Clark had to depend on Plains diplomacy enacted by Plains people speaking for them.

Even though this moment seems ominous in light of what would happen to these Cheyennes later, as Jeffery Ostler pointed out, the Plains Indians who returned "had real reason for hope as they rode toward the Red Cloud Agency."[7] In the eyes of the Lakotas and the Cheyennes, they had negotiated terms of peace with the United States. For the Northern Plains people, Crook was offering an alliance similar to the one Miles offered—an agreement that would reestablish the friendly relationship they had before fighting ensued over the Black Hills and that would guarantee them access to their territory. The Northern Cheyennes did not see themselves as a defeated people.[8] Crook had authorized Spotted Tail and Red Cloud to bring gifts of tobacco, assurances that they would be well fed and safe at the agencies, guarantees that the military would not retaliate, and promises of a northern reservation.[9] When Spotted Tail encountered a large group of Northern Cheyennes as he was riding toward Crazy Horse's camp, he was able to convince them to return to Red Cloud Agency.[10] The Cheyenne and Lakota leaders of these bands had no reason to doubt that Crook would be true to his word. They had previous friendly agreements with the United States that had only begun to unravel in the past few years with the relatively recent flood of Americans into the Black Hills. Finally, like Miles, Crook had sealed his promises with tobacco.[11]

Despite the binding nature of his promises in the eyes of the Cheyennes and Lakotas, Crook presumed that by coming into the agency, these groups had surrendered to the United States. Crook apparently did suggest a northern agency for the people who had come in, proposing that the Red Cloud and Spotted Tail Agencies be moved to the mouth of the Tongue and Powder Rivers. Of course, nothing came of this. Ostler has proposed that Crook tried to manipulate the situation by sending a proposal to federal officials, attempting to appear as if he were keeping his promise to maintain order at the agency but knowing that the federal government would never act on the request.[12] In this way, he achieved his overarching priority—to maintain control over Plains peoples. For Crook, these negotiations were simply a means to contain all Plains Indians and establish order at the agencies. Once they arrived at Red Cloud Agency, Crook treated these Plains peoples as prisoners of war.

While General Miles needed to enlist Native scouts that knew the country for his military campaigns, Crook already had scouts and had no need to establish this kind of relationship with those that came to Red Cloud Agency. Instead, it was in his best interest to show the government he could maintain control by submitting the Cheyennes and Lakotas to the surveillance of the state. For many government officials, the safety of the plains lay in the spatial control of its Native population. Chris C. Cox, a special Indian commissioner who reported on the Great Sioux Reservation in 1874, illustrated this view, stating, "The Indian should be kept within limited bounds, and, as far as consistent with his comfort and necessities, his nomadic life abridged. Depredations will never cease, the savage will never be controlled until he is either induced or compelled to give up his migratory habits and confine himself to the boundaries designated and furnished by the government."[13] At Red Cloud Agency, the Cheyennes and Lakotas lived in a bounded landscape where their lives could be tracked and restricted by Indian agents and military personnel. As soon as the people came into Red Cloud Agency, these officials attempted to control them using methods of surveillance such as regulating the population through censuses, controlling diet through rations, and enforcing immobility through spatial confinement.

Nevertheless, the Cheyennes, Arapahos, and Lakotas at Red Cloud Agency proved difficult to bind. The agent at Red Cloud in 1875, J. J. Saville, described the people who refused to comply with these colonial forms of control as wild and vicious. He reported that the Plains Indians at the agency "could not be made to understand the necessity of regular issues of food, but insisted on their own lawless way of giving every man as much as wanted."[14] Saville claimed that these newcomers vehemently opposed any effort to control the distribution of rations. He also reported that attempting a census raised bitter opposition, almost leading to violence.[15] The people must have been aware that these actions took power from Cheyenne and Lakota leaders and placed it in the hands of Euro-American agents, stripping the people of both cultural and political autonomy. Although they most likely did not realize the full implications of the surveillance the agent wished to place them under, they apparently were aware that losing control of the distribution of their food and allowing the agent to have a precise record of their population would give the United States power over their lives that threatened their ability to live according to their own cultural order.

What is more, the Northern Cheyennes at Red Cloud Agency soon had to deal with a more powerful attack on their autonomy. The Office of Indian Affairs threatened them with removal. In 1877 the commissioner of Indian affairs, in his annual report to the secretary of the interior, referred to the Northern Cheyennes and Arapahos, declaring, "These Indians for several years past have been reported as receiving rations with the Sioux at Red Cloud agency, but as 'belonging' with their southern brethren in the Indian Territory, whom they could not be induced to join by any persuasion or command unsupported by force."[16] Before the wars on the northern plains, the federal government endeavored to place the Northern Cheyennes on the Southern Cheyenne and Arapaho Agency in Indian Territory but could not obtain their consent. Cheyenne participation in the war, particularly in the Battle of the Little Bighorn, provided the federal government with a justification to continue removal without consent.

In September 1876 federal officials announced that because they fought in this battle, all Northern Cheyennes would be sent as they were caught to Indian Territory.[17] This decision was made just after the Battle of the Little Bighorn but months before the Northern Cheyennes living in the Powder River region had come to the agencies.

Crook obfuscated this plan during peace negotiations. Yet the commissioner of Indian affairs wrote in his report for 1877 that when the major portion of the northern camps arrived at Red Cloud Agency, "the Cheyennes were suddenly seized by a desire to remove to the Indian Territory."[18] This surely thrilled officials in Washington, who had been trying to effect this removal for years. Those in charge at Fort Robinson knew the Northern Cheyennes resisted removal to Indian Territory, but they seized the opportunity to fulfill the plans that had already been laid in September. Even after the full tragedy of Cheyenne removal had played out, government officials frequently argued that the Northern Cheyennes had agreed to go south.

The Senate Report of 1880 on the Removal of the Northern Cheyenne explained their desire to leave for Indian Territory as a need to escape "the troubles into which they had fallen." The report was referring to the battles with the military that they assumed had left the Cheyennes destitute. It also argued that they felt endangered by the Spotted Tail Sioux. The Cheyennes related none of these motivations, but such arguments supported federal officials' need to justify the removal as the best outcome for the people. The report also disputed Cheyenne claims that they were misled about the quality of the southern country or that they were promised that they could return north, arguing there was no proof of these promises.[19] The report referred to a lack of written evidence. Yet officials had made these promises during negotiations and the Northern Cheyennes were depending on them, regardless of the justifications presented by the report.[20]

Wooden Leg, who was present at Red Cloud Agency, described the events that transpired around the decision to remove to Indian Territory very differently from the description in official documents. He stated:

> There was some dissatisfaction among the Cheyennes on account of talk of them being taken to the South. The agent and the soldier chiefs had said we ought to go there and be joined as one tribe with the Southern Cheyennes. Our people did not like this talk. All of us wanted to stay in this country near the Black Hills.

But we had one big chief, Standing Elk, who kept saying it would be better if we should go there. I think there were not as many as ten Cheyennes in our whole tribe who agreed with him. The white men chiefs would not talk much to any Cheyenne chief but him. They gave him presents and treated him as if he were the only chief in the tribe, when he was but one of our forty tribal big chiefs. One day he went about telling everybody, "All get ready to move. The soldiers are going to take us from here tomorrow." Lots of Cheyennes were angry.[21]

In a council with Crook and Mackenzie after their arrival at the fort, these officials gave the Northern Cheyennes three options: go south, go to the Shoshone and Arapaho agency, or stay at Red Cloud Agency for a year and then let the authorities decide. Most Northern Cheyennes wished to remain at the agency, in the land they knew, close to their Lakota relatives and other Northern Cheyenne families still living in the north off the reservation. George Bird Grinnell believed that when Standing Elk made his positive declaration to the agency officials, the people were so astonished that they kept silent and eventually they simply agreed to go.[22]

The Northern Cheyennes may have also acquiesced to this decision because they did not believe that the removal would be permanent. This belief was justified for several reasons. In the agreement that some Lakotas, Cheyennes, and Arapahos had signed with the United States ceding the Black Hills in 1876, Article 4 declared that the peoples who signed the document would agree to visit the Indian Territory and look for land to make a permanent home. It stated, "If such delegation shall make a selection which shall be satisfactory to themselves . . . then the said Indians agree that they will remove to the country."[23] If the delegation decided they did not like the land, the agreement implied, they were not required to remove. In the 1880 Senate report, Wild Hog gave testimony referring to this agreement. He stated that during the council in which they agreed to go south, Generals Crook and Mackenzie told them, "You can go down and look at the country, and if you do not find it as we say it is, you can come back and live here again."[24] Wild Hog stated that he was at the council with Little Wolf, Dull Knife, Standing Elk, and Living Bear, and they all understood the same thing. William Rowland had interpreted the words of the council to them. He was a trusted interpreter, married into the community, who spoke both Cheyenne and English fluently. Considering the 1876 agreement as well as the statements made in this council, these Cheyenne leaders had every reason to believe that they would be allowed to remain in the north if that was what they wanted.

In fact, two Northern Cheyenne headmen, Spotted Elk and Yellow Calfskin Shirt, had already traveled with a Lakota delegation, established in conjunction with this agreement, to Indian Territory to examine the landscape in the fall of 1876. According to Old Crow, who was interviewed for the Senate report, Calfskin Shirt and Spotted Elk advised the Cheyennes to go south, saying that it was a nice country.[25] These two men had closer kin ties with the Southern Cheyennes than most Northern families, so for them, traveling to Indian Territory would be less disruptive. For the Northern Cheyennes who had close kin ties with the Lakotas, however, leaving would have interrupted the relationships with family and land on which they depended for so many aspects of their lives.

American officials ignored these fine distinctions. Both federal and agency officials, who assumed the Cheyenne nation was homogenous, believed that the Cheyennes belonged on the southern agency with other Cheyenne. For example, Crook and Mackenzie told the Northern Cheyennes, "When you get down there [to the southern reservation] you will find the rest of the Cheyennes, the Southern Cheyennes, who have been living in that country for many years; it will be very pleasant for you all to get together again in that country."[26] Furthermore, in the eyes of the United States, if the chiefs who traveled with the delegation decided Indian Territory was a good place, this opinion surely reflected the views of the people. Notice, however, that these chiefs traveled south in the fall of 1876, months before most of the Northern Cheyennes had returned to the agency from the Powder River region. These chiefs did not participate with the Lakotas in the fighting in the north, reflecting that they held different alliances. Furthermore, for the Cheyennes, one or two chiefs did not have authority to make decisions for the entire nation. The Council of Forty-Four was required to meet, discuss the issues, and make their decision together. For most Northern Cheyennes, the decision to go south was not authorized by their legal system. Furthermore, it contradicted the terms by which they had made peace with Crook.

Because they had kin ties in the north and a connection to that landscape, the Northern Cheyennes as a people had focused their political goals on remaining in their northern homeland since the 1860s. While many had kin ties to Southern Cheyennes, they also had negotiated a different relationship with U.S. officials than their southern relatives. In an 1880 interview, Wild Hog stated that only a small portion of Northern Cheyennes at Red Cloud Agency were willing to remove to the south; most of the Cheyennes preferred not to go but believed that because it was the will of the government, they had little choice.[27] Wooden Leg described similar sentiments about the decision to move south, stating: "We had understood that when we surrendered we were to live on our same White River reservation. We had given up our guns and our horses and had quit fighting because of this promise. Now after we had put ourselves at this great disadvantage, the promise was to be broken. But we could not do anything except obey."[28] Wooden Leg considered Red Cloud Agency at Fort Robinson the Northern Cheyennes' agency; in fact, he understood that the government had promised it to them. Crook had made the promise of a northern reservation to all the Cheyennes, Arapahos, or Lakotas that came into Red Cloud. He had proposed a reservation in the Powder River region, but the Northern Cheyennes had no reason to think that if that did not work out, they would not be able to live on the Great Sioux Reservation. U.S. officials had continuously negotiated with both the Cheyennes and Lakotas together since the 1868 treaty. The Cheyennes had no reason to think that they would be treated differently from the Lakotas. Federal officials, however, simply ignored the promises Crook made and imposed their will, ultimately removing as many Northern Cheyennes as they could from Red Cloud Agency.

While still in the north, some people managed to use their kinship ties to avoid removal altogether. On May 28, 1877, a group of 972 Cheyennes left Red Cloud Agency to head south. They arrived on August 5, 1877, but only 937 Northern Cheyennes were enrolled at Darlington Agency on arrival.[29] Apparently around thirty-five Cheyennes had taken off en route, most likely to return to the camps of their Lakota relatives or to the Tongue River region to join their Northern Cheyenne relatives who were scouting for General Miles. What's more unusual is that in his annual report of 1877, Agent James Irwin reported that on July 1, when he arrived at Red Cloud Agency, he found between ten and fifteen lodges of Northern Cheyennes camping there who were perhaps associated with Crazy Horse's band.[30] Crazy Horse's band came into Red Cloud Agency on May 6, 1877, a few weeks before the Northern Cheyennes were removed.[31] These families were intermarried with the Lakotas and could have blended in with them in the eyes of the agents, particularly because they spoke Lakota. It is highly likely that they realized the danger of being removed to Indian Territory and used their position within Crazy Horse's band to camouflage their Cheyenne identity until this danger had passed.[32] Mr. BC explained to me that these Cheyennes living in a predominantly Lakota band had simply spoke to officials in Lakota. In order to save their families, they assumed a Lakota identity. The officials could not distinguish between subtle indicators of identity such as beadwork patterns or cuts of moccasins and had no idea these Lakota speakers were actually Cheyennes. They had used their network of kin to strategically shift their identity. In an 1880 interview, Old Crow mentioned that there were about fifty-six or fifty-seven women and children who were captured from Dull Knife's camp and who also lived at Red Cloud Agency with the Lakotas.[33] These Cheyennes asserted their autonomy using their kinship to remain outside the grasp of the U.S. government.

Even though Irwin discovered that there were lodges of Cheyennes who had not joined the trip south, he allowed them to remain where they were camped. On November 1, 1877, a large group of Arapahos were escorted from Red Cloud Agency to Fort Casper, Wyoming, and about fifty Cheyennes, mostly women and children separated from Dull Knife's village after Mackenzie's attack, joined this group.[34] These people, identified as Cheyennes, certainly had relatives among the Arapahos to whom they could turn in their moment of need after the Mackenzie battle. These Northern Cheyennes also utilized kin ties in order to remain in the north with their Arapaho relatives as Cheyenne relatives were being removed to Indian Territory. While resisting removal and remaining in the north may not seem like an expression of autonomy, in fact this action not only helped people remain connected to their northern homeland but also maintained the widespread web of kin ties that diasporic Cheyennes could draw on to support their efforts to return. By connecting with relatives to remain in the north, Cheyenne families had established themselves in Wyoming and on the Sioux reservation, as well as at Fort Keogh.

Despite promises of a northern reservation, nearly all the Northern Cheyennes residing at Red Cloud Agency, totaling almost a thousand people, were forced to make the long journey to Indian Territory in early spring of 1877. Once these Cheyennes arrived at Darlington Agency, some acclimated to their new home. In his 1878 annual report, John D. Miles, the agent there, stated that although they had been issuing separate rations to the Northern and Southern Cheyennes, in July he decided to issue them together. At this time, "the Southern Cheyennes were encouraged to blend the Northern Cheyennes with their own people, in which they were successful to the extent of over 550 people, under Living Bear, Yellow Calfskin Shirt, Standing Elk, Turkey Legs, American Horse, and others, who accepting this country as their permanent homes, have placed their children in school and are well behaved."[35]

Many Northern Cheyennes had kin among the Southern Cheyennes. The families Miles spoke of had found relatives to help make their transition easier and to encourage them to remain. When asked why Standing Elk and the people with him wanted to stay in the south, while he wanted to return north, Little Chief responded, "The people of his band have always had some relatives down here among these Southern Cheyennes. They had been thinking of coming here a long time before they did; they were predisposed in favor of this country." Little Chief's response clearly demonstrated how important kinship was to helping Cheyenne families feel contented on the reservation. Living Bear, one of the Northern Cheyennes who came south, described his situation, stating, "I have been satisfied here ever since coming down; when I first came down here the Southern Cheyenne met me and took me by the hand, and told me they were glad I had come down; and I have felt at home ever since." When asked why he believed some Cheyenne would want to stay in Indian Territory and others would want to return to the north, General Nelson Miles stated, "The relatives of some of them, who were already down there, treated them hospitably and made it as comfortable as possible for them. That would naturally have a tendency to make them like it better down there."[36] The families with close kin ties that could immediately be activated had a smoother transition and most elected to stay. They made the adjustment to Indian Territory not because of anything the government did, but because of their binding family connections.

Not all the Northern Cheyennes who came south had this welcoming experience. Many were closer to their Lakota, Arapaho, and Cheyenne relatives in the north and had only distant relatives in the south. In his history of the Southern Cheyenne and Arapaho Reservation, Donald Berthrong declared that when the Northern people came south, the two groups began to bicker and belittle each other almost right away. He stated that the young men from each group also competed over beef rations, insisting that they distribute the rations instead of the agent.[37] These groups struggled to find a place in the south. The Northern Cheyennes who had more difficulty activating kin relationships among the Southern Cheyennes described their experiences in the south in much more negative terms.

Little Chief noted that Dull Knife's people had not gotten along with the Southern Cheyennes and stated of his own band, "We do not get along very pleasantly with these other Indians; we do not feel good to be among them." Wild Hog related a harsher experience with the Southern Cheyennes. He declared, "No sooner had the Northern Cheyennes got down there than the Southern Cheyennes began to show dislike for them. They said, 'What are you Sioux doing here?' Little Rogue pointed his finger at me and asked that. After that there was quarreling between the Northern and the Southern Cheyennes all the time."[38] The Southern Cheyennes made a distinction that the government and agency officials failed to recognize. While the government believed that all Cheyennes could easily be categorized by what they believed were rigid ethnic borders marked by language, culture, and shared history, the Southern Cheyennes saw some Northern Cheyennes as more closely related to themselves and some as more closely related to the Lakotas. If all the Northern Cheyennes in the south had attempted to acquiesce to the agency life, activating even distant kin connections, this may have eased the tensions some, but the Northern Cheyennes who wished to return north resolved to remain separate in hopes that they might accomplish this goal. John Miles declared that when these Northern Cheyennes separated themselves from the rest and camped four or five miles away from the agency, "they became like two tribes . . . and then our Southern Cheyennes called those who had separated from them the Sioux Cheyennes."[39] For a nation bound by kin, such divisions were common, and different bands in the past had always been free to maintain different alliances from the rest of the nation. Yet when they were confined to a reservation, without true freedom to organize their own political processes, these distinctions led to pronounced tensions.

Relations were understandably strained between the Southern Cheyennes and the Cheyennes dedicated to returning north. Furthermore, the influx of nine hundred new mouths to feed strained government rations, increasing the possibility of violence. While some Cheyennes interviewed in 1880 complained of how the Southern Cheyennes treated them, no one stated this as the reason they wanted to return north. These tensions are not part of the reason given in oral histories today, either. Ms. DG, whose ancestors formed part of the group taken from Red Cloud Agency to Indian Territory, stated that she had never heard of fighting between the Southern and Northern Cheyennes; it was never part of the story told to her.[40] It is possible that modern Cheyennes might want to represent the Cheyenne people as a unified entity, but this would not explain why Cheyennes in 1880 would not point to these tensions as a reason to return.

If scholars assume that the Cheyenne nation was unified by the same types of categories as the state, then they can logically draw the conclusion that such tensions would indicate factionalism among a people, leading to a permanent divide. The Cheyennes, on the other hand, had frequently dealt with tensions caused by multiple ethnic alliances in the past. Sometimes these tensions escalated into military skirmishes, and sometimes families left the political body of the Cheyennes; however, because the nation did not maintain unity through rigid boundaries, such tensions did not lead to permanent destruction of the sociopolitical body. Instead, the Cheyennes depended on kinship ties to maintain connections between members even during disruptions. Once encased within the confines of the reservation, they did face the imposition of rigid nation-state boundaries and the flexibility of kinship hardened under the strain. Nevertheless, it did not break, and the Northern and Southern Cheyennes continued to maintain their sense of autonomous nationhood through kinship ties that crossed these boundaries.

Although the agents on the southern reservation showed concern over these tensions, the federal government reports emphasized illness and lack of rations as the reasons that the Cheyennes wanted to return north. General Sheridan revealed that the Northern Cheyennes received "insufficient food and irregularity in its supply."[41] In the Senate report, John D. Miles pointed to discontentment over rations and to the rampant sickness among the northern people.[42] J. K. Mizner, a commanding officer in the Fourth Cavalry at Fort Reno, declared in a letter to the secretary of war that the Northern Cheyennes found the southern country sickly, with no game, and their rations were poor in quality and quantity, and they did not get enough to eat.[43] Hunger coupled with new climatic conditions led to much sickness among the Northern Cheyennes. Once in the south, many died from diseases they had not encountered in the north, such as malaria and yellow fever. The inadequate rations they received increased the severe health conditions. The reservation doctor estimated that at one point around 2,000 Cheyennes were sick.[44] Although such depredations embarrassed federal officials, illness and hunger did not encourage them to question the ethnic and physical boundaries Indian agents attempted to impose to control the Cheyenne people. Federal documents de-emphasized the tensions between the Northern and Southern Cheyennes and completely ignored the close ties between the Northern Cheyennes and their Lakota and Arapaho relatives to retain the bounded understanding of this nation that they needed to justify the containment of the people.

Such physical suffering, illness, and lack of food, surely tested the Northern Cheyennes and made them less eager to remain in Indian Territory, but what drove them north was not illness or hunger, nor was it a desire to break from their southern relatives—it was instead their allegiance to a different people and land. Their home drew them north, where they could live with close relatives in a familiar landscape. When the Northern Cheyennes interviewed by the Senate committee were asked why they wanted to return north, they did not ignore their physical suffering, but almost all of them emphasized their homeland. Wild Hog stated,

> We could not forget our native country anyway—where we grew up from childhood, and knew all the hills and valleys and creeks and places we had hunted over; where the climate was cooler, the air purer and healthier, the water sweeter and better, than in the southern country to which we had been sent by the government; and finding that the promises which had been made to us by the government were not fulfilled, that instead of being better than the land we had left, everything was so much worse, we got homesick for our own country again.

Little Chief reiterated what Wild Hog had said, stating that the northern country was where he had been born and it was better than the south in every way. When asked what is better in the northern country, Wild Hog's wife answered simply, "Everything is better."[45]

In the summer of 2005, Ms. DG spoke to me about her ancestors' desire to return north. She stated that the people were more comfortable in the north because they knew the plants and animals, they knew the weather, and they knew the landscape.[46] It is no small matter to be taken from a land where every hill, valley, and spring has meaning and history, where each family knows where the deer go when it gets cold, how to find clean water, collect berries, and gather medicinal plants. Disconnection from the land meant more than a loss of resources and a disturbing sense of disorientation for the Northern Cheyennes, which in itself was no small matter. Yet by becoming entirely dependent on the agency in a way they had never been before, these Cheyennes lost control over their choices. They could no longer decide where to camp or even what to eat. They were in danger of losing their autonomy completely.

It is no surprise that the people longed for their homeland. This feeling of homesickness was so strong that Northern Cheyenne people today tell a powerful story about the sadness of their ancestors. Elva Stands In Timber related this story to me when we were talking about the Cheyennes who fled from the southern agency. She stated that a very old woman who had not wanted to be taken to Indian Territory lived in the camp of Northern Cheyennes that had separated itself from the rest of the agency. She grew very ill in the south, longing for her home. One day, with her last breath, she said, "Right now, up north, the wind is whistling in the pine trees," and she laid back and died.[47] Ms. Stands In Timber emphasized that, like this woman, some people died of homesickness.

The people suffered separation from not only the land but also their relatives, both human and nonhuman. They had been pulled from a landscape where their ancestors were buried and their spirits dwelled. They had made kin with each plant and animal in the north. The places filled with power that gave the nation strength and sustenance were in the north. The people now lived far from Bear Butte and the Yellowstone River, and they had no evidence that their agents would allow them to return to these important places to pray. They must have realized that these American men would not understand the painful separation from nonhuman relatives because they only discussed their human kin, but their longing for the landscape of their ancestors so obvious in their interviews implies a deep affiliation with the nonhuman entities that inhabited it.

When Old Crow, interviewed in 1879 while still in Indian Territory, was asked why he did not want to remain in the south, he related that the country was better in the north. He continued, "Almost all my relatives and friends are up there; I have a mother up there yet, and I have a daughter up there who is married; and I must live separated from them all the rest of my life." When asked whether families had been divided by this removal, Old Crow stated that the Northern Cheyennes who were removed had family at Tongue River, on the Yellowstone, on White River, "and all through that region." He declared that young people were separated from their parents, parents from their children, and women from their brothers.[48] This was not only because they had been intermarried with the Sioux and some of their relatives were living in these bands, but also because many Cheyennes had stayed north with General Miles. Furthermore, Wooden Leg related that some Cheyennes had not even come into Red Cloud Agency before the people started for Indian Territory, and others fled as soon as the decision was made to go south.[49]

Considering the important responsibilities that parents had for their children and that siblings had for each other and their sibling's children, Old Crow's statement is quite significant. Women depended on their brothers as male supporters of their families. Their children looked to their uncles to fulfill important functions in their lives. A woman without a brother would struggle. Extended family was central to the functioning of Cheyenne cultural life. Americans may not have understood the severity of this experience for Cheyenne families. While extended families chose to separate, usually such separations were assumed to be temporary. Furthermore, unlike Euro-American families who would withstand a husband leaving to take a homestead or pan for gold or children moving from their natal homes for work, Cheyenne families saw little sense in separating husbands from wives or children from parents, even in times of war.

Dull Knife and Little Wolf knew that the people who had removed themselves from the southern agency were struggling. They suffered from illness, hunger, dislocation, homesickness, and confinement. This was not the life these families envisioned for their children or those yet to come. Separated from their land and their relatives, these Northern Cheyennes could not eat, govern, or practice their religion in the way they were accustomed. Not only had they lost political power, but they no longer had access to places of spiritual power. For these families, living in diaspora was simply unbearable.

Dull Knife and Little Wolf felt their only solution was to return to their home in the north. Berthrong declared that because they had just come from successful military encounters with troops and the U.S. military had a limited force in Indian Territory, the Northern Cheyennes were "confident in their own ability to cope with the government."[50] I propose that this confidence extended beyond their military prowess. The Cheyennes felt that they were justified in returning north for two reasons. First, the government failed them in the promises regarding their life in the south. Wild Hog stated that they had been promised much better rations in the south and that there would be plenty of buffalo to hunt, neither of which turned out to be true.[51] Second, they had been told that if they did not like the country in the south, they could return north. The Northern Cheyennes acted based on their own understanding of this agreement. Although some Cheyennes said that they went south because they believed they had to, they did not believe they should have to remain. In fact, many Cheyennes believed that they could leave if they wished based on promises made during negotiations for peace. They had been guaranteed a place in the northern territory, based not only on their own understandings of land tenure as negotiated in Plains diplomacy but also on treaties signed with the U.S. government.

According to George Bird Grinnell, Little Wolf visited Agent Miles around July 4, 1878, to discuss returning north. Miles told him to wait a year and that there was nothing else that could be done. After a long conversation that got Little Wolf nowhere, the Cheyenne headman finally stood up and responded,

> My friends, I am now going back to my camp. I do not wish the ground about this agency to be made bloody, but now listen to what I say to you. I am going to leave here; I am going north to my own country. I do not want to see blood spilt about this agency. If you are going to send your soldiers after me, I wish that you would first let me get a little distance away from this agency. Then if you want to fight, I will fight you, and we can make the ground bloody at that place.[52]

Even in his declaration to defy Miles and return north, Little Wolf was thinking of the well-being of Cheyenne families. He did not want bloodshed at the agency, surely aware that such a battle would endanger Cheyenne families who chose to remain. In fact, some of those fleeing were forced to leave family members behind. Dull Knife's family decided to leave their youngest child, George Dull Knife, in the care of relatives, suspecting the journey would be too difficult for him. He probably came north with extended family in the summer of 1883 when many of those Cheyennes who decided not to flee were allowed to return to Pine Ridge.[53] Even during desperate times, both

Little Wolf and Dull Knife knew that as headmen they had a responsibility to protect all their people and safeguard their future whether they decided to stay or leave.

Miles was fully aware that many Northern Cheyennes were unhappy enough to leave. Four young men had already left the reservation, and the rest of the Northern Cheyennes who were planning to leave camped quite far from the agency. In an effort to control this camp using the tools of state domination, Miles called the northern bands to Darlington for a census, but they refused to come in. He set a deadline to arrive by the nightfall of September 7, 1878, but the people did not respond. Three days later those living in this camp were gone, though they had left their tipis standing to fool the Indian police. Although Little Wolf declared his intentions to the agent months before he left, Miles was still surprised when American Horse and a member of the Indian police woke him at three o'clock on the morning of September 10, 1878, to tell him that Dull Knife and Little Wolf's camp left the Cheyenne-Arapaho reservation.[54] Miles's first estimate of the number missing was 353 people—92 men, 120 women, 69 boys, and 72 girls.[55]

Within a few days of their departure, more than 2,000 troops were closing in on the group. Lieutenant General Sheridan's orders to General Crook were blunt. He was told to "spare no measures . . . to kill or capture the band of Cheyennes on the way north."[56] In a telegram from Sheridan to General Townsend about the fleeing Cheyennes, Sheridan stated, "There is a strong hope that the troops will be able to meet with them and capture or destroy them. It is important for the peace of the plains and the success of the reservation system that these Indians be captured, and every effort will be made to accomplish that purpose."[57] Here the government stated their purpose clearly: the plains were not safe if the Cheyennes were roaming; they must be contained within the boundaries of the reservation. In the eyes of American military officials, this small party of men, women with little children, and elders threatened to explode the plains into warfare and destroy the entire reservation system. To the casual modern observer, it seems unlikely that these few Cheyennes would be able to single-handedly destroy the entire reservation system simply by walking north. The power of the U.S. government over

Plains nations, however, relied on containment. Any Indigenous people living outside the reservation system, without evidence of assimilation into Euro-American lifeways, questioned the ability of government officials to retain control over the people within its geographical boundaries.

In the discourse of the period, this act of leaving the reservation was considered an "outbreak." According to Philip Deloria, the concept of "outbreak" became common during the beginning of the reservation period when the institutions of the state only partially controlled Native populations. This term revealed the American fear that Native people would escape "the spatial, economic, political, social, and military restrictions placed on them by the reservation regime."[58] The Northern Cheyennes who had fled exposed the government's inability to contain the Cheyennes as a nation and force them to accept the boundaries imposed by the state. This party posed a serious threat, not a physical or military threat but, as Sheridan's letter indicates, an ideological threat to the dream of control held by the federal government.[59] The military power of this small party clearly did not threaten the United States; they only had ninety-two men to defend their band against thousands of soldiers. The threat came from the party's mobility and flexibility. If the people could move according to their own free will, the government would not be able to control them. The concept of "outbreak" demonstrates that not only did officials fear escape from state-based restrictions imposed on Native people, but also that Native people's lack of rigid boundaries undermined the state's efforts at containment. The Cheyennes were able to maintain this flexibility through their wide-ranging network of kin.

On the journey, the people battled with troops several times, but they managed to survive and continued to evade the military.[60] Some of the most famous violent exchanges along this harrowing trail occurred in Kansas, not with troops but with settlers. Several scholars have detailed these raids. While some have argued that Cheyenne warriors carried out these attacks against small settlements in retaliation for massacres against their own relatives, James Leiker and Ramon Powers claim it was a response to the Euro-American invasion of their homeland, noting the unusual damage done to property along with the violence perpetrated against these settlers.[61] While these young warriors might have had relatives who had been harmed by U.S. troops at some point, Leiker and Powers have convincingly argued that the disturbance created by Euro-American settlements in a landscape that Cheyenne people understood to be their own could have incited anger, especially for people who were under the stress of literally being hunted by the military. Perhaps the violent acts against these settlers were an attempt to articulate the anger these young Cheyenne men felt at being forced from their home, as the landscape they depended on to provide for their families was taken over by non-Native settlers.

Monnett points out that it was not in the best interest of these fleeing Cheyenne to ransack farms and ranches on their way north—it drew unwanted attention. After the Battle at Punished Woman's Fork, however, the people were in desperate need of supplies and fresh horses. These warriors mostly took food and warm clothing from the settlements, demonstrating the main purpose of the raids.[62] Little Wolf testified that he often harangued the young men, "telling them not to kill citizens, but to leave them alone." He admitted, however, that he knew that some men had attacked settlements, although they had never told him about it.[63] Leiker and Powers remind us that the immigrant families who had sought homesteads in the newly opened Kansas Territory had been encouraged to build their homes in a war zone.[64] While federal officials could philosophize about the best course of action from the safety of their offices, both Cheyenne and settler families bore the violent brunt of these decisions. The newspaper reports of the time certainly sensationalized the disturbance, however, whipping the region into a frenzy of terrified settlers and vindictive vigilantes. Alan Boye aptly points out that because of this, today there is no way of knowing exactly what happened during this part of the trek north.[65]

It is nothing short of a miracle that a little party of three hundred people could avoid the thousands of troops scouring the plains as much as they did. Iron Teeth, a Cheyenne woman who made this journey, described what it was like.

> Day after day, through more than a month, I kept my youngest daughter strapped to my body, in front of me, on my horse. I led

another horse carrying the next youngest daughter. We dodged the soldiers during most of our long journey. But always they were near to us, trying to catch us. Our young men fought them off in seven different battles. At each fight, some of our people were killed, women and children the same as men. I do not know how many of our grown-up people were killed. But I know that more than 60 of our children were gone when we got to the Dakota country.[66]

Iron Teeth related the strains of this journey for a woman with young children. Her account reminds readers that this flight was not a military action but an effort to return home and reunite families. The group was not a war party, and the effort to return was not carried by young warriors alone but by entire families. Iron Teeth did not relate any battles, nor did she know how many adults died, but she remembered the little children.

In October 1878, after a long month of running, hungry and tired, Dull Knife and Little Wolf camped somewhere north of the Platte, possibly in the Sand Hills but also perhaps on White Tail Creek.[67] There the people decided to split into two groups. Many reasons have been given for this split. Some have argued that Dull Knife split with Little Wolf because Dull Knife wanted to return to Red Cloud and his Lakota camp, to be with relatives where they would be well taken care of, and Little Wolf wanted to continue heading north.[68] Scholars have portrayed this as a dispute, but bands often divided for pragmatic reasons. Ms. DG stated that she believed that the people separated because they thought it would give them a better chance of survival to be in smaller groups.[69] Some scholars have argued that Dull Knife acted as a decoy to draw the troops away from the others.[70] Furthermore, Little Wolf suggested a plan that would take much more stamina than some in the group had. Undoubtedly, many people wanted to join their relatives with Red Cloud where they would be well fed and safe, instead of facing the military's unabated pursuit, the impending winter, and the longer journey north. Dull Knife's suggestion would have certainly been appealing, although it would be risky to approach an agency. Little Wolf's plan had the safety of escape; they would not go to an agency but instead would stay out in the country and try to make it through the winter in their homeland.

Portrait of the war chief
Old Little Wolf, taken by
Elizabeth Curtis Grinnell or
Julia E. Tuell, ca. 1910.
Image N13558, Smithsonian
Institution, Washington, D.C.

After the group separated, Little Wolf's band successfully disap-
peared into the Sand Hills of Nebraska.[71] The military trying to catch
their trail had no idea that the escaping Cheyennes had split into two
groups. Little Wolf's people were able to depart while the military
tracked Dull Knife and those following him. Little Wolf found a little
valley near the lower fork of the Niobrara River, which was well hidden and stocked with game.[72] This small group passed the winter
there, concealed from the soldiers who continued to search but did not
find them. By early spring, when the snow and ice were beginning
to melt, Little Wolf and his camp set off for the northern country. They
traveled past the Black Hills and up to the Powder River, where they
were camped in March 1879. Most likely, they headed north in an
attempt to join their relatives who lived at Fort Keogh and scouted
with Lieutenant Casey. They had already experienced the treatment
at Red Cloud Agency, and they knew that some Northern Cheyennes
had managed to remain at Fort Keogh. There was no agent there; it
was a military post, so perhaps Little Wolf and his followers felt they

had a better chance to live the life they loved with their northern relatives who were not attached to an agency but instead to the military.[73] By this point, they knew that at the agencies, federal officials were attempting to return all Cheyennes to Indian Territory, but they had reason to believe that those who scouted at Fort Keogh were not being sent south.

By the spring, the U.S. military had regained a sense of where Little Wolf was headed. As Little Wolf's people traveled to the Powder River, Lt. William P. Clark traveled from Fort Keogh with orders to intercept the party. Clark brought Lakota and Cheyenne scouts, and when he reached the Powder River, he sent a Lakota scout named Red War Bonnet, an interpreter, and another scout named George Fleury to search for the Cheyenne camp.[74] These men found Little Wolf's village, declared their presence, and were allowed to enter. After a few days, Red War Bonnet was able to ride back to Clark and report the location of the camp. When he left, Little Wolf moved the people again. Clark decided to attempt to meet Little Wolf, sending several scouts out ahead of the slow-moving military column. The scout, Wolf Voice, happened to be the one who came across Little Wolf's camp.[75] "I am Cheyenne," he had called out to the people so that they would not be afraid to come out and talk to him. Little Wolf agreed to meet with Lieutenant Clark to discuss terms for peace and rode out with Wolf Voice to meet him. Once the two met and declared their friendly intentions, Clark moved into Little Wolf's camp and distributed rations while his medical officer attended to the sick and injured. After they had camped together for three days, Clark began to forge an agreement with Little Wolf. He suggested that Little Wolf and his young men join their relatives at Fort Keogh and become scouts so that they could remain in the north.

Clark asked Little Wolf to give up his guns and his horses, as the price of peace. He wanted the guns immediately but offered to allow them to wait to surrender their horses until they got to Fort Keogh. Little Wolf responded to Clark, saying,

> Since I left you at Red Cloud, we have been south, and we have suffered a great deal down there. Many have died of diseases we have no name for. Our hearts looked and longed for this country

where we were born. There are only a few of us left, and we only wanted a little ground, where we could live. We left our lodges standing, and ran away in the night. The troops followed us. I rode out and told the troops we did not want to fight; we only wanted to go north, and if they would let us alone we would kill no one. The only reply we got was a volley. After that we had to fight our way, but we killed none who did not fire at us first. My brother, Morning Star, took one-half of the band and surrendered near Camp Robinson. He thought you were still there and would look out for him. They gave up their guns and then the whites killed them all. I am out in the prairie, and need my guns here. When I get to Keogh I will give you the guns and ponies, but I cannot give up the guns now. You are the only one who has offered to talk before fighting, and it looks as though the wind, which has made our hearts flutter for so long, would not go down. I am very glad that we did not fight, and that none of my people or yours have been killed. My young men are brave, and would be glad to go with you to fight the Sioux.[76]

Little Wolf's speech as it was recorded is very important. Although it is hard to know whether his actual words were recorded as spoken or if they were recorded from memory, this speech as it is demonstrates, first, that Little Wolf had knowledge of Dull Knife's band after they had split, coming from the people who traveled to meet his band. This is evidence that people continued to use mobility to remain connected when opportunities arose even during this very restrictive era. Second, Little Wolf asked for land and stated this as his reason for leaving Indian Territory. Third, he prepared his relationship with Lieutenant Clark for establishing an alliance, pointing out that he was the only one who had offered to talk and stating that he was willing to fight with Clark—in other words, to create an alliance—through talking, making an agreement, and then fighting together. Clark had also offered gifts, in the form of rations, as part of the initial peace negotiations. Little Wolf had every reason to believe that Clark offered an alliance. This would also guarantee the people access to land in the Powder River region, as all involved must have realized, especially since many of Two Moons's people still lived in the north. Clark agreed to let the Cheyennes keep their guns, and on March 25, 1879, Little Wolf succeeded in forging an agreement with Clark. On April 1, his people arrived at Fort Keogh, and the young men became scouts with the army. Little Wolf would live out the rest of his life in the north country to which he fought so desperately to return.

Dull Knife and those with him did not fare as well as those who followed Little Wolf. Fearing the trip north with Little Wolf was too dangerous and longing for the security that living among relatives provided, Dull Knife came into Fort Robinson in Nebraska. This small group of 149 people arrived at the fort on October 26, 1878. They believed they were returning to Red Cloud Agency where their Lakota relatives usually camped, yet in the time they had been in the south, the agency had been moved. On July 11, 1878, the Lakota chief Red Cloud and some of the other chiefs traveled with the commissioner of Indian affairs to Wounded Knee and White Clay Creek and chose this area as the location for a new agency.[77] The commissioner agreed to this location, moving his entire operation, even tearing down the buildings of Red Cloud Agency in Nebraska and transporting them to the new location to be rebuilt again. By the time Dull Knife reached the old location in Nebraska, Red Cloud and the Lakotas who had been living there were already settled in their new agency, which had been called Pine Ridge. When he arrived at the location of the old agency, he found no agency or Lakota camps of his relatives; instead, he found a fully operational military fort.

Capt. J. B. Johnson had been searching for Dull Knife on a large plateau on the high plains of northeastern Nebraska, in a place called The Table. October 23, 1878, was a foggy, snowy day, and as the captain searched in vain, doubting he could find a Cheyenne camp in such miserable conditions, it appeared in front of him out of the mist. Dull Knife, Wild Hog, and several other headmen signaled to the troops that they wanted to talk, and Captain Johnson met them halfway to shake their hands. According to Carter P. Johnson, a sergeant in the Third Cavalry at Fort Robinson, Dull Knife told the captain that he had arrived in the country he had started out for, and his entire band, who had left Indian Territory with him, were cold and hungry, and they were ready to join the soldiers on the condition that they be taken to the agency.[78] Dull Knife neglected to tell the captain about Little Wolf, certainly intending to draw the military away from his friends and relatives who still struggled to make their way north. Furthermore, he agreed to end the fighting and go peacefully with Captain Johnson as long as he was going to Red Cloud Agency. Johnson understandably was anxious to extract the surrender himself on the spot, since these Cheyennes had been chased by most of the U.S. troops on the plains, and this difficulty had been on the mind of the War Department for months. He agreed to Dull Knife's terms and asked him to bring his people to his camp on Chadron Creek to eat and rest. He set his own terms that the men give up their weapons the next day. Dull Knife agreed, and late in the evening of October 23, this group of Cheyenne families traveled through a heavy snowstorm to Johnson's camp on Chadron Creek.[79]

Dull Knife surely believed that if he traveled with these troops back to Fort Robinson, he would also be returning to Red Cloud Agency, so he joined Johnson with few misgivings. He would be reunited with relatives who would make him much safer than he was with the military. The next morning, Lakota scouts arrived at the camp and told Dull Knife and his people that Red Cloud Agency had been moved and their relatives now lived at Pine Ridge, but the men had already given up their weapons when they received this news. Once Johnson finished collecting several old, broken guns, he started the Cheyennes for Fort Robinson. Apparently the people realized that they were not being taken toward their relatives among Red Cloud's people, now living at Pine Ridge, because they began to protest that they were not going in the right direction. Dull Knife called for another talk and asked Captain Johnson to tell them what was going to happen. Sgt. Carter P. Johnson recalled that Captain Johnson told Dull Knife that they were going toward Red Cloud and that's where he wanted to go. Sergeant Johnson continued, "He said he didn't care anything about Red Cloud Agency; he wanted to go to Chief Red Cloud; he didn't want to go to Fort Robinson at all and he wasn't going to go there."[80] He was told that then a fight would start and he said he was willing to fight. Apparently at this time, both sides retreated and began to prepare for a battle, digging rifle pits and building breastworks.[81] After a few tense hours staring across at each other, Dull Knife and his people decided to back down and continue with the captain.

Interestingly, C. P. Johnson and George Bird Grinnell gave different reasons for the people's resignation. C. P. Johnson's account was based on his own memory of the events, as a soldier under Captain Johnson. He stated that the captain threatened the people with a six-pound gun, assuming that its destructive power frightened them into submission. There is little evidence, however, that this group felt threatened by the idea of death. C. P. Johnson's account emphasized the U.S. power to contain Native peoples, reiterating one of the goals of the state and claiming it had been accomplished in this case. Grinnell's account was mainly based on oral histories he gathered from the Cheyennes present at this encounter. He stated that the people were convinced to comply because one of the officers kept telling them that once they reached the fort, they would have plenty of food and be well cared for and that they intended to send the people on to the agency.[82] Dull Knife certainly wanted to get his people home safely, and although perhaps not intimidated by the gun, he must have felt that the opportunity provided to them offered more hope than another bloody battle. Perhaps he decided that since the alternative was more fighting, he should attempt to trust the officer. After all, they were so close to their relatives now.

Grinnell's account reflected a response interpreted through the centrality of kinship. If an agreement could be made, the first priority was to keep these families safe. In a Native nation, such negotiations depended on interpersonal relationships bound together by speaking honestly and keeping one's word, not the mechanisms of an impersonal governmental system. While officials had misrepresented their intentions in the past, these officers were new to this band. Apparently, Dull Knife's people decided to risk trusting them. Ironically, the officer in Grinnell's account did not lie outright; the United States did plan to send the people to the agency, but not to Pine Ridge Agency. Unbeknownst to any of these men, federal officials planned to send this group of Northern Cheyennes back to the agency in Indian Territory.

These Cheyennes had traveled hundreds of miles to come to their homeland in the north. They fought hunger, cold, the military, and settlers to return home. Many historians reported that during these negotiations with Captain Johnson, Dull Knife said, "We are back on our own ground and we are safe."[83] Yet he still demanded to return to Red Cloud, and the two sides almost came to blows over it. It might seem that once he was home, one government-run location would be as good as another for Dull Knife and his people, if not for the importance of kin to both physical survival and cultural maintenance. Dull Knife and his people were willing to fight for the chance to be reunited with Red Cloud's people because they were relatives.[84] They certainly realized that among relatives they would have had much more protection from the whims of the government. They would have been able to blend into this band, and once there, they could not so easily be singled out for removal again.

In fact, some of those who chose to travel with Dull Knife never went to Fort Robinson, instead successfully reaching Red Cloud's camp. Iron Teeth related, "At Salt Creek, as we got to the old Red Cloud Agency, my younger son and the oldest daughter set off with some other Cheyennes, to go forward to the agency [Pine Ridge]. Some of our friends warned them not to do this, that the Pawnee and Arapahoes who belonged to the soldiers would kill them along the way. But they were determined to go. It turned out they did what was best. They got through without any serious trouble." These young people took the dangerous opportunity that presented itself to sneak away to their relatives at Pine Ridge once they found out they would be taken to Fort Robinson by the military. After describing the journey of her son and daughter, Iron Teeth added, "I and my three remaining children and the other people with us had before us many other days of hard trial."[85]

Perhaps Bull Hump's wife sensed the terror that was to come. After Dull Knife's meeting with Johnson, as the group headed toward Fort Robinson, she wrapped herself up in a blanket and rolled off the wagon into a deep snowbank. The Lakota scouts who had accompanied the military contingency that had traveled to meet Dull Knife's group quickly gathered around her, protecting her from view. They did not report her escape. Later, with a small group of Lakota scouts and disguised as a Lakota man, she would visit the group locked in the barracks.[86] While these scouts were employed by the U.S. military, they used their position to do what they could to help their Cheyenne relatives.

Monnett has reported that even though Red Cloud knew about the circumstances of Dull Knife, he responded with cold disinterest, remaining unwilling to help them. Considering the close ties between the groups, this is highly unlikely. Red Cloud was involved in the same dangerous game with the government that so many other Northern Plains leaders played at this time. It was to his advantage not to appear too eager to help the fleeing Northern Cheyennes so that the government would not get suspicious and so that he could remain in a position to help his relatives. Apparently Red Cloud told a reporter, "I do not think the Cheyennes will come near us, but if they do, I will attend to them as the Great Father asks."[87] This is exactly what agency officials wanted to hear, and yet certainly Red Cloud knew that the Cheyennes were doing everything they could to get to his camp. A small group, including Iron Teeth's children, had already arrived. He also must have been prepared to take these relatives in, and by discouraging the surveillance of the agents, he helped create an environment that would allow any Cheyenne people headed for his camp the space to evade the government's watchful eye.

There is evidence that Red Cloud actually tried everything in his power to help these people come to him safely. Before the Northern Cheyennes had been spotted by the military, Red Cloud met with officials at Sheridan, Nebraska, about a potential uprising of young Lakota warriors sparked by the Northern Cheyenne flight. Clearly, he had to keep these officials calm, not only for the sake of his people but for the fleeing Cheyennes as well. Red Cloud told the officers that he would do all in his power to discourage the warriors' aggression, but C. P. Johnson reported,

He [Red Cloud] stated that many of his young men were very much excited by the rumors of the war that was going on between the Cheyennes and the troops: that many of them had inter-married with the Cheyenne band that was then in the field and were firm friends and that he did not deny that there was danger, some of them would desire to side with the Cheyennes, but that the presence of so many troops only served to further excite them and render them less easy to control, and that he did not doubt his own ability to handle them provided this large encampment of regulars was disposed of, or at least moved to a greater distance.[88]

The military did as Red Cloud wished, which gave the Lakota leader more freedom to take in the Cheyennes who successfully fled the military.[89] Furthermore, according to Johnson, once Red Cloud's people left Sheridan, they promptly set fire to a huge swath of prairie because they were trying to prevent different bodies of troops from meeting.[90] According to Powell, once Dull Knife's people arrived at Fort Robinson, the Lakotas at Pine Ridge sent over a hundred pairs of moccasins to their captured friends and relatives.[91] Although these moccasins surely eased their discomfort, extra pairs of moccasins were also essential for traveling long distances. As both of these efforts demonstrate, clearly Red Cloud was doing what he could to aid his Cheyenne relatives while not raising the suspicions of the military.

Despite Red Cloud's veiled efforts and Dull Knife's insistence to go to join him, he and his people were taken to Fort Robinson. Federal officials remained dedicated to returning these Northern Cheyennes to Indian Territory. Captain Johnson left Chadron Creek with 46 men, 61 women, and 42 children to travel to Fort Robinson.[92] When they reached the fort, the army placed them in an old barracks building because they had no other place for them to stay. George Grinnell portrayed their first weeks at Fort Robinson as pleasant. He stated that the people had plenty to eat and were allowed to walk to the stream and even farther away to the hills as long as they returned in the evening.[93] Once they arrived, the people began to feel safe at Fort Robinson. They knew the country because they had been coming to the agency at that location for years. They had finally arrived in their homeland with their kin approximately a day's travel away.

After almost two months at the fort, the military officials began to try to persuade them to go south again, but federal agents had not officially declared they would have to leave. Nevertheless, the people were soon confined to their barracks. Grinnell stated that this happened because Bull Hump left for Pine Ridge to visit his wife.[94] Once his absence was discovered, the rest of the people were locked into the barracks and guarded. Bull Hump was found and brought back. He probably had assumed that he was free to come and go from the agency as they had been in the past, especially to visit such a close relative. The officers at the fort, however, were committed to keeping this group of Cheyennes contained, so the instant one of them challenged this containment, the officials intensified their hold.

By mid-December the officers had escalated their efforts to convince the Northern Cheyennes to return to Indian Territory. Despite the fort officials' persistence, Dull Knife and his people insisted that they would never return south. Federal officials were so determined to bring the people back to Indian Territory that the officers at Fort Robinson tried to force their compliance. In January Capt. Henry W. Wessels, the commanding officer, received the federal order to remove the Cheyennes at Fort Robinson to Indian Territory. The headmen of the Cheyennes were informed of this decision on January 3, 1879.[95] Dull Knife responded, "This is the home of the Northern Cheyenne, our fathers are buried here, our children have been raised here."[96] Wild Hog reiterated this sentiment. Dull Knife finally told Wessels, "No, I am here on my own ground and I will never go back. You may kill me here but you cannot make me go back."[97]

Wessels wrote to the quartermaster at the Department of the Platte stating, "I want no more stores for [the] Cheyennes. [They] are ready to move all but the clothes and their consent."[98] Material preparations had been made for the removal to take place in the dead of an unusually harsh winter, but the Cheyennes refused to budge. All the local officials clearly understood that the federal government demanded this removal and that they must carry it out, by force if necessary. Nevertheless, Captain Wessels attempted to extract consent from the Cheyenne headmen at all cost. He ordered their rations to be cut off. Then he induced Wild Hog, Crow, and Strong Left Hand to come out of the barracks and attempted to lock them in the guardhouse in order to separate these military leaders from the others. Wild Hog fought back, and in the confusion Strong Left Hand ran inside the barracks shouting that they had taken Wild Hog and would put him in irons. The wives and children of Wild Hog and Crow and some of the old women left the barracks, opting to stay in the guardhouse with their husbands. Once they had left, Wessels ordered that no food, water, or fuel should be given to the Cheyennes. It was midwinter and the temperature outside had reached zero. Some Cheyennes said they had no food or water for eight days; others said they had no food for five days and no water for three.[99] Captain Wessels encouraged the women and children to come out so that they could be fed, but they would not. Many accounts stated that the men did not hold them back, but knowing the determination to send the people south, families did not want to be separated in case the army were to use the women and children to convince the men to consent.

Even with guards surrounding the barracks day and night, the people decided to fight instead of submitting to return south. They kept talking to each other about it and finally declared, "It is true that we must die, but we will not die shut up here like dogs; we will die on the prairie; we will die fighting."[100] They began to prepare to flee that night. Angeline Johnson, the wife of an officer living at the fort at the time, wrote to her sister, "The rest of that day we could hear them tearing up the floor and smashing things generally and occasionally singing their death song, knowing that some of them would probably be killed when they made their attempt to escape."[101] Those locked in the barracks had covered the windows and were tearing up the floor and digging rifle pits in case the fighting came inside. They also retrieved the guns they had smuggled in and hidden under the floorboards. When forced to disarm, they had dismantled as many as they could, hiding the hammers, triggers, springs, and screws on the women and children as jewelry and hair ornaments. That evening, they began to piece their weapons back together.[102]

At about ten o'clock in the bitterly cold evening of January 9, 1879, the young Cheyenne men broke the windows out and fired on the guards, attempting to clear a safe passage. Then everyone poured out of the windows and the front door. Men, women, and little children rushed into the snowy night made silvery by a full moon. The guards dashed toward them, shooting as they ran. More soldiers scrambled from their quarters into the night only half dressed and fresh from bed. Most Cheyenne prisoners headed for the creek behind the barracks. After going without water for at least three days, many stopped to drink. As the people crossed the river, their clothes got wet and quickly froze in the night air. The thermometer read fifteen to twenty degrees below zero that night.[103] They headed as fast as they could for the buttes in the distance, but they were weak with hunger and thirst and were slowed by their frozen clothes. Many people, mostly women and children, were shot down between the barracks and the buttes.

Iron Teeth related the events she and her children suffered, stating: "After the night bugle sounded, my son smashed a window with the gun I had given him. Others broke the other window and tore down the door. We all jumped out. My son took the younger of the two daughters upon his back. The older daughter and I each carried a small pack. It was expected the soldiers would be asleep, except the few guards. But bands of them came hurrying to shoot at us. One of them fired a gun almost in my face, but I was not harmed."[104] She recalled that her son and her little girl went one way while she and her older daughter went the other and they had no plan of how to meet again. She and her daughter found a cave to hide in. They heard shooting and soldiers all around them outside. They stayed hidden in that cave for seven days, afraid to build a fire, eating tiny bits of the small stores of dried meat they had carried and using snow for water. On the seventh day, a soldier called to them promising not to hurt them, and they were taken back to the fort. Iron Teeth's toes and fingers were frozen through.

George Grinnell described another scene the soldiers came upon in their pursuit of the fleeing Cheyennes. James Rowland, a man married to a Cheyenne woman who had acted as an interpreter at the fort during this period, had followed the soldiers toward the bluffs. Just before the people's trail turned up into the bluffs, he came across a little party of five women who had been carrying babies and little children. These women, who had labored with their charges, were all shot dead but one, Dull Knife's daughter. The beautiful girl, who had been admired and honored by the officers during the time at the fort, lay gasping for breath. So near death, she could no longer speak, though Rowland tried to talk to her. She was still holding a little child she had carried for some other mother who had no more strength.[105] These young women died with the children they had struggled one last time to bring home safely.

Grinnell also interviewed a man who, at thirteen, had been at Fort Robinson and attempted to escape with the others. He described running through soldiers as they fired at him and escaping toward the sandstone bluffs where he hid with many others in large holes along the stone walls. He described hiding in the rock alcove:

> There were five of us, and we had one gun and one pistol. The troops began to shoot into the holes where we were and kept shooting, and presently all had been killed except me. When I looked about and saw that every one of my friends was dead, I did not know what to do. I waited, and at length the soldiers stopped firing. I thought then that I might as well go out and be killed as stay in there, and I walked out of the hole in which I had been hidden and went toward the soldiers. The officer called up his soldiers and they surrounded me. I was not tied up, but was helped up behind a soldier on his horse and taken into the post.[106]

Days later a small group of fifteen men, women, and children who had survived and evaded capture continued to make their way toward the new Pine Ridge Agency to join their relatives among Red Cloud's people. Finally the military caught up with them in the Badlands and chased them out onto the open plains. There this small party made a last attempt to fight, hiding for protection from the continuous gunfire in a buffalo wallow. When the shooting stopped, only three women remained alive.

Another small group was luckier. Dull Knife, his wife, Slow Woman, and son, Buffalo Hump, his son's wife and her child, and another young man had found a hole to hide in away from the soldiers and remained there undiscovered for ten days. They had chosen a different route than most of the fleeing Cheyennes, after pausing on their way to the White River. One of Dull Knife's daughters had been hit by a bullet and fallen. The group had paused to help her, but she pleaded with them to continue. Just north of the river, they decided not to follow those who had taken a more direct route into the bluffs. Instead, they followed a shallow gully, attempting to hide their tracks once they reached the rocky outcroppings. Then they wandered for eighteen more days toward Pine Ridge and finally came to the cabin of William Rowland, who at the time was the interpreter at Pine Ridge and who had relatives among the Northern Cheyennes. He immediately took in the small party of ragged survivors, fed them, and nursed them to health again. Guy Dull Knife Jr. described Dull Knife's party when they arrived, remembering what his grandfather had told him of the night: "They looked like dead people. They were nothing but skin and bone. Their faces were hollow and they were half naked, wearing next to nothing. Some were barefoot and their hands and feet had frozen. Chief Dull Knife was then about seventy years old and at first some of the people did not recognize him. When they found out what had happened to them, the men and women in the camp were so sad, they started to cry." Those who made it to Pine Ridge hid among Lakota friends and relatives until the army stopped looking for them.[107] Even in their most dire circumstances, these Cheyennes could depend on their network of kin.

Of the approximately 150 Cheyennes who fled Fort Robinson that night, sixty-four were killed.[108] Very few made it to Pine Ridge on their own. The survivors who were captured by the soldiers were taken on wagons back to the fort to await their fate at the hands of U.S. officials. Each of these narratives, related by people who survived what transpired on January 9, 1878, provides a sense of the terror that the Cheyennes who lived through this massacre experienced.

Almost immediately after the massacre, Pine Ridge relatives of the Northern Cheyenne survivors began asking for their family. Rowland had already taken in Dull Knife and some of his family, so they had surely heard of the horrors the people had experienced. Although they had been cautious to hide their support of the Northern Cheyennes previously, once the violence was over, they felt empowered in a new way to demand that their relatives to be sent to them. It began with specific requests for certain relatives. On January 15, 1879, Woman's Dress, an Ogallala headman, asked for his sister, her daughter, and an infant who were among the wounded Cheyenne.[109] The next day, the commissioner of Indian affairs sent a letter to the secretary of the interior asking for their release. Toward the end of January, General Crook began to consent, sending thirty-three women and twenty-two children to the Lakota agency. In early February the general sent another twenty-one Cheyennes, seven men and fourteen women and children—along with wagons and provisions—to Pine Ridge Agency.[110] On February 2, Captain P. D. Vroom of Fort Robinson sent a telegram to the War Department requesting that Wild Hog's wife and children be allowed to go to Pine Ridge because this woman was the sister of the Ogallala named American Horse. He also recommended that the remaining women and children be permitted to go to Red Cloud's people.[111] Red Cloud took up this demand, urging the officials to bring all captured women and children to Pine Ridge.

The bloody massacre of Cheyenne men, women, and children during and after the breakout at Fort Robinson forced the federal government to reconsider its position on this removal. The newspapers of the day quickly took up the story, announcing a "Cheyenne outbreak." This second "outbreak" did not inspire the fear that the first one had; this time the newspapers, particularly those in the East, were full of pity for the Northern Cheyennes. In a letter to the editor, someone from Fort Robinson wrote to the *New York Herald* and reported in detail the suffering of the Cheyennes held at the fort, concluding, "The history of the removal of the Northern Cheyenne . . . and their inhuman massacre will all be made known in due time and will prove a lasting disgrace."[112] According to the *Atlanta Constitution*, "The affair was a brutal and inhuman massacre, a dastardly outrage upon humanity and a lasting disgrace to our boasted civilization."[113] Only a year earlier, Americans had feared the lack of containment represented in the flight from the southern reservation. Once they had read about the suffering of the Cheyennes at the fort and the killing of women and children, they no longer saw this "outbreak" as a frightening lack of containment but as evidence that, in spite of the breaking of boundaries, these Plains people could easily be contained. This inspired pity, not because the Cheyennes should not be contained but because they suffered so much in their containment. Now that Americans were convinced of their country's power to control the Cheyenne people, they were able to show sympathy for people they had so recently feared as hostiles.

The events at Fort Robinson did generate pressure on the United States to allow these Cheyennes to remain in the north. The sympathetic attention the newspapers gave to Dull Knife and his struggle to return home helped sway opinions in Washington and throughout the country, and support developed for the Northern Cheyennes' campaign to remain in the north.[114] For many Americans, this incident characterized the failure of the current Indian policy. During this era, because of this and similar incidents, the public sentiment shifted away from consolidating American Indian people on single reservations, as was attempted with the Cheyennes and Arapahos.[115] Although the bloody headlines in the newspapers surely helped, ultimately it was the insistence that they be reunited with their kin that brought Dull Knife and other Northern Cheyennes home.

In their final report, the members of the Senate committee that investigated the Northern Cheyennes' removal declared, "The government must choose the alternative of forcing them to submit to a lifelong imprisonment, under which they will resent and resist all efforts to civilize them, or else allow them to return North and unite with their kindred there in their voluntary and successful efforts to become self-supporting and share in their contentment."[116] The writers of the report used testimony from the Cheyennes to bolster this view, and the officials who had the power to determine the fate of the Northern Cheyennes finally recognized that many of them would only be content living with their relatives in the north country that they knew as their home. General Miles put in a request to have Dull Knife and his people transferred to Fort Keogh in Montana, and in the fall of 1879, the commissioner of Indian affairs approved it.[117] The agent at Pine Ridge at the time, Valentine T. McGillicuddy, reported that he was glad to be rid of these Cheyennes because they mourned continuously for their relatives killed during the breakout. Those who had suffered at Fort Robinson, including Dull Knife, his wife, his eldest son, Buffalo Hump, and several daughters, were finally allowed to join Two Moons and Little Wolf and all their other relatives along the Tongue River in Montana.[118]

Today, the Fort Robinson breakout and the massacre that ensued hold a powerful place in Northern Cheyenne national history. A Northern Cheyenne man named Tall Bull told the anthropologist John

Bobtail Horse (with revolver; *left*) and Dull Knife (*right*). This photo was taken by Laton A. Huffman outside his studio in Fort Keogh, Montana, between 1879 and 1881. While some have argued that the person on the right is Bull Hump, Dull Knife's son, the figures were identified as Bobtail Horse and Dull Knife by Northern Cheyennes in 1953. Image 2199, W. S. Campbell Collection, Western History Collections, University of Oklahoma Libraries.

Moore that his reservation was "bought with the blood of the men, women, and little children who died that night so that the rest of their people could come home again." The story is often told in literature produced by the Cheyenne nation for outside consumption.[119] The Northern Cheyennes today call this important event in their people's history "the breakout." The people have consciously chosen to reshape the conventional "Fort Robinson outbreak" into "the Fort Robinson breakout." Ms. DG discussed these terms, stating that the word "outbreak" sounds like the Northern Cheyennes were a disease that would infest the territory if it got loose. She said that the term "breakout" was better because that is exactly what the people did: they broke out of their prison.[120] Ms. DG related her critical analysis to me well before Deloria published his interpretations, and she poignantly delineated the impact this term has on how outsiders view the history of her people. The Northern Cheyennes continue to fight the dominant narrative of their own history by disrupting its familiar terminology in their own tellings. When relating public narratives of their history, many Northern Cheyennes point to the breakout as the event that spurred the establishment of their reservation, using it to illustrate the struggle of the Northern Cheyenne people to remain with their relatives in their homeland.

When Dull Knife and Little Wolf's actions are viewed through the lens of Cheyenne social organization, it becomes clear how important the web of family was to surviving diaspora, to returning home, and even to maintaining a Northern Cheyenne sense of autonomy. Many historians have reiterated the government's emphasis on lack of rations and insufficient supplies to explain the people's action. This argument, however, does not consider the cultural motivators for the Cheyennes, and it paints the people as helpless victims of American colonialism. Although hunger and sickness had profound effects on the well-being of the Northern Cheyennes living on the southern reservation, the loss of their kin and their landscape was the catalyst that spurred such drastic action. Many of those interviewed in 1880 linked illness and hunger not with poor rations but with the loss of their homeland. These Cheyenne people had formed kin ties not just with northern peoples but with the northern landscape. To live in the south was to live among distant relatives and strangers in the landscape. This loss was so powerful that once the Northern Cheyennes with Dull Knife and Little Wolf realized the federal government would not grant them permission to leave Indian Territory, they began waiting for the best moment to make their escape back to family and homeland.

Both Dull Knife and Little Wolf were able to use kin strategically to gain an advantage in their efforts to return home; however, in the political environment surrounding removal created by federal and local government officials, this became a dangerous strategy. Little Wolf depended on people from the Lakota agency to give him news of events while he was in hiding. When he negotiated with Clark, there were Northern Cheyenne scouts among the soldiers who supported him.[121] Officials at Fort Keogh were more disposed to offer Little Wolf and his young men positions as scouts in the military because they already had been fighting with other Northern Cheyennes for several years. Dull Knife and his people also depended heavily on relatives, particularly after their escape from Fort Robinson. Those who successfully fled the fort were taken in by relatives in Red Cloud's camp where they hid from the authorities. He attempted to help these refugees as soon as he realized they were headed north. Relatives at Pine Ridge began asking for their family members remaining at Fort Robinson almost immediately after the massacre. Red Cloud asked for all the women and children, indicating that they belonged in his camp at Pine Ridge. Eventually, Dull Knife and his people left Pine Ridge and returned to Fort Keogh in Montana, a move that federal officials never would have considered if they did not have relatives who worked successfully as scouts for General Miles. The survival of the Northern Cheyennes following Little Wolf and Dull Knife during their diaspora depended heavily on their widespread kin network.

The cost of their success was high for both Dull Knife's and Little Wolf's followers. Unlike the relationship between Two Moons's people and General Miles, Crook's agenda could not accommodate the needs of the Northern Cheyennes. In the political climate of the moment, Crook could only demonstrate military success by forcing the Northern Plains peoples to surrender and removing the Cheyennes. These actions supported the agenda of federal government officials to end the war on the plains and open up the Black Hills and Powder River country for settlement by Americans. By the fall of 1876, both local agents and federal officials had a reason to remove the Northern Cheyennes to Indian Territory that could be justified in terms of the tenants of the nation-state. The Northern Cheyennes had instigated violence and made it difficult for local officials to contain and control them. To regain control officials of the state attempted to force a surrender. Even though they never succeeded, the act of coming into the agency was constructed as a surrender, in order to give U.S. officials justification to assume control over the Northern Cheyennes as prisoners of war. Furthermore, the drive to control Plains Indians justified allowing one leader, such as Standing Elk, to agree to go south for all the people. The question remains, however: why take the expense to remove the Northern Cheyennes when they could have been confined to the Great Sioux Reservation with their Lakota relatives?

It is probable that Crook realized that the Cheyennes were no more of a physical disturbance to American settlers than the Lakotas. Both groups had proved difficult to contain, and he likely believed that if he separated the two, each group would be easier to control. Furthermore, Crook could use the removal of the Cheyennes as an example to threaten the Lakotas into more complete complacency. The Northern Cheyennes were a much smaller group and more easy to remove than the Lakotas. By forcing the Cheyenne camps south, Crook succeeded in separating military society men from their brothers and in carrying out a threat that had been leveled on the Lakotas as well. This threat of removal would be much more effective against the Lakotas once their relatives had been removed. Crook's immediate political agenda was to gain control over the Indian people on the Great Sioux Reservation. Like other U.S. officials, Crook certainly believed that the flexible Plains social organization lacked order and therefore embodied a potential for violence. His actions demonstrate that he believed only representatives of the United States had the power to contain this potential by imposing the rigid boundaries of the state, particularly territorial and ethnic boundaries.

With the goal of control in mind, it made sense to contain all Cheyenne people in a bounded territory, and the southern reservation appeared to be the logical choice. Although local agents in direct contact with the Northern Cheyennes knew they had relatives among the Lakotas as well, categorically, for federal officials, it made sense to group the Northern people with the Southern Cheyennes. The 1868 treaty stipulated that the Northern Cheyennes could accept a permanent agency on the Crow reservation, but this alternative for removal from Red Cloud Agency was never even considered. According to the fixed ethnic categories that Euro-Americans understood as natural social divisions, the Northern Cheyennes did not belong at Red Cloud Agency or in the north on the Crow reservation. While other Native nations had been forced to share a reservation with their enemies, placing the Cheyennes on a reservation with their enemies was surely too volatile, and allowing them to remain with their northern allies was as well. Because these officials believed the Cheyennes were a homogenous ethnic unit, their permanent reservation could only be the Southern Cheyenne and Arapaho Reservation.

Throughout their history, the Northern Cheyennes confounded U.S. efforts to impose rigid boundaries because, as their social organization was intertwined with many other Native nations and they were a mobile people, they were difficult to contain. By activating these social relationships to move across the plains, they were able to fly under the radar of agents and military officers. The Northern Cheyennes were also hard for both military officers and Indian agents to control because the Plains nation eluded the rigid boundaries of ethnic and geographic definitions that these officials attempted to impose. The Northern Cheyennes did not need to maintain rigid borders based on ethnicity, language, or territory to assert an autonomous sense of nationhood. Furthermore, the members of such a nation could utilize kin ties to remain mobile and evade the control of the state. For U.S. officials who were trying to open the plains for American settlers and control the happenings within the geographic boundaries of the state, this kind of flexibility could not be tolerated. Although the Cheyennes did not wield a more dangerous military power than the Lakotas, local officials insisted that they must be separated because their interaction instigated violence. It did instigate violence, but not necessarily physical violence; instead, their interaction disintegrated the rigid boundaries U.S. officials so carefully attempted to build with agencies, censuses, rations, and other state-based institutions. Herein lay the violence that officials feared most: the destruction of the hegemony that maintained the United States as a nation-state. By resisting these boundaries through the maintenance of flexible kin ties across space and ethnicity, the Cheyennes could survive diaspora and accommodate new ways of living without losing their sense of Indigenous cultural identity or autonomous nationhood.

Like Two Moons, Dull Knife and Little Wolf acted based on their cultural perspective of the situation, but unlike Two Moons, they failed to develop a sustained dialogue with government officials that supported their point of view. They pressed their own understanding, insisting that they belonged in the north, living with their Cheyenne and Lakota relatives in a territory they saw as their own. Ultimately, instead of allowing the state to control them, they continued to act based on their own cultural understandings: that they were not subject to the U.S. government, that they were free to leave Indian Territory, that the northern country was their home, that they were justified in living there, and that they would be able to find help with relatives as they traveled. While Crook and the other officials attempting to control the northern people clearly did not recognize the political assertions embedded in the Cheyenne discourse around kin, Dull Knife and Little Wolf still used this language when arguing to return home. Demanding that webs of kinship remain intact was the most powerful way the people had for asserting political autonomy during that tumultuous period. Although their pleas to reunite with their family members fell on deaf ears until after Americans discovered the atrocities of Fort Robinson, these refugees still depended on their networks of relatives as they fled. While government officials vacillated in their recognition of Cheyenne assertions of autonomy, as long as the people retained their familial connections, they were able to maintain their political mechanisms. In the end, even after all the blood and death, this Native nation survived, woven together by webs of kinship.

CHAPTER SIX

WE ARE NOT ALL FOOLS
Little Chief's People and the Language of Kin

Ms. WL and I sat at the kitchen table in her small house in Lame Deer. We had a loaf of white bread and a tall package of bologna in front of us, and we were swiping mayonnaise across the bread and smacking all the pieces together into a pile of sandwiches for whoever was hungry. It was the beginning of my summer on the reservation, and she and I finally had found a quiet time to get together and catch up. We chatted casually about what we had been up to over the last few months, leading her to ask me how my research was going. "Oh, fine," I told her. "Actually, I was pretty excited," I said, "because this past year I found a cache of letters by Little Chief. They are really cool. He was writing to the president. All the time. And no one writes about him. You know, I've only seen his name mentioned in books a couple of times." As usual, I wasn't expecting her response at all.

"He was my relative," she said.

"Really!" I burst out. For me, being a descendant of Dull Knife or Little Chief is being related to a famous person. No one has spent volume after volume analyzing every movement of my ancestors as they crossed the plains. If any of them once did write letters to the president, surely no one has ever paid attention to them. Of course, as exciting as this attention might seem to be, it's not always a blessing, especially not for Indigenous peoples.

"Yeah, but I've only learned a little about him in my research," she told me. "I want to know more."

"Well, I'll give you copies of the letters," I told her, knowing she would be interested, but also knowing they were not nearly as

202

important to her family's history as the long narratives her ancestors must have told about Little Chief. Those narratives almost certainly painted Little Chief in a different light than American history has, particularly since scholarship has almost forgotten him. In fact, telling the story of this man disrupts the hegemonic narrative of popular U.S. western history because he fully embraced Scott Richard Lyons's x mark. Although Little Chief, along with several hundred other Cheyennes, was removed to Indian Territory, he successfully retained a connection to his homeland and kin during diaspora and ultimately returned home, but not through open resistance or a show of military might. Instead, Little Chief fought with the pen—his strategy to return home was a letter-writing campaign. Flooding the U.S. president with a storm of letters does not fit the stereotype of a nineteenth-century Cheyenne warrior fighting for his freedom. Yet he negotiated with a foreign political system, making concessions while adeptly wielding American assumptions about Native people to his benefit, all without losing sight of his cultural identity or Cheyenne constructions of Native nationhood.

In 1879, when Two Moons's people had begun to make permanent homes for themselves in Montana, and Dull Knife and Little Wolf were in the midst of their journey home, the struggle of Little Chief and his people had just begun. As Dull Knife and Little Wolf fled north from Indian Territory, Little Chief and his band were being taken to the same southern agency. These Cheyennes were actually part of the group who had made peace with General Nelson A. Miles at Fort Keogh. Some of these men had also become scouts for Miles, and although the general had promised them a home in the northern country, he had little actual power to follow through. When the order came from Washington to remove the Northern Cheyennes at Fort Keogh, Miles managed to retain some scouts and their families by arguing that they were essential to his military operations. While his efforts ensured that around a hundred Cheyenne people could remain in the region, the U.S. government still removed a party of more than two hundred people to Indian Territory. Even after Dull Knife's flight, or perhaps because of it, the War Department and the Office of Indian Affairs remained committed to their mission to contain all Cheyenne people on the southern reservation. Little Chief's group faced head-on the contradictions and ambiguities that arose as federal officials tried to force state-based boundaries on Northern Cheyenne people, including the consequences of the discrepancies between the agendas of local officials such as Miles and those of federal officials. Little Chief's story reveals yet another way that the Northern Cheyenne people strategically employed the language of kin with representatives of the United States. It also demonstrates that this strategy resulted in varying levels of success for different groups.

Even though the Northern Cheyennes living at Fort Keogh believed they had not surrendered to Miles but instead had formed an alliance, federal officials in the War Department and the Office of Indian Affairs did not share this perspective. They asserted that the Cheyennes at Fort Keogh had surrendered and become prisoners of war, despite their status as scouts. As prisoners, they were at the mercy of the state. Miles did convince federal officials that the classification of prisoner should not apply, but only for a few men. By arguing that these scouts were essential to military success on the plains, he succeeded in retaining these men as enlisted members of the U.S. military, allowing them to remain at the fort with their families. The rest of the Cheyennes were classified as prisoners in the eyes of the federal officials and as such could be removed.

Of course, it would have been much less costly and time-consuming to settle these Cheyenne families on the Crow reservation next door or with their relatives on the Pine Ridge reservation only a short ride away. To federal officials of this period, removed from the complexity of Plains relations on the ground, however, the dream of containment mattered more. According to their understanding, the Cheyennes belonged together on one reservation because they were conceived of as uniform in ethnicity, language, religion, culture, and territory. These officials proscribed to a divide-and-conquer ideology—divide Cheyenne warriors from their Lakota and Arapaho allies and conquer them with imposed boundaries, both physical and psychic. In order to control the Cheyennes, they had to be contained both ethnically and territorially. Although Dull Knife and Little Wolf had already shattered this containment by fleeing the Indian Territory reservation, federal officials remained determined to complete their goal of holding all Cheyenne people on one reservation, even if it meant one removal after another.

Despite these efforts, the Cheyennes still maintained far-reaching kinship ties that they could use to evade the boundaries imposed by the nation-state. Like those following Two Moons, Little Wolf, and Dull Knife, Little Chief would also use kinship strategically to return to the north. Unlike these other Cheyennes, Little Chief and his people depended mainly on rhetoric based in kinship to convince federal officials they should be allowed to return north. This group was not able to depend on kinship ties for the physical support to move to the Tongue River valley until they actually arrived at Pine Ridge.

While in Indian Territory and at Pine Ridge, Little Chief sent a barrage of letters to federal officials, including the president of the United States, emphasizing his kin relationships with the Cheyennes living in the north and using the argument that his people should be reunited with their families. Little Chief also emphasized the president's obligation to his people as their "Great Father" and as their leader. In his political relationships with U.S. officials, Little Chief relied on the kin-based political strategies that had previously guided the interactions between Native nations just as the other Cheyenne headmen had. Little Chief, however, was not dealing with another Plains nation, nor was he negotiating with local agents driven by personal agendas. He was dealing with federal officials whose main goal was to contain and control his people. Even so, Little Chief's letters to the president reflect his adeptness at combining kinship as a strategy with manipulating the expectations of the state to negotiate for the needs of his people. By using kin terminology with the president and by emphasizing that the Northern Cheyennes should be united with their families, ultimately Little Chief succeeded in his efforts to return his people to the Tongue River valley.

In the fall of 1877, only a few months after Little Chief, Two Moons, and other Cheyenne leaders made peace with Gen. Nelson Miles, the order came to remove all the Northern Cheyennes at Fort Keogh to Indian Territory. Miles had taken thirty Cheyenne scouts with him to help bring in Chief Joseph and the Nez Perces. When he returned to Fort Keogh, he discovered the order asking him to send all the

Little Chief, 1879. Cabinet card created by A. Bogardus. Written on the back of the photo: "Photo given by John D. Miles, Indian Agent." Kansas State Historical Society, Topeka, Kansas.

American Indians living there to Fort Abraham Lincoln in present-day North Dakota.[1] Miles petitioned to retain about thirty Northern Cheyenne families, arguing that he needed the men to remain at the fort as scouts and guides. In 1880 the Senate committee interviewed both Little Chief and General Miles. In his statement, Little Chief himself declared that Miles wanted to keep them all at the fort but was only able to retain about thirty men because they were enlisted as scouts when the order was given.[2] It is possible that Miles made his feelings clear to the Northern Cheyenne headmen in an attempt to explain his failure to stop the removal because of his promise to White Bull (Ice) after the Lame Deer battle that he would do what he could to help the Cheyennes remain in Montana. For the moment, however, he could do little more than petition to retain these scouts.

Speaking of Little Chief's people to the Senate committee, Miles stated, "The Indians took the order to go to Fort Lincoln very hard;

they were very much opposed to being sent away from that country. They pleaded for a week to remain." According to Little Chief, Miles told the Northern Cheyennes facing removal that they should go to the southern reservation peacefully but also gave them hope that they would be able to return. Little Chief recalled his conversation with Miles, stating, "He said if we did not like the country we could get our relatives together who had come down ahead of us and go back north again; if we were not satisfied, he said, he would have it arranged so that we could go north again; there would not be much trouble in doing that, because, he said, the government knew the valuable services we had rendered helping him." Little Chief and his people left for Indian Territory believing not only that they would be able to return but also that they would be able to bring the rest of the Northern Cheyennes back with them. When the Senate committee asked Miles about Little Chief's statement, the general responded that he had only told Little Chief to keep his people together, remain peaceful, and prevent his people from committing any depredations, so that he could ask the president to be allowed to return. Miles told Little Chief that because of their cooperation with the government as scouts they might be allowed to return, encouraging him to take his request to the highest power in the United States. Miles then reminded the Senate committee that he had no power to promise Little Chief that he could return, emphasizing that he did not commit the federal government to act.[3]

Diplomatically, Miles carefully reassured the Senate committee that he had not obligated the United States to allow Little Chief's people to return north, safeguarding his own position. Nevertheless, he had put a concerted effort into keeping some Northern Cheyenne families with him at Fort Keogh and into bringing home those forced to Indian Territory. Even at the time of the removal, Miles made it known that Little Chief's people played an important role as scouts. He was quoted in the *Dodge City Times* as having said, "He never could have accomplished what he did against the Nez Perce, except for the service of this portion of the Northern Cheyenne."[4]

Miles also showed his commitment to the Northern Cheyennes in his interview with the Senate committee. When asked his private opinion about the removal of the Northern Cheyennes to Indian

Territory, he stated that he considered "the banishment . . . to be unwise, unjust, and cruel." When asked if it was advisable to return the Northern Cheyennes to their homes in the north, Miles declared, "I think it would be. I believe it would do no harm to do what seems right."[5] When addressing the Senate committee, Miles did argue that American Indian people as a population should not be confined on large reservations nor be subjected to regulated rations. These statements supported his insistence that the Cheyennes be allowed to return north, arguing that such controls were not necessary in a way that could be understood by the state.

Despite Miles's efforts to prevent removal of the scouts, many Cheyenne families had to leave Fort Keogh for Fort Lincoln in the fall of 1877. The party was assigned a military escort on this journey, and apparently some Northern Cheyenne scouts who had been retained at Fort Keogh participated in this escort.[6] This is a powerful example of the contradictions in the imposition of federal policy. Some men in Little Chief's party had very recently scouted for the government, yet they faced removal. Riding beside these men, in the role of a military escort, were their Northern Cheyenne relatives who had been allowed to remain in the north. Ben Clark was asked to meet Little Chief's people at Fort Lincoln and escort them to Indian Territory, ultimately placing them at Fort Reno on the Cheyenne and Arapaho reservation. In a letter to the anthropologist James Mooney, Clark described his role in removing this group. He frequently acted as a translator to the Cheyenne people and had settled in Fort Reno himself. He stated that when Little Chief found out that he was to be removed to the south, he "begged permission to interview General Sheridan."[7] This was arranged, and in November 1877 Clark, Little Chief, and five others traveled to Chicago to meet with the general. In 1880 Clark related the events of this meeting to the Senate committee. He stated that Little Chief expressed his unwillingness to remove and told Sheridan that he would do anything the government asked, including fighting against the government's enemies, if they could remain in the Tongue River country.[8] Little Chief never told Sheridan he would not go south, but he diligently tried to negotiate for his people's continued presence in the Tongue River valley.

Knowing that other Cheyenne families remained at Fort Keogh through the young men's roles as scouts, he wisely offered military service.

Little Chief's negotiation to stop the removal failed, but he did successfully negotiate the terms of it to help his people. Ben Clark stated that they had agreed to put off the move and winter the band at Fort Lincoln, and that he would be in charge of moving the band south in the spring. Little Chief convinced Sheridan to allow the Northern Cheyennes to travel in the way they were accustomed. Instead of taking railroad cars or steamships, they would travel on horseback, pitching tents every day and moving slowly so that their horses would make the journey with little loss.[9] Although Little Chief accepted that his people would have to go south, he left this meeting with Sheridan continuing to believe that Miles had said he would be able to bring his people back north again. The band was to leave the fort as early as possible in the spring of 1878. The departure was delayed, however, when Ben Clark was called away to travel to Canada to confer with Chief White Bird and bring back a party of Nez Perces, camping near Sitting Bull's band at the time.[10] Clark did not start with Little Chief's band on the journey south until July 21, 1878.

This group reached Sidney, Nebraska, on September 14, 1878. There Clark received a telegram from Gen. George Crook relating that Dull Knife had broken away from the agency near Reno. Clark sent word back, asking if it would be advisable to continue the journey south.[11] Considering the volatile situation, General Crook decided to hold a meeting with Little Chief and the headmen and warriors with him. Crook, Lieutenants Bourke and Schuyier, and Ben Clark met with Little Chief, Crazy Mule, Gray Head, Red Hat, Ridge Bear, Big Wolf, and others. An article in the *Army and Navy Journal* reported on the council meeting, stating that Little Chief's people were sorry to hear about what had happened to Dull Knife on the southern reservation because many had relatives among that band and were afraid they would be killed.[12] Little Chief and his people were certainly aware of the conditions in Indian Territory; they knew that the country was poor and that many Northern Cheyennes had died there.

At the council, Little Chief's people expressed some of their concerns about traveling to the southern agency, particularly after their relatives had left. The *Army and Navy Journal* reflected the sentiments the Cheyennes expressed to Crook, stating, "They were leaving their own hunting grounds, where they were born, where their fathers were buried, and were sad on that account. The Black Hills belonged to the Cheyenne as long ago as they could remember and before the Sioux owned them."[13] An article in the *Sidney Telegraph* asserted the same and reported that Little Chief argued that they would be leaving a healthy country with ample hunting and grazing for a poor country full of sickness, chills, and fever.[14]

These articles reveal that Little Chief's people were careful to assert their connection with the northern lands not only to officials but to the press as well, reminding everyone with any power to affect their future that the Black Hills belonged to them. Furthermore, they asserted an ownership that superseded that of the Lakota Sioux, who had been granted a reservation near the Black Hills in Dakota Territory. Although the journals showed no sign of recognizing it, Little Chief and those with him were crafting a strategic discourse to exert their primary relationship with the northern territory. The *Army and Navy* article emphasized that Little Chief was anxious to obey the government, while the *Sidney Telegraph* article stated that the Cheyennes were embittered against the government because they had been led to believe that they would be allowed to stay in the north.[15] At first glance, these newspaper articles seemed to contradict each other, but on closer examination, it appears that each newspaper had simply emphasized different aspects of Little Chief's political strategy. While this leader might have appeared compliant at this meeting, he was also clearly asserting his people's ownership of the northern territory.

The *Sidney Telegraph* printed a full transcription of Little Chief's speech to General Crook a week later, demonstrating that Little Chief did not believe that traveling to the southern reservation was permanent. The newspaper reported him saying, "We understood when we got to Indian Territory if we couldn't get along with the Southern Cheyennes—if they were all fools—we could go back to our own country. The Black Hills . . . belonged to us. They belonged to us before the Sioux owned them. Our fathers for many generations belonged there and the country is very dear to us. But because it is the will of the government, we are going blindly away. We are not all fools but are going because we have to."[16] Little Chief was very clear that the land in and around the Black Hills belonged to the Northern Cheyennes and that their relationship superseded that of the people who had been granted this land through treaty. He clearly asserted a privileged relationship with the northern territory based not only on the cultural power embedded in it but also on the longevity of this relationship. His logic was powerfully elegant: U.S. officials recognized Lakota rights to this territory, but the Cheyenne relationship was longer and therefore deserving of recognition as well.

Little Chief also emphasized again that the people had been told that if they did not like Indian Territory, they would be allowed to return north, referring to his conversation with General Miles. Many Northern Cheyennes today say that the old people never believed any removal to be permanent. They always understood that they would be allowed to move if they did not want to live in a certain area.[17] For a people who thought of movement as a vital part of their place in the world, as renewal, to settle in one area would have made little sense. These Cheyennes had always determined their own movements, from the Great Lakes to the Great Plains to the agencies where they would accept annuities. They had much reason to believe that while they had to negotiate with U.S. officials, ultimately they still had some control over their own fate. Still, Dull Knife and Little Wolf's flight must have given them pause, suggesting a need for concern. Considering the circumstances, Little Chief wisely kept reminding whomever might listen—including newspaper reporters—that he had been promised that he could return north.

Clark decided to keep Little Chief's people in Sidney much later than planned. He had mapped their journey from there to Dodge and believed the route he had chosen would almost certainly be the course that Dull Knife would choose as well. He strongly believed that a meeting of the two bands would lead to disaster, stating, "My band was only reconciled to the idea of going to Indian Territory because they expected to meet the Dull Knife band there. If we met the hostile band I would have lost my band and maybe myself."[18] Finally, by late October, Clark left for Indian Territory with Little Chief and the rest of this band of Northern Cheyennes. The *Sidney Plaindealer* surely exaggerated the relief of the town's citizenry when it declared, on

October 24, that they no longer had to fear the stealing, peeping, kidnapping, loafing "red-faced savage." Unlike the *Sidney Telegraph,* which reported that this band of Cheyennes was being taken from their homeland, the *Plaindealer* reported that these Cheyennes were runaways and the government was returning them to "their old territory, at Fort Reno, Indian Territory."[19] This statement surely reflected the strain that Dull Knife and Little Wolf's journey north had caused for federal officials, local agents, and the local American settler population. For the *Plaindealer,* all Cheyenne Indians off the reservation were dangerous and likely to attack at any moment, regardless of their actual circumstances. These journalists and their readers had certainly heard the reports that came out of Kansas. Perhaps they wanted to use the sensationalism of this previous unrest to sell papers, or perhaps the stereotyped images they held of Plains Indians stirred genuine fear that the people with Little Chief were prone to random outbursts of violence simply because they were Cheyennes. Those driven by profit and fear cared little about which region this party of Cheyennes came from; if they were outside of a reservation, then they believed they should be contained for the safety of the Americans in the area.

With the fate of Dull Knife, Little Wolf, and their people still unknown, on December 9, 1878, a group of 221 people arrived at the Cheyenne-Arapaho agency in Darlington, Indian Territory, led by Little Chief, Crazy Mule, Ridge Bear, Iron Shirt, and Black Bear.[20] Once there, they discovered that there were still 640 Northern Cheyennes at the southern agency who did not leave with Dull Knife.[21] When Little Chief's group arrived, twelve families broke off, contented to join southern relatives. At the same time, about thirty families of Northern Cheyennes already living at the agency joined Little Chief's people in the hope that they might be able to return to their home in the north.[22] The new arrivals encountered the same problems that other Northern Cheyennes before them had. They struggled with the climate and suffered from the low beef rations. Nevertheless, Little Chief refused to leave Indian Territory until government officials consented to his wish to return north. He was determined to find a way to convince them without disobeying orders or breaking free from the agency. He knew how Dull Knife and Little Wolf had been chased and did not want to subject his people to these cruel hardships. On May 9, 1879, Little

Chief and five other Northern Cheyennes traveled to Washington, D.C., in an effort to get permission to return north. They met with the commissioner of Indian affairs, the secretary of the interior, and President Rutherford B. Hayes. The only thing that came of this delegation's trip was the promise that all the Northern Cheyennes would be settled together, but the location was left undetermined, to be either in the north (Pine Ridge) or the south (Indian Territory).[23]

Little Chief was quite insistent about the miserable condition of his people almost from the moment he arrived, causing the southern agent, John Miles, to worry about another "outbreak." Most Northern Cheyennes in Indian Territory who did not have close relatives among the Southerners refused to incorporate their lives with the agency. For example, they did not send their children to school.[24] Little Chief had promised Agent Miles that he would not allow members of his band to flee as Little Wolf and Dull Knife had done, but he reminded Miles that he had much difficulty controlling the young men. In April 1881 Agent Miles sent a letter to the commissioner of Indian affairs relating his concerns. He stated, "The present attitude of the Little Chief and Black Wolf bands of Northern Cheyennes is one exciting considerable suspicion and a little uneasiness."[25] John Miles believed that this particular group of Northern Cheyennes were continually prepared to leave the agency, preventing them from settling into life there. His efforts to contain the Cheyennes on the reservation through the institutions of the state were met with resistance at every step. Little Chief's people refused to be bound together with the Southern Cheyennes and Arapahos to create a uniform, homogenous ethnic body that state officials could more easily control.

Miles's fear that some of the Northern Cheyennes would leave the agency was not unfounded. On March 19, 1881, he wrote to the commissioner of Indian affairs detailing a hunting trip that Black Wolf, one of the Cheyennes with the Little Chief group, had taken with a party of fifty-five men, women, and children. This party had been granted permission to travel to Fort Supply and hunt in that area for deer and turkey. After thirty days away, Black Wolf applied to have his pass renewed and was granted an extension. After his time was up, he was ordered back to the southern agency, but he would not return because his horses were too weak and the weather was bad.

Miles did not find these excuses to be valid and believed that Black Wolf was planning to leave Indian Territory with this small party and return to the north. Miles stated that he would continue to be suspicious because "until the present unsatisfactory and unsettled condition of the Northern Cheyenne is changed" they would always be "determined to proceed north at the first favorable opportunity."[26]

Little Chief asserted over and over again that his people did not belong at the southern agency. He told Miles that Colonel John K. Mizner, the commanding officer at Fort Reno, had promised him a speedy return to the north with the help of the government. He also stated that when he arrived north, he would send the children to school and enlist his men as army scouts. In a letter to the commissioner of Indian affairs, Miles declared that the commanding officer's promise was a complete falsehood, but that the belief in these promises had united the Northern Cheyennes and therefore any attempts to settle them had failed. He went on to argue that these attempts "will continue to fail so long as the present unsettled, vacillating policy continues in the treatment of these Indians."[27]

Miles recognized that the inconsistent nature of Indian policy at the time worked to the advantage of the Northern Cheyennes by undermining the authority of the United States. In his letter, he pointed out that the Northern Cheyennes at his agency would retain hope that they could return north as long as any portion of their people remained there. By 1881 the bands of Dull Knife, Little Wolf, and Two Moons all had returned successfully to their homeland. Miles reminded the commissioner that many government officials had given Little Chief's group hope by stating that they might be able to work something out and by not removing all of the Cheyennes to the south, including Dull Knife and Little Wolf's people.[28]

In fact, it is probable that Colonel Mizner did suggest he would help Little Chief return home. He apparently was impressed that this headman had exercised great control over his men, encouraging them not to fight but instead to remain patient. In April 1881 Mizner wrote a letter to the headquarters of the Department of Arkansas, stating that Little Chief had been "instrumental in keeping the bad element down" among his people and that many believed it would be wise for the government to send this band of Northern Cheyennes back north.[29]

Miles, who was charged with containing the Cheyennes at the southern agency, instead expressed his concern about the trouble that Little
Chief and his people potentially could cause, requiring that the Indian
Office take action to settle this group. Miles reiterated the ideology
supported by those in the Indian Office, of containment and control
as a primary strategy for U.S. relations with Plains people. Colonel
Mizner, however, reflected the perspective held by most officers in the
U.S. military familiar with the struggles between the United States
and Plains people. These officers believed moving Indian Affairs out
of the War Department and into the Interior Department to be a colos-
sal mistake. They argued that the military infrastructure was much
more adept at dealing with Native people, and they went so far as to
blame many of the spectacular failures in policy of the time period
on this shift.[30]

Little Chief certainly was no fool. As a prominent Cheyenne man,
he had experience navigating the fissures created by political negotiations within his own kin-centric Native nation, and he would have
been adept at interacting with people representing multiple political
perspectives in order to build consensus. Within Native nations, these
moments of factionalism often led to dynamic reinvention of the
current sociopolitical system. He must have realized that he could take
advantage of the debate between the War Department and the Indian
Office, pressing the fissures to open a space for negotiation and ultimately steering the process toward the best interest of his people. From
the perspective of leaders used to kin-centric politics, such scuffling
created ruptures from which positive change could emerge. Little
Chief surely used the tension to his advantage, carefully massaging
it to convince officials that his people must be allowed to return to
their northern homeland.

Despite his emphasis on containment, Miles's letter encouraged
the Indian Office to give consideration to Little Chief's frustrated band.
The office responded by asking for an exact report of the number who
would be returning north if such a trip would be undertaken. Miles
stated that 222 people, including women and children, arrived at the
agency in 1878, but that from this number some had settled down and
should not be removed. He listed these families by their most prominent male members, Crazy Mule, William Rowland, and Bear's Lariat,

for a total of nineteen people. By subtracting this number and adding the births that had occurred since the group had arrived, Miles calculated that 238 people should be allowed to return north. He stated that those who came to Indian Territory with Dull Knife would want to be added, and even though it would create dissatisfaction, they had to drawn the line and the best place to do it was Little Chief's people.[31]

When Commissioner Hiram Price presented Miles's concerns to the secretary of Indian affairs, he indicated that he understood the urgent necessity of taking decisive action in relation to Little Chief's band considering "their evident determination to desert and go north, and the injurious effect of their presence upon the other Indians at that Agency." The commissioner reinforced his argument by noting that this particular group of Northern Cheyennes never signed any treaty or presented any other evidence of a desire to remain in the Indian Territory. Commissioner Price stated that the Northern Cheyennes should be moved either to the Shoshone and Bannock reservation, "where their friends, the Northern Arapahoes, were located," or to Fort Keogh, "where some thirty lodges of Little Chief's people were temporarily located"—people who had been allowed to remain there through General Miles's efforts.[32] These suggestions seem to align with the ideology in opposition to the removal of Plains peoples from their homelands held by most military officials of the time. Although Miles believed strongly in containment on the reservation, he realized that the removal plan for the Northern Cheyennes had failed in the case of Dull Knife and Little Wolf and could head down a similar path with Little Chief's band if he did not act soon and with careful consideration.

In the attempt to decide on a resettlement location for this group, John Miles consulted with Little Chief and reported his words to the commissioner. According to Miles, Little Chief did not want to speak for the Cheyennes already in the north but for himself and his party. He asked for a separate agency for the Cheyennes at the junction of the Rosebud and Yellowstone Rivers in Montana and believed it would be best to go north and have a council with the other Cheyennes already in the north.[33] Little Chief clearly stated his people's desire to return to their homeland in the Powder River region and join their relatives who remained there. He also indicated that he would be willing to settle at either the Crow agency or at White River on the Pine Ridge reservation, but that he would consider these alternatives inadequate, suggesting that he would view them as temporary solutions and continue to fight to rejoin the Cheyennes at Fort Keogh.

While contemplating Little Chief's request, the Indian Office decided to consult the War Department. The secretary of war at the time, William Tecumseh Sherman, replied sternly that the Northern Cheyennes should remain in Indian Territory. He argued that it would not be wise to increase the number of Plains people at Fort Keogh or at the Shoshone and Bannock reserve. Finally he stated, "The consent of Indians should not be material or conclusive as to the location of any particular family or tribe. They are notoriously restless and dissatisfied."[34] For Sherman, moving this group of Northern Cheyennes to another reservation was not worth the trouble it would cause by disrupting the established order at these locations.

Luckily for Little Chief, few others felt as Sherman did, because by June 1881 the Indian Office had decided to aid Little Chief and those who had traveled south with him in returning north. On June 27 S. J. Kirkwood, the secretary of the interior, addressed a letter directly to Little Chief, stating that "a hope was given to you, which you construed as a promise, that if you and they went quietly to the Territory and stayed there for a time, you would be allowed to return to your own country again." Kirkwood acknowledged that Little Chief and his people had all remained quiet and orderly and had put their faith in this promise. He stated, "The government desires always to keep faith with the Indians and now redeems the promise you have relied upon."[35] Kirkwood implied that because Little Chief and his people did not cause problems for the government, they would grant the request. Nevertheless, the secretary first spoke about the promise as only existing in the minds of Little Chief and his people, but then he switched his language, speaking as if there were an agreement between this band and certain government officials that would now be fulfilled.

The officials decided on Pine Ridge as an appropriate destination and began making preparations for the trip. While Little Chief's people preferred Fort Keogh, fully aware that many of their relatives had settled there successfully as scouts, they knew that they would also be welcomed by family at Pine Ridge. They might not be returning to the heart of their homeland, but at least they were headed north. The Indian Office would even furnish twelve mule teams and wagons to transport the flour, sugar, coffee, bacon, and other supplies that would be needed for the journey.[36] Just as the preparations were completed and Little Chief and his people were ready to leave, another complication arose. Miles was set to enforce his decision that only those who journeyed south with Little Chief could return north with him. Little Chief, on the other hand, claimed that the secretary of the interior had promised that he could take thirty of Red Cloud's relatives with him.[37] The interpreter Ben Clark was with Little Chief at the time and vouched for the truth of this statement. Little Chief's claim stalled the journey north. No one was allowed to leave until the matter was settled to the agent's satisfaction.

After much debate, the Indian Office finally decided to take action. The commissioner of Indian affairs asked Little Chief to come to Washington, D.C., yet again to meet with a delegation of Lakota Indians to discuss a transfer to the north and the possibility of moving to Pine Ridge.[38] In July 1881 the commissioner received word that Little Chief had consented to go.[39] The Cheyenne leader arrived in Washington in August, met with the Lakota delegation, and received permission to settle at the Pine Ridge reservation with those Lakotas who recognized Red Cloud as their headman. In his report, the commissioner stated that he encouraged the move because Little Chief's people were extensively intermarried with Red Cloud's people and they spoke the same language. As with the survivors of the Fort Robinson breakout, Red Cloud's people again became the port in the storm for Northern Cheyenne people trying to get home. While he had the ear of the commissioner, Little Chief repeated his request to allow all the Northern Cheyennes who had been removed south to settle at Pine Ridge. The commissioner told the Cheyenne headman that the decision had been made to move only those who came down with Little Chief, but he promised to place the request before Congress.[40]

Little Chief's strategic use of the language of kin certainly helped his people journey home. Nevertheless, his impact was limited; he could not win a homecoming for all the Northern Cheyennes in Indian

Territory because his proposals challenged the ability of the state to maintain rigid boundaries and retain dominance. For the Northern Cheyennes, continuing an autonomous sense of nationhood meant maintaining the social relationships that held it together. Being severed from family and not being allowed to travel to reunite, even occasionally, threatened Cheyenne nationhood. Therefore, it was central that the Cheyennes be free to return north to visit or even live permanently if they wished.

It seemed senseless to those remaining in Indian Territory that Congress would not allow all the Cheyennes to move together. If the move had been approved for the Northern Cheyenne people, there would be no reason to exclude some of the people who wanted to come. In fact, Little Chief, according to the conventions of kinship, had quite a good reason to bring home those who did not originally journey south with him. The Northern Cheyennes who wished to journey north felt a strong affinity with the Lakotas at Pine Ridge. Some were related to Red Cloud, the Lakota chief, and they should be allowed to return to their families. Although the commissioner was convinced, he could not authorize the move of all the Northern Cheyennes in Indian Territory. The state's need for containment simply lacked the flexibility to accommodate what Little Chief saw as a simple matter. By recognizing the Cheyenne freedom of movement across the plains, Congress would be legitimizing their Native nationhood. Keeping tight control through setting limits on the group allowed U.S. officials to assert dominance.

Despite the insistence that only those who came down with Little Chief would be allowed to return north and the effort to impose this through censuses, many unauthorized people joined the journey without the knowledge of officials. At the southern agency, John Miles authorized 237 people to leave. On December 2, 1881, a group of 317 Northern Cheyennes arrived at the Pine Ridge Agency in Dakota Territory, totaling eighty-two more people than had been allowed to leave.[41] One of Dull Knife's sons, George Dull Knife, was probably among this unauthorized group. According to his grandson, Guy Dull Knife Jr., George had been with his parents on the removal from Red Cloud Agency to Indian Territory, but when they decided to return home, he was left with extended family. As a toddler of only three, his parents probably felt that he was too young to make such a dangerous journey.[42] The story of this little boy illustrates that the Cheyennes depended on extended kin to navigate the dramatic changes created by diaspora.

A census of those who arrived at Pine Ridge uncovered the extra people, and there was an immediate uproar among the officials. Valentine T. McGillycuddy, the agent at Pine Ridge, wrote to the commissioner of Indian affairs, Hiram Price, demanding to know why so many Cheyennes had left the southern agency without authorization. He stated, "Little Chief gives as a reason that there was an error in the count as made before starting, and that there were a large number of children in transit."[43] Little Chief and his people were quite adept at flying under the radar of the U.S. government. Of course, he did not admit that unauthorized people had joined his group, but they surely must have with his knowledge.

In an attempt to explain the number of Cheyenne arrivals, John Miles wrote to the commissioner of Indian affairs stating that only 235 people were transferred because he had required all Cheyennes wishing to leave to gather in a separate camp near the agency and away from other camps, and he and his men counted this camp, totaling 252, and then he insisted that Little Chief choose seventeen people to remain, which he did.[44] Miles and his men made a list of those who were allowed to go, and Captain Thomas, who traveled with Little Chief, was told to let no others join and to count the group three separate times on the journey. Miles stated that there would have been no way to know if people had left the reservation on their own, but he had expected to find stowaways by taking several censuses throughout the journey. Apparently, the Northern Cheyennes understood such mechanisms of control utilized by the state, realizing how important it was to dodge these efforts at containment in order to retain some sense of autonomy. No Cheyennes who remained would ever report those who had left without permission or revealed their hidden relatives. Little Chief might have seemed too compliant with government officials to be politically effective, but his adept ability to manipulate the system through establishing personal relationships with many people in power proves otherwise.

Miles blamed the officers who were on the march, yet they probably never even knew this hidden resistance was happening. If these Cheyenne did not want to be counted, they would not be. Yet they chose to be counted when they reached Pine Ridge. It would have been even easier for those not on the census to escape another count once they arrived at the agency by blending into the Lakota camps. They probably realized, however, that if they did not allow a census at that point, they would not be issued rations. Most likely they had been told by their relatives that Agent McGillycuddy did not provide rations for people he could not account for. In a letter to the commissioner of Indian affairs, the agent stated that Cheyenne and Sioux families were continually arriving at his agency from other areas asking for enrollment and rations, but because they did not have passes or transfers, he refused to provide for them. In explaining their ability to remain at Pine Ridge, he declared, "I presume that they are being cared for by their relations here."[45] He presumed correctly, but most likely many of the Northern Cheyennes who arrived from Indian Territory did not want to overburden their already undernourished relatives. At the same time, McGillycuddy failed to realize that by ignoring those who came to his reservation and keeping them off his books, he allowed them to exist outside the surveillance of the government and therefore maintain a sense of freedom.

Some Northern Cheyennes remained in Indian Territory who wished to return north and who had surely been told by Little Chief about the promise the commissioner had made to petition Congress for their return. John Miles reported to the commissioner that 684 Cheyennes and 19 Arapahos still wished to return north. These Northern Cheyennes met in council and asked for an answer to their request. They encouraged the agent to allow them to return that summer and told Miles that they were having trouble holding their young men back.[46] They also continued to remind their agent that they had been separated from their families in the north. Miles related this grievance to the commissioner of Indian affairs, stating, "It is a fact that a great many families are separated—a portion being north and down here—this fact coupled with the decided preference for the north makes them very unhappy and prevents their effort at any progress here."[47]

The commissioner drew on Miles's argument to support the Northern Cheyennes' efforts to return north. He stated that he believed that the Northern Cheyennes would never find contentment at the southern agency and argued that separating the Southern Cheyennes from the Northern Cheyennes would bring harmony to the reservation, allowing the Southern Cheyennes to progress toward civilization more rapidly. He also stated, "The Northern Cheyenne who return will be contented and do far better among their kindred and friends at their old homes among the Sioux."[48] Once again, the commissioner used the people's own argument that they should be allowed to return so that they could be in their homeland amongst their relatives. Finally, in July 1883, Congress provided the funding to remove the remaining Northern Cheyennes to Pine Ridge.[49] McGillycuddy reported that in September 1883, about 360 men, women, and children arrived at the agency from Indian Territory. The last Northern Cheyennes holding out hope to return north had finally come home.

Although Little Chief's people had returned north, their struggles continued. They were still separated from their families living in the Tongue River valley and were determined to make their way farther north to be with them. On December 6, 1881, only four days after they had arrived at Pine Ridge, the agent sent a letter to the commissioner of Indian affairs reporting that Little Chief's people had requested passes to visit their relatives at Fort Keogh. McGillycuddy denied them these passes, stating it would "be against the interests of the [Indian] service." The commissioner approved his decision, responding, "Give the Indians distinctly to understand that they must now settle down to business and give up all expectation of being permitted to roam at large and visit. They must take steps to become self-sustaining."[50] The Northern Cheyennes again threatened the state's goal of containment by their mobility, supported by their far-reaching network of kin. Officials in the Office of Indian Affairs had given up hope that they could contain the Cheyennes in Indian Territory, but they believed that controlling the people was possible if they moved Little Chief's group to Pine Ridge. Much to the frustration of federal officials, however, the Cheyennes had barely arrived when they began asking to leave.

Little Chief's people had two advantages in their quest to join the rest of the Northern Cheyennes living in the Tongue River valley.

First, they had family who had physically aided their movements north and who petitioned sympathetic local officials to support bringing the people home. Second, in their time dealing with local and federal officials, Little Chief's people had gained an understanding of the goals of the Office of Indian Affairs that they could use in their petitions. By June 1882 the people were not just petitioning to visit their relatives; they had begun to ask to settle with their family members who were engaged in farming. In his letter about this petition, McGillycuddy stated that Black Wolf, along with eighty-five other people, wanted to join their relatives who supported themselves by their own labor along the Rosebud River. He stated that they understood that they would receive no rations and would have to farm, and he recommended that they be allowed to go.[51] Black Wolf's people knew that their relatives living in the Tongue River valley would take them in and help them settle in the area. They also knew that the Office of Indian Affairs might be willing to support their move north if they believed the Cheyennes would adopt a sedentary way of life by beginning to farm. Although McGillycuddy supported Black Wolf's petition to move to the Tongue River valley, the Office of Indian Affairs did not. Federal officials insisted that all Northern Cheyennes should remain where they were.

Others who had taken an interest in the struggles of the Cheyennes in the Tongue River valley also petitioned the move. In the summer of 1882 George Yoakam, the soldier at Fort Keogh in charge of teaching Northern Cheyennes to farm, began to send letters addressed to President Chester A. Arthur declaring that Little Chief's people were very anxious to settle along the Tongue River. He argued that they should be encouraged in their desire to take homesteads and to support themselves through farming.[52] The commissioner of Indian affairs responded to Yoakam, stating that Little Chief's people had every right to homestead in the Tongue River valley, but the Office of Indian Affairs had no funds to help them do so.[53] By this point, the commissioner had decided not to forbid Black Wolf's people to go north, but he would not support them, either.

The Northern Cheyennes living in the Tongue River valley also petitioned to bring their relatives to the region. E. P. Ewers, an adjutant general in the Fifth Infantry at Fort Keogh, had been ordered to take charge of this group. White Bull, a Cheyenne man living in the area, asked him to contact Agent McGillycuddy. In his letter, Ewers described the houses and farms the Northern Cheyennes had built on the Rosebud River, the Tongue River, and Otter Creek, stating that they had been successful. Then he declared that the Cheyennes living there were anxious for Little Chief's people to settle with them. He also stated that he believed the Cheyennes would make more progress if they were allowed to live together in one place.[54] This letter demonstrated to the Office of Indian Affairs that the Cheyennes living in the Tongue River valley had enough resources to help their relatives, and had the support of military officers at Fort Keogh. Ewers used two arguments that federal officials would consider valid: moving north could contain all the Cheyennes in one place and would also further their progress as farmers. At the same time, his letter revealed a Cheyenne philosophical framework that valued reunification of families and a return to their homeland.

Black Wolf and his people settled in the Tongue River valley much earlier than Little Chief and those following him. Black Wolf took risks by disobeying the agent that Little Chief refused to take. In October 1882 McGillycuddy wrote to the commissioner of Indian affairs convinced that Black Wolf could not be contained at Pine Ridge without force. According to McGillycuddy, Black Wolf did not submit to Little Chief's authority. Black Wolf had insisted that he never agreed to remain at Pine Ridge and had always required that his people should be sent to Fort Keogh. McGillycuddy declared that the Cheyennes with Black Wolf would never be contented no matter where they settled because they had continued to travel between the agency and Fort Keogh throughout the fall. Little Chief had apparently remained at Pine Ridge during this period, and according to McGillycuddy, his people were "behaving themselves."[55]

Although both federal and local officials assumed that Little Chief was the leader of all the Cheyennes at Pine Ridge, the Northern Cheyennes understood their situation based on their own conceptions of leadership and social organization. Black Wolf did not feel the need to follow Little Chief because Little Chief was the headman of a camp, not a chief of the Council of Forty-Four. While Little Chief had been the primary negotiator when the people remained in Indian Territory, now that they lived in the north, Black Wolf had become a leader in his own camp and made decisions separately from Little Chief. Little Chief decided to pursue the need to return home by continuing his barrage of petitions, reminding officials that his people belonged with their relatives in the north. Black Wolf decided to join his northern relatives without negotiating with the agent or Little Chief. One leader placated the representatives of the state by refraining from shattering their dream of containment; the other opposed these agents and their dream by openly asserting the autonomy of his camp to come and go as they pleased. Each leader pressured state officials using different tactics, but both strategies emerged from kin-centric understandings of exercising political autonomy. One simply emphasized the relationship-building component of this political system, while the other emphasized the flexibility to fracture.

McGillycuddy drew on these circumstances to blame the Northern Cheyennes for many of the problems he encountered at Pine Ridge. When preparing for the transfer of Little Chief's people from the south, he wrote that in former years, the troubles at Red Cloud Agency were often caused by the Northern Cheyennes because they would "not submit to agency discipline and restraint." In 1882, when McGillycuddy was trying to prevent Black Wolf's movements between Pine Ridge and Montana, he declared the people were "an insubordinate, uncontrollable, and migratory lot of aborigines."[56] McGillycuddy disregarded Black Wolf's authority and represented him as restless and uncontrollable because his people remained mobile and would not follow Little Chief's less confrontational political tactics. Other officials at the federal level shared McGillycuddy's opinion. In 1882, as secretary of war, William Tecumseh Sherman wrote of the Northern Cheyennes living at Pine Ridge, "These restless Indians never were and never will be content to stay where they are, and where their treaty compels them to be."[57] For Sherman and McGillycuddy, the Northern Cheyennes had to be contained by force; to attempt to please them would only end in folly.

Despite the uproar his mobility caused certain government officials, Black Wolf eventually convinced the Office of Indian Affairs to allow him to remain in the north. In November 1882, without permission from his agent, Black Wolf traveled to the Tongue River valley with 127 Northern Cheyennes and camped along the river. He visited Fort Keogh and requested permission to keep his people in the area. Black Wolf's speech to the commanding officer there was recorded. He used similar arguments to demonstrate his connection to the Tongue River as those before him had, stating: "I am glad to get back here. This is the place I first made peace with the whites. My heart is glad to get back here where I surrendered." Black Wolf noted that General Miles was not at the fort anymore, but he stated, "I believe [the new officers] are all as good men as they were the first time I came here." He then declared his desire to "live like white men." He ended his speech stating, "Many years ago when my tribe lived here all of this country including Powder and Tongue River belonged to us. First the Sioux came and took it. Now white men have it. We want to be helped now."[58]

In this speech, Black Wolf first drew attention to the agreement his people made with Miles when they came in after the Battle of the Little Bighorn, then he stated that he believed the men there to be just as good, insinuating that they should carry on the political relationship that had been formed through personal obligations. When networks of kin wove together to form political alliances among Plains people, those relationships could stretch for generations. This new generation at the fort had every reason to honor General Miles's agreement. Black Wolf then demonstrated his people's connection to the land, noting that it had belonged to them. He argued that as the Lakotas moved into the territory, they took possession of it, but he does not imply that the Cheyennes were disenfranchised from the land—particularly since they had allied themselves with the Lakotas. Black Wolf proposed, now that the white men owned it, that the Cheyennes should receive help. The logic of this argument reflected the understanding that they had established a relationship with the Americans at Fort Keogh who controlled it, and such a relationship legitimated the authority to access land. Black Wolf claimed that the Cheyennes were willing to be a part of this group—to live like white men—as long as the agreement they had made with Miles would remain intact, underscoring the relationship between the two groups. In this speech, he reminded the officials at the fort of Cheyenne connections to the landscape by reiterating the alliance his people had established with General Miles.

By the end of November, both the secretary of the interior and the commissioner of Indian affairs supported Black Wolf's permanent residence along the Tongue River.[59] That December, George Yoakam reported to the commissioner of Indian affairs that when Black Wolf's people arrived, they began to follow the other Cheyenne and to build houses in the area. In another letter, Yoakam recommended to the commissioner that he send the rest of Little Chief's people to the Tongue River because those who had already come had made so much progress.[60] Black Wolf's people were finally able to make permanent homes with their relatives in the Tongue River valley with the approval of government officials. While these officials probably focused more on Black Wolf's apparent willingness to assimilate and not on honoring the webs of relationship that tied them to the Northern Cheyennes, his people still succeeded in returning home while continuing to honor these networks. Yet the officials were swayed by the logic of kin, recognizing that these Cheyennes would be more content if reunited with their families. Their actions did not represent a recognition of Cheyenne cultural autonomy, however; instead, these officials recognized that reuniting families seemed to further their efforts at containment. The Cheyennes had less need to travel when living among family.

Regardless, Little Chief would have to wait for almost a decade to return permanently to live with his Cheyenne relatives. By 1883 nearly all the other Cheyennes who wished to had established permanent homes in the Tongue River valley, but he continued to seek permission to return to the northern country with his Northern Cheyenne relatives. An executive order designated reservation boundaries for the Northern Cheyenne people in 1884, strengthening Little Chief's argument to return. His passive strategy prolonged the process. He had been told by Miles before his people were removed to Indian Territory to remain obedient to the government, and after he had heard what had happened to Dull Knife's people, perhaps he took this warning seriously. Because he was willing to wait, however, the government was able to ignore his needs for much longer.

In March 1886 Little Chief wrote to a friend, Red Wolf, asking about the life he lived in the Tongue River valley. His friend wrote him back, stating that he collected rations every week, and that he had received a cook stove, clothes, blankets, and some farming implements. Red Wolf told his friend that he would soon take a ranch on Lame Deer Creek, and that he wanted Little Chief to come up north.[61] A few months later, Little Chief again began barraging the commissioner of Indian affairs and the president of the United States with letters petitioning to be allowed to return north. In May 1886 he sent a copy of Red Wolf's letter to the commissioner as evidence that the people at Tongue River were supported in their endeavors to farm, declaring that his people were not. He told the commissioner that they had no agricultural tools to work with, "and in view of this fact, myself and band [sic] will be forced to move back to our people at the Cheyenne Agency in Montana." In this letter, he told the commissioner that he wanted to better his people, and the only place he could do that was in the Tongue River valley, where he could obtain support.[62] Little Chief used an argument that would be compelling to federal officials, stating that his people were hindered in their progress at Pine Ridge but could become farmers if they moved. At the same time, he used his relationship with Red Wolf to bolster his argument. His connection to the people at Tongue River helped him construct petitions that federal officials were more likely to accept.

Little Chief also remembered that Miles had told him to ask the president to be allowed to return to the north, so in October 1886 he asked the commissioner of Indian affairs for permission to go to Washington to bring his request in person. Little Chief dictated this letter to his grandson, E. C. Dawson, who had been a student at the Carlisle School in Pennsylvania and could transcribe his grandfather's words into English.[63] Little Chief again complained of the lack of tools and resources to begin farming and asked to be allowed to move to a better place. This time, he did not directly ask to be moved to Tongue River, but he did indicate his displeasure with the condition of his people at Pine Ridge, stating that it would improve if they were allowed to move. He baldly stated that he wanted to be given the things he had been promised for himself and his people. He then noted that many in the Indian Office had said that the Northern Cheyennes were continually moving from place to place. He addressed head-on the frustration with this that Agent McGillycuddy had expressed, stating that his people did not move for their own enjoyment but because they were tired of waiting to receive help from the government. He assured the commissioner that once they received what they had been promised, they would settle down in one place.[64] In this letter Little Chief acknowledged the goals of the state to keep his people contained on one reservation and to teach them to farm. He demonstrated his willingness to work toward these goals, but not entirely on the government's terms. The federal office had to provide his people with the help they had promised and permit them to live in a place that was suitable to them.

As the months passed, his requests became more pointed. In July 1887 Little Chief penned a letter to President Grover Cleveland directly. He had learned to write and no longer needed his grandson to transcribe his thoughts. He stated: "You wanted to let all the Cheyennes follow the ways of the whites. Now I ask you one thing; it is this, how do you expect us to become like you white people when we do not have anything. All the promise[s] I receive from A Great Father are not given to me. Do you know anything about why the Cheyennes do not get any horses that [are] given to the Indians from [the] Great Father?" He then asked about the Cheyennes living on the Tongue River and if they had a good life. He stated that the Cheyennes at Pine Ridge take care of themselves and have good homes but nothing to work with, so they would never reach "the rich life." He also brought up promises about a schoolhouse and a sawmill that had not been fulfilled. Then he continued: "Please write to me soon for I obey your orders now. Tell all the news you know about at Washington. We are willing to obey your orders. I don't want to disobey your orders. They [his band of Cheyennes] do not want to stay because the agent does not treat them well for we like our agent very well but still he does not treat us well. I would like to come and see our Great Father [and] talk [these] things over ourselves. Write to me soon."[65] The letter was signed "Your Friend, Little Chief." Little Chief spoke to the president as if he were a head chief, stating that he accepted his authority. He made it apparent that he would not have to but that he had chosen to. As with a Cheyenne chief, he assumed that authority was granted by the people—obedience was not obligatory. Furthermore, Little Chief noted that his people were upholding their responsibilities within this political order by attempting to get along with an agent who treated them unfairly. He took the opportunity to remind the president that by falling short as a head chief, he had disappointed a constituency deserving respect. He made promises that he had not kept. He said he would provide a school, a sawmill, and particularly horses. To promise a gift and not follow through was not a chiefly act.

Little Chief did not directly accuse the president of being stingy, but he did ask if he knew why they had not received any horses. He reminded the president of his obligation to the Cheyenne people as their chief. He also reminded him that his people were very poor, indicating that they fell squarely into the category of people who should be helped by a leader. In his letter, Little Chief utilized Cheyenne understandings of social obligations and responsibilities, political in nature yet based in the kin-centric understanding of reciprocity, to convince the president to meet the needs of his people. His comments also posed a subtle critique of American leadership over Cheyenne people that U.S. officials assumed they possessed. If the president was not fulfilling his role as a leader by ensuring the well-being of his entire community, the Cheyennes would have no reason to recognize him as such. He (and the government with him) could wrest control through domination, but this would not have equated to leadership within a Cheyenne framework. If the president did not respond to the needs of his people, Little Chief insinuated, the Cheyennes had no obligation to him. Most likely, the president had no idea Little Chief questioned his right to rule when he listed the promises the government had failed to keep.

Finally, in 1888 Little Chief began to ask directly that his people be reunited with the rest of the Northern Cheyennes living in the Tongue River valley. In a letter to Pine Ridge agent H. D. Gallagher, he stated, "We also want to combine with those Cheyennes at Tongue River . . . so we wouldn't have any trouble much in visiting each other."[66] In a letter written in March 1890, Little Chief told the commissioner of Indian affairs that he had visited the Tongue River valley to see friends and family and that there were good farms there. He stated that this would be a good place for his people, and he wanted to know when he would be able to move there.[67] He always traveled with permission and was wary to disobey government officials, but he was tireless in his petitions to be allowed to return north. He continued to emphasize the desire for farms, using progress toward civilization as an argument, knowing it would appeal to federal officials. He also drew on Cheyenne political frameworks based on social organization, telling federal officials that his people should live closer to their relatives and also reminding high-ranking officials of their obligations to his people.

Finally, almost a year later, in January 1891, Little Chief and his people were granted permission to leave Pine Ridge for Montana to live permanently. Although the headman had been petitioning government officials at all levels for nearly a decade, these letters were probably not the deciding factor. In 1890 the events surrounding the Ghost Dance movement among the Lakotas and the American fear of violence affected the Cheyennes at Pine Ridge. By that time, Edward W. Casey had taken charge of the Cheyenne scouts at Fort Keogh, and on November 27, 1890, he received orders to enlist as many scouts as he could and then head south towards Pine Ridge to patrol the area around the Little Missouri River, watching for any people trying to leave the Fort Peck reservation.[68] In an interview conducted by Thomas Marquis, James Tangled Yellow Hair declared that the Cheyenne men at Fort Keogh had been told that the Lakotas had been hostile toward the Cheyennes living at Pine Ridge because they would not fight against the whites. Tangled Yellow Hair stated that the Lakotas had always been their friends, but they were worried about their Cheyenne relatives and decided to go with Casey to protect their own people.[69] Again the safety net of family supported the Cheyenne people living in diaspora. Although the Ghost Dance movement among the Lakotas acted as a catalyst to bring Little Chief's people back to the Tongue River country, if their relatives had not been living in the region and scouting for the army, they would have had little hope of returning to this part of their homeland permanently.

Tensions were high when the Cheyenne scouts arrived at Pine Ridge. While there is no evidence that the Cheyennes living among their Lakota relatives had been in any serious danger, certainly the atmosphere in the area was explosive. Agency officials were concerned that Lakota Ghost Dancers might turn hostile at any moment. While the Ghost Dance was a peaceful revitalization movement, Euro-Americans on the northern plains were frightened by their sudden lack of control over the situation. This tinderbox of fear exploded in the Wounded Knee massacre on December 29, 1890.[70] While Cheyenne scouts did not participate in any part of the massacre, they were in the area when it happened. After this horrific slaughter of mostly unarmed families, some Lakotas attempted to retaliate and began building fortifications far from the agency. Casey's Cheyenne scouts became central to the negotiation efforts to regain peace on the reservation. These scouts were camped on White Clay Creek and kept an eye on the rebel village, meeting often with Lakota warriors between the two camps.[71] Eventually, a peace was brokered in no small part due to Cheyenne scouts who could travel between the camps and interpret.

After a relative calm returned to Pine Ridge, General Miles asked the adjutant general of the army, Maj. Gen. John M. Schofield, for permission to transfer the Cheyennes living at Pine Ridge to Fort Keogh under the escort of Casey's scouts. The commissioner of Indian affairs, Thomas J. Morgan, consented to the transfer a few days later, believing that it was necessary for their safety, considering that Cheyenne scouts had been on the reservation during the turmoil.[72] In early February, Casey arrived with 517 Northern Cheyennes at Fort Keogh.[73] Little Chief's people only had permission to remain at the fort, however, and were not yet allowed to join their relatives living in the Tongue River valley. Nevertheless, they traveled regularly between the fort and their families once they arrived. By July 1891 around 250 of Little Chief's people were staying with relatives in the Tongue River valley, and neither the agent nor the officials at the fort could entice them back.[74] Finally, the War Department and the secretary of the interior agreed that it would be best to allow the transfer of Little Chief's people to the Northern Cheyenne reservation.[75] A group of 276 people settled on the reservation on October 3, 1891.[76] Thirteen years after Little Chief's people arrived in Indian Territory, those Northern Cheyennes who sought to be reunited with their relatives in the heart of their homeland had returned.

The history of Little Chief and his people is just one example of how the fluidity of Northern Cheyenne social organization not only helped the people maintain connections to dispersed family groups during removal but also pushed the boundaries of and finally broke the structures imposed on the people by the state. The Cheyennes needed relatives spread across the plains to facilitate any effort—U.S.-sanctioned or otherwise—to return home. Without Lakota relatives, most Cheyennes leaving Indian Territory would not have had support or refuge on their journey north. The fact that some families managed to avoid diaspora by making an alliance with General Miles proved to be a saving grace for those who were forced from their homeland. If all the Northern Cheyennes living at Fort Keogh had been removed to Indian Territory, Dull Knife, Little Wolf, and Little Chief would not have had relatives living in the Tongue River valley who could help them return.

Little Chief's journey to the Tongue River valley, however, took much longer than those of the other Northern Cheyennes. Like Two Moons and the scouts who remained with Miles, Little Chief attempted to work with local and federal officials to reunite Northern Cheyenne families in their homeland. Unlike Two Moons, Little Chief's people found themselves far from home, struggling to convince disinterested federal and local officials of the importance of homeland and kin. This seemingly minor difference created an untenable task for Little Chief. His arguments for Cheyenne autonomy were based on an Indigenous intellectual framework that emphasized reciprocity over dominance and balanced social relations over hierarchical institutionalized ones. The officials he negotiated with never even imagined such a framework to be political. Little Chief had no personal relationships with these officials to facilitate his petitions, like the relationship Cheyenne scouts developed with Miles.

Using any rhetorical resource available, Little Chief did attempt to sway officials by convincing them that his people were ready to assimilate. At the same time, he argued for an autonomous Cheyenne nationhood by constructing his arguments in terms of kinship, emphasizing that his people could only assimilate if they were living with their relatives. Because Cheyenne nationhood was not based on fixing hierarchical relations of power through establishing boundaries, adopting new housing, dress styles, subsistence methods, or language could not undermine it. By insisting on the continuation of family, reciprocity, and respectful relationships between U.S. leaders and the people they presumed to lead, Little Chief called on American officials to respect Cheyenne nationhood. What is more, he attempted to convince federal and local officials that his people's political choices deserved respect during a decade when the ambiguities and contradictions in Indian policy had erupted in tragedy for many Northern Plains nations.

After Dull Knife and Little Wolf's flight from the southern agency, the difficult military struggle, the terror of settlers along their path, and the final tragedy at Fort Robinson, the secretary of Indian affairs became wary of any tension that might have resulted in similar turmoil. Both he and the commissioner of Indian affairs began to declare in official correspondence that all the Northern Cheyennes belonged in the north with their relatives. They had shifted away from the idea of the Cheyennes as one bounded ethnic group that federal officials had been using for a long time to justify moving them all to Indian Territory. Under extreme circumstances, these two federal officials began to understand that members of this Native nation had been pulled in different directions and had different affinities. As the construction of a bounded Cheyenne nation became a less effective part of the political agenda to find and contain its members, new American constructions of the Cheyenne nation emerged that accepted that the Northern Cheyennes belonged in the north and not on the southern reservation. Thus, federal officials consented to returning Little Chief's people to the north because they believed the Cheyennes would be easier to contain and control if they were content with their relatives in their homeland. The upheaval at Pine Ridge surrounding the Wounded Knee massacre had worried officials that keeping Cheyenne people from their relatives might lead to more hostilities. Although they still did not realize the political importance of the kinship systems that united the Cheyenne people at many levels and helped them maintain autonomy across vast distances, U.S. officials did recognize that the Northern Cheyennes would continue their efforts to return to their families in the north unabated.

While Little Chief and his people used the language of kin with federal officials to convince them to acknowledge their autonomy to return north, they also used the flexible nature of kin relationships to cross state-imposed boundaries. Sometimes these crossings remained undetected, as with the extra families that traveled north with Little Chief. Other times local agents fought to prevent these crossings, as with Black Wolf's trips from Pine Ridge to the Tongue River. In each case, the support of kin made containment, and therefore the assertion of state dominance, a constant struggle for federal and local officials. As with Two Moons, Dull Knife, and Little Wolf, government officials never fully understood the strategic ways Little Chief used kinship. Even so, eventually they realized that because of the pull, the strength, and the flexibility of kin, they had to reconsider their efforts to subdue the Northern Cheyennes. Federal officials never questioned their assumptions that the Cheyennes should be contained and controlled. They did question, however, the best way to contain them, and they ultimately realized that they would have to allow the Cheyennes to return home to their relatives if they were to maintain any sense of control.

Little Chief also attempted to temper his demands with language and mechanisms the state would understand. Like Two Moons, Little Chief made an x mark through his letter-writing campaigns in an attempt to create a better life for his people. As Lyons has pointed out, this kind of accommodation does not undermine political autonomy or cultural identity.[77] Little Chief clearly continued to prioritize Northern Cheyenne values even while he remained obedient to agency officials. Furthermore, although his accommodations, including learning to read and write in English, could appear to be concessions in the eyes of the state, they were in fact assertions of Native nationhood. Adapting to the ways of others threatens the nation-state because it has been built on controlling boundaries. The colonial imposition of such boundaries has continually failed to undermine Native nationhood while Native peoples maintained their web of relationships. Because such political expressions are built on reciprocal relationships, with and between the peoples, the land, and all who dwell on it, establishing new relationships and incorporating new cultural practices only strengthens a Native nation.

CHAPTER SEVEN

IT BELONGED TO US

Northern Cheyenne Homesteading as an Assertion of Autonomy

One summer evening, I was helping the young women of Ms. JS's family prepare a large meal for the many people who had come to their house to sweat and pray. We chatted about food and joked about boyfriends and husbands as I sliced hard-boiled eggs into the potato salad. They cut chunks of meat and peeled potatoes for the stew as I stirred mayonnaise into my creation. The sky outside slowly turned from blue to pink to grey as we finished our work and settled in at the kitchen table for cigarettes and more conversation. Still learning to relax about getting things done "on time" and developing a sense of getting things done "as needed," I asked, "Should I slice the watermelon?"

"Maybe," Ms. JS said. "Let's see what round they're on. I'll have my son check." This young woman walked to the door and I followed her, nosy as always. She called in a clear, loud voice that carried across the brown yard and into the hills, "Sonny, sonny, come over here." As I watched her second son, the oldest boy in the group of cousins playing in the bluffs, come over the hill, I heard one of Ms. JS's sisters say, "You can always tell a Muddy girl." The group in the house laughed. I looked at her and then looked back out at the kids, now following their brother, curious to know why he had been called. I wondered if the girls had been playing in the pump.

"Did the kids get muddy or something?" I asked, walking back to the kitchen table and picking up the heavy watermelon. The sisters looked at each other and laughed again.

"No, no," one of them said. "We're from Muddy district. And people from Muddy are just like that."

I'm still not quite sure what people from Muddy are like, exactly, but I do have a better idea now than I did that second summer. Being from a certain district at Northern Cheyenne means something about who you are and where you came from—not just recently but in the early days of Cheyenne resettlement in the area. People's identities are connected to their districts.

Once, when I was walking the circuit with a friend of mine at the annual Fourth of July powwow, we took a detour on our way to the Indian taco stand to speak with one of her childhood friends. The two women made small talk, chatting about how they had been and the most recent events that had affected their own personal lives, like grandchildren growing up and finding a new mattress. After the two women parted, and we continued on the path toward our greasy treat, my friend turned to me and said, "She's another Birney girl. I always stop to talk when I see her."

Birney is a tiny town along the banks of the Tongue River far to the southeast of Lame Deer. When my friend was a girl, it took a full day by wagon to come into town for groceries and supplies and visiting. The Northern Cheyenne reservation is divided into several districts: Busby, Muddy, Ree, Rosebud, Lame Deer, Birney, and Ashland. Everyone knows these districts because they dictate the areas represented on tribal council and therefore have elected representatives. But districts have a more powerful pull on people's identity than a hometown or a high school affiliation does on most Euro-Americans. Growing up in a certain district shapes people's perceptions of you. Cheyennes talk about people from Muddy as boisterous and people from Ashland as private. Each district also has its own history of settlement originally structured by familial relationships, which plays a role in shaping who you are and how others see you. Relatives settled near relatives. Bands settled together in one place. These histories are remembered, demonstrating that family remains an important factor in both spatial and political organization.

While familial ties certainly shaped Cheyenne settlement patterns in the area that would become the reservation, the Northern Cheyennes did not neglect kinship as a political strategy once they established themselves in the Tongue River valley. Although some men became scouts for the U.S. military and many families took up homesteading and attempted to farm, the people did not adopt the political constructions of the state to order their own social world, nor did they adopt these constructions in their continued negotiations with U.S. officials. Even though the Cheyennes in the Tongue River valley adapted to American ways of making a living and accepted some nation-state borders, such as those established by homesteading or a reservation, these adaptations did not displace previous forms of social organization and expressions of political autonomy. Adopting Euro-American farming practices proved no threat to assertions of nationhood based on reciprocal social relationships because it did not threaten the relationships themselves. Although Cheyenne leaders realized that asserting rights to a specific territory was important because this is how Americans constructed sovereignty, the people continued to fight for freedom of movement as central to asserting their kinship to each other and the land and maintaining these relationships through ceremonies and visiting. In this way, Northern Cheyennes continued to exercise their sense of political autonomy.

Even though many Cheyenne families lived in the Tongue River valley before 1884, their legal right to this territory had not yet been recognized by the federal system. They could not depend on a treaty to gain them their own reservation. They had none that granted land just to them. Federal officials had dedicated themselves to removing the Northern Cheyennes to Indian Territory since at least 1874, and many local officials sought to contain the people there or in Pine Ridge, forbidding travel. In addition, the Cheyenne strategy of securing land for themselves in hopes that this would allow them the freedom they needed to live on their own terms was at odds with the federal government's plan of containing all Cheyenne people on first one and then two reservations. Only General Miles and the other local officials at Fort Keogh fought to retain land in the Tongue River valley for the Northern Cheyennes. Those who scouted for Miles became central figures in the people's quest to remain in their homeland, politically distinct from other Plains nations. Through their roles as scouts, these men developed a personal relationship with Miles that obligated him to fight for a permanent home for them in the north.[1] These scouts eventually convinced other federal officials that they could assimilate into American culture, reassuring them that they could live on their own land.

Before the Civil War, federal officials believed they could successfully keep Native peoples separate from the rest of the American population. Confining American Indians to reservations supposedly helped populate the land with Americans faster and with less violence while giving Native peoples time to become civilized in the Western definition. The Grant and Hayes administrations developed a peace policy meant to continue this separation strategy. Government officials revamped the Indian Office with the hope that their new policies and programs would civilize Native peoples before they were overrun by American settlement.[2] This peace policy held a lot of promise for both reformers and politicians who believed that they had solved what they understood to be their "Indian problem." Yet the massacre of Northern Cheyenne families at Fort Robinson on a cold January night in 1879 was the first of a series of catastrophes that brought the success of the peace policy into question.[3] Several tragic events throughout Native America in 1879, including those at Fort Robinson, as well as American Indian people themselves vocally calling for change, vividly brought the country's attention to the devastation and suffering of Natives living on reservations.

Americans attacked the current Indian policy and called for an end to the reservation system, arguing that the only real solution was total assimilation.[4] This seemed to be the one goal that would satisfy all Euro-American factions. Those who were concerned for the suffering of Native people were soothed with the belief that they would soon be as happy and successful as any other American. The opening up of reservation land that total assimilation would bring soothed those concerned about land for farming and ranching. Military officials were relieved at the prospect of no longer having to contain Native people and then explain themselves when containment turned to massacre. Federal congressmen were soothed by the promise of no longer having to provide American Indian people with rations, agents, schools, doctors, and the many other costs associated with reservation life.

Most importantly, assimilating American Indian people into a booming American society would make up for dispossession and would reaffirm the American ability to incorporate all peoples into one unified nation at a time when many other groups attempting to assimilate—including freed slaves and immigrants from Europe and Asia—revealed the cracks in the democratic assumptions of the United States. Assimilation of American Indians would prove to both American citizens and the watching world that acquiescing to the norms and requirements of the majority would be rewarded with social equality. Initially, homesteading was the means by which Native people would attain total assimilation, because officials believed social evolutionary theories that stated that land owned and passed down within nuclear families created private wealth, which in turn created the stability and social sophistication needed for civilization.[5] Those who supported dividing reservations into individual acreages believed the reservation system was too gradual because the land was still tribal. Only individual ownership of land would spur American Indian peoples toward what Americans saw as civilization.

This change in fashion relating to U.S. Indian policy actually helped the Northern Cheyennes stay in their homeland, but in quite a roundabout way. These same Cheyennes had defeated Custer at the Little Bighorn, in an attack that the United States represented as pure savagery. To be able to turn them into successful farmers and ranchers on quiet homesteads would be the ultimate display of American power. Indian policy supporters could satiate their critics by displaying the savages who had killed Custer as successfully working toward assimilation. The Cheyennes living in the Tongue River valley during this period were adapting to military life as scouts and to sedentary life as homesteaders. Despite the debates going on around them, it seems the people were relatively confident in their position in the valley. They had begun settling on the land and had the support of the local agents. They had upheld their end of the military alliance with General Miles as scouts, and he had not indicated he would fail to uphold his end.

These Northern Cheyennes had a well-established relationship with this landscape that not only stretched far back into their own history but also was secured by their political relationship with General Miles. According to Cheyenne historical and political constructions of territory, the Northern Cheyennes belonged on this land. Furthermore, by living in the Tongue River valley, maintaining a sacred relationship with the plants and animals living with them, continuing to travel to visit relatives, and welcoming family to their homes for extended visits, the Cheyennes asserted that they had never severed their relationship with the landscape. These relationships through which the Cheyenne nation expressed political autonomy remained intact.

Surprisingly, although federal officials debated Cheyenne rights to the territory during this period, ultimately they never denied them. Finally in 1884, the Northern Cheyennes secured a tenuous recognition of their homeland. The president of the United States had acknowledged their rights to this land by establishing a small reservation through executive order. Nevertheless, this order did not settle the debate over the land or even over the fate of the people. The establishment of the 1884 reservation boundaries seemed to be a temporary solution to a struggle taking place between the local officials working with the Cheyennes, the local ranchers who wanted access to Cheyenne lands, and federal officials who were trying to decide whether homesteading or reservation life was the best method of assimilating Native people. While American officials understood a nation's connection to land in terms of rights and Plains people saw it as a relationship, ultimately the Cheyennes were able to convince federal officials that their people should remain in their northern homeland. Throughout the debate, the Northern Cheyennes continued to use kinship as a political strategy, and once again this strategy paid off.

The Northern Cheyennes scouting for Miles lived contentedly at Fort Keogh for months before they began to settle in the region that would eventually become their reservation. Several historical sources suggest that Little Wolf was the first to begin the slow trickle of families from the fort to the Tongue River valley in Montana. Because he had killed Starving Elk, another Cheyenne man, in the winter of 1880, Little Wolf banished himself from the community.[6] He moved with his family along the Yellowstone until he reached the Rosebud River.

He then followed this river south until he reached a spot on Muddy Creek just a few miles from where the town of Lame Deer is today.[7] Muddy Creek was a known camping spot that the Cheyennes had used in the past. Little Wolf stopped traveling when he reached the cabin of William Rowland and his family.[8] Rowland had married a Cheyenne woman and lived and moved with the Cheyennes for most of his life.[9] Ms. DG pointed out that the Rowlands were really the first to settle permanently in the area of the present-day reservation.[10] Even in his banishment, Little Wolf was able to turn to other members of his community.

Northern Cheyennes today also point to Little Wolf as the one who began the Cheyennes' movement to settle in the area of the modern reservation. Once he had been camping along Muddy Creek for a little while, people began to follow him into this area and join his camp. When speaking of Little Wolf, Mr. BC stated that Little Wolf had hoped to always be free, and he believed that he would be when he left the southern agency and refused to come into Fort Robinson.[11] Even though Little Wolf ultimately lost the resources to continue moving across the plains, he did succeed in his long struggle to return home. He moved to a familiar camping spot in the landscape where he had grown up, a place he traveled through only four years earlier. Even though he committed a crime worthy of banishment, people continued to respect him and followed him as a chief. In this way he played an important role in helping the Northern Cheyennes settle permanently in their homeland.

While reservation agents viewed Native peoples as their charges and struggled to constantly contain them on their reservations, General Miles was not concerned with bringing these families back because he no longer had to provide space and food for them at the already crowded fort.[12] Although the Northern Cheyennes with Little Wolf were officially considered prisoners of war by the United States military, Miles did not hold them at his fort, just as he had not with Two Moons's people. He allowed them to stay beyond his immediate control in their own camps, where they had lived comfortably for several years. Miles and the other leaders at the fort did not seem to fear that the Northern Cheyennes with Little Wolf were hostile and trusted them to live away from the confines of the fort. Certainly, military officials could have used the fact that Little Wolf killed a man as a reason to retain him and even lock him in jail. Because the victim was Cheyenne, however, and no federal policy allowed involvement in the internal affairs of Native nations, the Cheyennes themselves issued their standard punishment for murder—banishment.[13]

Ultimately, Little Wolf's people owed their extraordinary freedom to the alliance that their Northern Cheyenne relatives had created with General Miles. Elva Stands In Timber described Miles's role in encouraging the Northern Cheyennes to settle in the Tongue River valley. She stated that when the people first arrived at Fort Keogh, they were placed in barracks, but the military was worried about them at the fort. They then began camping near the fort, but Miles did not like this, either. So he worked hard to find them their own land. Miles wanted them to be living away from the fort, so he encouraged them to move south and take homesteads. She declared that he was the one who really got the Northern Cheyennes settled in Montana and helped them stay in their homeland permanently.[14]

After the people had begun to move south from the fort, Miles began to strongly encourage Two Moons and his people to go into the country along the Tongue River to select places to live. In a council held in 1890, Howling Wolf remembered that after the Northern Cheyenne scouts helped apprehend Sitting Bull in 1881, "Miles must have written to Washington to ask about this country. After awhile General Miles heard from Washington that, now he and the Cheyennes were friends, he could put them where ever they wanted to go. After awhile General Miles sent for two head men and told them that he wanted us to go up on the Rosebud and settle down there, that it belonged to us."[15] The Northern Cheyenne families at Fort Keogh sought good home sites around Lame Deer and Muddy Creek. John Stands In Timber described the land: "You can't find country like this anywhere else no matter how far you go. There was plenty of wood, and good water, and range, and many kinds of game. It was the place they had in mind all the time." Miles kept his promise to the Northern Cheyennes who scouted with him and was true to their alliance; he helped them permanently retain legal rights to their land.[16]

Howling Wolf articulated the Cheyenne perception of this relationship in his speech, noting that their friendship with Miles, as recognized by officials in Washington, established their access to land. For the Northern Cheyennes, this friendship, as many called it, denoted an alliance between equals, securing the Cheyennes the ability to settle "where ever they wanted to go" in the region. Because the Northern Cheyennes had an alliance with Miles, they were able to remain connected to the heart of their homeland, not through the generosity of government officials but through their strategic use of kin relationships and their own perseverance. While it is doubtful that Miles recognized the autonomy embedded in the Cheyennes' quest to settle in their homeland, he did acknowledge his personal responsibility to the scouts who had helped build his career and safeguarded his life. Additionally, his strong belief that Plains peoples should be assimilated gradually in their traditional homeland facili-tated his support of Cheyenne families settling in the Tongue River valley. So while Miles's ultimate goal of assimilation contradicted Cheyenne efforts to remain autonomous, the language of reciprocal responsibility embedded in the kin-centric discourse surrounding this friendship brought peoples with dramatically different worldviews together in one purpose.

As the Northern Cheyennes began to camp, hunt, and live in the Tongue River valley, one official at Fort Keogh began petitioning the federal government to establish a reservation for them in the area. As early as December 1880, George Yoakam, the soldier who had been assigned to teach the Plains Indians at the fort how to farm, was writ-ing to the secretary of the interior asking him to deed land and give cattle to each Cheyenne and Lakota family living there.[17] In his first letter, he proposed the territory that should be given to "the Sioux and Cheyenne Indians now here or may here after come here" and "bounded on the east by Tongue River, on the south by Wyoming, on the west by the Crow reservation, and on the north by the Yellow-stone."[18] He asked that each of these Plains Indians be made citizens, that they be given schools and churches, and that they be provided with enough supplies to start farming. He also suggested that those living on the proposed reservation be allowed to decide which non-Indians could come there. He was suggesting a plan for not only assimilation but also self-determination, believing that with this aid and the stipulations he requested, the Northern Cheyennes would

Black Wolf by Laton A.
Huffman. From the
Collection of Gene and
Bev Allen, Helena,
Montana.

become self-supporting, successful at farming and ranching, and able
to oversee their own reservation. He argued that the best path for the
Cheyennes was assimilation, but he did not tout the federal agenda
of containment or control. Instead, he pressed for a limited autonomy
for the people he worked and served with.

The boundaries Yoakam proposed for the reservation reflected the
Northern Cheyennes' delineations of the territory they had secured
in their alliance with Miles. While discussing the establishment of the
reservation in the summer of 2005, Mr. BC stated that he believed
the boundaries of the land the United States recognized as Northern
Cheyenne during this period stretched from Miles City in the north
(which is along the Yellowstone), the Bighorn Mountains in the south
(the border of Wyoming), west to the Little Bighorn, and the Black
Hills in the east.[19] These delineations fit Cheyenne expectations of

the lands associated with their alliance, and there is some evidence that General Miles was aware of his scouts' perceptions. Miles stated in a letter written in 1880 that he walked the land with several Northern Cheyennes in order to discuss boundaries for a reservation.[20] The Northern Cheyennes still point to this trip as evidence that the United States recognized their rights to more land than they have today. In a later conversation that same summer, Mr. BC told me that when Two Moons was first at Fort Keogh, he and nine or ten other men walked with General Miles around the borders of what was to be the reservation; they walked all the way south to Wyoming and a lot farther east than what the boundary is today.[21] Therefore, considering their relationship with Miles, it is not surprising that the Northern Cheyennes believed these boundaries to be recognized as their territory by the United States.

Furthermore, these boundaries would have meshed with certain boundaries on the landscape that the people already recognized as securely Cheyenne territory. Although they reported to officials at Fort Keogh, they surely continued to travel the entire area mentioned to hunt, gather plants for food and medicine, visit relatives, and maintain ceremonial practices. The land they walked would have been the land they recognized as theirs, through their presence in that landscape for generations and reiterated by their alliance with the American newcomers who also claimed the land, particularly since they would have been traveling within this area while scouting for Miles before the reservation was established.

By the fall of 1881, George Yoakam began writing to officials in the federal government stating that the Cheyenne Indians at the fort wished to renounce their tribal relations so that they could take up homesteading near the Rosebud River.[22] In order to legally settle the Cheyennes who had moved into the area around Tongue River, General Miles had encouraged them to take land under the Indian Homestead Act. Congress had passed the act in 1875, stating that Native people could apply for homesteads provided that they had abandoned their tribal relations, or would at some point in the future.[23] It is unclear exactly what the government meant by abandoning tribal relations, but even though many Northern Cheyennes took homesteads, they never abandoned their tribal relations, nor did they ever intend to.

Just like the Homestead Act of 1862, which allowed American citizens to take land, this act allowed each Native person to claim 160 acres with the expectation of owning the land after paying the filing fees, living on the land, and making improvements on it, such as building a house and beginning to farm. Miles himself hoped that this was the solution to resisting the push and pull of the federal government, including the constant threat of removal. He also believed strongly in assimilation and thought homesteading would provide the stability that might help the Cheyennes incorporate fully into an American way of life.[24]

Federal officials processed the Northern Cheyennes' applications for homesteads, apparently assuming the Cheyennes had abandoned their tribal relations, or at least would sometime in the near future. For them and most other Americans, Natives who were bound together by ethnicity and territory on a reservation existed as a tribe. People who were scattered across space and who adopted certain components of Western culture, particularly intensive agriculture, did not fit their conception of a tribe. Therefore, the Northern Cheyennes at Fort Keogh seemed to be American Indians who had abandoned their tribal relations. The first Northern Cheyennes to homestead in the region were scouts in the U.S. military. As scouts, they appeared as individual citizens loyal to the United States, not as members of a tribal entity separate from the United States. The ambiguous status of the Cheyennes in the eyes of federal officials worked to their advantage in this case. They had been imagined as members of other tribes—the Lakotas or the Southern Cheyennes and Arapahos—who had abandoned their tribes when they chose to live in Montana. This construction gave the Cheyennes the opportunity to use a law of the state meant to break apart the tribal order to instead preserve their sense of autonomy and secure their presence in the heart of their homeland.

Once they received permission from Washington, E. P. Ewers, Captain of the Fifth Infantry at Fort Keogh and the man in charge of the Cheyennes, went with several Cheyennes to the Rosebud River, Lame Deer Creek, and Muddy Creek to examine the landscape and choose the best places to locate homesteads. Many Cheyennes selected sites along the Rosebud and Muddy, drove in stakes to mark the land, and built log foundations for houses. Other Cheyennes wished to locate where there was more water, so Ewers helped them select sites at the mouth of Otter Creek on the Tongue River.[25] Although some Cheyennes settled in the fall of 1881, many people went back to the fort even if they were not enlisted as scouts and then returned to their sites in the spring of 1882 to begin homesteading. The Cheyenne people chose the land around the Tongue River because they knew this land intimately. It was a favored hunting ground where they had camped for generations. Cheyenne families had left the agency to come to these lands just before the Battle of the Little Bighorn. Many of the scouts' families had been freely camping in the region only six years earlier and knew the landscape well. They had grown up in the area and therefore knew which places were sheltered from the weather with lots of water and wood. The region that the people had chosen as a good place to settle certainly did not encompass the entirety of the Cheyenne homeland, but it contained a valuable landscape for the people.

The Northern Cheyennes living near Fort Keogh decided to use the Indian Homestead Act to their advantage for two reasons. First, they could remain in their homeland using the security of legal precedence established by the nation-state in spite of the treaties that placed them elsewhere. Second, they could live independently without rations or an agent. They did not have to ask permission to leave a reservation or go hunting because there were no imposed boundaries. Homesteading emerged as a way to live as a people with autonomy that was sanctioned by federal policy and made sense in terms of the ideals of the nation-state. Of course, the goals of the Indian Homestead Act contradicted the purposes for which Cheyenne people used it. While the act was meant to turn politically autonomous Native nations toward capitalistic individualism and American citizenship, it allowed the Northern Cheyennes to remain independent by avoiding the restrictions that a reservation would have forced on them.

Although many Northern Cheyenne homesteaders worked hard to fulfill the requirements of the Indian Homestead Act, the land had to be registered before it could gain the full legitimacy of the state. Ewers tried several times to have entries made of the Cheyenne homestead claims at the land office in Miles City, but he was continually told that this was impossible because the land had yet to be surveyed.[26] The officials at Fort Keogh hoped to keep these Northern Cheyennes stable on their homesteads long enough to be ready when the surveyor finally came through.

In August 1882 George Yoakam declared in a letter to the president that he had succeeded in settling a number of Cheyennes on homesteads in the Tongue River valley.[27] By October 1882 there were enough Cheyenne homesteaders that Captain Ewers made an inspection of these claims for the assistant adjutant general of the Department of Dakota. The emphasis of his letter was the progress that these homesteaders were making toward civilization. Ewers pointed out that they had been self-sustaining for three years, they were gradually becoming more civilized, and many were beginning to speak English. He found ten houses on Muddy Creek, sixteen above the mouth of Muddy Creek on the Rosebud River, and many more on the Tongue River and Otter Creek. At this time, the homesteads were spaced so that each family would have 160 acres. Ewers reported that the houses were well built, but the gardens were not yet profitable because the people had gotten settled too late in the year to plant. He stated, "I believe that all of these Indians will do better next year, as they are very anxious to live like white men and remain in this country."[28]

It is hard to know whether the Northern Cheyennes were indeed anxious to live like white men; perhaps they were simply interested in establishing a new way of subsistence that would be successful for them. It is certain, however, that they were anxious to remain in their homeland. Throughout their history, the Cheyennes had adapted to new ways of life in order both to take advantage of new productive endeavors and to preserve their autonomous political identity as Cheyenne people. They had adapted to a new way of life when they moved onto the plains, changing their cultural life and even giving up small-scale agriculture but not severing their kin-based social organization. The flexibility of kinship allowed the Cheyennes to adapt and migrate without destroying their sociopolitical body. As they took up homesteading, the Northern Cheyennes were again adapting to the new world that was upon them while maintaining their

own cultural perspectives and securing themselves as an autonomous people. Just because Cheyenne people lived in cabins and grew
gardens did not mean they had abandoned their tribal relations.
Government officials simply lacked the flexibility to understand this
at the time.

For federal and local officials alike, homesteading would only be
a success if it severed their national autonomy and assimilated the
Northern Cheyenne settlers into a Euro-American way of life. In
February 1883 the commissioner of Indian affairs, Hiram Price, received
the report he had requested from Special Agent George Milburn on
the conditions of the Cheyenne settlements. Milburn reported that
Two Moons, Little Wolf, and Dull Knife and their people were all
settled around the Rosebud in May 1882. Some members of Little
Chief's band who had followed Black Wolf camped on Hanging Woman
Creek after they left the Pine Ridge agency in October 1882.[29]

Milburn apparently made an effort to educate the Northern Cheyenne homesteaders about how to secure the land they had claimed
under the Indian Homestead Act. He stressed to them, through interpreter William Rowland, that they had to occupy and cultivate the
land on a continuous basis. He explained the fees and how to file
for claims, and he stressed that it was essential that they space their
houses far enough apart that their claims would not overlap once the
land had been surveyed. He also told them that they "must forsake
tribal relations, wild habits and pursuits and should take on the ways
of white men, and, in short, be civilized."[30] For Milburn, as indeed
for the other Euro-Americans overseeing the Northern Cheyennes,
forsaking tribal relations equated to living like white men: subsisting
on farming rather than hunting, building permanent homes and giving
up mobility, and not living in camps but spreading out. Milburn
stressed to these Cheyenne homesteaders that if they did not follow
the letter of the law, there would be Euro-American settlers who would
watch for every opportunity to defeat their patents for their claims.
He admitted he was impressed by the efforts of the Cheyenne homesteading along the Rosebud, noting that they all had houses and had
begun to farm successfully.

Milburn compared the Cheyennes on the Rosebud, who he claimed
"excite some admiration for what an Indian can do when given even

meager opportunity coupled with wise counsel," to the Cheyennes along Hanging Woman and Otter Creeks, who he claimed "show how helpless they are when misguided."[31] Only two members of Black Wolf's camp had built houses; the rest still lived in tipis and subsisted on hunting. They also kept their horses because they needed them to hunt, and they remained highly mobile. In his 1883 report S. W. Millen, a member of the Fifth Infantry stationed at Fort Keogh who was assigned to oversee these homesteaders, mentioned that at the time of his visit, Black Wolf and White Bull were both visiting the Arapahos on their reservation.[32] The Cheyennes of White Bull's camp did not build their own houses. Yoakam either purchased the structures for them, or they paid Euro-American settlers to build them. Those who had built houses crowded them close together, neglecting the entreaty to build them far enough apart to conform to the regulations of the Homestead Act.

The numerous reports demanded by federal officials and Milburn's comparison of these two groups makes one thing clear: in 1883 officials were interested in supporting those Cheyennes who were conforming their settlements to the Homestead Act but still felt the need to contain those who were not. Milburn divided them into two groups: the Rosebud Cheyennes, who he claimed had already succeeded, and the Hanging Woman and Otter Creek Cheyennes, who he claimed had not been given the opportunity to succeed. His solution was to get rid of George Yoakam, whom he believed had misguided these Cheyennes. He recommended the appointment of a trustworthy white man to direct those who selected claims and the removal to a reservation of those who did not.[33]

Later in 1883, S. W. Millen submitted another report about the Northern Cheyenne homesteaders. From his tour of the Cheyenne homesteads, Millen concluded that although the people had good houses and gardens, they were not able to support themselves from these efforts. He argued, "These people have been encouraged to locate on ranches by Government Officials in high authority and now that they have done as advised they should receive some help." He went on to relate that many of the Cheyennes living in the area had been led to believe that they would receive some sort of help from the government. Millen argued that without this aid, they would be less likely to succeed and become self-sufficient. He reiterated much of Milburn's report, declaring that the Cheyennes on the Rosebud were succeeding but the Cheyennes on Hanging Woman and Otter Creeks needed assistance. In fact, he lambasted Black Wolf's band as lazy with no desire to take homesteads and work the land. Millen also agreed with Milburn, arguing that Black Wolf's band had an ill effect on the others settled in the area, suggesting that they be sent back to Pine Ridge.[34]

These reports indicate that although the idea of a reservation had been proposed, these officials had not seriously considered it. Officials at the time sought to incorporate all Native people within U.S. geopolitical boundaries under the umbrella of the state. According to the thought of the period, homesteading severed American Indian people from their sense of group identity. In the eyes of these officials, assimilating them into the state involved building permanent homes meant to hold nuclear families, spacing these homes far from each other, forcing each nuclear family to become self-supporting using their own land and labor, and ending dependence on the extended family network that was central to Native social and political organization.[35] In this way, homesteading, like the allotment policy that followed, was meant to break apart Native nations and incorporate the members into the state. Government officials believed that they had to divest potential homesteaders of anything disruptive to these activities. They felt the need to control Black Wolf and White Bull because the Northern Cheyennes following these leaders did not put effort into their homesteads, but more dangerous than their unwillingness to take up the accouterments of civilization was their continued dependence on mobility and kinship networks. While government officials might not have recognized the full political ramifications of kinship as it pertained to Native nationhood, they certainly recognized that extended kin networks gave Plains people an autonomy that allowed them to forgo incorporation into the state. For many government officials, Plains people resistant to full assimilation belonged on reservations where they could be more rigidly contained and where they could more gradually learn to accept the boundaries of U.S. citizenship.

None of the Northern Cheyennes abandoned their kinship networks, but officials were blinded to this among those who appeared to adopt the lifestyles approved by the state. Establishing the Cheyennes in permanent houses, farms, and nuclear families was seen as a path to American citizenship. Although the Cheyennes on the Rosebud continued to leave their camps to hunt, including buffalo hunts, and to visit family on other reservations, they had built homes and were attempting to farm. In the eyes of U.S. officials, the houses and fields symbolized the severing of Cheyenne nationhood and the adoption of American individualism. To them, the evidence of these severed relations lay in lifestyle. Once Native people adopted a Euro-American lifestyle, officials believed they automatically severed their widespread kin networks—in other words, their tribal relations. They never realized that the flexibility of Native social organization could accommodate this new way of life. Their state-based assumptions of political organization blinded officials to the fact that homesteading did not actually dismantle the Cheyenne nation.

Instead, the flexibility homesteading granted these Cheyenne families fed their Native nation. Some Northern Cheyennes built cabins and fences and began growing gardens. Others simply put up tents or tipis on land they hoped to claim. Still others camped near another family who was working a homestead. Yet even people who had cabins continued to travel, leaving their homesteads to visit family and friends in distant places and attend important events. They did not let the boundary of a homestead pin them in place as the reservations were meant to do. In this way, many Northern Cheyennes maintained their freedom by taking up homesteads and beginning to garden and ranch, often supporting themselves entirely. These families were last issued rations in December 1877, and they did not receive more until January 1884 with the establishment of the reservation. Ewers stated, "They fed and clothed themselves, bought their wagons and harnesses, built and furnished their houses, with money received from the sale of buffalo robes, produce and ponies and what was earned by work and scouting."[36] This spatial and economic freedom allowed them to come and go as they pleased. By adopting homesteading, an institution of the nation-state, they had secured land in the heart of their homeland, freedom to hunt and continue ceremonies, and the ability to maintain their own social life and kin ties with family far away. They also managed to live outside the constant surveillance of the U.S. government. It surely looked to many federal officials as if these Plains peoples had given up their tribal life, when in fact they had used an institution the federal government created to continue their Native nation by maintaining land, mobility, and kin ties.

Nevertheless, homesteading did not become the ultimate solution to the Northern Cheyenne people's fight to remain in their homeland. Because the territory was not yet surveyed, when American settlers chose land in the area, their claims began to overlap with Cheyenne claims.[37] Once American settlers came into conflict with Cheyenne families over this land, homestead boundaries lost their previous stability. By 1883 these settlers were beginning to voice complaints about their Northern Cheyenne neighbors. When Black Wolf's band arrived in Montana from the Pine Ridge reservation, more Cheyennes moved from Fort Keogh into the Tongue River area, and American homesteaders became restless at the growing Cheyenne population. A small group of American ranchers launched a complaint out of Miles City that these homesteaders were irresponsible and that they killed cattle. They argued that these Northern Cheyenne settlers must have killed and consumed their cattle because there was no wild game to be had in the area and they did not grow enough of their own food to subsist. In his 1883 report, Milburn investigated the claims of these cattlemen and found them to be unsubstantiated, stating that the ranchers failed to provide any evidence. Furthermore, when he visited with the Northern Cheyenne and the non-Native skin dealers in the area, he saw that these Cheyennes had procured hundreds of deerskins, as well as antelope and buffalo hides.[38] From these hides, he determined that there was plenty of game to sustain all the Cheyennes who were living there. Clearly the American settlers had committed themselves to driving out the Cheyenne homesteaders any way they could in order to gain this prime ranching land.

American settlers also fought against a Northern Cheyenne reservation in the Tongue River valley. They did not want to see land carved out from what they believed to be their ranch lands and began crying for yet another removal. A new inspector, named M. R. Barr, was sent to the region to examine the conditions there and report on prospects for removal. He found that actually not all American Montanans were eager for a removal. For example, local merchants opposed it because they feared that if the Cheyennes were removed, the military would depart from Fort Keogh, dramatically decreasing their clientele. In fact, only ranchers involved in large-scale cattle interests that required open range actively sought removal; small-scale ranchers who combined raising stock with farming were indifferent on the matter.[39]

The Cheyennes who spoke with Barr were adamant about their legitimacy in the area. Barr wrote a report that spoke fondly of the Northern Cheyennes and discouraged removal. He related that Two Moons reminded him that his people had been born in the Tongue River country and that their relationship with General Miles ensured their rights to live in their homeland. He recommended that a reservation be established along the Rosebud, which he stated had the best farmland. He argued that they required an agent who would live with them and ensure their success at farming.[40] Removal would have solved the dispute between American and Cheyenne settlers in the Tongue River valley, but government officials remained unconvinced of the benefits, particularly since removal had proved to be such a devastating failure only a few years earlier.

At the same time, homesteading also had problems government officials were not able to solve. Some of the Northern Cheyennes took homesteads and began gardening and ranching quite successfully, while others built houses they abandoned, and still others simply camped in tipis as they always had. Captain Ewers, Special Agent Milburn, and Millen all emphasized in their reports that while some Cheyenne homesteaders flourished, all the Northern Cheyennes in the Tongue River region could use an agent of some kind to oversee their progress and provide them with the supplies they needed. In August 1884 Captain Ewers sent another letter to the commissioner of Indian affairs, attempting to settle the situation one more time. He reminded the commissioner that the condition of the people was constantly improving and argued that a reliable agent living among them would be invaluable. He noted again that only some homesteads were progressing and that game would run out at some point; without learning to farm and ranch, the Northern Cheyennes would be in great want of food and clothing. He stated that the agents had been residing at Miles City and argued that this was simply too far for them to be of much use. Ewers recommended that an agent live with the Northern Cheyennes and that "a sufficient amount of land on the Rosebud and its tributaries in the vicinity of the Cheyenne settlement be set aside for the Northern Cheyenne Indians, and that each Indian be given one hundred and sixty acres of land."[41] He believed that the Cheyennes living along Otter Creek and Tongue River should move closer to the Rosebud so that they could all easily get help from an agent.

For these officials, the Rosebud was naturally the place to set aside land. The Cheyenne homesteaders living there fit their current definition of successful assimilation, while at Otter Creek and Tongue River, many Cheyennes were still living in tipis and subsisting from the game they hunted. It surely made sense to protect the Cheyennes who would represent American success at assimilation and bring the ones who were still wayward into the same fold. Establishing a reservation that would preserve the already established homesteads and encourage others to take up plots of land seemed the best way to keep the whole group on the path to civilization. It had proven difficult to convince all the Cheyennes in the area to take up homesteads, and it was steadily becoming more difficult to ensure that the people who had homesteads would be able to file for a patent in the time the law allowed. For these officials, the solution was a reservation.

By October, Price, the commissioner of Indian affairs, had sent Milburn back to investigate the possible imposition of reservation boundaries. Milburn reiterated that even the Northern Cheyennes on the Rosebud had not cultivated that much land, but he stated that he would preserve the Rosebud homesteads in the reservation as he was instructed to do. Government officials seemed concerned that homesteading through patents would fail, and so a small reservation, where the Cheyennes could be instructed on how to farm on individual plots of land, was the solution. Yet in his plan, Milburn did not carve out 160 acres per family, on the basis that this was simply too much land. He suggested that the Northern Cheyennes move to the nearby Crow reservation, where they would already have an agent and the land was better.[42] Inspector Barr had previously established that this was not to the liking of either the Crows or the Cheyennes, yet this suggestion would continue to haunt the people for sixteen years.

Despite the ever-present phantom of removal, on November 26, 1884, President Chester A. Arthur passed the executive order that established the boundaries of the Northern Cheyenne reservation.[43] The executive order followed the suggestion of Barr and others to include the land around the Rosebud River and Muddy Creek, but it did not stretch east to include the Northern Cheyennes who had settled along both banks of the Tongue River. On paper the government recognized the boundaries of a Northern Cheyenne reservation, yet the land had still not been surveyed. Non-Cheyenne homesteaders often did not bother to discover where the reservation boundaries were located when claiming land. In fact, Ewers stated that as late as 1887, "the reservation lines were not known by citizens living on and near the same."[44] Although many Northern Cheyennes most likely did not know, either, undoubtedly it mattered little to them. They were more interested in establishing a presence in the area that was recognized by the United States than ensuring the sanctity of boundary lines. Regardless of American boundaries, they knew where their land ended and began and surely felt that they could travel across their homeland no matter what kind of boundaries the United States had set up. They had established this precedent with General Miles since 1880 and certainly understood boundaries as representative of these social relations and not as lines created by documents. At this point, they were more interested in securing a place to live where they would not be removed. The reservation set such a precedent regardless of its physical boundaries.

Just after Chester Arthur passed this executive order, a group of ranchers claiming to represent the citizens of Montana sent a memorandum to the president arguing that he should revoke it. The letter declared that the order was ineffective and that the land was unsuitable for the Cheyennes. It concluded by insisting that the Cheyennes did not need a northern reservation, claiming, "These few Indians who have attempted to avail themselves of the benefits of the Act of March 3, 1875, need no protection, and those who are wild and roving should be sent back to the reservations from which they broke, in defiance of the United States."[45] They argued that the Cheyennes who had taken homesteads did not need a reservation because they were protected under the Indian Homestead Act. All other Cheyennes in the area, and they specifically named Black Wolf and those following him, were there illegally according to their argument and should be sent to other reservations.

According to the letter, "wild Cheyennes," or those who roved and had no houses, belonged on reservations. Those who had built homes and had apparently attempted to live like white men should be left alone to sink or swim. The conclusion reiterated this point, stating, "The policy of the Department has been to cut down Indian Reserves, not to increase them; to force or encourage Indians to take lands in severalty or by allotment, not to herd them on reserves." The argument at first glance appears to be most concerned about the Northern Cheyennes' progress toward civilization, yet a closer look reveals these ranchers' concerns about loss of land. They argued that because these Cheyennes were free to take homesteads, there was no reason to create reservation boundaries and close thoroughfares. They worried about being shut off of the land where they ran their cattle, and they saw these reservation borders as unfair restrictions on their access. In the conclusion they stated that they never believed that one day "they should be forced to warn their friends at home not to join them in Montana on Government land, for fear that the Government might imprison them within an Indian Reservation among savages." They closed with, "This is a calamity and is a bar to our development."[46] For these ranchers, development required open land therefore establishing reservation borders hampered this flow of Western progress. They did not refuse the Northern Cheyennes the right to participate, but they resented any encouragement from the government. They argued that if the Northern Cheyennes could not succeed at ranching or farming, they should be taken away from the area and contained so that they would not get in the way of the progress of others.

The argument put forth by this handful of Montana ranchers followed American ideologies of manifest destiny through taming the landscape. For this group, the federal government had adopted a plan to assimilate American Indian people in hopes that they would eventually no longer need to maintain reservations. Why establish a new reservation? Why not force the Northern Cheyennes to return to the reservations they escaped? Although the Northern Cheyennes had no reservation of their own and were designated by treaties to Pine Ridge and Indian Territory, U.S. officials continued to support their presence in Montana even though they would take prime ranch land.

It is tempting to turn to the Fort Robinson breakout as an explanation, but there is little evidence to suggest that this tragedy forced the hand of the government. Although the events of 1879 and activists' outcries about them surely had an effect on policy, the breakout did not end the conversation about removal. Furthermore, the United States waited for five years after the massacre to establish the reservation. They did not seem eager to purge their guilt over the tragedy by protecting the Cheyennes' presence in their homeland. In fact, officials clearly disagreed over the best course of action when it came to the Northern Cheyennes. Yoakam argued for a reservation from the beginning, while Miles and other officers at Fort Keogh believed homesteading was the answer. Still others in Montana and Washington, D.C., considered removal to the Crow reservation. Furthermore, Little Chief remained at Pine Ridge, waiting for any indication he would be allowed to join his relatives in the north for almost a decade. Although some local and federal government officials seemed ready to accept a Cheyenne presence in Montana, they argued over exactly the best spot and the best method for years.

Even after the 1884 executive order passed and was put into effect, the Northern Cheyenne reservation still required a compromise between several factions. Because the reservation land was not surveyed and no official boundary lines were drawn, little changed on the ground, and the Cheyennes' presence in the area was still under threat by American settlers. The government did not assign an Indian agent to the reservation until 1886, and the people living inside the reservation continued to travel outside of its boundaries to the Tongue River or Fort Keogh or even Pine Ridge to accept rations. The boundary lines had little meaning because they were never enforced with the Cheyennes or the American settlers. Although Inspector Barr stated that he had convinced the Cheyennes living on the Tongue River to move within the confines of the reservation, nothing ever came of this; they were not asked to move and did not volunteer to do so.[47] Furthermore, some American settlers persisted in their push for removal to the Crow reservation, and government officials continued to consider this recourse. In hindsight, it is easy to assume that the 1884 executive order was the final step to settling the Northern Cheyennes in Montana, but this was really only one step in a long process continuing through the 1900 executive order and into the twentieth century.

So if the 1884 executive order failed to end the debate, then why pass it in the first place? If the Northern Cheyennes managed to settle in the heart of their homeland, why establish a reservation? It seems there were two concerns, one for Miles and Yoakam that white settlers would usurp the land and thereby drive the Cheyennes into dependency, and the other for government officials in Washington that the Northern Cheyennes would not be able to maintain their homesteads or demonstrate that they were assimilating without the security and guidance of an agent and a reservation. Although George Yoakam's barrage of letters surely had some effect on the decision, the encroachment of white settlers onto Northern Cheyenne claims sealed the need for a protected land base. At a time when federal officials proclaimed wholeheartedly Native people's desire to completely assimilate into what they considered civilized society, they certainly did not want to risk the surefire success story of the Northern Cheyenne warriors-turned-scouts by allowing white settlers to usurp land. By this point in time, it seemed that this group who fought at Little Bighorn would assimilate, proving to the United States that their Indian policy was finally on course. They also knew, however, that these Northern Cheyennes would need more support than they had been given.

So the government attempted to move established homesteaders to a reservation. They had tried homesteading and it was working for some, but not for everyone. In the 1880s the government shifted their policy about Native land because they began to link economic development in the West to total assimilation. The anthropologist Alice Fletcher helped to convince the United States of the importance of land in severalty, arguing that division of reservation lands into homesteads would protect American Indian populations from removal and dispossession so that they could concentrate on learning to support themselves through farming.[48] Surely the federal government saw the same situation but in reverse with the Northern Cheyennes. They had homesteads but no legally recognized right to that land, and a reservation would help protect those homesteads. With a reservation and an agent, Cheyenne settlers could go on working their homesteads and therefore progressing, but the American homesteaders would no longer have legal recourse to push them out.

Although government officials were caught in an undercurrent of assimilation at the time, many also believed that the Northern Cheyennes had a right to live in the Tongue River valley. In part, they were convinced by the arguments of Two Moons and others who insisted that the Cheyennes belonged on this land for two reasons: one, that they were born here and their ancestors were buried here, and two, that it was promised to them by General Miles. Military and other federal officials certainly justified these arguments in a different way from the Northern Cheyennes' understanding. Most likely they found these statements convincing because they could understand the desire to be in the place your forefathers lived, but not because they believed that relatedness equated to a political relationship with the landscape. They also surely believed that because these scouts had aided in subduing those whom American officials saw as some of the most significant hostile Native holdouts, finally making the West safe for settlement, the United States should honor Miles's promise of land. After all, these negotiations were taking place in a time when the United States emphasized not just assimilation but also honor in relationships with Native nations.[49] Some U.S. officials identified with Cheyenne arguments about homeland, family, and honor. While these officials certainly did not support Cheyenne political autonomy, there was enough commonality in the language of kin to convince them to safeguard the Cheyenne people's home in the north.

Ironically, over time, many reservations became a way for American Indian peoples to retain their political autonomy instead of a means to destroy it.[50] This was true for the Northern Cheyenne reservation from the start. The people were fighting for a permanent home on land they recognized as their own and were willing to accept a certain amount of American administration to accomplish that end, but they certainly never gave up their own sense of nationhood in the process. Ms. DG described her ancestors' determination to me, saying that the people wanted to remain independent on their own land. She explained that the Northern Cheyennes wanted a place of their own, and they knew that if they lived on any of their treaty reservations with either the Southern Cheyennes and Arapahos in Indian Territory, the Northern Arapahos at Wind River, or the Lakotas at Pine Ridge, they would still have to share an agent and resources and most importantly live by rules made for someone else, even though all these peoples were their relatives.[51] While they had political ties with each of these groups and never thought of themselves as a separate nation from their southern relatives, they wanted to be able to make decisions on their own and not be affected by the needs, wants, and pressures of another group. She pointed out that the Northern Arapahos had to compromise with the Shoshones, and the Southern Cheyennes had to compromise with the Southern Arapahos. If the Northern Cheyennes stayed in the south, they would have had to consider the Southerners, and if they stayed at Pine Ridge, they would have had to consider the Lakotas. Any reservation federal officials offered would tie the fate of the people to another community; they saw how bad this was for the Northern Arapahos and had tried in Indian Territory to deal with this themselves.[52]

The Northern Cheyennes wanted their own space where they could remain autonomous. The people who had fought so hard to stay in the Tongue River valley believed it was best to have their own reservation, Ms. DG said, so that they could be in charge of their own land and have their own agency and in this way retain independence.[53] If they could make their own decisions, they could be sure what they did was best for their people.[54] From the way that Northern Cheyenne people talk about their reservation today, it is clear that they do not see the place as a loss but a gain. The reservation provided them with the chance to remain securely in their homeland and with the opportunity for a certain degree of autonomy. It seems apparent that the Northern Cheyennes at the time believed that securing land would ensure their ability to shape their destiny, and they still do today. Certainly, reservations were a colonial imposition created to contain and control Native people, but by strategically manipulating these boundaries, the Northern Cheyennes continued to assert an autonomous sense of Native nationhood even while living under the domination of a foreign state.

By maintaining their ties to kin regardless of what government officials did, the Northern Cheyennes were able to return to and remain in their homeland. This determination did not end with the establishment of the reservation. Despite the introduction of reservation boundaries, the Northern Cheyennes strove to continue to live according to their own cultural order. It seems that their alliance with Miles, their ability to navigate the restrictions of the nation-state, and their ability to redirect these restrictions to comply with their own cultural order had served them well. At the heart of each of these struggles was the family, the solid relationship with Miles, the kinship ties that allowed the Cheyennes to circumvent the restrictions imposed by government officials, and the strength of intergenerational familial support to continue to maintain their own cultural order while acculturating to life under American domination.

Today some Northern Cheyennes point to the acculturation required to establish the relationship with General Miles as central to the founding of the reservation. Ms. DG stated that those who scouted for Miles made a great sacrifice. She said that they gave up some of their old ways, stopped moving across the plains, and stayed in one place. They also fought for the U.S. military at times against their own friends. She pointed to these sacrifices as the way the Northern Cheyennes eventually obtained their own reservation in Montana. She also indicated that their relationship with Miles helped them win their land. She stated that the Northern Cheyennes at Fort Keogh had a very close relationship with the general; he was their good friend and they placed a lot of trust in him. In turn, he upheld that relationship and the obligations that came with it, fighting hard to win the Northern Cheyennes a reservation of their own.[55] This Northern Cheyenne elder spoke of these Cheyenne scouts who gave up so much with high esteem. Ms. DG did not characterize their actions as assimilationist or as traitorous to her people but instead spoke of these sacrifices with respect and recognition of their ultimate power.

When the Northern Cheyennes became scouts, they were no longer able to travel the plains as freely as they once had. Nevertheless, life at Fort Keogh and on homesteads did not limit their mobility like reservation boundaries did for most Native nations. Again the people used their fluid social structure to remain mobile. Under these circumstances, the Northern Cheyennes could maintain their kin relations with those outside of their immediate community without being regulated by an agent. Furthermore, because the Northern Cheyennes had no agent and therefore received no rations, many who had connections at Pine Ridge continued to travel from their homes in the Tongue River area to Pine Ridge to collect rations and bring them back.[56] Even during the reservation period, Cheyenne peoples depended on far-reaching familial ties to sustain their presence in their homeland.

Despite the reservation boundaries and vigilant assimilating efforts of the government, the Northern Cheyennes continued using their mobility and their kinship relations in order not simply to survive but to survive as an autonomous people. They lived in the Tongue River valley and established homes there, but they remained free to travel and thus maintained their kin connections. This mobility, which kept them connected, also prevented excessive U.S. control over their lives. The safety net of off-reservation family provided the people with a certain amount of autonomy. Homesteads were an important part of this independence, and by refusing to acquiesce to the reservation border, by continuing to live on homesteads outside of it, and by moving freely on and off the reservation, the Northern Cheyennes maintained leverage to circumvent government policy. Ironically, while the government officials, policy makers, social scientists, and activists of the time believed dividing property by the nuclear family would connect people to the land in a way that would lead them to Western civilization, the Northern Cheyennes continued to maintain ties to extended family through mobility, which kept them connected to their land and ensured their continuance as a people despite the assimilationist tactics of the government. By maintaining their relationships while appearing to sever them, the Northern Cheyennes could retain their land and therefore assert some political autonomy over their lives, even if it was limited by the state.

CHAPTER EIGHT

Make Us Strong on This Reservation

The Northern Cheyennes' Struggle to Remain in Their Homeland

Mr. BC and I had just finished balling up newspapers and stuffing them between logs, carefully stacked in a pyramid around a pile of lava rocks. He taught me that you only need to hold your lighter to a couple of pieces of the newspaper and the dry wood will catch easily. We retreated to the plastic chairs that looked like they had come from an elementary school and watched the results of our handiwork. We had time to relax, smoke, and chat before we needed to fix the blankets on the lodge and get ready for the sweat. Sitting side by side, staring out at the road, our conversation wandered from the hot weather to the struggles of romantic relationships to my research.

"I still don't understand why the government expanded the reservation in 1900," I mused. "It just seems so strange."

"Well, they didn't expand it far enough," Mr. BC told me. I assumed he was simply commenting on the fact that the reservation failed to cover what the Northern Cheyennes saw as their true territory. I had no idea that I was missing the point. By then, I did know enough to let go of my assumptions and keep asking questions.

"They didn't?" I replied, hopeful.

"No, they didn't," he responded. "They drove a bunch of Indians living east of the Tongue River off their allotments."

"What?" I asked, sitting up and looking him in the eye for the first time since we sat down. Now I was completely confused. I could hear the frustration in his voice. He obviously felt this was a true injustice committed by the U.S. government. I hadn't heard anything about Cheyenne landholders east of the Tongue River, and I had spent a lot of time in the archives. I was also confused because I thought that the Cheyennes were not allotted until after the 1900 expansion. Later I discovered that I was correct about this. The Northern Cheyennes were not allotted until 1926. He was using allotment as a general marker to refer to land in private Cheyenne ownership.

As we watched the fire climb on that hot summer afternoon, Mr. BC told me that in 1900 there were Northern Cheyennes who had settled and taken homesteads on the east bank of the Tongue River. When the government expanded the reservation, these people were forced to give up their homesteads and move across the river onto the new reservation. He stated that they had signed a paper that they did not understand and only got twenty-five dollars to move. He remembered that his grandparents and others of that generation repeatedly asked about that land. They wondered why they had been forced to leave and why they had never been allowed to return. He realized the rocks were getting hotter and suggested that we start to fix the blankets and get ready for the sweat, but before we got up he said to me, "It would be good if you wrote about this; it would be really good."

After this conversation, I looked for evidence in the archives about what had happened to these Cheyenne homesteaders. I was especially curious about the twenty-five-dollar payment for their land. It seemed such a pathetic amount that I could not believe it was true. Maybe he meant $2,500, I thought, as I searched. In the end, I discovered he was correct about the payment, and that the people were dramatically underpaid at the time. Mr. BC had helped me uncover another moment forgotten by most history books.[1] Apparently, the establishment of the Northern Cheyenne reservation in 1884 had not ended the threats to a permanent Cheyenne land base in the north. From 1884 until 1900, American ranchers continued to challenge the reservation boundaries, hoping for access to more land. These boundaries were essentially ignored by the Northern Cheyennes who continued to live in the patterns they had established on returning to this part of their homeland. Their agents struggled to impose the reservation boundaries to keep ranchers out but never pressured the Cheyenne families homesteading outside of the boundaries. Contradictions emerged as local agents tried to carry out the federal policy of the first executive order while at the same time attempting to do what they believed was best for the Cheyenne. In order to end the confusion, President William McKinley expanded the boundaries with another executive order in 1900. This expansion was the culmination of a process in which kinship again played an important role. Although the expansion ultimately brought all Northern Cheyennes within the boundaries of the reservation, the people continued to utilize kinship in their negotiations with the United States because they continued to understand their relationship to the land as legitimated by social organization based on kin.

U.S. officials finally recognized the Northern Cheyennes' need to live in the Tongue River valley, first by encouraging homesteading and then by establishing a reservation. Yet even as the turn of the nineteenth century approached, the people continued to be threatened with removal. Despite the protests of local officials, federal policy makers pressed the idea that these Cheyennes should be removed from the Tongue River reservation and settled on the Crow reservation. Federal officials proposed to move them only a short distance onto land with which the Northern Cheyennes had a lasting relationship; it also contained favored camping sites.[2] Nevertheless, they would lose the independence of having their own reservation and an agent who only considered the interests of the Northern Cheyenne people. Even though removal to the Crow reservation allowed the Northern Cheyennes to remain in the north within the heart of their homeland, the Cheyenne people stood firmly against it. They did not want to share a reservation, especially not with their old enemies. They needed their own space to make their own decisions and maintain their own sense of Native nationhood.

Although the Northern Cheyennes obtained recognition of their legal rights to a small piece of their northern homeland through the 1884 executive order, the reservation boundaries certainly did not confine them. The Cheyenne people crossed them to hunt, work, and visit relatives. Some Northern Cheyennes even built homes and lived outside this boundary. Social ties had more power determining their relationship to the landscape than geopolitical boundaries. In the eyes of Americans, however, geopolitical boundaries were essential to defining a relationship to territory. Officials believed that Native people were under the power of the state and had to acquiesce to whatever boundary lines were drawn.[3] Defining Indian lands often became an ambiguous activity, as federal officials attempted to establish a permanent bounded landscape to contain Native peoples, while continually having to shift these boundaries for other political reasons. Although U.S. representatives had established the border of the 1884 reservation, the local officials disregarded the boundary because it was too impractical to enforce.

By 1900, the Northern Cheyenne people had not only escaped removal to the Crow reservation, they had convinced the United States to grant them a new executive order expanding the reservation to encompass more Cheyenne homesteaders. Nevertheless, this expansion was not an unequivocal victory for them. The reservation gained 204,000 acres, so that with the 1900 executive order, it contained a total of 460,000 acres.[4] But the Northern Cheyennes lost recognition of ownership of land to which they had laid claim through homesteading on the east side of the Tongue River. The Cheyennes who had built homesteads on the east bank lost their land, houses, barns, and any other work they had put into their claims, receiving almost no compensation for their loss.

Officials continued to apply American Indian policy in contradictory ways. Both federal and local agents had encouraged homesteading for the Northern Cheyennes as an effort to assimilate the people into the polity of the United States. At the same time, the efforts of both federal and local officials to solidify the reservation boundaries undermined Northern Cheyenne efforts at homesteading. As the twentieth century unfolded, the people would face more threats to their land base. Throughout these struggles, they continued to exercise their autonomy, using both Euro-American political mechanisms and social relations based on kinship. The Northern Cheyennes have always emphasized the centrality of their northern landscape to their survival as a nation. Regardless of the fluctuations and whims of changing federal administrations, they have managed to maintain their relationship to the land through kin-based connections.

As early as 1882, George Yoakam began fighting to keep non-Native settlers away from the homesteads the Northern Cheyennes had started along the Tongue River. In December 1882 a town site was being proposed in the area, and Yoakam wrote to President Arthur in an attempt to prevent it. He noted that there were 610 Cheyennes who had taken homesteads in the area and "if white men should start a town within the limits of the Cheyenne settlement that they would be overrunning the Indians' settlement." He continued that because non-Native settlers had the same rights as Native settlers to homestead in the area, the Cheyennes would be difficult to protect without a reservation.[5] Yoakam asked for this land to be reserved for them because believed that the Northern Cheyennes needed protection from American settlers so they could establish homesteads, not to retain their autonomy but to begin their path toward Western civilized life. As the farm educator for the Plains peoples at Fort Keogh, he also had a strong personal interest in preventing their removal. Permanent settlement in the region would secure his post.

Establishing a reservation in 1884, however, did not solve the problems with American settlers overrunning the land the Northern Cheyennes had claimed. These boundaries only encompassed some Northern Cheyenne homesteads. Many families had settled on both banks of the Tongue River, miles away from the new eastern reservation border. In December 1884, one month after the executive order established the Northern Cheyenne reservation, George Yoakam was pleading for a larger reservation. He asked President Arthur to set aside a space large enough for all the Cheyennes in Montana as well as all those still residing at Pine Ridge. This reservation would encompass both banks of the Tongue River, and even extend down Hanging Woman and Otter Creeks. He asked that the Northern Cheyennes have an agent of their own and not be attached to the Crow agent because there was enough to do among the Cheyennes alone. Yoakam proclaimed that, "The chief reason that the Indians are not progressing more rapidly is because of insufficient Indian appropriations."[6] Yoakam's proposal would bring all Northern Cheyenne homesteads within the boundaries of the reservation and provide an agent who would concentrate only on Northern Cheyenne needs.

From the sincerity of his letters and the sheer volume of them, apparently Yoakam believed he had the best interests of the Northern Cheyennes at heart. In 1884 he was fighting to bring the Cheyennes living at Pine Ridge back to Montana. He asked for reservation boundaries that suited the needs of the Cheyenne people, not the government or the American settlers in the area. Most importantly, he wanted appropriations from the Indian Office, which he believed would allow the Cheyennes to succeed at farming. Yoakam would also personally benefit from larger boundaries, as well as a more populous reservation. As an employee of the Indian Office, his job depended on federal support for teaching Native people to establish Euro-American-style farming operations. If he could succeed in the eyes of federal officials, perhaps he would be granted a higher position. This young officer worked closely with Cheyenne households, which certainly must have affected his suggestions. Surely Cheyenne homesteaders took advantage of the captive audience, especially to impress on him the importance of safeguarding Cheyenne lands. While Yoakam's ultimate goal was probably to build his career, he could also become a mouthpiece for some of the things the Cheyennes wanted for their own community.

Although many Northern Cheyennes lived outside the reservation border, they did not believe they were unprotected on their land. They did not seek to move their homesteads within the boundaries; they simply stayed where they were and continued the work they had begun a few years earlier. As Cheyennes, they held an inalienable relationship to this land for many reasons. First, they had been camping in the area for generations. When the military sought to remove them in the 1870s, they fought and won two decisive battles, the Battle Where the Girl Saved Her Brother and the Battle of the Little Bighorn. Most importantly, they did not surrender to the U.S. government after Crook and Mackenzie's winter campaign; instead, they created an alliance with Generals Miles and Crook, which Miles had honored. This alliance meant that the Northern Cheyennes had retained the privilege to hunt, travel, and live within the territory that Miles oversaw. The Cheyennes living in the area could not have believed the reservation boundaries were of much importance in comparison with the people's long-established relationship with this land. They knew that reservation boundaries were physical evidence that the federal government recognized the Cheyennes had a relationship with this territory, but these boundaries certainly did not encompass or define that relationship.

Federal officials knew that there were Northern Cheyennes living outside the reservation boundary whose land was protected by the Indian Homestead Act. Some officials endeavored to find a way to remove these families from their claims. By the summer of 1885, the commissioner of Indian affairs had already sent another investigator, E. D. Banister, U.S. special Indian agent, to the reservation with the purpose of selecting a land base for the Northern Cheyennes. The commissioner declared that Milburn's earlier report was marred because he had recently become the attorney for the citizens of Montana who were calling for the revocation of the reservation he himself had recommended.[7] The commissioner sent Banister in an effort to create a less biased report. One of Banister's stated goals was to bring all the Northern Cheyennes within the boundaries of the reservation. In June the Northern Cheyennes living along the Tongue and Rosebud Rivers held a council with Banister, and he convinced them to sign an agreement to remove "at any time we may be ordered and . . . to any location which may be selected."[8]

In July of the same year, Banister had prepared a report for the commissioner of Indian affairs. He stated that he told the Cheyennes in the council meeting that they would not be able to receive rations unless they agreed to remove to any location the commissioner of Indian affairs chose. Not even a year after the reservation had been established, the Indian Office was trying to lay groundwork for the removal of all Northern Cheyennes. Banister recommended that all the Northern Cheyennes in the Tongue River valley be placed on a reservation and given allotments, so that "they can then be fully protected from the white settler and encouraged in farming and grazing."[9] The recommendation of a reservation was meant to safeguard the process of establishing the Cheyennes as farmers and to protect Cheyenne homesteaders. Regardless, Banister's plan would strip many Northern Cheyennes of their homesteads—lands they had legally claimed through the mechanisms of the state.

Banister reiterated Milburn's suggestion that the Northern Cheyennes be moved onto the Crow reservation, arguing that none of the land along the Rosebud where many people had homesteaded was suitable for farming. He recommended that the president revoke the

1884 executive order and open negotiations with the Crow Indians to purchase part of their reservation.[10] This suggestion solved several problems for representatives in the federal government. They would not have to worry about disgruntled white settlers, they could encourage the Northern Cheyennes to become farmers, and they would not have to carve out more land to reserve.

In June the commissioner of Indian affairs, John D. C. Atkins, pointed out that Banister's plan was not as simple as it appeared because the Cheyennes who had taken homesteads had plenty of protection. Their lands were inalienable and not taxable for twenty years, the Cheyennes could make homestead entries without paying fees, and white settlers were not allowed to take up claims on Indian homesteads.[11] In a dramatic swing to the other side of the debate, the same commissioner suggested in October 1885 that the Northern Cheyenne reservation be returned to public domain because the people did not need a reservation. He recommended that the Cheyennes in the area be allowed to retain and improve their land, but he had also composed an executive order to revoke the reservation which he recommended to the president.[12] The secretary of the interior, L. C. Larson, responded that because many investigations had been made, he was postponing the decision.

Larson explained that many of the Cheyennes appeared unwilling to leave their residences, and most who lived outside the current reservation boundaries refused to move onto it. He proposed that in order to satisfy the Cheyennes who refused to move and the American settlers who feared a reservation, the department should have sufficient land surveyed where the Cheyennes were living to locate those living outside the reservation on homesteads, restore the reservation to public domain, survey these lands, and place the Cheyennes there on homesteads as well. No American settlers would be allowed to settle in the area until all the Cheyennes had homesteads, and once they were located on individual tracts, the department would have to put effort into helping them build houses and farm.[13] Despite the many suggestions, the Cheyennes were never moved to the Crow reservation, nor was Larson's plan carried out. Although the land was finally surveyed in 1888 with the intention of removing all the Northern Cheyennes on the east bank of the Tongue River onto homesteads on the west bank, the original executive order was never revoked.

The discussions over the Northern Cheyenne reservation clearly exposed the tensions embedded in the ideals of the nation-state when dealing with its Indigenous inhabitants. Certain federal officials believed that the government should revoke the reservation so that the Northern Cheyennes could be more quickly incorporated as U.S. citizens. With homesteads and without a reservation, these officials believed the Northern Cheyennes would give up their autonomous sense of nationhood, including their cultural beliefs and customs, for an American way of life. Ultimately, they would be fully incorporated members of the nation-state, eventually taking on the role of citizen. This plan, however, never came to fruition. On the other side of the debate, officials believed that because Native people were incapable of full incorporation, the Cheyennes should be contained on a reservation under the tight control of an agent, and the land should be given to non-Natives who would know how to make it productive in a capitalist economy.

Eventually these two perspectives found a compromise. When R. L. Upshaw became the first Indian agent for the Northern Cheyennes in January 1886, there were 795 Cheyenne people living off the reservation in tipis and log cabins on Rosebud Creek, on the Tongue River from the mouth of the Otter Creek to the mouth of Hanging Woman Creek, and a short distance up both Otter and Hanging Woman Creeks.[14] Immediately, Upshaw launched a forceful letter campaign to the commissioner of Indian affairs to extend the reservation. In February 1886 he recommended against moving the Cheyennes to the Crow reservation and suggested instead that the reservation be extended east to the Tongue River and that American settlers in the area be removed. He provided six reasons, one being "to satisfy the Indians." Finally, the Cheyennes had a permanent agent living on the reservation, dealing with daily problems. Upshaw realized that the instability of the reservation boundaries made any other task difficult. He told the commissioner that he was living with his family in a one-room shack but did not want a permanent home until the reservation boundaries were settled.[15] He believed that there was no sense in building something if the reservation might be revoked or everyone removed. Upshaw noted that the Cheyennes were well aware of the plans for removal and were as unsettled about it as he was.[16] Some Cheyennes felt there was little point in building cabins and becoming established, while others continued to maintain and improve their homesteads, perhaps with the hope that a solid homestead would deter removal.

Soon after, George Yoakam sent a letter to the secretary of the interior asking that the reservation be extended three miles east of the Tongue River because "many Cheyennes have continued to reside on the east side of Tongue River since 1882 and for the past four years their church and school has also been on Tongue River."[17] These Cheyennes received rations there and were served by a Catholic mission, which included this church and school.[18] Yoakam specifically pointed to the civilizing effect of a reservation, stating, "The only way to civilize any tribe of Indians is to adopt the reservation system."[19] By 1886 Yoakam had developed a reputation at the federal level of being a little fanatical, which made him less convincing. Coupled with Upshaw, however, the two reiterated the current thinking in the Indian Department, that the Cheyennes would need a reservation if they were to become civilized. Federal officials were also dealing with heavy resistance from the Cheyennes themselves. They certainly did not want to go to the Crow reservation, and those on the Tongue River refused to move. The Cheyennes along the river were as solidly established as if they had been on a reservation and held land in severalty. Yoakam and Upshaw used these homesteads to anchor their position that the Indian Office should discard plans for revocation and removal and should instead consider a larger reservation. In an era when policy makers supported total assimilation as the solution to their "Indian Problem," Yoakam and Upshaw argued that expanding the reservation would cause the least disruption to the civilizing process that had already been so successful among the Northern Cheyennes.

The situation became more complicated in 1886 because while Yoakam and Upshaw were whispering in the commissioner's right ear to extend the reservation, others were whispering in his left to settle the Cheyennes onto homesteads. By 1888 the land on the reservation and along the Tongue River had been surveyed, so Northern Cheyenne homesteads were finally on the map. In 1889 Upshaw wrote to the new commissioner of Indian affairs, John H. Oberly, concerned that

these homesteads were not in compliance with the law and thus settlers would easily be able to take away Northern Cheyenne lands.
He reminded the commissioner that after the land was surveyed, it
was supposed to be withheld from American settlement. Then he
stated, "American entries had already been made of land on which
Indians were living and which the Indians supposed belonged to
them."[20] He informed the commissioner that the surveys taken in
1886 were meant to help the Cheyennes take homesteads, but no
further action had been taken. By 1889 Upshaw had realized that the
homesteading situation had become difficult to sort out, and he began
fighting for the security of a reservation. He then asked for maps of
the surveyed land so that he could help the Cheyennes file claims on
their homesteads. He wrote again to the commissioner in 1890, but
nothing came of his requests.

Upshaw involved Northern Cheyenne leaders in these debates over
the fate of the reservation as well. When provided the opportunity
to speak about their concerns, these men continued to implement the
alliance forged between themselves and Miles to legitimate their access
to the northern lands. In a council held in 1890, Howling Wolf, who
scouted at Fort Keogh, brought up the forging of the original alliance
with General Miles, speaking of Sweet Woman to invoke its legitimacy. He began by declaring that the soldiers and the Cheyennes had
been friends for a long time, pointing to the beginning of their friendship as the negotiation initiated by Miles and facilitated by Sweet
Woman. Howling Wolf stated, "He [Miles] didn't abuse her but took
good care of her."[21] He spoke highly of Miles, noting that he treated
Sweet Woman well and that Miles took the people in, allowing them
to live in their home country. Notice the language of friendship, just
as above when Elva Stands In Timber used the word "friend" to describe the relationship between Sweet Woman and General Miles.
To say that Miles was their friend was to indicate once again that they
had formed an alliance with him.

About a month later, in another meeting about the status of the
reservation, Brave Wolf pointed again to General Miles for proof of
their connection to the Tongue River valley lands. He said, "You ask
us about our land. I will tell you the truth. General Miles is our friend.
I feel as if he was our brother. My people have always helped him.

Group portrait of Col. Nelson Appleton Miles in council with Cheyenne Indian chiefs in Lame Deer, Montana, 1889. Written on the back of the photo: General Miles and Indian Commission at Tongue River Agency. Miles is posed sitting at a table, Two Moons is posed sitting and wearing a white shirt, and army lieutenant Edward W. Casey is immediately behind him. Photographs by Christian Barthelmess of people and places in New Mexico, Colorado, and Montana, 1881–1903. Yale Collection of Western Americana, Beinecke Rare Book and Manuscript Library.

General Miles put us here." At the same council, White Bull stated, "You are talking about General Miles. He promised we should live here until we are all old men."[22] For the Northern Cheyennes, so much rested on Miles's promise to reserve Cheyenne land, so they remembered it and continued to refer to it throughout their negotiations with the U.S. government. To these headmen, the alliance they had created with Miles guaranteed their continued presence in their northern homeland. They had maintained their relationship with the landscape throughout their wars with the United States, but when those wars ended, it was the alliance that sealed their ability to remain. Like alliances with other newcomers to the plains in the past, this relationship with Miles—expressed in White Bull's use of the word "brother"—established a shared landscape between Miles's people and their own. The Northern Cheyennes refused to allow their autonomy on this landscape, underscored by this alliance, to be whipped away.

In 1891 the new Northern Cheyenne agent, John Tully, sent a letter asking for clarification. He described the confusion over the land situation in and around the Northern Cheyenne reservation, stating that American settlers had little idea whether their claims were on or off the reservation and that the land office in Miles City did not even recognize that there was a reservation. He stated, "A number of persons have taken up land on what has all along been known as the reservation both by homestead, perception, and the land act. Much of this land is now occupied by Indians who will be dispossessed if the claims of the whites are recognized by the law as being valid."[23] Tully explained that even though the land along the Tongue River was set aside for Cheyenne homesteading, many non-Cheyennes had been allowed to settle there. He also called for another survey because no one in the area seemed to know any boundary lines. Tully insisted that everyone in the area understood the land belonged to the Cheyennes according to their legal status as homesteaders.

Yet the delayed surveying of the land, the mishmash of American and Cheyenne settlements, and the lack of recognition by the Miles City land office left the federal government in a state of confusion over what to do. In the mind of the agent, land had been set aside for the settlement of the Northern Cheyennes who lived outside the reservation boundaries, and he was simply ensuring that the Northern Cheyennes became successful homesteaders. The Cheyennes themselves insisted that the land was theirs, so much so that Agent Tully reiterated that the land on which they were living had been considered part of their reservation. Because there were no actual boundary lines, the Northern Cheyennes had more power to impose their own understandings of the boundaries. During this period the federal government's ambiguity about its role toward American Indian people worked to the advantage of the Northern Cheyennes. The confusion this ambiguity wrought among officials continued for years, until finally in 1898 another inspector was sent to try to straighten it out.

James McLaughlin, who had been the agent at Standing Rock during the Wounded Knee massacre, was appointed to investigate the situation at the Tongue River reservation and determine whether it was advisable to move the Cheyennes onto the Crow reservation.[24] He arrived at the agency on August 13, 1898, and promptly called together a council to discuss the matter with the Cheyennes themselves. He determined from speaking with the Cheyennes and Crows that neither wanted to live on the same reservation and reported that "although the Crows and Northern Cheyennes are neighbors, there is not the most cordial feeling between them." McLaughlin only spent a few sentences of his report discussing the enmity between the Crows and the Cheyennes. He was more concerned with the connection the Cheyennes insisted they had to the land. He stated, "The Northern Cheyenne Indians are very much attached to the country they now occupy, many of them having been born and reached manhood within its borders; besides they have had the assurance of government officials from time to time that they would be permitted to remain there undisturbed."[25] Their connection to the land seemed to impress McLaughlin. As a veteran of Plains-U.S. relations, he did not simply dismiss the promises they obtained from government officials to remain in the area of the Tongue River as many others had.

McLaughlin told Congress that several Cheyennes had either originals or copies of letters from officials that they had kept as evidence of the government's reliability. He cites two of these letters in full, one from Gen. Nelson A. Miles and the other from T. J. Morgan, commissioner of Indian affairs at the time. In his 1889 letter, General Miles recounted the many services the Northern Cheyennes at Tongue River provided for the government, beginning with their negotiations at his fort, stating that it paved the way for the end of the War on the Plains. Miles continued by describing in detail their service as scouts against Lame Deer and Chief Joseph. He then argued, "They were told that if they remained at peace and did what they were directed to do, the Government would treat them fairly and justly. They have fulfilled their part of the compact, and it would be but justice for the Government to allow them to remain where it has placed them."[26]

For General Miles, the Northern Cheyennes' claim to the territory around the Tongue River valley existed regardless of the reservation. He stated in his letter, "They have an undoubted right, legally and morally, to remain where they are now located."[27] He declared that this was because they surrendered their tribal relations to take up homesteads. Yet Miles did not justify the Northern Cheyennes' presence in the Tongue River valley in terms of the progress toward civilization made on their homesteads. In fact, he never mentioned assimilation. He was arguing from an even stronger position, the promises from the government.

Miles had consciously used the word "compact" to describe the relationship he had established with the Northern Cheyennes. Archival documents created by U.S. representatives used the term "surrender" to describe the moments when Plains people came into the agencies. This terminology often obscures the actuality that the Northern Cheyennes who came into Fort Keogh did not believe they had surrendered and that Miles did not consider these men, women, and children to be prisoners of war. The two parties had made an agreement, which surely looked to the Northern Cheyennes like the alliances they had made with other Native nations in the past. Miles implied that this compact substantiated Northern Cheyenne rights to the territory. By the 1890s his perception of Cheyenne expectations about their place on the land presented in this letter reflected the kind of social order that Plains peoples used in the past when creating alliances.

Although he did not go so far as to say that he had promised the
Northern Cheyennes this land, he posed a convincing argument in
support of the Native nation by combining the state-centric discourse of rights with Plains understandings of access to land as based
on relationships.

In this letter Miles underscored the importance of the social relationship he had developed with the Northern Cheyennes by relating
the events of what he called "surrender," stating it was in good faith,
and then describing Northern Cheyenne military service at Fort
Keogh.[28] Clearly, Miles understood Northern Cheyenne military service as pivotal to their rights to the Tongue River valley. Whether he
realized that the Northern Cheyennes around Fort Keogh understood
their friendship as an equal military alliance, which would allow them
joint access to the territory, is unclear. In his letter, however, his use
of words such as "compact" and "justice and morality" clearly supported the Northern Cheyennes' desire to settle in the Tongue River
valley. Regardless of what Miles apprehended about the cultural
political expectations of the relationship he established with these
scouts, he felt responsible to them because of the social bonds they
shared. It is easy to see why Cheyenne people held onto Miles's letter
as proof of their ability to remain in their homeland. They had fought
in alliance with him, even saving his life. According to their own
sociopolitical order, the compact they had with Miles guaranteed their
permanent presence on the land around the Tongue River, and they
argued that his letter supported this claim.

In their two councils with McLaughlin, the first held on August 17,
1898, and the second on October 6, 1898, the Northern Cheyennes
present referred to their agreement with Miles regularly.[29] Two Moons's
statement is worth quoting in its entirety:

> My friend, we are glad to see you and have you with us. You
> were a long time with our friends, the Sioux, and we have heard
> of you and that you are a good friend of the Indians. We don't
> want you to try and get land for us any place away from here.
> This is our country, and we want to remain here, and have our
> children continue to live here after we old men are gone. General
> Miles promised us that we would never be sent away from here,
> and I hope that you will now make us strong on this reservation.[30]

Two Moons opened with a warm greeting that not only welcomed McLaughlin but also reminded him of the Cheyennes' expectations of him. He had worked to do good things for the Sioux, who were the Cheyennes' friends, allies, and relatives, and so they expected him to do good things for the Cheyennes as well. He also called McLaughlin a friend, again invoking the responsibility of social relationships. Two Moons then emphasized, "This is our country," underscoring that the people wanted to remain there, invoking future generations in the mention of children. He sealed his argument by reminding all gathered that Miles had promised that they never would have to leave.

The Northern Cheyennes surely believed that the Tongue River country was their country for many reasons: they had been living in the area for generations, they had close ties with the Lakotas with whom they shared the territory, and they fought hard to keep enemies out of that country—including the U.S. Army, whom they defeated only miles from the Tongue River at the Battle of the Little Bighorn. Yet the speakers did not bring up their military victories; they referred only to their long presence in the area and their alliance. Medicine Bear stated, "Leave us here that we may live and die in a country in which we were born and grew up." He emphasized that the Cheyennes' relationship with this land had stretched for generations, their parents lived there and gave birth to them there, and their people should continue in that country as new generations are born. Both American Horse and Hairy Hand also reminded the inspector that the country was promised to them. White Elk made the explicit connection between Northern Cheyenne permanence on the land and their alliance with General Miles when he stated, "We first made peace with the whites on Tongue River, and we want to make our permanent home here."[31]

Bobtail Horse and Little Chief reiterated White Elk's understanding of the connection between making peace and settling in a specific landscape in the second council. Bobtail Horse stated that the Northern Cheyennes made peace with the whites in that region and then reminded all gathered of their military service and how they fought other tribes who were at war with the U.S. government while living in that country. Little Chief reminded McLaughlin that General Miles put them on the land where they fought against their own friends, the Lakotas.[32] These speakers each underscored the alliance they had with General Miles and illustrated how it sealed their continued relationship with this land. The Euro-American officials still presented themselves as friends of the Northern Cheyennes, so the alliance was still good. The Cheyennes continued to assert their connection to that territory based on these facts.

McLaughlin must have taken what he heard in these council meetings into careful consideration because he recommended another executive order to expand the Northern Cheyenne reservation to the Tongue River. This expansion would more than double the size of the reservation, but it would not encompass the homesteads of the Cheyennes who had settled on the eastern banks of the river. In 1898 McLaughlin set out to make an agreement with all the Northern Cheyennes living on the east side of the Tongue River to move onto the reservation.[33] Forty-four Northern Cheyenne men and two women signed their names on this document declaring that they would abandon their homesteads and move west in exchange for twenty-five dollars to cover their losses.

During this period of ambiguity leading up to the expansion, the Northern Cheyennes continued to rely on kinship to maintain their relationship with their land and to convince government officials to recognize it. They emphasized their lack of friendly relations with the Crows and utilized their alliance with the Lakotas, particularly to invoke McLaughlin's responsibility to help the Cheyenne people. These Cheyenne councilmen realized that their most powerful alliance was with General Miles. This relationship proved incredibly valuable to their cause, not because Cheyenne men had fought for the U.S. military—many Native men had done that—but because Miles himself had upheld his oral compact with the people. He had devoted himself to convincing the federal government that the Northern Cheyenne people deserved to remain in their own little valley along the Rosebud and Tongue Rivers. Ultimately, the force of his arguments, the letters of Northern Cheyenne agents, and the moving speeches of the Northern Cheyenne people themselves convinced federal officials that removal would be a mistake.

In order to complete the expansion, many American homesteaders would be forced to move outside the proposed reservation boundaries and would receive compensation for their homesteads as well.

McLaughlin negotiated forty-one agreements with American settlers living within the proposed boundaries of the reservation. He divided these agreements into four types: bona fide settlers, equitable rights, legal landowners, and squatters and illegal settlers. He defined bona fide settlers as those who had valid titles to their land, equitable rights as those who had final receiver's receipts but doubtful rights, legal owners as those who came into their land in a legal way other than homesteading, and squatters as those who occupied the land illegally. According to McLaughlin's calculations of the values of these parcels of land, the government would owe the fifteen settlers $91,310, the five equitable rights settlers $12,770, the eight legal landowners $34,670, and the eleven illegal settlers $11,625. The U.S. government planned to pay eleven illegal squatters more than $11,000 for improvements made on land they did not own, yet they planned to force forty-six Cheyenne families from their homes, giving them a total of $1,150 to cover the houses, barns, and fences they built on land that had always been theirs.[34]

Orlan Svingen stated that the land the American homesteaders would vacate was meant to serve as an inducement for the forty-six Cheyenne families living on the east side of the Tongue River to move west.[35] Clearly the Northern Cheyennes did not find this inducement very compelling. McLaughlin admitted himself, "They were reluctant to leave the east side of Tongue River, but to show their good will and desire to meet the wishes of the Government in having these matters amicably adjusted they all consented."[36] McLaughlin's statement obscured the negative response he received from the Northern Cheyennes settled on the east side of the Tongue River. Their signatures provide evidence that they did consent but not as amicably as McLaughlin wanted to portray.

In a council meeting with the inspector, American Horse, Little Chief, and George Standing Elk all stated that they wanted the reservation to be larger than the one that had been proposed, declaring that it should extend beyond the divide east of the Tongue River. Bobtail Horse stated, "We fought all Indian tribes in this country who were at war with the government when we were soldiers of the government, and we would wish a larger reservation than you propose."[37] He reminded the government that in making peace on the

Tongue River and taking up an alliance with the United States, they had a claim to the territory, not just because it had always been theirs but also because they were in alliance with the other people who claimed it as their own land. He directly connected fighting with the United States to Cheyenne claims to the territory, justifying a larger reservation.

Despite the protests, on March 19, 1900, President William McKinley signed the executive order that expanded the Northern Cheyenne reservation to its current eastern boundary, the Tongue River.[38] McLaughlin had worked hard to establish reservation boundaries that would suit both the Northern Cheyennes and the U.S. government. This executive order did recognize Northern Cheyenne rights to this territory, securing their presence in the Tongue River valley and ending the discussion over removal to the Crow reservation. To the Cheyennes, however, it made little sense to relocate from the successful homesteads that government officials had encouraged them to take in the first place. Regardless of Cheyenne opinion, in the process of expanding the reservation, forty-six families lost their homesteads, fields, houses, and barns, and they received only twenty-five dollars per homestead in compensation—practically nothing.

Although the Northern Cheyennes living on the east side of the Tongue River had signed the contracts McLaughlin presented them, these papers did not have the same meaning to the Cheyennes that they had to the government. Northern Cheyennes today still talk about the move across the Tongue River and question its legitimacy. For example, Mr. BC said his grandparents repeatedly asked about that land, wondered why they were moved off of it, and lamented the fact that they were never allowed to return. The issue of this lost land has weighed heavily on the Northern Cheyennes, and they passed their trepidation and suspicion about this move to their children and grandchildren. Mr. BC stated that the people who lived across the Tongue River believed they would be allowed to return to their homesteads within five years. He said they never understood why they had to move or why they were never allowed to return.[39] William Rowland, who signed the agreement as the interpreter, claimed that he fully explained the purpose of the move.[40] Nevertheless, it is evident from oral history that despite a competent interpreter, the Northern Cheyennes only partially understood the implications of the agreement. Considering the ambiguity of Indian policy throughout the nineteenth century and its often painful impact on the Cheyenne people, it is not surprising that they did not believe this move was permanent. According to Cheyenne oral history, a Cheyenne man who had heard about the agreement rode out early in the morning to try to warn Cheyenne homesteaders not to sign; on the way, he had to stop and eat and the government officials got there first.[41] The loss of this land lives on in Cheyenne memory as a heavy injustice.

An essentially unrecorded event in American history is detailed quite clearly in Northern Cheyenne history, emphasized by the retelling of this story on the reservation. The omission of this event from most histories suggests that, to mainstream historians, the movement of the Northern Cheyennes within reservation boundaries is insignificant. Euro-American histories focus on the establishment of the reservation boundaries, while Cheyenne oral histories emphasize a severed connection to a specific landscape. The Northern Cheyennes highlighted their relationship to this land, stretching back for generations. They also asserted that this relationship was guaranteed by their alliance with General Miles, which he confirmed by letter. Such pieces of paper were the physical evidence of their long-standing relationship to this landscape and of the oral agreements affirming that relationship between the representatives of two nations—the Cheyennes and the United States. It is not surprising that the Northern Cheyennes found the end result of the expansion dubious.

Yet while forty-six Northern Cheyenne families lost their homesteads, the nation had taken another step toward U.S. recognition of their right to live in their homeland. At a moment in American history when Indian policy concentrated on completely dismantling the reservation system through allotment, the Northern Cheyennes successfully won a reservation and then its expansion. Between 1880 and 1895, Native nations lost 60 percent of the total amount of land the allotment policy would rob from American Indian peoples. By the time allotment ended, Native nations had lost most of the land they had been guaranteed through the reservation system.[42] During a period when federal officials attempted to rid themselves of the responsibility of reservations, they created a new one for the Northern Cheyennes, even providing an agent and rations. This reservation emerged as an overwhelming success for the Northern Cheyennes who had fought to secure their position in their northern territory. Like so many earlier successes, however, this one required unjust sacrifice the Cheyennes had not anticipated.

Local and federal officials probably failed to recognize the political responsibility their social relationships with Native people demanded; however, they certainly understood the social value of reciprocity and the importance of honor in agreements.[43] Perhaps they were enticed by romantic arguments of the pull of family and homeland, as long as they did not undermine U.S. control. They must have also been persuaded of the important role these Northern Cheyennes played as scouts and that they ought to have their own reservation to support the assimilation process. By 1900 both federal and local officials had shifted away from their previous divide-and-conquer strategy. Euro-Americans had come to view the frontier as closed and the Indigenous peoples of the Plains as conquered. Now that Native people had been subdued, government agents had turned to the assimilationist agenda as the mechanism for controlling the American Indian population. As scouts and homesteaders, the Northern Cheyennes appeared to be well on the path to assimilation into Euro-American society. By this time, the only reason to force them onto the Crow reservation would have been to clear the landscape for settlement, and many local and federal officials recognized the injustice of such an act.

Although the arguments the Northern Cheyennes presented in their councils with McLaughlin certainly made an impact, U.S. representatives never adopted the political understandings of land or kin that guided the Cheyenne nation. American officials could still be compelled by what they saw as honorable or sympathetic actions while at the same time usurping the land belonging to forty-six Northern Cheyenne families by setting the 1900 boundary line. For representatives of the nation-state, a people's territory was defined by boundaries, so these officials believed that solidifying the boundaries of a reservation satisfied the Cheyennes' desire to remain on the land. It also supported the assimilationist agenda and ended the conflict over removal. The families who were forced to move were not seen as important in relation to the state's wider goals.

For the Cheyennes, the relationship to a landscape encompassed their presence as well as their historical and spiritual connection, and the social relationships that defined these connections. This was an important part of the matrix of factors that supported their autonomous sense of nationhood. Unlike the state, which overrode the personal experiences of individuals and families to emphasize institutional goals, the Native nation was affected by the decisions of each family. No organization within the Native nation existed beyond the reach of familial relationships, so such actions could not be taken without considering the effects on the social fabric of the nation woven from kin. Moving across a line did not end the web of relationships connecting people to animals, plants, and the land. Severing a standing relationship to the landscape by inserting a boundary line surely seemed simply preposterous. No piece of paper could end a living relationship with the land and animals and plants within it. No signature could sever generations of relationships between the people and the land they loved.

CONCLUSION

For the Unborn

"Imagine what the world would be like if all our leaders made their decisions with the unborn in mind," I said. Ms. DG and I looked at each other and then out the window at the pine trees and bluffs of the reservation. I assumed we were both pondering this awesome thought. She and I had again been talking about the importance of family to Northern Cheyenne ways of life. We were enjoying our coffees, I from the couch and she from an overstuffed recliner. We discussed Cheyenne leadership and the responsibility of the chiefs to consider all the unborn in their decisions. It is a profound idea. Today politicians and corporate leaders make decisions based on the next election or the next fiscal quarter. If their choices were based on the needs of the unborn, our entire world would look different. How would we think about the oil industry if we had to consider how our choices would affect four generations in the future? How would we make political decisions if we were building a world for our great-great-grandchildren? The repercussions would be staggering.

The next evening, Mr. SD asked me if I wanted to go with him to a sweat. I hadn't been to a sweat in a while, so I was a little nervous, but he told me, "This is a really welcoming group." As I sat on their front porch thirty minutes later, eating a frozen ice pop handed to me by a boy barely five years old and listening to sweet stories about grandchildren, I knew I was in good hands. It would be a good sweat. At the end of the night, as I was lying on the ground, catching my breath, watching the stars, and wondering if the storm rumbling in the distance would roll our way, I recalled that once Mr. SD had told me that when he prays, he always tries to remember the unborn. They are the ones we are preparing the world for, I thought to myself. What does that even mean?

Ms. DG had been telling me for years that Dull Knife had a family. It has taken me just as long to begin to have a sense of what this means. In many different ways, she was trying to explain to me who a people are when they make political and economic decisions with the unborn in mind. She talked about the preparations she makes for her own grandchildren, thinking about both the knowledge and the objects that she will leave them, that they in turn can pass to their grand-children. She also told me about the long struggles that the Chey-enne people have fought over land. I have learned about not only the efforts to establish the reservation but also the fights to safeguard the landscape from standard allotment policy, sale to non-Cheyennes, and destruction by the coal industry. The Cheyennes have resisted short-term economic development time and again in favor of long-term investment in their people. This has meant buying back the reservation as well as buying land off the reservation in places such as Bear Butte to preserve it for generations to come.

When Dull Knife and Little Wolf fled Indian Territory pursued by hundreds of soldiers, when Two Moons traveled to Fort Keogh and spoke to Miles, when White Bull asked Miles to safeguard the Chey-ennes in their northern homeland after the battle on Lame Deer Creek, and when Little Chief penned his letters to the president, these men were thinking of their great-great-grandchildren. They were not build-ing their own legacies. Western history made their names famous, erasing their children and grandchildren who followed them north, who put on scout uniforms, who built barns and fences, who tran-scribed their thoughts onto the page, and who took their letters to the post. These relationships were important because Cheyennes both defined their political identity and exercised their autonomy through them. For these leaders, making decisions with future generations in mind was not simply a romantic exercise; it was the best way to protect the people's political and economic interests. Unlike the state, there were no arbitrary boundaries on the landscape or contractual obligations written on paper to unify Cheyennes as a people. To be Cheyenne was and still is to be a relative. To assert a claim to a landscape meant demonstrating your relatedness, to all of its inhabitants, human and nonhuman, and maintaining the reciprocal relationship that a relative would. As the heirs of these relationships, the unborn are central to political discourse in this world.

Although the Northern Cheyennes fought for a reservation in their homeland, they never allowed their relationship with the landscape to be severed by these boundaries. As Craig Howe demonstrated, the landscape has primacy over human beings for American Indian people, while at the same time landscape and people are intimately connected.[1] This connection did not fall apart or get set aside because reservation boundaries had been established. The responsibility Native peoples have to the landscape, to the spiritual world connected to it, and to their relatives to maintain a relationship with it drew people across reservation boundaries to continue what they have done for centuries.

The Northern Cheyenne landscape has been constructed by kin ties from the distant past until the present moment. The people live where their ancestors were born, traveled, died, and are buried. They travel to sites their ancestors visited, learning about them through their parents and grandparents. They have worked to maintain a relationship with this entire landscape for all those yet to come. Northern Cheyenne tribal members state that their landscape should not just be maintained for the people and their children but for all the unborn.[2] By traveling to historical and spiritual sites on the reservation, the people maintain a relationship to their ancestors by remembering, retelling, and honoring their families' connections to these places with their children. The Northern Cheyennes also maintain their wide-ranging kin ties across reservation boundaries. They travel off the reservation to visit relatives, whether living in Indian Territory or other places, to share ceremonies and celebrations. In the case of travel for spiritual reasons, they carry with them the needs and prayers of their family who can't come. And all the family who can come support the person who is undertaking a spiritual task by cooking for them, camping with them, and caring for them emotionally and spiritually. Family makes it possible even today for the people to continue their relationship with their known geographic universe regardless of reservation boundaries.

The Northern Cheyennes are also well aware, and have been since removal, of how important it is to reassert their connectedness to their landscape in the eyes of the United States. Because the reservation was established by two executive orders and because they had been threatened by removal so often in the past, the 1900 executive order did little to ease the people's concerns that they still might be subject to a removal. Ms. DG explained that because the reservation had been established by executive order, the people worried that a later president would be able to revoke the order.[3] These fears were certainly justified by experience because removal and land loss were still on the table for the Northern Cheyennes between 1884 and 1900. So even after the 1900 expansion, they continued to seek a more secure recognition by the federal government to their rights to this land. In the 1920s the Northern Cheyenne people began to petition the U.S. Indian Office to allot their reservation. When speaking about the Northern Cheyennes' struggle for their reservation in the summer of 2005, Ms. DG argued that the people believed that allotment would guarantee the recognition they sought. She said that the people asked the federal government to allot them, but they also ensured that the government did not sell the extra land.[4] "Many people fight over a lot of things on the reservation," she said, "but they always come together over land."[5]

Considering all the scholarship about the destruction that allotment caused to American Indian communities, it seems counterintuitive that the Northern Cheyennes would petition for it as a way to preserve their relationship to their landscape. In most communities, allotment checkerboarded the land, led to land loss, and opened the door for sale of Native lands and white settlement. Across most of Indian Country, allotment destroyed the tribal land base and had devastating cultural effects. Yet by 1920 the Northern Cheyennes had the advantage of hindsight because they had watched Pine Ridge fall prey to the excesses of allotment. They were determined that their experience would be a different one. Furthermore, they had a very compelling reason to face the risks of allotment for the acknowledgement of their legal rights to the land that it would bring.

During the 1920s the U.S. courts began to debate the status of reservation lands. According to the Public Land Leasing Act of February 25,

Indian Camp at Lame Deer by Laton A. Huffman. From the Collection of Gene and Bev Allen, Helena, Montana.

1920, the title to lands within the boundaries of reservations created by executive order belonged to the United States. This was only true, however, for unallotted land.[6] In an interview for the American Indian Tribal Histories Project, Rubie Sooktis declared, "There are those that say they wanted the allotments because they were always under constant threat of being removed to the Indian Territory, even after the reservation was established."[7] The people had fought hard to win their land and believed allotment was a way to secure it.[8] Because the unallotted lands on executive order reservations had been declared the property of the United States and because the Northern Cheyennes had suffered the threat of removal in their recent history, the people decided to allot the reservation in hopes of permanently establishing rights that the U.S. government would recognize as valid.

Unexpectedly, the Northern Cheyennes had to fight for allotment as well. In 1923 the superintendent at Lame Deer wrote to the commissioner of Indian affairs, stating that he believed it was the policy of the Indian Office to allot the Northern Cheyenne Indians. He continued, "It is the almost unanimous wish of the Indians to have the entire reservation allotted at one time."[9] Despite the past popularity of allotment, the Office of Indian Affairs flatly refused to allot the reservation, stating simply that it was not advantageous on that specific piece of land.[10] But the Cheyennes were persistent with the U.S. government about securing their land. When the commissioner of Indian affairs visited the Northern Cheyenne reservation later in the fall, the people petitioned him personally to allot their reservation.[11] Their persistence paid off because in 1926 Congress finally enacted an allotment act for the Northern Cheyenne reservation.

Wisely, the Northern Cheyennes refused to allot under the original Allotment Act of 1887, instead convincing Congress to script an act tailored to their specific needs. Through this act, the people secured their land, believing the United States would not be able to revoke it. Two things stand out about this act. First, "the unallotted lands of said tribe of Indians shall be held in common, subject to the control and management thereof as Congress may deem expedient for the benefit of said Indians." Although Congress managed the excess lands, they were not allowed to be sold to non-Cheyennes as had happened with so many other allotted reservations. Furthermore, all timber, coal, or other minerals, including oil and gas, would be reserved for the benefit of the people and could only be leased with the consent of the tribal council under the rules prescribed by the secretary of the interior. Again the government retained management, but the people secured ownership over their mineral resources. Furthermore, the act stated that after fifty years all the mentioned resources "of said allotments shall become the property of the respective allottees or their heirs."[12] In 1976 all mineral rights would transfer to the allottee or his or her descendants, even if the lands were sold. Ultimately, this act gave the Northern Cheyennes even more control over their land than they previously had. Strange as it may seem, allotment was a victory for the people.

Yet, as with many of their victories, the Northern Cheyennes had to continue fighting to maintain it. The allottees could not sell their land for twenty-five years, so the people felt their reservation was safe. John Woodenlegs, the tribal chairman in the 1950s, said, "Nobody worried until 1955—except white ranchers and speculators. They were waiting to defeat my hungry people with dollars the way the soldiers defeated them with bullets."[13] When individual allottees became able to sell their allotments, some allottees put their land up for sale. As Woodenlegs's statement attested, some of these allottees lived in extreme poverty, making selling their land an immediate solution for a desperate personal situation.

In 1955 the Bureau of Indian Affairs put the first tracts of Northern Cheyenne land up for sale. Woodenlegs recalled that many Northern Cheyenne people told the tribal council to save their land any way they could. The tribal council, wishing to secure its land base, passed a resolution to buy any land its allottees wished to sell. The council planned to sell cattle from their own herd to collect enough money to buy land up for sale. The Bureau of Indian Affairs had to release the funds the nation planned to use to purchase the land and flatly refused. Sadly, nearly a thousand acres of Northern Cheyenne land fell out of Cheyenne ownership at the auction in October 1958. Once they had finally received the money from their cattle, the nation used that money to buy land as fast as possible. Between 1958 and 1959, the tribal council managed to hold the reservation together by bidding on every piece of land that came up for sale, but they knew that they would not be able to sustain this approach with the money they had.[14] They needed a new plan to save their homeland.

Finally, the tribal council announced what Woodenlegs called "The Northern Cheyenne Fifty-Year Unallotment Program." After much prayer and thought, the council decided they would ask the Bureau of Indian Affairs to grant them a loan of over $500,000 that they could use to purchase any land that came up for sale. The council obligated itself to buy back all the land that individual tribal members wanted to sell, using the land they purchased to make the money to pay back the government. They also asked the bureau to hold all land sales until they received their loan. Much to the tribal council's surprise, the federal government actually did order all sales to stop.

The introduction penned by the council and submitted to the U.S. Department of the Interior made clear the connection between their well-being as a people and their land:

Today we are a tribe of Indians, and we use that word, tribe, in the old way. Sometimes we are divided against each other inside the Tribe, but we are divided about who will lead the people and not about where to lead them. . . . Our people are still united by the memory of how we fought for and won this land we live on. We are united by certain ways of acting, by belief in holy things, by our Cheyenne language as few tribes in allotted areas are united today. We are one people because our lands are still almost intact. . . . The land is the only place where we are welcome as we are today, the only place where we can love and take pity on each other now and join our strength to make a decent future life for all of us and each of us. One and all we want a chance to save our homeland that makes it possible for us to be united Cheyennes.[15]

The tribal council clearly delineated that they were united in their land. The introduction explained that the people held beliefs and actions in common, and it emphasized the memory of how the people won their land. It asserted that their land base helped them maintain a common language and cultural identity. Without the land, the Northern Cheyennes would risk losing their autonomy as a people.

John Woodenlegs described the land as the only place where Northern Cheyenne people remember the same things together and stated, "We remember our grandfathers paid for it [the land]—with their life." He recounted Cheyenne removal, stating,

> They took them to Oklahoma. The people were sick there in all that heat and dust. They asked to go home again, but they were locked up in military prison instead. Then Little Wolf and Dull Knife broke out of the prison, and they led the people on the long walk home. Montana is far away from Oklahoma, and they had no horses. They had no warm clothes, and many froze to death in the snow. They had nothing to fight with, and most of them were shot by the soldiers. A whole army hunted them all the way. My grandmother told me she walked holding a little girl by the hand on each side. She had to keep pulling them out of the line of the soldiers' bullets. 300 of my people left Oklahoma. 100 came home. After that the Government gave us the reservation we live on now. Now you can understand why we are fighting to save our land today.[16]

Although Woodenlegs conflated the journey from Oklahoma with the Fort Robinson breakout, this does not diminish the power of his narrative. By relating the impact of the journey on Cheyenne families, he demonstrated that the experience of their ancestors within a specific landscape was powerful documentation of Northern Cheyenne rights to that land. Even in the mid-twentieth century, Woodenlegs strategically utilized the kin-based connection of the Northern Cheyennes to these ancestors who fought to return to the Tongue River Valley, demonstrating their rights to their territory as established through the struggles of their ancestors.

This is why the tribal council, with the Northern Cheyenne people behind them, was prepared to take out a loan from the government to buy land that they had always considered their own. John Woodenlegs stated himself that "we do not think it is just that we Northern Cheyennes have to spend all the funds we could use for community development to buy back allotments so that our tribe will keep its home."[17] He stated emphatically, however, that the tribe would buy up every inch of allotted land if they had to in order to save the reservation. After extreme sacrifice, ultimately, the nation safeguarded their land once again. Today the reservation covers approximately 444,000 acres and the people own 99 percent of it; only 1 percent has been lost to non-Cheyenne owners.[18]

It is common to hear people say that they had to pay for their reservation three times; the first time they bought the land with their own blood, then with money they had borrowed from the United States, and then they had to pay for it again with their own money.[19] Despite all the hardships the people suffered to remain in their homeland, they had to convince the United States to recognize their connection to this territory over and over again. This battle for recognition lasted from the time Two Moons's people first made an alliance with General Miles until they finally settled the question of legal ownership in the 1950s. For the Northern Cheyennes, however, this landscape always was theirs based on both their reciprocal kin relationships with the nonhuman entities living in it and their long-held alliances with other nations going all the way back to their earliest days in the Black Hills. They had maintained these connections for generations, and the presence of the United States did not usurp them. Yet according to the nation-state model held by the United States, the Cheyennes had lost their right to their territory at the moment of contact, through the doctrine of discovery. Treaties and other institutions of the state continued to negate the Cheyennes' rights to their territory, until finally a reservation was established in 1884. From this first, unstable recognition by the federal government, the Northern Cheyennes built a strong base. Throughout this long struggle, the people's kin relationships remained an important way to articulate a distinctly Cheyenne connection to the landscape, even when addressing non-Cheyennes.

Each time the Northern Cheyennes accepted a nation-state boundary, however, they lost some of their power to force the United States to acknowledge their own cultural constructions of land and social organization. This was true of both the 1900 boundary and the allotment. The United States, for its part, waffled on the best course for Native peoples, displaying ambiguity in the face of many of the decisions concerning the Northern Cheyennes. Although the federal government had encouraged homesteading for Native people, they also took Northern Cheyenne homesteads, providing no financial or institutional encouragement to rebuild. Twenty years later they discouraged allotment, a policy they had enforced with fervor only decades before. Twenty-five years after that, in the 1950s, the Northern Cheyennes were barely able to save the land they had fought so desperately to return to a little less than one hundred years earlier.

Over the course of their relationship with the United States, sometimes the ambiguity of U.S. Indian policy caused suffering and strife for the people. At other times these contradictions benefited the people, providing an opening for government officials to accept Northern Cheyenne actions based on the people's own political assertions. Nevertheless, decades after the United States began its efforts to contain the Northern Cheyennes within the rigid boundaries of the nation-state, this Native nation still understood its relationship to landscape and collective identity as based in part on the social relationships it maintained.

The Northern Cheyennes today are very proud of their reservation, located in one of the people's favorite camping regions, along the Tongue and Rosebud Rivers, favored for its mild climate, ample game, water, grazing, and productive gathering. Their pride in their homeland is apparent in the way tribal members remember their long struggle to obtain the reservation. Some recount the battles and massacres of the 1870s. Others discuss the fight to keep the reservation lands tribally owned in the twentieth century. Still others relate the negotiations their relatives entered into in an effort to ensure that the United States would recognize the connection they already had to these lands. The Northern Cheyenne narrative of the origins of this reservation have evolved into a proud national history for the people, but it also illuminates a deeper understanding of the relationship between American Indian nations and the United States.

Assuming that the rigid boundaries that define the nation-state apply to American Indian social organization has left scholars with few explanations for the establishment of the Northern Cheyenne reservation. Many scholars have argued that the Fort Robinson breakout led to the establishment of the Northern Cheyenne reservation.[20] Although the breakout had a dramatic effect on Northern Cheyenne history, it is highly unlikely that this event convinced the United States to establish a reservation.[21] If this had been the case, Little Chief's people would not have been removed. Implying that the breakout caused the United States to create a reservation robs the Northern Cheyennes of their agency in establishing themselves in their homeland. Furthermore, this narrative explains the Northern Cheyenne reservation as the outcome of a singular event that spurred the generosity of a benevolent but all-powerful state. Such a narrative overlooks the importance of the negotiations that took place between the United States and the Northern Cheyennes.

One author, Orlan J. Svingen, has illustrated that other factors besides the breakout were involved in the establishment of the reservation. For Svingen, many historical factors combined to create an environment in which Northern Cheyenne rights to remain in their northern homeland could be recognized by the United States. These historical factors included the passing of a violent frontier, widespread popular sympathy for the struggles of the Northern Cheyennes, military support of the scouts at Fort Keogh, and the push for reform in American Indian policy. Svingen has also argued that the unity of the Northern Cheyennes was an important historical factor.[22] He contended that the Northern Cheyennes spoke with one voice, resisted factionalism, and fought for the single goal of keeping their people together on one reservation.

As Svingen demonstrated, scholars often cite the distinguishing elements of Cheyenne history, assuming the Northern Cheyennes remained in their homeland only through a set of auspicious circumstances particular to this group alone. Yet Svingen neglected the two factors by which scholars might be able to conceptualize how Northern Cheyenne history fits into the larger history of the U.S. relationship with Native nations: that kinship is central to Native assertions of political autonomy and that the implementation of U.S. Indian policy by federal and local officials has been marked by contradiction. Incorporating these factors illustrates that the Northern Cheyenne reservation, though created in a precise historical moment from the culmination of a specific series of events, is also only one outcome of the type of negotiations that regularly took place on the plains between the United States and Native nations.

Regardless of the differing cultural components of specific Native nations, each acted through a sense of political autonomy built on kinship. These kin-based political formations ordered each nation internally, in their relationships with other Native nations, and in their relationships with nation-states. While Native nations used kin ties to establish and maintain their social, political, and economic relationships with other nations, nation-states used rigid social, physical, and political boundaries to delineate their relationships with other nations. Because the rigid boundaries of the state are difficult to impose and maintain on groups with flexible social organization, Native nations have found space to respond to the United States based on their own sociopolitical understandings.

The Northern Cheyennes used the ambiguity created by the space between the state-centric definition of tribe and their own kin-centric understanding of themselves as a Native nation to assert their perspectives in negotiations with the United States, to varying degrees of success. Often local officials who worked closely with the Cheyenne people contradicted federal policy in their actions, seeing the sense in Cheyenne arguments and siding with people they had come to know personally. Throughout their history, the Cheyennes sometimes won concessions from the state but at other times received harsh physical and social treatment for their persistence in maintaining their Native nation.

There is no evidence that Northern Cheyenne leaders failed to understand nation-state political constructions. Instead, these leaders could skillfully manipulate such constructions, filtering them through their own political discourse, establishing themselves as full participants in the interplay of power relations on the plains. By understanding the centrality of kinship to political action for Plains nations, the establishment of the Northern Cheyenne reservation no longer appears as an anomaly in American Indian history but as a reasonable outcome of the negotiations as they occurred between one Native nation and the United States.

Understanding the importance of kinship to the Cheyenne nation also produces a narrative centered in Cheyenne cultural perspectives that further supports the inherent autonomy of the Cheyenne nation. Cheyenne emphasis on kin to structure membership as well as access to resources and territory created an autonomous sense of nationhood that transcended the nationalistic tribal group identity placed on Native nations by the United States. Because national identity was expressed in terms of kin relationships, the Northern Cheyennes had the flexibility to adopt certain state-based institutions while maintaining their own nationhood. Moving away from a nation-state model of Native nations to a theoretical approach that recognizes the importance of kinship channels and flexible social organization to maintaining a sense of nationhood builds a case for Indigenous political autonomy not dependent on the state and therefore self-sustaining.

As is apparent from their continual struggle to return to and live in the heart of their homeland, the Northern Cheyennes resisted efforts by American officials to define them. For a time, officials sought to group all Cheyennes together on one reservation in Indian Territory—a strategy that appealed to the rigidly bounded definitions of Native nations that most Americans held. The Northern Cheyennes conceived of their nation in more flexible terms, and despite their social and cultural ties to the Southern Cheyennes, they felt they belonged with their human and nonhuman relatives in the north. The Northern Cheyennes responded to U.S. efforts at containment with strategic political action based in kin, demonstrating that their connection to the landscape was constructed through these relationships. Those who were removed to Indian Territory explicitly referenced kinship in their negotiations with government officials, emphasizing it as the reason they belonged in the north. Arguments about illness emphasized the threat this new land posed to children and grandchildren—the future generations. Discussions of the strangeness of the land articulated to officials that the northern people had not established kin relationships with all the inhabitants of this southern landscape.

The Northern Cheyennes who wanted to return relied on their kinship relationships with the Lakotas at Pine Ridge, on their relatives who lived in the Tongue River valley, and on the alliance they created with General Miles. The kin-based actions had varying levels of success, but ultimately all of the groups were able to join their relatives in their Tongue River homeland. The Northern Cheyennes also used kinship as a powerful part of the discourse they presented to

American officials to secure their presence in their homeland during
the early reservation era. The Northern Cheyennes drew on both the
kin-based alliance they established with Miles and their historic kinship to the landscape as the place where they were born and where
their ancestors were buried.

Northern Cheyenne history also demonstrates the power of kin-
based political action to evade rigid nation-state boundaries. Although
Northern Cheyennes actively participated in nation-state activities
such as scouting, homesteading, and the establishment of the reservation, they never neglected their kinship and alliance networks, and
they continued to draw on them when government officials attempted
to impose rigid boundaries that threatened to disrupt the community. They demonstrated this by accepting some boundaries of the
state and not others. Most prominently, they deemphasized their
treaties with the U.S. government to return to Montana. No treaty
with the Cheyennes recognized their rights to any land outside the
Indian Territory or the Lakota reservations. The people had to overcome the fact that these treaties disregarded the Cheyennes' understanding of their own nationhood. In establishing boundaries through
treaties, federal officials often ignored the complexities of intermarriage and alliance between American Indian nations and the flexibility of access to territory as practiced by Native peoples. Instead,
these officials relied on treaty designations to solidify the idea of the
tribe as a rigidly bounded entity with a unified ethnic identity and a
delineated territory, similar to the nation-state. The Northern Cheyennes, for their part, disregarded these attempts to define them and
insisted that they be reunited in their homeland in Montana despite
the efforts of federal and local officials to keep them in Indian Territory
and later at Pine Ridge.

For Cheyennes, both political identity and its inscription on the
landscape was constructed through relations within and between
families, between ancestors and the unborn, between allied nations,
and between people and the plants, animals, and rock formations
within a particular landscape.[23] These kin-based networks constructed
the people's relationship to their landscape even after the reservation boundaries were established, and they continue to do so today.
Jacki Rand has noted that more scholars have begun to indirectly

challenge "the reservation boundary as a fixed and impermeable temporal marker, as well as a social, cultural, and political barrier."[24] In the case of the Northern Cheyennes, delineating the continuance of these networks of relationships directly challenges the reservation boundary as an impermeable barrier. Reservation boundaries failed to erase Cheyenne relationships with relatives beyond them; the people maintained their wider sense of community across these borders.

Even after the people arrived at Pine Ridge from the south, they would not allow the reservation boundaries to define their relationship to their kin and landscape. They traveled back and forth to the Tongue River valley, often without permission from the agent. When the Northern Cheyenne reservation boundaries were first established in 1884, the people did not acquiesce to them, either. Those living in the Tongue River valley ignored this boundary and continued to homestead and camp outside of it. They asserted their connection to their landscape beyond the boundary in their daily lives and their discourse with government officials. Ultimately, the president shifted the borders of the reservation in 1900 so that they would reflect the residence patterns the Cheyennes had established.

From the perspective of government officials, a nation maintained its identity and its relationship to land through the creation of boundaries that mark these relationships as distinct; therefore, once a reservation boundary was established and accepted, it severed the people from claiming land and identity beyond the boundaries. For the Cheyennes, however, relationships to landscape and identity persisted through kin relationships that could be maintained across the rigid boundaries set by the state. Under this system of political autonomy, relationships to landscape extend as far as a group's kin connections would allow.

The role the Northern Cheyennes had in the establishment of their own reservation can further scholarly conversations about Indigenous autonomy in four ways. First, the Northern Cheyenne case encourages a deeper examination of the importance of kinship for Native nations in organizing strategic political action in ways very different from the nation-state. Second, this history raises questions about the ways Native nations have used kinship to circumvent the inscription of nation-state boundaries and, in doing so, have made kin ties essential to resistance and persistence. Third, this study encourages scholarship on the way that the flexibility of kin-based sociopolitical organization provides Indigenous peoples space to negotiate with the nation-state, and the ability to adopt some trappings of the state and redefine or discard others. Fourth, the Northern Cheyenne case demonstrates that Native nations have an inherent political autonomy that depends on each group's own delineation of sociopolitical organization, that can be recognized by others outside the nation, and that exists independent of the limited sovereignty granted by a nation-state. By using Northern Cheyenne history as an example, I wish to propose a theoretical framework for understanding kin-based relations as a method that Indigenous populations in general have used to negotiate with nation-states, to cross the physical and social boundaries states impose, and to maintain control over their own cultural identity. Ultimately, I propose that using kinship as a theoretical approach for understanding nationhood can provide scholars with a way to conceptualize the persistence of political autonomy among Indigenous peoples.

An exploration of Cheyenne autonomy as it has been exercised through networks of kin demonstrates that Native nations, including those who have accepted some of the trappings of the state, are not dependent on the recognition of the nation-state and can exist both within and outside of it at the same time. The Northern Cheyennes' struggle to be recognized according to their own social and political definitions was a struggle against erasure by the state. At the same time, the Cheyennes possessed agency in this struggle because the state never attained an all-encompassing power over their ability to define who they are. Focusing on an Indigenous understanding of social organization reveals that historically, Native nations exercised a political autonomy more flexible and often more powerful than the sovereignty based in the state and assigned to them by nation-state governments, because this autonomy recognizes claims to identity, territory, and resources that the state is unable to acknowledge.

Although today the Cheyennes use the ethnic definition of a bounded, statelike entity imposed on them because the United States has invested it with political power, they also resist the boundaries of space and social relations implied by the ethnic definition. The creation of reservations, enrollment, and allotment not only pushed the Cheyennes into bounded territorial space but also forced individuals with mixed backgrounds to choose one tribal affiliation. The Cheyennes continued to resist the imposition of such boundaries through maintaining intertribal relations through kin and drawing on them to cross territorial boundaries. The fixed borders imposed by the nation-state had consequences for the people, so to mitigate these consequences the Cheyennes built and rebuilt kin ties that resisted these colonial borders. Viewing the Cheyennes from this perspective reveals a political autonomy that was not devastated by U.S. colonial might but instead was maintained into the reservation era and continues to exist without the nation-state today, although in a weakened form.

Today many groups assert political power from beyond the boundaries of the state, affecting its stability. Undocumented immigrants, migrant labor, refugees, Indigenous peoples, and international extremist groups undermine the power of the state to contain and homogenize, some on a daily basis. Multinational corporations circumvent national regulations by maintaining multiple and shifting locations. There is a general sense that such fluid political relations emerged as a result of globalization. Yet Cheyenne history reveals that Indigenous peoples were using flexible social organization to exercise political power from multiple and shifting locations to undermine state formations long before the era of the multinational corporation or the global terror network.

In the end, does including Two Moons's or Little Chief's or Dull Knife's family change the Northern Cheyenne story that dramatically? These new characters demonstrate that Cheyenne people and their allies exercised political autonomy through establishing and activating kinship ties. They also show that these means of expressing political power provide a flexibility that can be very useful when attempting to negotiate the imposition of state-based boundaries. So the story is different. It is no longer simply about retaining sovereignty or succumbing to assimilation. It is about a kind of nationhood that supersedes these categories, a kind of political mechanism that negotiates colonial impositions while retaining autonomy. The political autonomy that emerges from reciprocal social relationships can meet almost any changing circumstance, as long as the webs of kinship survive.

Even today, kin relationships are primary to the political actions of Native nations. The restorative justice practiced in tribal courts is about repairing relationships. Native environmental activists, working to restore tribal lands and traditional foodways, emphasize the relatedness of people to nonhuman beings and the reciprocal responsibilities these relationships entail. Native people continue to depend on networks of family for economic support. The primacy of the extended family in Native communities is even recognized by the Indian Child Welfare Act, which seeks to place Native children in foster care within their broad network of family members. The web of kin might look different today than it did in the past. It has been woven and rewoven each time it was torn by removal, colonialism, missionization, and forced assimilation, but Native nations repair each tear, sometimes slowly, but always with the goal of sustaining relationships.

In a world where essentially all Indigenous peoples must navigate their position within the boundaries of the states where they live, these stories about the power of Cheyenne kinship might just inspire new ways to construct political relationships, both within Indigenous communities and between these communities and the state. I have no idea what this might look like. But it is clear, even to me, that Native people still find strength, life, and political power in their families and in their stories. Some elders still remember what their political life looked like when it drew its power mainly from kin relationships. Both scholars and political pundits have begun to wonder if the nation-state is in fact as eternal as it claims to be. Perhaps the state is in decline, they lament. Instead of worrying about the future, we might look to the past, allowing Indigenous history to lead the way. There we can find stories about political autonomy that is flexible enough to handle shifting localities and fluid membership, and in its flexibility, strong enough to withstand a five-hundred-year storm of oppression and assimilation. In these stories, we see exemplified a decision-making process that incorporates perspectives from the ancestors while considering the needs of the unborn. In my humble opinion, the possibility for new life to emerge from such stories is simply immense.

APPENDIX

The 1874 Agreement with the Northern Cheyennes

Federal officials pointed to this document when they argued that the Northern Cheyennes had agreed to reside permanently at the Southern Cheyenne and Arapaho Reservation in Indian Territory. Notice the language that states the people agreed only to travel south, not to live there permanently.

Reproduced from J. J. Saville, "Treaty with Northern Cheyenne and Arapaho Indians: Red Cloud Agency, DT," November 17, 1874, Letters Received, Red Cloud Agency, Kansas City National Archives.

TREATY WITH NORTHERN CHEYENNE AND ARAPAHO INDIANS: RED CLOUD AGENCY, DT

We the undersigned chiefs and headmen of the Northern Cheyenne and Arapahoe Indians do hereby agree to go to the Southern Reservation whenever the President of the United States may so direct provided we are allowed to remain at Red Cloud Agency and receive rations and annuity goods until that time arrives.

Red Cloud Agency

November 12, 1874

CHEYENNES	ARAPAHOES
Little Wolf	Black Cloud
Limber	Eagle Dress
Big Wolf	White Breast
Standing Elk	Plenty Bear
	Red Eagle

We certify that we have interpreted the above to the chiefs and headmen before they signed and entrusted their signatures to this agreement.

WITNESSES	INTERPRETERS
I. W. Faugh	William Rowland
James Roberts	Friday

We the undersigned witnesses certify that we were present and saw the chiefs and headmen sign the above agreement.

I certify on honor that the above is correct.

J. J. Saville
U.S. Indian Agent

Notes

Introduction

1. Starita, *Dull Knifes*, 29. For other descriptions of the origins of Dull Knife's name, see Eastman, *Indian Heroes*, 82; Dusenberry, "Northern Cheyenne," 27–28; Stands In Timber and Liberty, *Cheyenne Memories*, 214.

2. I use the term "American" throughout to refer to a person who identifies him- or herself with the political entity of the United States, accepting membership in the nation regardless of race or heritage. Although I employ this term, I recognize historically that the term "American" in reference to residents of the United States can sometimes become a monolithic reference that either subsumes or erases other American nations, such as Mexico, Brazil, or Canada. I have chosen the term for its ease of use and employ it in a very specific sense. I use "American" to refer to all people who imagine themselves to be a part of what Benedict Anderson terms the deep, horizontal comradeship of the nation. See Anderson, *Imagined Communities*. This term refers not only to people the U.S. government recognizes as citizens but to all people who claim membership in the nation as well. At a certain point in history, most American Indian people become Americans in the way that I use the term. However, American Indian membership in the United States is complicated by their continuing membership in their own nations. At the same time, Native people are not immune to the kinds of representations we see of American Indian people employed to legitimize the U.S. hegemonic nationalist narrative. They also find the heroic but tragic narratives constructed around their ancestors appealing and have sometimes used them to make their continued presence known to non-Natives and to bolster their own national claims.

3. The General Allotment Act, or the Dawes Act of 1887, divided reservation lands into 160-acre parcels. Heads of households chose parcels of land, and the government opened reservation land not claimed by tribal members

for settlement by non-Natives. For more on the Allotment Act, see Chang, "Enclosures of Land"; Genetin-Pilawa, *Crooked Paths*; Greenwald, *Reconfiguring the Reservation*; Otis, *Dawes Act*.

4. Hoig, *Perilous Pursuit*; Monnett, *Tell Them*.

5. Monnett, *Tell Them*; Leiker and Powers, *Northern Cheyenne Exodus*; Sandoz, *Cheyenne Autumn*; Hoig, *Perilous Pursuit*.

6. King, *Truth about Stories*, 2.

7. Ibid., 10–23.

8. Silko, *Ceremony*, 132–38.

<h2 style="text-align:center">CHAPTER 1</h2>

1. For a discussion of polyphonic cultural representations, see Clifford, *Predicament of Culture*, 46.

2. The Northern Cheyenne nation today is recognized by the United States as a sovereign government. Like other Native sovereign nations in the United States, the Northern Cheyenne nation projects a unified tribal history, complete with monuments, museums, great men, and national narratives, to strengthen the claim to sovereign nation status.

3. Clifford, "Introduction: Partial Truths," in Clifford and Marcus, *Writing Culture*, 8.

4. For a discussion of history and the state, see Anderson, *Imagined Communities*. For a description of how Native histories operate to connect peoples within a nation but also to express the divergent histories of particular bands and families, see Basso, *Wisdom Sits in Places*.

5. Boye, *Holding Stone Hands*, 116.

6. See Brown, *Strangers in Blood*; Perdue, *Cherokee Women*; Kidwell, "Indian Women as Cultural Mediators"; Shoemaker, *Negotiators of Change*; Sleeper-Smith, *Indian Women and French Men*; Thorne, *Many Hands*; Van Kirk, *Many Tender Ties*. Some scholars have begun to directly address the implementation of kinship as a part of Indigenous political discourse, such as Braun, "Against Procedural Landscapes," 201; Hyde, *Empires, Nations, and Families*; Innes, *Elder Brother*; Lakomäki, *Gathering Together*; Miles, *Ties That Bind*; Rand, *Kiowa Humanity*; Rzeczkowski, *Uniting the Tribes*; Witgen, "The Rituals of Possession"; Witgen, *Infinity of Nations*.

7. Fixico, *American Indian Mind*, 22.

8. Fogelson, "Ethnohistory of Events and Non-Events," 134; DeMallie, "'These Have No Ears,'" 533; Nabokov, *Forest of Time*; Shoemaker, *Clearing a Path*, xii.

9. Shoemaker, *Clearing a Path*, xii. Indigenous theory has been developed more extensively since it was proposed by Shoemaker. See Simpson and Smith, *Theorizing Native Studies*.

10. Smith, *Decolonizing Methodologies*, 4.

11. White, "Memory Moments," 331.

12. Aleiss, *Making the White Man's Indian*; Bergland, *National Uncanny*; Berkhofer, *White Man's Indian*; Kilpatrick, *Celluloid Indians*; Rollins, *Hollywood's Indian*; Slapin and Seale, *Through Indian Eyes*.

13. Deloria, *Playing Indian*, 4.

14. Hoxie, "Retrieving the Red Continent."

15. Clifford and Marcus, *Writing Culture*, 16. See also Rosaldo, *Ilongot Headhunting*; Wolf, *Europe*.

16. Fabian, *Time and the Other*.

17. Lakomäki, *Gathering Together*. Several scholars have made important contributions to the process of recognizing the impact American Indian historical action has had on American history, including Blackhawk, *Violence*; Calloway, *New Worlds for All*; Calloway, *One Vast Winter Count*; DuVal, *Native Ground*; Hämäläinen, *Comanche Empire*; Merrell, *Indians' New World*; Richter, *Facing East*; Taylor, *American Colonies*; West, *Contested Plains*; White, *Middle Ground*; Witgen, *Infinity of Nations*.

18. Blackhawk, *Violence*; Rand, *Kiowa Humanity*.

19. Blackhawk, *Violence*, 5 (emphasis in the original). In 1969 Vine Deloria Jr. also warned scholars that it is inadequate to simply incorporate Native people into American narratives without reconfiguring their boundaries. Deloria, *Custer Died for Your Sins*.

20. Hardt and Negri, *Empire*, 87, 98.

21. Hobbes, *Leviathan*, 78.

22. Hobbes, *On the Citizen*, 76.

23. Morgan, *Ancient Society*.

24. Morgan, *Systems of Consanguinity*, 14.

25. Foucault, *"Society Must Be Defended,"* 26.

26. Reyes and Kaufman, "Sovereignty, Indigeneity, Territory," 511.

27. Anderson, *Imagined Communities*.

28. Alonso, "Politics of Space"; Bell, *Cult of the Nation in France*, 5–7.

29. Some recent scholarship concerning the constructed nature of the nation-state has begun to explore the limitations of historical narratives that emerge from a nation-state perspective. See, for example, Scott, *Seeing Like a State*; Willinsky, *Learning to Divide the World*; Rowe, *Post-Nationalist American Studies*; Noble, *Death of a Nation*. Furthermore, some scholars have questioned these assumptions for understanding Indigenous group formations. See Sharrock, "Crees, Cree-Assiniboines, and Assiniboines," 95; Witgen, *Infinity of Nations*; Wolf, *Europe*, 6.

30. Wolf, *Europe*, 6. For further exploration of the connection between the construction of human societies as bounded objects and the rise of the social and natural sciences, see Willinsky, *Learning to Divide the World*.

31. Sharrock, "Crees, Cree-Assiniboines, and Assiniboines," 95.

32. Fried, "On the Concept of 'Tribe,'" 8–9, 14.

33. Eggan, "Cheyenne and Arapaho Kinship System"; Grinnell, *Cheyenne Indians*, 2:4–13; Hoebel, *Cheyennes*; Llewellyn and Hoebel, *Cheyenne Way*, 21.

34. For a more detailed discussion, see Berndt, "Kinship as an Assertion."

35. For a discussion of the nation-state as a colonizing political entity that seeks to incorporate all peoples within its borders, see Anderson, *Imagined Communities*.

36. Deloria, *Indians in Unexpected Places*, 15–28; Hoxie, *Final Promise*, 2–39; Rand, *Kiowa Humanity*. David E. Wilkins has demonstrated how this ambiguity has played out historically, tracing several U.S. Supreme Court rulings as they swing in their constructions of Native peoples from nationlike tribes to chaotic savages. See Wilkins, *American Indian Sovereignty*. For an in-depth discussion of the ambiguity of the nation-state and how it allows Europeans and Americans to transpose the conception of a bounded ethnicity onto Indigenous groups while at the same time viewing Indigenous peoples as chaotic and irrational, see Anderson, *Imagined Communities*.

37. Deloria and Clifford, *Nations Within*.

38. Lyons, *X-Marks*, 135–36.

39. Barker, *Sovereignty Matters*, 21, 26.

40. Holm, Pearson, and Chavis, "Peoplehood"; Alfred, *Peace, Power, Righteousness*; Alfred, *Wasáse*; Barker, *Sovereignty Matters*; Turner, *This Is Not a Peace Pipe*; Kauanui, *Hawaiian Blood*; Smith, "Indigeneity"; Weaver, "Indigenousness and Indigeneity."

41. For example, DuVal, *Native Ground*; Hyde, *Empires, Nations, and Families*; Hämäläinen, *Comanche Empire*; Raibmon, *Authentic Indians*; Rand, *Kiowa Humanity*; Smoak, *Ghost Dances and Identity*; Lyons, *X-Marks*; White, *Middle Ground*; Witgen, *Infinity of Nations*.

42. Sami Lakomäki, *Gathering Together*, 4.

43. Alfred, *Wasáse*; Simpson, *Mohawk Interruptus*; Smith, "Indigeneity"; Stark, "Nenabozho's Smart Berries"; Williams, *Like a Loaded Weapon*.

44. Fixico, *Indian Resilience*, 12; Scott, *Seeing Like a State*; Spivak, "Nationalism and the Imagination"; Zaum, *Sovereignty Paradox*.

45. Deloria and Lytle, *Nations Within*, 2–8; Deloria and Wilkins, *Tribes*, 7. Early in the period of European exploration of the Americas, the Catholic Church articulated the Doctrine of Discovery, which was designed to secure title to land through discovery by Europeans but marked Native nations as the original occupants and required them to give up the land willingly, establishing a frame for Europe to legally recognize Native nations as sovereign entities. For more on the Doctrine of Discovery, see Robertson, *Conquest by Law*; Banner, *How the Indians Lost Their Land*; Miller, *Native America*.

46. Josephy, *500 Nations*, 50, 52–53; Schaaf, "From the Great Law"; Tooker, "United States Constitution"; Howe, "Story of America," 164.

47. Deloria and Lytle, *Nations Within*, 3; Wilkins, *American Indian Sovereignty*, 4, 21–25.

48. Deloria and Lytle, *Nations Within*, 4.

49. Deloria and Wilkins, *Tribes*, 7; Deloria and Lytle, *Nations Within*, 8. See also Wilkins, *American Indian Sovereignty*.

50. Wilkins and Lomawaima, *Uneven Ground*, 5.

51. Deloria and Lytle, *Nations Within*, 8.

52. Ibid., 8–14.

53. Grinnell, *Cheyenne Indians*; Powell, *Sweet Medicine*.

54. Holm, Pearson, and Chavis, "Peoplehood," 12, 17.

55. Sundstrom, "Mirror of Heaven."

56. I use the term "Cheyenne" to refer to this Native nation throughout because although its organization shifted over time, the Cheyenne people have seen themselves as a sociopolitical collective and have been recognized as such by outsiders for at least several hundred years. Today Northern Cheyenne people use the term "Cheyenne," which refers to both Tsitsitsas and Suhtaio peoples, when speaking in English to refer to their own collective cultural identity and the political entity of their nation. They also use "Cheyenne" to encompass both Northern and Southern Cheyenne peoples as one nation. While the Northern Cheyenne reservation has its own government, as does the Southern Cheyenne reservation, the people see these two reservations as parts of one larger Cheyenne nation.

57. Albers and James, "On the Dialectics of Ethnicity"; Barth, *Ethnic Groups and Boundaries*; Fried, "On the Concept of 'Tribe'"; Sharrock, "Interethnic Social Organization."

58. Lyons, *X-Marks*, 138–39.

59. See Harmon, *Indians in the Making*; Fowler, *Shared Symbols*, 3; Blu, *Lumbee Problem*, 2.

60. Harmon, *Indians in the Making*; Wright, *Creeks and Seminoles*; Merrell, *Indians' New World*; Lyons, *X-Marks*.

61. Alfred, "Sovereignty"; Reyes and Kaufman, "Sovereignty, Indigeneity, Territory."

62. Agamben, *Homo Sacer*, 18.

63. Reyes and Kaufman, "Sovereignty, Indigeneity, Territory," 508–9.

64. Alfred, "Sovereignty."

65. Reyes and Kaufman, "Sovereignty, Indigeneity, Territory," 512.

66. Lomawaima, "Mutuality of Citizenship," 345.

67. DuVal, *Native Ground*, 4.

68. Hyde, *Empires, Nations, and Families*.

69. Blackhawk, *Violence*, 6.

70. Rand, *Kiowa Humanity*, 9.

71. Hämäläinen, *Comanche Empire*; Hyde, *Empires, Nations, and Families*.

72. Hämäläinen, *Comanche Empire*; Aikau, "Indigeneity in the Diaspora"; Byrd, *Transit of Empire*; Gallay, *Indian Slave Trade*; Brooks, "Captives and Cousins"; Barr, *Peace Came.*

73. DuVal, *Native Ground*, 9; Hyde, *Empires, Nations, and Families*, 293.

74. A few scholars have sought to incorporate the flexibility of Native social organization and the chaos of conquest while describing a Native nation's ability to sustain its autonomous political status. See Lakomäki, *Gathering Together*; Rand, *Kiowa Humanity*; Rzeczkowski, *Uniting the Tribes.*

75. Moore, *Cheyenne Nation*; Grinnell, *Cheyenne Indians*; Hoebel, *Cheyennes*; Eggan, *American Indian.*

76. Eggan, *American Indian.*

77. This is true for all federally recognized American Indian peoples in the United States as well as First Nations peoples in Canada who hold treaties with the crown. It is also true for the Maori of New Zealand and the Aboriginals of Australia. There are other peoples who exist as recognized nations separate from the states in which they live, but with less clearly defined legal statuses, such as the Sami of Northern Europe, the Ainu of Japan, and the San of Botswana.

78. Deloria and Lytle, *Nations Within*, 14.

79. Reyes and Kaufman, "Sovereignty, Indigeneity, Territory," 515.

80. Silko, "Language and Literature."

81. Wolf, *Europe*, 99.

82. Braun, "Against Procedural Landscapes," 201; DuVal, *Native Ground*; Hyde, *Empires, Nations, and Families*; Sami, *Gathering Together*; Innes, *Elder Brother.*

83. Scholars have made clear the importance of kinship to Indigenous identity, including Kauanui, *Hawaiian Blood*; Klopotek, *Recognition Odysseys*; Rifkin, *When Did Indians*; Wightman, *Honoring Kin.*

84. DuVal, *Native Ground*, 7.

85. Deloria, "Kinship with the World," 224.

86. Ibid., 227.

87. Alfred, "Sovereignty," 48.

CHAPTER 2

1. Fixico has mentioned the centrality of generosity to Indigenous moral economies, as well as its importance to maintaining positive relationships both within the family and beyond. *Indian Resilience*, 23–24.

2. Forest describes this ripple effect in "Return of the Ancient Council Ways," 238.

3. Fixico, *American Indian Mind*, 75.

4. Deloria, *Speaking of Indians*, 31.

5. DeMallie, "Kinship and Biology," 125–26.

6. Ibid., 131; Deloria in *Speaking of Indians* articulates this same sense of reciprocal obligation embedded in kinship terminology (30).

7. For more details, see Berndt, "Kinship," 312–16, Appendix A.

8. John Moore has described the importance of the nisson among the Cheyennes historically as well as the centrality of groups of sisters to taking care of children even today. See Moore, *Cheyenne Nation*, 272, 281; Moore, "Cheyenne Polygyny," 315.

9. Anderson, *Four Hills*, 20. DeMallie made this point in relations to Lakota and Dakota peoples as well in "Kinship and Biology."

10. See Kan, *Strangers to Relatives*.

11. Jeffrey D. Anderson describes this for the Arapahos as well in *Four Hills*, 21.

12. Albers and Kay, "Sharing the Land," 50.

13. Albers, "Changing Patterns," 91.

14. Moore, *Cheyenne Nation*, 204, 221.

15. Stands In Timber and Liberty, *Cheyenne Voice*, 102, 247–48. Little Wolf told Grinnell he did what he could to prevent the young men from raiding the settlements. See Grinnell, *Fighting Cheyennes*, 413.

16. For more on these moments of strife, see Monnett, *Tell Them*, 95–97, 165; Leiker and Powers, *Northern Cheyenne Exodus*, 61.

17. For a discussion of these shifting kinship expectations, see Moore, "Cheyenne Polygyny"; Nugent, "Property Relations."

18. Moore, *The Cheyenne*, 13–29; Gussow, "Aboriginal Occupation," 24; Hoebel, *Cheyennes*, 4–11; Hyde, *Life of George Bent*, 3–8; Weist, *History*. For a more detailed discussion of Cheyenne origins around the Great Lakes and origin narratives, see Berndt, "Kinship," 62–69.

19. Grinnell, *Cheyenne Indians*, 1:4. Michelson recorded that Left Hand Bull's great-grandfather was born in Canada around 1740–50. Moore, *Cheyenne Nation*, 115.

20. Grinnell, *Cheyenne Indians*, 1:3.

21. Moore, *The Cheyenne*, 1–5.

22. Hyde, *Life of George Bent*, 4.

23. Moore, *The Cheyenne*, 13.

24. Neil McKay, Dakota language teacher at the University of Minnesota, e-mail with author, May 8, 2007.

25. Grinnell, *Cheyenne Indians*, 1:2n2.

26. For a more detailed discussion of Cheyenne migrations onto the Plains, see Berndt, "Kinship," 74–78.

27. Grinnell, *By Cheyenne Campfires*, 263–78; Moore, *Cheyenne Nation*, 102–6. Stands In Timber also related detailed narratives about Sweet Medicine,

his life, and his instructions to the Cheyenne people. Stands In Timber and Liberty, *Cheyenne Voice*, 6–26.

28. For a detailed discussion of the purpose of these bundles and their origins, see Moore, *Cheyenne Nation*; Grinnell, *Cheyenne Indians*; Powell, *Sweet Medicine*. For narratives about the Sacred Arrows bundle, see Stands In Timber and Liberty, *Cheyenne Voice*, 27–31, 316–20.

29. American Indian Tribal Histories Project, "The Origin of the Suhtaio," *Northern Cheyenne Educational DVD Set*.

30. Stands In Timber and Liberty, *Cheyenne Memories*, 19–24. Stands In Timber also recounted the Great Race narrative in *Cheyenne Voice*, 253. Interviews by the author, Lame Deer, Northern Cheyenne Indian Reservation, summers of 2004, 2005, and 2006.

31. DeMallie has noted that the impact of kinship on Plains social organization is so strong that newcomers to a community would be assigned a place within the kin network so that their connection to the community would be clear. DeMallie, "Kinship and Biology," 131–33. Other scholars have written about the centrality of kinship to American Indian social organization, including Miller, "Kinship"; Deloria, *Speaking of Indians*; Fixico, *American Indian Mind*.

32. Rifkin, *When Did Indians*.

33. Stands In Timber and Liberty, *Cheyenne Voice*, 462. Rifkin also discusses the efforts of reservation officials to break up polygamous marriages. Rifkin, "Romancing Kinship"; Rifkin, *When Did Indians*.

34. Roscoe, *Changing Ones*; Rifkin, *When Did Indians*; Jacobs, Thomas, and Lang, *Two-Spirit People*.

35. See Berndt, "Kinship," figure 18 in appendix B; Stands In Timber and Liberty, *Cheyenne Voice*, 191–92, 255, 320–21, 355; Moore, *Cheyenne Nation*, 99.

36. American Indian Tribal Histories Project, "The Origin of the Tsistsistas," *Northern Cheyenne Educational DVD Set*; Hyde, *Life of George Bent*, 13; Weist, *History*, 24.

37. American Indian Tribal Histories Project, "The Origin of the Tsistsistas"; Hyde, *Life of George Bent*, 13. Elva Stands In Timber also told a version of this story. Elva Stands In Timber, interview by the author, Lame Deer, Northern Cheyenne Indian Reservation, July 31, 2006. Some Cheyenne oral histories relate that the Suhtaios and the Tsistsistas were once the same people who had separated; when they found each other again generations later and discovered they spoke the same language, they reunited.

38. Hyde, *Life of George Bent*, 13.

39. Moore, *Cheyenne Nation*, 99.

40. Weist, *History*, 24; Hoebel, *Cheyennes*, 9. Weist puts the date at 1830.

41. For a more detailed explanation of the organization of Cheyenne kindreds, camps, and bands, see Berndt, "Kinship," appendix B.

42. Moore, "Cheyenne Polygyny," 314–15.

43. Grinnell, *Cheyenne Indians*, 1:91; Ms. DG, interview by the author, Lame Deer, Northern Cheyenne Indian Reservation, summer 2005 and 2006.

44. Grinnell, "Social Organization," 137.

45. Ibid., 138. This was a rare circumstance. Usually a motherless infant was given to the mother's family to raise.

46. For a detailed description of Cheyenne band formation historically, see Moore, *Cheyenne Nation*, 177–250. Moore uses the term "bunch" to describe a group who traveled and camped together, oriented around a group of sisters, because the Cheyenne speakers he interviewed used this term in English to describe this arrangement. He distinguishes between clans, bunches, and camps, arguing that "clan" has been used to refer to military societies, "camps" to residence units, and "bunches" to groups led by council chiefs. These bunches created the core of the named bands and were made up mainly of the relatives of the council chiefs, while other members of these bands often lived in scattered camps.

47. Interviews by the author, Lame Deer, Northern Cheyenne Indian Reservation, summers of 2004, 2005, and 2006. Also see American Indian Tribal Histories Project, "Cheyenne Leadership."

48. Moore, *Cheyenne Nation*, 46–47. See also Grinnell, *Cheyenne Indians*, 1:48–86. Grinnell listed seven societies including Kit Fox Men, Elk Horn Scrapers, Dog Men, Red Shields, Crazy Dogs, Bowstrings, and Chief Soldiers. He stated that originally there were only four bands and that the Crazy Dogs and Bowstrings were recent additions (49). Hoebel listed five original military societies, including the Fox, Elk, Shield, Dog, and Bowstring (*Cheyennes*, 40). Possibly these two authors listed other societies because military organizations have shifted slightly in makeup over time.

49. Stands In Timber and Liberty, *Cheyenne Voice*, 107. Stands In Timber described the origins of each of these societies as well (23–24). He described the Swift Fox society in detail as well as the Crazy Dogs (38–40, 42–45, 309–10). For a discussion of the difference between the names scholars have given for military societies among the Cheyennes and also of the shifting in these societies over time, see Llewellyn and Hoebel, *Cheyenne Way*, 99–100.

50. For more on the operations of this society, see Santina, "Recreating the World"; Grinnell, *The Cheyenne*, 229; Schneider, "Women's Work," 114.

51. Research conducted on the Northern Cheyenne Indian Reservation by the author, summers of 2004, 2005, and 2006. Stands In Timber mentioned the chiefs' society as well and stated that they upheld the laws and were responsible for renewing the Sacred Arrows. See Stands In Timber and Liberty, *Cheyenne Voice*, 23, 107–11.

52. I do not address the Council of Forty-Four in great detail here. Although these head chiefs had a part in connecting the Cheyenne people as a Native nation, they did not form kin relationships across bands directly as a council in the way that military society men did. Chiefs formed relationships

across bands through the marriages they made for their children. For more information on the Council of Forty-Four, see Moore, *Cheyenne Nation*, 106–7; Llewellyn and Hoebel, *Cheyenne Way*, 67–98; Grinnell, *Cheyenne Indians*, 1:336–58; Hoebel, *Cheyennes*, 43–53.

53. Grinnell, *Cheyenne Indians*, 1:50–51; Llewellyn and Hoebel, *Cheyenne Way*, 103; Moore, *Cheyenne Nation*, 107. Stands In Timber discussed the mechanism for appointing new chiefs to the Council of Forty-Four (*Cheyenne Voice*, 107–8).

54. Grinnell, *Cheyenne Indians*, 1:50.

55. Hoebel, *Cheyennes*, 40.

56. Ibid.; Grinnell, *Cheyenne Indians*, 1:49.

57. Eggan, "Cheyenne Kinship," 86–88.

58. Hoebel, *Cheyennes*, 41; Grinnell, *Cheyenne Indians*, 1:50. Stands In Timber described this practice for the Swift Fox society. See Stands In Timber and Liberty, *Cheyenne Voice*, 45–46.

59. Hoebel, *Cheyennes*, 41; Grinnell, *Cheyenne Indians*, 1:50.

60. Ms. DG, interview by the author, Lame Deer, Northern Cheyenne Indian Reservation, summer 2006.

61. Hoebel, *Cheyennes*, 40; Eggan, "Cheyenne Kinship," 85.

62. Moore, *Cheyenne Nation*, 106. Grinnell claimed that each of the ten bands had four chiefs on the council and that the council had four principle chiefs (*Cheyenne Indians*, 337). Henrietta Mann supported Grinnell's statement; see American Indian Tribal Histories Project, "Cheyenne Leadership." Having four chiefs from each band represents the ideal and did not always equate to the distribution of chiefs in each band at any given time. Further, because the members of a bunch did not always claim a unitary band identity, each band might have four chiefs, but a bunch could have any number.

63. American Indian Tribal Histories Project, "Cheyenne Leadership."

64. Moore, *Cheyenne Nation*, 109.

65. American Indian Tribal Histories Project, "Cheyenne Leadership."

66. Grinnell, *Cheyenne Indians*, 1:336–37; interviews by the author, Lame Deer, Northern Cheyenne Indian Reservation, summers 2005 and 2006. Stands In Timber related a powerful story of a chief who refused to seek revenge after his son was murdered, stating that a true chief must always avoid getting angry. Stands In Timber and Liberty, *Cheyenne Voice*, 102.

67. Grinnell, *Cheyenne Indians*, 1:53. For a detailed discussion of both the ceremonial and political activities of the military societies, see Llewellyn and Hoebel, *Cheyenne Way*, 99–131; Grinnell, *Cheyenne Indians*, 1:48–79.

68. Moore, *Cheyenne Nation*, 106. For a detailed discussion of the story of Sweet Medicine as a foundation for Cheyenne political organization, see Moore, *Cheyenne Nation*, 102–9.

69. Stands In Timber and Liberty, *Cheyenne Memories*, 36; Grinnell, *Cheyenne Indians*, 1:345. Both of these sources tell versions of this part of the Sweet Medicine story. Also see American Indian Tribal Histories Project, "Cheyenne Leadership."

70. Stands In Timber and Liberty, *Cheyenne Memories*, 36.

71. American Indian Tribal Histories Project, "Cheyenne Leadership."

72. Eggan, *American Indian*, 53.

73. Moore, *Cheyenne Nation*, 46–49.

74. Ibid., 48.

75. This duality is very common in the organization of nations speaking Algonquian languages, such as the Shawnees and the Mesquakies. Fred Gearing has demonstrated that dual social organization was not unusual at all in eastern North America. See Gearing, *Priests and Warriors*.

76. Straus, "Northern Cheyenne Ethnopsychology," 329–30. Straus also discusses how these qualities are manifested in women.

77. Ibid., 329n6.

78. Moore stated that both the Dog Men and the Foxes formed separate bands that had their own locations in the camp circle when the United States warred with the Cheyennes. See Moore, *Cheyenne Nation*, 48–49.

79. Ibid., 191.

80. Interviews by the author, Lame Deer, Northern Cheyenne Indian Reservation, summers of 2005 and 2006. The term "full blood" as it is used in this instance by Cheyenne people does not represent biological descendancy but cultural identity. Raymond DeMallie has discussed the use of "blood" to refer to identity among Lakota and Dakota peoples as well, and he has argued that this terminology has been influenced by the Bureau of Indian Affairs's tendency to use "blood" to acknowledge tribal enrollment. DeMallie, "Kinship and Biology," 132.

81. Several authors have discussed the importance of kinship for establishing interethnic relationships on the plains, including Albers and Kay, "Sharing the Land"; Sharrock, "Interethnic Social Organization"; Anderson, *Kinsmen of Another Kind*; Moore, *Cheyenne Nation*; Albers, "Symbiosis, Merger, and War."

82. See Berndt, "Kinship," appendix A for a full description.

83. Moore, *Cheyenne Nation*, 9. For a detailed discussion of band exogamy among the Cheyennes, see 251–63.

84. Hyde, *Life of George Bent*, 15.

85. Pierre Antoine Tabeau specifically mentions that the Cheyennes brought horses laden with wild turnips to trade with the Arikaras, who highly valued the root. Albers, *Home of the Bison*, 1:403–4.

86. Moore, *Cheyenne Nation*, 115.

87. Hyde, *Life of George Bent*, 16.

88. Jablow, *Plains Indian Trade Relations*, 42.

89. Weist, *History*, 25.

90. Modern nations, of course, incorporate outsiders of differing national affiliations. The United States prides itself on being considered a multicultural nation. At the same time, the United States considers foreign nationals who are not fully incorporated into the nation-state a threat to national unity. Consider the fear over undocumented immigration. Undocumented immigrants participate in the national life of the United States on many levels. Yet not only are they considered outsiders by many Americans, who believe they should not be granted the benefits of citizenship, many also see them as a threat to the stability of the state and therefore a chaotic force to be contained.

91. Patricia Albers has distinguished three types of intertribal relationships: those "based on war (competition), merger (cooperation), and symbiosis (complementarity)." Albers, "Symbiosis, Merger, and War," 99.

92. Albers and Kay, "Sharing the Land," 74.

93. Jablow, *Plains Indian Trade Relations*, 146–50. In her *Women of the Earth Lodges*, Virginia Peters also presented a detailed description of this encounter and its aftermath.

94. Jablow, *Plains Indian Trade Relations*, 50.

95. Peters, *Women of the Earth Lodges*, 146–47.

96. Ibid.

97. See Berndt, "Kinship," appendix A for further explanation of groupings of sisters and appendix B for a discussion of how these groups of sisters built uterine bands.

98. Hyde, *Life of George Bent*, 59–60. The exact date is debated; see Berthrong, *Southern Cheyennes*, 25–26.

99. Moore, *Cheyenne Nation*, 235.

100. Jablow, *Plains Indian Trade Relations*, 64.

101. For a discussion of the processes associated with merger, see Albers, "Symbiosis, Merger, and War," 112–14.

102. Albers and Kay, "Sharing the Land," 74.

103. Grinnell, *Cheyenne Indians*, 1:313.

104. Moore, *Cheyenne Nation*, 9. For a discussion of the three ways in which hybrid bands can be formed, see 54. Moore also presents a compelling argument that in the 1860s, the Dog Men were on the path to complete merger of Lakota and Cheyenne families through brother-brother adoptions that brought Lakota men into Cheyenne Dog Soldier societies. They might have broken from their larger Native nations had they not suffered a military disaster at Summit Springs in 1869. Moore, *Cheyenne Nation*, 202.

105. Albers, *Home of the Bison*, 1:37–51; Hyde, *Life of George Bent*, 20.

106. Hyde, *Life of George Bent*, 21.

107. Albers, *Home of the Bison*, 1:37; Hyde, *Life of George Bent*, 21.

108. Albers, *Home of the Bison*, 1:51; Weist, *History*, 27.

109. Powell, *Sweet Medicine*, 416. As European and American travelers, traders, and explorers entered the area, they made a record of the peoples they met. In 1801 Perrin du Lac spoke of the Cheyennes sharing the area of the Black Hills and the Cheyenne River with the Kiowas, Arapahos, and others. Another European who had entered the territory, Jean Valle, had visited with the Cheyennes in the Black Hills in the winter of 1801. Pierre-Antoine Tabeau recorded that in the winter of 1804–5, he spent time with a Cheyenne band in the eastern part of the Black Hills. Lewis and Clark's account of their visit to the region in 1804 emphasized that there was Cheyenne presence in the Black Hills as well. Lewis and Clark sent a map back to Washington in 1805 labeled "Cheyenne Nation, 110 lodges and 300 warriors, rove," in the area of the Black Hills. Grinnell, *Cheyenne Indians*, 1:31; Moore, *Cheyenne Nation*, 56; Weist, *History*, 28; Gussow, "Aboriginal Occupation," 28; Hurt, *Sioux Indians*, 162; Worcester, *Forked Tongues*, 110–11. Schoolcraft, who collected ethnographic information for the U.S. government, created a table that estimated the Indian population in 1850. He reported that the Cheyennes had "300 lodges and 3000 souls," and they resided "principally west of the Black Hills." Schoolcraft and Eastman, *Historical and Statistical Information*, 630.

110. Hyde, *Life of George Bent*, 17.

111. Moore, *Cheyenne Nation*, 321.

112. Stands In Timber agreed that Sweet Medicine acquired his teachings for the Cheyenne people around the Black Hills. The prophet lived a long time and asked the people to build him a wooden tipi where he stayed until he was no longer with them. According to Stands In Timber, the location of the tipi was marked somewhere west of Bear Butte. He believed that the marker still exists. Stands In Timber and Liberty, *Cheyenne Voice*, 107.

113. Moore, *Cheyenne Nation*, 314. It is important to note that although Moore argues that the four original Cheyenne bands were united by Sweet Medicine, including the Suhtaios, some oral histories state that the Tsistsistas already had the arrows when they met the Suhtaios. That Moore points to Sweet Medicine and the Black Hills as the location and moment of a great political shift for the Cheyenne people is correct, I believe; however, the exact chronology of this shift remains unclear and is not a topic of exploration here. Furthermore, it is important to note that the Council of Forty-Four is associated with not only Sweet Medicine but also a Cheyenne captive woman who brought the council from the Assiniboines. I do not try to reconcile these two oral narratives here but instead explore them both, giving them each equal weight as important explanations about the political and social life of the Cheyenne nation.

114. Peattie, *Black Hills*, 43; Weist, *History*, 25; Hyde, *Life of George Bent*, 16; Grinnell, *Fighting Cheyennes*, 36–37. Both Hurt and Moore cited Collet's map of 1796 showing the Cheyennes on the Cheyenne River that flows around

the Black Hills. Hurt, *Sioux Indians*, 78; Moore, *Cheyenne Nation*, 133. There is evidence that some Cheyenne groups had a more continued presence in the Black Hills at an earlier date as well. Albers, *Home of the Bison*, 1:39, 51.

115. Albers, *Home of the Bison*, 1:53.

116. Stands In Timber and Liberty, *Cheyenne Voice*, 355.

117. Weist, *History*, 25; Powell, *Sacred Mountain*, 27–28; Hyde, *Life of George Bent*, 21.

118. Albers, *Home of the Bison*, 1:41.

119. Moore, *Cheyenne Nation*, 218–19. Moore argued that this group is marked on the Lewis and Clark map camped with the Kiowas on the North Platte. In 1820 Major Long, who was leading an expedition to the Rocky Mountains, came across a camp of Kiowas, Comanches, Arapahos, Kiowa-Apaches, and Cheyennes on the Arkansas River. For more detailed accounts, see Jablow, *Plains Indian Trade Relations*, 60; Grinnell, *Cheyenne Indians*, 1:38–39; Berthrong, *Southern Cheyennes*, 20–21. A member of the expedition, Capt. John R. Bell, stated that these Cheyennes were a "band of seceders [*sic*] from their own nation," explaining that "since on the occurrence of a serious dispute with their kindred on the Shienne [*sic*] River of the Missouri, they flew their country and placed themselves under the protection of Bear Tooth [a leader among the Arapahos]." Bell clearly was speaking about the Wotapios. Berthrong, *Southern Cheyennes*, 21.

120. For details, see Moore, *Cheyenne Nation*, 121–25.

121. Ibid., 235.

122. Hyde, *Life of George Bent*, 22. This was not a unified action by the Cheyennes. Some Cheyennes traveled south out of the Black Hills with their Kiowa allies.

123. Weist, *History*, 29. For an alternative perspective on Crow and Cheyenne relations through the 1860s, see Liberty, "Cheyenne Primacy."

124. Albers, *Home of the Bison*, 1:41; Moore, *Cheyenne Nation*, 218–37.

125. The main body of the Cheyennes, including the Tsistsistas, Heviksnipahis, Hevhaitaneos, Oivimanas, and Hotametaneos, occupied the forks of the Cheyenne River on the eastern edge of the Black Hills from the late eighteenth century to the early nineteenth century. Berthrong noted that between 1776 and 1836, the Cheyennes and certain groups of Lakotas clashed periodically, driving the Cheyennes into an alliance with the Arapahos, who themselves were allied with the Kiowas in the south. By 1812 considerable numbers of Arapahos were moving south to the Arkansas River. Some Cheyennes moved with them to act as middlemen in trade between their Arapaho friends and the nations on the Missouri River. Berthrong, *Southern Cheyennes*, 18–19; Jablow, *Plains Indian Trade Relations*, 58–60. Between 1815 and 1825, the Cheyennes proper moved south as a block from the forks of the Cheyenne to the forks of the Platte. Other bands of Cheyennes had spread out around

the Black Hills, living and camping both northwest and south of the main body. The Omisis and Totoimanas, as well as some Suhtaios, lived on the northern and western edge of the Black Hills. These groups had intermarried with the Lakotas and together would come to dominate a large expanse of territory that stretched from the Black Hills to the Powder River region. The Masikota band lived southeast of the Black Hills along the White River where some intermarried with Ogalala and Sicangu bands of Lakotas. The Hisiometaneos also had close ties with the Ogalalas and Sicangus and lived on the Niobrara River, just south of the Masikotas. Some Suhtaios lived in the area southeast of the Black Hills as well, indicating that the Suhtaios had split at some point, some people moving north while others moved south. By 1820 the Wotapios had moved to the Arkansas in Colorado and were living and camping there with their Kiowa allies. See Albers, *Home of the Bison*, 1:69; Moore, *Cheyenne Nation*, 218–21.

126. For example, see West, *Contested Plains*, 83; Hoig, *Peace Chiefs*, 28; Hoebel, *Cheyennes*, 10–11; Grinnell, *Cheyenne Indians*, 1:40–41; Weist, *History*, 32. Grinnell, however, does acknowledge that intercourse continued between Northern and Southern peoples.

127. Hoebel, *Cheyennes*; Jablow, *Plains Indian Trade Relations*, 63–65, 80; Berthrong, *Southern Cheyennes*, 18–26. Jablow argued that around 1830, the Cheyennes became divided into northern and southern bands because part of the nation wanted to follow the fur traders and moved south to trade with Bent; those that remained in the area of the Black Hills became the Northern Cheyennes. He demonstrated that Bent's Fort allowed the Cheyennes to give up the role of the middleman, negotiating between Native groups to obtain European goods, and to begin trading directly with the whites. Jablow and Berthrong both mentioned Bent's Fort and William Bent's marriage to the Cheyenne woman named Owl Woman as factors in the division between Northern and Southern Cheyennes, but both noted that determining a catalyst must account for several complex factors. For a detailed discussion of Bent's Fort and the intermarriages between the Bent family and Cheyenne families, see Hyde, *Empires, Nations, and Families*.

128. Albers, *Home of the Bison*, 1:68.

129. For a description of the process of making peace, see Grinnell, *Fighting Cheyennes*, 63–69; Llewellyn and Hoebel, *Cheyenne Way*, 91–95; Jablow, *Plains Indian Trade Relations*, 73; Weist, *History*, 42.

130. Albers, "Symbiosis, Merger, and War," 122–23. For a detailed description of the Cheyennes' role in trade among Plains nations, see Jablow, *Plains Indian Trade Relations*.

131. Stands In Timber and Liberty, *Cheyenne Voice*, 244.

132. For more information on the practice of exchanging captives and both Native and Euro-American perspectives, see Barr, *Peace Came*; Brooks, *Captives*

and Cousins; DuVal, "Indian Intermarriage"; Igler, "Captive-Taking"; Rushforth, "Origins of Indian Slavery."

133. Albers, "Symbiosis, Merger, and War," 127. Stands In Timber discussed these kinds of visits between the Crows and Cheyennes in *Cheyenne Voice*, 275–76.

134. Albers, "Symbiosis, Merger, and War," 128.

135. Straus, "Northern Cheyenne Ethnopsychology," 346.

136. Straus, "Tell Your Sister," 175–76.

137. Moore, *Cheyenne Nation*, 189.

138. Anderson, *Four Hills*, 20; Fowler, *Tribal Sovereignty*.

139. Fixico, *Indian Resilience*, 24.

140. Moore, *Cheyenne Nation*, 202.

141. For a more detailed process of the Dog Men's role in reshaping Cheyenne social organization, see Moore, *Cheyenne Nation*, 203; Moore, "Cheyenne Political History."

142. Moore, *Cheyenne Nation*, 197.

143. In *The Cheyennes* Hoebel describes in detail the loss of privileges such a Cheyenne would suffer on his return. Interviews conducted by the author on the Northern Cheyenne Indian Reservation indicate that four years was the usual period of time before a murderer would be allowed to return from exile (50–52). For a more detailed description of Cheyenne laws surrounding murder, see also Hoebel and Llewellyn, *Cheyenne Way*.

144. Grinnell, *Fighting Cheyennes*, 42–60; Hoebel, *Cheyennes*, 38; Moore, *Cheyenne Nation*, 197.

145. Moore, "Cheyenne Political History."

146. Starita, *Dull Knifes*, 76.

147. Rzeczkowski, *Uniting the Tribes*.

148. For example, Stands In Timber related the story of a Mexican captive child who grew up among the Northern Cheyennes and received an allotment in 1926. He also talked about a German woman who had been taken prisoner and then married White Frog, who ended up with an allotment as well. See Stands In Timber and Liberty, *Cheyenne Voice*, 218, 268, 391. The Lakotas and Cheyennes have been intermarried for quite some time; see Stands In Timber and Liberty, *Cheyenne Voice*, 355, and Starita, *Dull Knifes*, 34. The families I have worked with at Northern Cheyenne have relatives from multiple Native nations, not only from Plains nations but also nations in the East and the Southwest. They also have Euro-American and European relatives.

CHAPTER 3

1. Eggan, "Cheyenne and Arapaho Kinship System," 37; Weist, *History*, 38; Hoebel, *Cheyennes*, 37.

2. For a detailed discussion of band convergence and dispersion in relation to the environment of the plains, see Moore, *Cheyenne Nation*, 127–75.

3. Eggan, *American Indian*, 54.

4. Elva Stands In Timber, interviews by the author, Lame Deer, Northern Cheyenne Indian Reservation, summer 2006. Stands In Timber mentioned a similar ceremony a narrator performed before telling his or her story. See Stands In Timber and Liberty, *Cheyenne Voice*, 189.

5. Nelson, *Original Instructions*; Nabokov, *Where the Lightning Strikes*.

6. While Native people have articulated intimate relationships to the land using kin terminology and recognized the spiritual power of these connections, it is important to recognize that Native peoples also developed sophisticated ecological knowledge about the landscapes in which they lived. This knowledge was based on generations of careful observation and was passed on through complex forms of intergenerational narrative preservation. See Kidwell, "Native American Systems of Knowledge," 87–102. Such detailed knowledge mirrors scientific observation in many ways and must have added to the specificity of narratives describing the landscape.

7. Scott Richard Lyons coined the term "removes," defining it in opposition to removals. He envisions this type of migration as not only a choice but a movement driven by hope and the promise for something better in a new place. Along the way, people often experience several awakenings, finding new ways of life. Lyons, *X-Marks*, 3–7.

8. American Indian Tribal Histories Project, "The Origin of the Tsistsistas." The narrator was referring to the Suhtaios and Tsistsistas. Stands In Timber also attempted to explain why Suhtaio, Tsistsistas, and even Arapaho people all spoke similar languages by pointing to a narrative that tells of how bands were separated during their migrations. Stands In Timber and Liberty, *Cheyenne Voice*, 3.

9. American Indian Tribal Histories Project, "The Cheyenne Creation Story."

10. To read or hear these stories in their original, see ibid.; Grinnell, *By Cheyenne Campfires*; Stands in Timber and Liberty, *Cheyenne Memories*; Moore, *Cheyenne Nation*, 93–96; Grinnell, *Cheyenne Indians*, 1:6–8.

11. For example, the narratives told by Cheyenne elders in the American Indian Tribal Histories Project DVDs share many of the same elements as the narratives Grinnell recorded.

12. Grinnell, *By Cheyenne Campfires*, 243–44. With the exception of Ben Clark, Grinnell did not reveal the tellers of the other narratives he related.

13. Stands In Timber and Liberty, *Cheyenne Memories*, 13, 14.

14. Ibid., 19–24. Elva Stands In Timber also talked about this narrative. Interview by the author, Lame Deer, Northern Cheyenne Indian Reservation, summer 2006.

15. American Indian Tribal Histories Project, "The Cheyenne Creation Story."

16. Moore, *Cheyenne Nation*, 93–96. Moore noted that many versions of early Cheyenne oral histories recorded by scholars are incomplete and have omitted large pieces of the histories. The band origins of the stories are difficult to uncover because ethnographers rarely recorded the names of the storytellers. Furthermore, for the Cheyennes, there is a marked difference between talking about these early histories and actually telling the narratives of them. Telling the narrative is highly ritualized and regulated; it must be done precisely and in a ceremonial manner by specific practitioners who have learned the proper way to tell the stories. Stands In Timber and Liberty, *Cheyenne Voice*, 189. Anyone can talk about a story, and in their conversation he or she will probably leave out pieces or talk about it in a nonconsecutive order.

17. American Indian Tribal Histories Project, "The Origin of the Tsistsistas."

18. Mr. BC, interview by the author, Lame Deer, Northern Cheyenne Indian Reservation, July 31, 2006; American Indian Tribal Histories Project, "The Origin of the Suhtaio."

19. American Indian Tribal Histories Project, "The Origin of the Suhtaio."

20. Hyde, *Life of George Bent*, 7; Stands in Timber and Liberty, *Cheyenne Memories*, 80–81. Stands In Timber declared that both the Suhtaios and the Tsistsistas learned about and used the quarry when they lived in Minnesota, but he admitted that he did not know whether one showed the other its location or if they both learned of it independently. For Stands In Timber's detailed narrative about Pipestone, see Stands In Timber and Liberty, *Cheyenne Voice*, 16–17, 216–18.

21. Ms. DG and Mr. BC, interview by the author, Lame Deer, Northern Cheyenne Indian Reservation, June 16, 2006.

22. Aikau, *Indians in the Diaspora*, 491–92.

23. Vizenor, *Fugitive Poses*, 15.

24. Basso, *Wisdom Sits in Places*; Brooks, *Common Pot*; Witgen, *Infinity of Nations*.

25. Moore, *Cheyenne Nation*; Moore, "Cheyenne Polygyny," 311–28.

26. Fixico, *American Indian Mind*, 53.

27. For full tellings, see Stands In Timber and Liberty, *Cheyenne Voice*, 253; Stands in Timber and Liberty, *Cheyenne Memories*, 19–24; Sundstrom, "Mirror of Heaven."

28. Elva Stands In Timber, interview by the author, Lame Deer, Northern Cheyenne Indian Reservation, 2006.

29. This racetrack formation can be seen clearly on the landscape when entering the Black Hills complex. It is marked by ridges of land on either side and runs around the hills proper. Today Interstate 90 follows a portion of it. It is also important to note that the Cheyennes are not the only peoples who benefited from the Great Race, and therefore honor the magpie. The Lakotas do as well.

30. Mr. SD, interview by the author, Lame Deer, Northern Cheyenne Indian Reservation, summer 2007; Sundstrom, "Mirror of Heaven." Sundstrom noted that Kiowa, Arapaho, and Lakota people all tell similar narratives about these distinctive formations in the Black Hills.

31. Howe, "Above the Trees," 165.

32. Fixico, *American Indian Mind*, 52.

33. Schlesier, *Wolves of Heaven*, 76–83; Nabokov, *Forest of Time*, 180. I was also told about the existence of this ceremony by several Northern Cheyenne people. Mr. SD essentially described it in the same way as above. Mr. SD, interview by the author, Lame Deer, Northern Cheyenne Indian Reservation, August 2007.

34. Albers and Kay, "Sharing the Land," 49.

35. Interviews conducted by the author, Northern Cheyenne Indian Reservation, summer 2006. Stands In Timber also mentions these practices in Stands In Timber and Liberty, *Cheyenne Voice*, 103, 105.

36. Albers and Kay, "Sharing the Land," 55, 52.

37. Stands In Timber described in detail the territorial markers that the Cheyenne nation used in the early nineteenth century to delineate their landscape, including the Missouri River, the Yellowstone River in eastern Montana, the Kansas River in the south, and the Rocky Mountains to the west. He stated that the people had even placed markers along these boundaries. Stands In Timber and Liberty, *Cheyenne Voice*, 105.

38. Lyons, *X-Marks*, 4.

39. For a full discussion of Cheyenne conceptions of land tenure, see Berndt, "Kinship," 84–87.

40. Anne Hyde has discussed the Bent family's intermarriage with Cheyenne families in detail in *Empires, Nations, and Families*. See also Van Kirk, *Many Tender Ties*; Brown, *Strangers in Blood*; Sleeper-Smith, "Women, Kin, and Catholicism"; DuVal, "Indian Intermarriage."

41. Hyde, *Empires, Nations, and Families*.

42. For a discussion of the ways that establishing boundaries between ethnic groups became part of a system of colonial domination, see Gupta and Ferguson, "Beyond 'Culture,'" 47; Rand, *Kiowa Humanity*; Rifkin, *Manifesting America*; Willinsky, *Learning to Divide the World*.

43. Anderson, *Imagined Communities*, 93.

44. Hoxie, *Final Promise*. Also see Rand, *Kiowa Humanity*.

45. See Banner, *How the Indians Lost Their Land*, 3. For regionally specific perspectives on land retention and loss in Native communities, see Brooks, *Common Pot*; Fisher, *Shadow Tribe*; Lakomäki, *Gathering Together*; O'Brien, *Dispossession by Degrees*; Liu, "Native Hawaiian Homesteaders," 85; Warren, "'To Show the Public,'" 1–28.

46. Prucha, *American Indian Treaties*, 237–39; Lazarus, *Black Hills*, 17.

47. Lazarus, *Black Hills*, 17.

48. Kappler, "Treaty of Fort Laramie with Sioux, Etc., 1851," *Indian Affairs*, 2:594–96.

49. Berthrong, *Southern Cheyennes*, 148.

50. Kappler, "Treaty with the Arapaho and Cheyenne, 1861," *Indian Affairs*, 2:807–11.

51. Prucha, *American Indian Treaties*, 269.

52. Weist, *History*, 48.

53. Loretta Fowler discussed the Arapaho presence and response to this massacre in *Wives and Husbands*, 24–28.

54. Much has been written about Sand Creek. See Berthrong, *Southern Cheyennes*, 152–223; Hyde, *Life of George Bent*, 110–63; Grinnell, *Fighting Cheyennes*, 165–80; Hoig, *Sand Creek Massacre*; Ortiz, *From Sand Creek*; Greene and Scott, *Finding Sand Creek*; Greene, *Washita*.

55. Berthrong, *Southern Cheyennes*, 224–25.

56. Hyde, *Life of George Bent*, 161–68. The head chiefs of the three main Arapaho bands, Medicine, Friday, and Black Bear, decided not to fight. Loretta Fowler stated that the Southern Arapahos kept their distance from the fighting, and Little Raven even attempted to negotiate for peace with the Americans. See *Wives and Husbands*, 25.

57. Hyde, *Life of George Bent*, 175.

58. Weist, *History*, 54; Hyde, *Life of George Bent*, 200.

59. Prucha, *American Indian Treaties*, 271.

60. Berthrong, *Southern Cheyennes*, 242.

61. Prucha, *American Indian Treaties*, 280.

62. Berthrong, *Southern Cheyennes*, 298.

63. Stands In Timber and Liberty, *Cheyenne Voice*, 344–45.

64. Kappler, "Treaty with the Sioux, Etc. 1868," *Indian Affairs*, 2:998–1007.

65. Kappler, "Treaty with the Northern Cheyenne and Northern Arapaho, 1868," *Indian Affairs*, 2:1012–15.

66. Stands In Timber and Liberty, *Cheyenne Voice*, 385–87.

67. Albers, *Home of the Bison*, 1:103. See figure 4 for locations of agencies and military forts.

68. Kappler, "Treaty with the Sioux, Etc. 1868," *Indian Affairs*.

69. To explore further the culturally negotiated process of treaty making, see Harjo, *Nation to Nation*.

70. Lyons, *X-Marks*.

71. Powell, *Sacred Mountain*, 763; Albers, *Home of the Bison*, 1:102.

72. See Powell, *Sacred Mountain*, 766.

73. Stands in Timber and Liberty, *Cheyenne Memories*, 54. See also Hoebel, *Cheyennes*, 51.

74. Kappler, "Treaty with the Cheyenne, 1825," *Indian Affairs*, 2:232–34.

75. Kappler, "Treaty with the Northern Cheyenne and Northern Arapaho, 1868," *Indian Affairs*.

76. Congress ended treaty making in 1871, so the Northern Cheyennes would not have been able to negotiate a treaty to gain recognition of their northern homeland. For more on the 1871 end to treaty making, see Prucha, *American Indian Treaties*; St. Germain, *Indian Treaty-Making*.

77. Shain and Sherman, "Dynamics of Disintegration," 339.

78. Tölölyan, "Contemporary Discourse."

79. Leiker and Powers, *Northern Cheyenne Exodus*, 19.

80. Tölölyan, "Contemporary Discourse."

81. Frank Rzeczkowski demonstrates that interethnic ties were central to Indigenous political action even after the reservations were imposed on the northern plains, noting that some of these intertribal political relationships were originally based on intermarriages that had taken place across tribal boundaries. This is only one example of the importance of kin ties as a mechanism to exercise political autonomy that continued into the late nineteenth and early twentieth centuries. See Rzeczkowski, *Uniting the Tribes*.

CHAPTER 4

1. Ostler, *Plains Sioux*, 78.

2. For accounts of this attack, see Grinnell, *Fighting Cheyennes*, 359–82; Marquis, *Wooden Leg*, 286–89; Stands in Timber and Liberty, *Cheyenne Memories*, 214–19; Powell, *Sacred Mountain*, 1056–71; Ricker, *Settler and Soldier Interviews*, 18–39.

3. Hoxie, *Final Promise*, 1–10.

4. United States, Annual Report of the Commissioner of Indian Affairs (1874), 46.

5. U.S. Senate, Report on the Removal of the Northern Cheyennes, 35.

6. Ibid., 17 (emphasis in the original).

7. Saville, "Treaty with Northern Cheyenne," given in appendix herein. Congress had ended treaty making with American Indian nations in 1871, so this was not an official treaty that had to be ratified. It was simply a written agreement.

8. United States, Annual Report of the Commissioner of Indian Affairs (1873), 244.

9. U.S. Senate, Report on the Removal of the Northern Cheyennes, 87, 88.

10. Albers, *Home of the Bison*, 1:103.

11. For a description of an expedition organized by Charles Collins and led by John Gordon that built a small settlement within the Black Hills and that was eventually escorted out by the U.S. military, see Albers, *Home of the Bison*, 1:120.

12. For all three letters quoted in full, see Wilkins, *American Indian Sovereignty*, 219–20.

13. Ostler, *Plains Sioux*, 60–61.

14. Ibid., 62.

15. Wilkins, *American Indian Sovereignty*, 220.

16. Marquis, *Cheyennes of Montana*, 69–70.

17. Grinnell, *Fighting Cheyennes*, 328–44. For accounts of this period in plains military history, see Bourke, *On the Border*; Ricker, *Settler and Soldier Interviews*; Grinnell, *Fighting Cheyennes*; Ostler, *Plains Sioux*; Utley, *Sioux Nation*.

18. She had traveled to the site of the battle with her brother. While he was riding in front of the line of soldiers, Chief Comes In Sight was knocked off his horse. When Buffalo Calf Road Woman saw this, she rode her horse straight toward the enemy line so that her brother could jump on behind her. In this way, Buffalo Calf Road Woman saved her brother. Grinnell, *Fighting Cheyennes*, 336.

19. Marquis, *Wooden Leg*, 204, 214–16.

20. Stands in Timber and Liberty, *Cheyenne Memories*, 191–92. For accounts of the battle from a Cheyenne perspective, see Marquis, *Wooden Leg*, 204–71; Agonito and Agonito, *Buffalo Calf Road Woman*; Hardorff, *Hokahey!*; Hardorff, *Cheyenne Memories*; Stekler, Welch, and McCullough, *Last Stand*.

21. Miles, *Personal Recollections*, 212.

22. Lazarus, *Black Hills*, 88–89.

23. Ibid., 80–83; Prucha, *American Indian Treaties*, 316–17.

24. Prucha, *Indian Treaties*, 317.

25. Ibid., 317; Lazarus, *Black Hills*, 92.

26. United States, Annual Report of the Commissioner of Indian Affairs (1876), 33.

27. United States, Annual Report of the Commissioner of Indian Affairs (1877), 19.

28. Ibid., 21.

29. Deloria, *Indians in Unexpected Places*, 26, 27.

30. Ostler, *Plains Sioux*, 66.

31. Grinnell, *Fighting Cheyenne*, 359.

32. Stands In Timber and Liberty, *Cheyenne Memories*, 214.

33. For a full description of this battle, see Stands In Timber and Liberty, *Cheyenne Memories*, 214–19; Ricker, *Indian Interviews*, 18–39; Ostler, *Plains Sioux*, 70–71; Grinnell, *Fighting Cheyennes*, 359–82; Powell, *Sweet Medicine*, 160–69; Marquis, *Wooden Leg*, 286–88.

34. Joe Starita has claimed that when Dull Knife signed the Fort Laramie Treaty of 1868, "he agreed never again to 'sharpen his knife' against the whites." Starita, *Dull Knifes*, 32–33. By not participating in the Battle of the Little Bighorn, he had kept this promise.

35. Ostler, *Plains Sioux*, 78.

36. Powell, *Sweet Medicine*, 169; Marquis, *Wooden Leg*, 286–88; Grinnell, *Fighting Cheyennes*, 359–82; Stands In Timber and Liberty, *Cheyenne Memories*, 218; Ostler, *Plains Sioux*, 71.

37. Lazarus, *Black Hills*, 93.

38. Monnett, *Tell Them*, 9.

39. Svingen, *Northern Cheyenne Indian Reservation*, 13.

40. In *Uniting the Tribes*, Frank Rzeczkowski has described the extensive visiting that continued among northern Plains nations after the establishment of reservations, even during the most confining periods.

41. Marquis, *Cheyennes of Montana*, 70. Note that Iron Teeth considered the Black Hills to belong to the Cheyennes as their "home country."

42. Ibid.

43. For a more detailed history of the choices made by individuals when deciding where to go, see Berndt, "Kinship"; Stands In Timber and Liberty, *Cheyenne Voice*, 446–48, 318–19.

44. Miles, *Personal Recollections*, 216.

45. Hill, "General Miles Put Us Here."

46. For a more detailed study of Miles's changing attitudes toward the relationship between plains people and the U.S. military, see Ostler, *Plains Sioux*, 289–312. See also Hill, "General Miles Put Us Here."

47. Miles, "Indian Problem," 305.

48. U.S. Senate, Report on the Removal of the Northern Cheyennes, 207.

49. Morgan, *Systems of Consanguinity*, 14.

50. This woman is mentioned in several accounts but sometimes by slightly different names. John Stands In Timber calls her "Sweet Woman" in *Cheyenne Memories*, but he uses "Sweet Woman" and "Sweet Taste Woman" interchangeably in *Cheyenne Voice*, 448–49. In *Sacred Mountain* Peter Powell calls her "Sweet Taste Woman" and acknowledges that she was also called "Wool Woman." Grinnell calls this woman "Old Wool Woman" in *Fighting Cheyennes*.

51. Grinnell claimed the men were away skinning a buffalo and that Miles's Crow scouts, who were looking out over the countryside, captured them. See Grinnell, *Fighting Cheyennes*, 384. John Stands In Timber named Big Horse as the man who accompanied this party and declares that he noticed black smoke rising and went ahead to scout their path. He stated that the women waited a long time and finally rode after him, but they rode into an army camp where they were captured. Stands in Timber and Liberty, *Cheyenne Memories*, 219.

52. For accounts of this attack, see Powell, *Sacred Mountain*, 1074–78; Grinnell, *Fighting Cheyennes*, 384; Marquis, *Wooden Leg*, 289–93; Stands In Timber and Liberty, *Cheyenne Voice*, 448–49; Stands In Timber and Liberty, *Cheyenne Memories*, 219–21.

53. Stands In Timber and Liberty, *Cheyenne Memories*, 221. Wooden Leg gives a different account, stating, "We were not sure, though, but some of them or all of them might have been wounded or killed." Marquis, *Wooden Leg*, 293.

54. Each account of the capture of Sweet Woman is slightly different, but they all describe the same event. To compare several accounts, see Stands In Timber and Liberty, *Cheyenne Memories*, 219–21; Dusenberry, "All

They Have Asked," 26; Grinnell, *Fighting Cheyennes*, 383–84; Marquis, *Wooden Leg*, 289–93; Powell, *Sacred Mountain*, 1074–78.

55. Elva Stands In Timber did not mention his name, but this man is prominent in the literature. John Broughier had one Euro-American and one Lakota parent. His name is spelled differently in different accounts: Grinnell used "Bruyere" in *Fighting Cheyennes*, Stands In Timber used "Broughier" in *Cheyenne Memories*, and Powell uses "Bruguier" in *Sacred Mountain*. Marquis and Powell claim he was also called White, and Stands In Timber claims he was called Big Leggings. It is possible that the Lakotas called him White and the Cheyennes called him Big Leggings. See Marquis, *Wooden Leg*, 295.

56. Elva Stands In Timber, interview by the author, Lame Deer, Northern Cheyenne Indian Reservation, July 28, 2005.

57. Stands In Timber and Liberty, *Cheyenne Voice*, 449.

58. Ostler, *Plains Sioux*, 78.

59. See particularly Albers, "Symbiosis, Merger, and War." For more on captivity as a political mechanism, see Barr, *Peace Came*; Brooks, *Captives and Cousins*; Ekberg, *Stealing Indian Women*; Rushforth, *Bonds of Alliance*; Snyder, *Slavery in Indian Country*. For a general discussion of Plains women's roles in warfare, see Medicine, "Warrior Women."

60. Albers, "Symbiosis, Merger, and War," 127–28. See also Shoemaker, *Strange Likeness*.

61. See Hill, "General Miles Put Us Here" for a more in-depth discussion of the competition between Generals Miles and Crook over bringing in these bands.

62. Stands in Timber and Liberty, *Cheyenne Memories*, 222. Stands In Timber states that Coal Bear was the Hat Keeper when Sweet Woman brought Miles's terms for peace to this camp. Stands in Timber and Liberty, *Cheyenne Voice*, 28.

63. Marquis, *Wooden Leg*, 295.

64. Ibid., 296; Powell, *Sacred Mountain*, 1090; Stands In Timber and Liberty, *Cheyenne Voice*, 467–69.

65. Sheridan to Sherman, March 23, 1877.

66. This list is compiled from these sources: Powell, *Sacred Mountain*, 1090; Grinnell, *Fighting Cheyennes*, 384; Stands In Timber and Liberty, *Cheyenne Memories*, 224; Ostler, *Plains Sioux*, 79.

67. Stands In Timber and Liberty, *Cheyenne Memories*, 224. Scholars have found no evidence for this statement in Miles's papers, but all Northern Cheyenne accounts, including the minutes of an 1890 council meeting recorded by government officials, noted that Miles promised the Northern Cheyennes a reservation of their own in the north.

68. Elva Stands In Timber, interview by the author, Lame Deer, Northern Cheyenne Indian Reservation, July 28, 2005.

69. For other accounts of Miles's first meeting with Two Moons, see Powell, *Sacred Mountain*, 1123–25; Grinnell, *Fighting Cheyennes*, 385; Marquis, *Wooden Leg*, 298; Stands In Timber and Liberty, *Cheyenne Memories*, 224–25; Stands

In Timber and Liberty, *Cheyenne Voice*, 467–68, 473; Dusenberry, "All They Have Asked," 26.

70. Sheridan to Sherman, March 23, 1877.

71. Ostler, *Plains Sioux*, 81.

72. Ricker, *Indian Interviews*, 328.

73. Marquis, *Wooden Leg*, 298.

74. Stands In Timber and Liberty, *Cheyenne Voice*, 467.

75. Marquis, *Wooden Leg*, 299.

76. Sheridan to Sherman, March 23, 1877.

77. Miles, *Personal Recollections*, 255.

78. In the secondary accounts, Stands In Timber mentioned Spotted Elk. Stands In Timber and Liberty, *Cheyenne Memories*, 223. Spotted Elk is also listed as surrendering at Fort Robinson; see Buecker and Paul, *Surrender Ledger*, 57. The last three names were only listed in Powell, *Sacred Mountain*, 1125; Buecker and Paul, *Surrender Ledger*, 59, 102.

79. For a description of these headmen and the effect their position had on the decision of the group, see Powell, *Sacred Mountain*, 1125.

80. In *Cheyenne Memories*, Stands In Timber stated that the first three of these men went straight to Indian Territory when the large camp on Powder River broke up, but I have found them listed on the *Crazy Horse Surrender Ledger* as arriving at Red Cloud Agency on February 16, 1877. In *A Cheyenne Voice*, however, Stands In Timber stated that these men signed the 1868 treaty as well as the agreement of 1876, indicating that they did come to Red Cloud Agency before traveling to Oklahoma. While his two statements seem to contradict each other, perhaps Stands In Timber wanted to emphasize the men's final destination in Indian Territory, not their journey there, to stress their southern kin connections. Stands In Timber and Liberty, *A Cheyenne Voice*, 215; Stands In Timber and Liberty, *Cheyenne Memories*, 223; Buecker and Paul, *Surrender Ledger*, 57. Powell stated that the last two of these men came into Red Cloud Agency and traveled to Indian Territory. Powell, *Sacred Mountain*, 1067. They were listed on the *Surrender Ledger* as well. Buecker and Paul, *Surrender Ledger*, 156, 212. This list is compiled from Powell, *Sacred Mountain*; Grinnell, *Fighting Cheyennes*; Marquis, *Wooden Leg*; Stands In Timber and Liberty; *Cheyenne Memories*; Ostler, *Plains Sioux*.

81. There is a possibility that Brave Wolf, Big Horse, and Star are a part of this group as Stands In Timber claims, but there is also a possibility that they came into the Red Cloud Agency because these names are on the *Surrender Ledger*. Big Horse is listed as Cheyenne on the list of the arrivals from the north. There is no Star listed, but there is a Bear Star and a Brave Wolf listed as part of Crazy Horse's band. It remains unclear, however, whether these are the same men Stands In Timber mentions.

82. Stands In Timber and Liberty, *Cheyenne Memories*, 223.

83. Marquis, *Wooden Leg*, 300.

84. Miles, *Personal Recollections*, 255.

85. This list is compiled from Powell, *Sacred Mountain*; Grinnell, *Fighting Cheyennes*; Marquis, *Wooden Leg*; Stands In Timber and Liberty, *Cheyenne Memories*; Ostler, *Plains Sioux*; Fredlund, Armstrong, and Sundstrom, "Crazy Mule's Maps."

86. Powell, *Sacred Mountain*, 1126.

87. One metaphor writers sometimes mention, "The Nation's hoop is broken and scattered," is attributed to Black Elk. Supposedly he ended his narrative about Wounded Knee with these now famous words. As recent scholarship has demonstrated, however, these words were in fact those of John G. Neihardt, the man who recorded Black Elk's narratives. This metaphor of Native peoples as divided, conquered, and vanishing had deep power for Americans. They could construct a comforting opposition of their nation-state as whole and unified and the Native nations that had threatened to disrupt it as broken and scattered. According to the transcripts of Neihardt's interviews, Black Elk actually ended his narrative with the statement, "Two years later I was married." See Svingen, *Northern Cheyenne Indian Reservation*, 361. I propose that instead of ending by describing a scattered nation, Black Elk ends by describing the persistence of his own personal life, and through marriage and the creation of his family, he emphasizes the importance of kinship to the persistence of his people.

88. Hyde, *Empires, Nations, and Families*.

89. For example, in a letter written on July 17, 1879, to the assistant adjutant general, the commanding officer referred to the Cheyennes at Fort Keogh as prisoners even though many had already enlisted as scouts. Fort Keogh Post Commissary Records, MS 15.

90. U.S. Senate, Report on the Removal of the Northern Cheyennes, 14.

91. General Hugh L. Scott, Notes on Sign Language.

92. An exception to this is Ostler, *Plains Sioux*, 78.

93. Hill, "General Miles Put Us Here."

94. Hoebel, *Cheyennes*, 43.

95. Interviews by the author, Lame Deer, Northern Cheyenne Indian Reservation, summers of 2005 and 2006.

96. Dunlay has discussed the importance of military officers embodying Plains expectations of leadership when they worked with Indian scouts. Dunlay, *Wolves*, 91–93.

97. For a detailed explanation of these political motivations, see Hill, "General Miles Put Us Here."

98. The battle was fought in the area of the modern Northern Cheyenne reservation town, Lame Deer, which was named after the battle.

99. John Stands In Timber listed White Hawk as one of the Cheyennes who came into Fort Keogh. Stands In Timber and Liberty, *Cheyenne Memories*,

223. He did eventually come to Fort Keogh, but Powell and Marquis both point out that he joined Lame Deer before coming in. We should not disregard Stands In Timber's account as inaccurate. He emphasizes where people ended up.

100. See his discussion of the Nez Perce capture as an example, in Liberty and Stands In Timber, *Cheyenne Voice*, 471–73.

101. Ibid. Grinnell, Powell, and Ricker all relate this story. See Grinnell, *Fighting Cheyennes*; Powell, *Sacred Mountain*; Ricker, *Settler and Soldier Interviews*, 144–45.

102. For more on intertribal alliances and territory, see Albers and Kay, "Sharing the Land."

103. See Stands In Timber's discussion of Two Moons's argument for coming into Fort Keogh in *Cheyenne Memories*, 240–41.

104. Miles, "Indian Problem," 305.

105. White, "Winning of the West," 320. White has also dealt with scholarly assumptions about Plains Indian warfare. He argued that this heroic military resistance representation of Plains Indian history has relegated Native peoples who did not organize armed resistance or who fought with the U.S. military to "the position of either foolish dupes of the whites or of traitors to their race." White disputed this idea, arguing that Native people had political and economic agendas for their military endeavors.

106. For a full description, see Liberty and Stands In Timber, *Cheyenne Voice*, 471–73.

107. "Report of Produce," Fort Keogh.

108. Miles, *Personal Recollections*, 255.

109. Lyons, *X-Marks*.

110. Ms. DG, interview by the author, Lame Deer, Northern Cheyenne Indian Reservation, August 27, 2005.

111. Stands In Timber and Liberty, *Cheyenne Memories*, 240–41.

112. Elva Stands In Timber, interview by the author, Lame Deer, Northern Cheyenne Indian Reservation, July 28, 2005.

113. Dunlay, *Wolves*.

CHAPTER 5

1. Kelman, *Misplaced Massacre*.

2. Vizenor, *Survivance*.

3. Hill, "General Miles Put Us Here."

4. Boye, *Holding Stone Hands*, 114–15.

5. Ostler, *Plains Sioux*. Ostler discussed what he called "the Indian's ability to avoid military defeat," arguing that it forced both Miles and Crook to rely on diplomacy (78).

6. Ricker, *Indian Interviews*, 17, 46.

7. Ostler, *Plains Sioux*, 84.

8. Elva Stands In Timber, interview by the author, Lame Deer, Northern Cheyenne Indian Reservation, July 28, 2005.

9. Ostler, *Plains Sioux*, 79–81, 87. Wooden Leg declared that there were Cheyennes with this delegation. See Marquis, *Wooden Leg*, 298.

10. Crazy Horse did not come into the agency until a few months after Spotted Tail found his camp and spoke with his people. Ostler, *Plains Sioux*, 82.

11. Crook had lived and worked with Plains Indians long enough at this point in his life that he certainly knew the power of making a promise with tobacco. Whether he took this practice seriously or not, he had to have assumed that the so-called hostiles would see this as a promise that he expected to keep.

12. Ostler, *Plains Sioux*, 87–88.

13. United States, Annual Report of the Commissioner of Indian Affairs (1874), 90.

14. United States, Annual Report of the Commissioner of Indian Affairs (1875), 250.

15. United States, Annual Report of the Commissioner of Indian Affairs (1874), 250.

16. United States, Annual Report of the Commissioner of Indian Affairs (1877), 19.

17. Dusenberry, "All They Have Asked," 23.

18. United States, Annual Report of the Commissioner of Indian Affairs (1877), 19.

19. U.S. Senate, Report on the Removal of the Northern Cheyennes, 5.

20. Jeffrey Ostler pointed out that both Crook and Miles made promises to the Cheyennes and Lakotas that they did not have the power to fulfill when they negotiated to bring them into the agencies. Ostler, *Plains Sioux*, 80.

21. Marquis, *Wooden Leg*, 309. Grinnell relates this same history in *Fighting Cheyennes*, 400.

22. Grinnell, *Fighting Cheyennes*, 400, 401.

23. Kappler, "Acts of Forty-Fourth Congress, Second Session, 1877," *Indian Affairs*, 1:168–72 (emphasis added).

24. U.S. Senate, Report on the Removal of the Northern Cheyennes, 9.

25. Ibid., 15.

26. Ibid., 14.

27. Ibid., 9.

28. Marquis, *Wooden Leg*, 309; Grinnell, *Fighting Cheyennes*, 400.

29. Monnett, *Tell Them*, 24; United States, Annual Report of the Commissioner of Indian Affairs (1877), 19.

30. United States, Annual Report of the Commissioner of Indian Affairs (1877), 62.

31. Date taken from Buecker and Paul, *Surrender Ledger*, 157.

32. Mr. BC, interviews by the author, Lame Deer, Northern Cheyenne Indian Reservation, summers of 2005 and 2006.

33. U.S. Senate, Report on the Removal of the Northern Cheyennes, 29.

34. "Fort Laramie," *Chicago Tribune*, November 26, 1877, in Ayer MS, John S. Gray Collection, Newberry Library, Chicago, Illinois.

35. United States, Annual Report of the Commissioner of Indian Affairs (1878), 49.

36. U.S. Senate, Report on the Removal of the Northern Cheyennes, xi, 42, 209.

37. Berthrong, *Cheyenne and Arapaho Ordeal*, 28; Fowler, *Tribal Sovereignty*, 19.

38. Berthrong, *Cheyenne and Arapaho Ordeal*, 20, 6.

39. Ibid., 256.

40. Ms. DG, interview by the author, Lame Deer, Northern Cheyenne Indian Reservation, summer 2006.

41. Sheridan to Townsend, September 19, 1878.

42. U.S. Senate, Report on the Removal of the Northern Cheyennes, 58.

43. United States, Annual Report of the Commissioner of Indian Affairs (1878), 48.

44. U.S. Senate, Report on the Removal of the Northern Cheyennes, 15.

45. Ibid., 5, 7, 34.

46. Ms. DG, interview by the author, Lame Deer, Northern Cheyenne Indian Reservation, August 27, 2005.

47. Elva Stands In Timber, interview by the author, Lame Deer, Northern Cheyenne Indian Reservation, August 21, 2005. See also Powell, *Sacred Mountain*, 1157; Powell, *Sweet Medicine*, 197.

48. U.S. Senate, Report on the Removal of the Northern Cheyennes, 26.

49. Marquis, *Wooden Leg*, 316.

50. Berthrong, *Cheyenne and Arapaho Ordeal*, 29.

51. U.S. Senate, Report on the Removal of the Northern Cheyennes, 4.

52. Grinnell, *Fighting Cheyennes*, 403.

53. Starita, *Dull Knifes*, 74.

54. U.S. Senate, Report on the Removal of the Northern Cheyennes, 62.

55. Berthrong, *Cheyenne and Arapaho Ordeal*, 33.

56. Ibid., 34.

57. P. H. Sheridan to Townsend, September 19, 1878, Letters Received, Bureau of Indian Affairs, RG 75, National Archives, Washington, D.C.

58. Deloria, *Indians in Unexpected Places*, 21.

59. Regardless, this group did pose a physical threat to the Americans living in their path. Although the leaders tried to hold back the young men, they did wreak havoc on many settlements in the Sappa Creek area of Kansas. See Leiker and Powers, *Cheyenne Exodus*; Monnett, *Tell Them*, 78–106; Powell, *Sweet Medicine*, 200–208.

60. For detailed military and historical accounts of these battles see Grinnell, *Fighting Cheyennes*; Monnett, *Tell Them*; Powell, *Sweet Medicine*; Powell, *Sacred Mountain*; Boye, *Holding Stone Hands*.

61. Leiker and Powers, *Cheyenne Exodus*, 64, 100; Powers, "Northern Cheyenne Trek," esp. 11. Monnett has related and critiqued the argument that these warriors acted in retaliation. Monnett, *Tell Them*, 91–97.

62. Monnett, *Tell Them*, 90–99.

63. Grinnell, *Fighting Cheyennes*, 413; Monnett, *Tell Them*, 92; Leiker and Powers, *Cheyenne Exodus*, 61.

64. Leiker and Powers, *Cheyenne Exodus*, 96.

65. Boye, *Holding Stone Hands*, 109.

66. Marquis, *Cheyennes of Montana*, 74–75.

67. Powell stated that they were camped on White Tail Creek. Powell, *Sacred Mountain*, 1174; see also Grinnell, *Fighting Cheyennes*, 410.

68. Boye, *Holding Stone Hands*, 237, 217.

69. Ms. DG, interview by the author, Lame Deer, Northern Cheyenne Indian Reservation, summer 2005.

70. Boye, *Holding Stone Hands*, 217.

71. For a detailed account of Little Wolf's winter in the Sand Hills, see Powell, *Sacred Mountain*.

72. Ibid., 1249. Some Cheyennes say that he was camped along Lost Chokecherry Creek in Nebraska. See American Indian Tribal Histories Project, "The Separation and Migration."

73. John H. Monnett stated that Little Wolf scouted for General Miles in 1877 before he traveled to Red Cloud Agency. See Monnett, *Tell Them*, 165. This is unlikely, however, because Miles reported that the Northern Cheyennes came to Fort Keogh on the April 22, but Little Wolf surrendered at Red Cloud Agency in February.

74. To compare three accounts of this search and encounter with Little Wolf, see Grinnell, *Fighting Cheyennes*, 410; Powell, *Sacred Mountain*, 1256; Monnett, *Tell Them*, 160.

75. Powell, *Sacred Mountain*, 1258.

76. U.S. Senate, Report on the Removal of the Northern Cheyennes, 249.

77. United States, Annual Report of the Commissioner of Indian Affairs (1878), 30.

78. Ricker, *Settler and Soldier Interviews*, 230.

79. Johnson to Sheridan, October 25, 1878. Also see Grinnell, *Fighting Cheyennes*, 414.

80. Ricker, *Settler and Soldier Interviews*, 231, 232.

81. Both Carter P. Johnson and George Bird Grinnell report this disagreement and standoff. Ricker, *Settler and Soldier Interviews*, 232; Grinnell, *Fighting Cheyennes*, 416.

82. Ibid.

83. Grinnell, *Fighting Cheyennes*; Monnett, *Tell Them*; Powell, *Sacred Mountain*.

84. Dull Knife and Red Cloud had been friends since before the Cheyennes were removed to Indian Territory. Steinacher and Carlson, "Cheyenne Outbreak Barracks."

85. Marquis, *Cheyennes of Montana*, 75.

86. Boye, *Holding Stone Hands*, 255, 264.

87. Monnett, *Tell Them*, 111.

88. Ricker, *Settler and Soldier Interviews*, 229.

89. Iron Teeth's daughter and those with her are an example of people who fled and safely made it to Red Cloud's camp.

90. Ricker, *Settler and Soldier Interviews*, 230.

91. Powell, *Sacred Mountain*, 228.

92. Monnett, *Tell Them*, 113.

93. Grinnell, *Fighting Cheyennes*, 417.

94. Ibid., 419.

95. United States, Annual Report of the Commissioner of Indian Affairs (1879), xvii.

96. Boye, *Holding Stone Hands*, 272.

97. Grinnell, *Fighting Cheyennes*, 418; Boye, *Holding Stone Hands*, 272.

98. Wessels to Quartermaster, January 6, 1879, Outbreak Rolls, Letters Received, Office of the Adjutant General, National Archives, Washington, D.C.

99. Grinnell, *Fighting Cheyennes*, 419.

100. Ibid., 420. For a detailed hour-by-hour description of the events leading up to the breakout and the event itself, see Boye, *Holding Stone Hands*, 260–97.

101. Twitchell, "Camp Robinson Letters," 94.

102. Grinnell, *Fighting Cheyennes*, 420.

103. Ricker, *Settler and Soldier Interviews*, 237.

104. Marquis, *Cheyennes of Montana*, 76.

105. Grinnell, *Fighting Cheyennes*, 422; Powell, *Sacred Mountain*, 1207. Carter P. Johnson also described the actions of Dull Knife's daughter. See Ricker, *Settler and Soldier Interviews*, 238.

106. Grinnell, *Fighting Cheyennes*, 424.

107. Starita, *Dull Knifes*, 66–67, 69, 74.

108. Grinnell, *Fighting Cheyennes*, 426.

109. Fort Robinson to Commissioner of Indian Affairs, January 15, 1879.

110. "Indians," *Army and Navy Journal*.

111. Commissioner of Indian Affairs to the Secretary of the Interior, January 16, 1879.

112. "Another View," *New York Herald*.

113. Quoted in Hoxie, *Final Promise*, 2.

114. Monnett, *Tell Them*, 191.

115. Hoxie, *Final Promise*, 3. Also see Leiker and Powers, *Cheyenne Exodus*, for a detailed discussion of these debates.

116. Monnett, *Tell Them*, xix.

117. United States, Annual Report of the Commissioner of Indian Affairs (1879), 39.

118. Starita, *Dull Knifes*, 84, 75. Starita named Pawnee Woman as the wife who survived the journey north, but in the histories Alan Boye collected at Northern Cheyenne, Dull Knife's descendants named the surviving wife as Slow Woman. Boye, *Holding Stone Hands*.

119. Interviews by the author, Lame Deer, Northern Cheyenne Indian Reservation, summers of 2004, 2005, and 2006.

120. Ms. DG, interview by the author, Lame Deer, Northern Cheyenne Indian Reservation, summer 2004.

121. Monnett, *Tell Them*, 167; American Indian Tribal Histories Project, "Separation and Migration."

CHAPTER 6

1. At this point in time, there were Northern Cheyennes, Lakotas, and Nez Perces living at Fort Keogh. The Lakotas and Nez Perces were to be sent to their reservations in the north, but the Cheyennes were ordered to remove to Indian Territory.

2. U.S. Senate, Report on the Removal of the Northern Cheyennes, xii, ix.

3. Ibid., xii, vii, viii.

4. "They Pass by Dodge City," *Dodge City Times*, 1.

5. U.S. Senate, Report on the Removal of the Northern Cheyennes, 206.

6. Fredlund et al., "Crazy Mule's Maps," 21.

7. Clark to Mooney, January 16, 1907.

8. U.S. Senate, Report on the Removal of the Northern Cheyennes, vi.

9. Ibid.

10. Clark to Mooney, January 16, 1907.

11. Ibid.

12. "Indian Affairs," *Army and Navy Journal*.

13. Ibid.

14. "Preparation at Sidney," *Sidney (Nebraska) Telegraph*.

15. Ibid.; "Indian Affairs," *Army and Navy Journal*.

16. "Little Chief States," *Sidney (Nebraska) Telegraph*.

17. Interviews by the author, Lame Deer, Northern Cheyenne Indian Reservation, summers of 2004, 2005, and 2006.

18. Clark to Mooney, January 16, 1907.

19. "Gone for Good," *Sidney Plaindealer*.

20. This count is taken from a census of Little Chief's people completed in 1879. See "Little Chief's Band," Annuity Payment Rolls 1841–1949. The 1879 commissioner of Indian affairs's report placed the number at "around 200"; see United States, Annual Report of the Commissioner of Indian Affairs (1879), xviii. In 1881 Miles stated that 222 people were removed to the southern

agency. See Miles to Commissioner of Indian Affairs, June 6, 1881. Donald Berthrong states that 186 people arrived at the southern agency. See Berthrong, *Cheyenne and Arapaho Ordeal*, 37.

21. Berthrong, *Cheyenne and Arapaho Ordeal*, 37. Fredlund, Armstrong, and Sundstrom demonstrated that a Crazy Mule was part of a scouting force from Fort Keogh that escorted Little Chief's people to Sidney Barracks. See Fredlund et al., "Crazy Mule's Maps," 21. Berthrong, however, obtained archival evidence that places a Crazy Mule in Indian Territory and indicates that he was actually part of the group that was removed. Evidently there are two Crazy Mules: one who took the name John Crazy Mule and remained at Fort Keogh scouting with Miles after Little Chief's removal, and the other who remained in Indian Territory. Crazy Mule's name does not appear on the census of Little Chief's people taken in 1879, nor does it appear on the censuses taken when Little Chief's people arrived at Pine Ridge. The Crazy Mule that remained in Indian Territory disengaged himself from Little Chief's people when he arrived. Berthrong noted that this Crazy Mule asked for land to begin farming. See Berthrong, *Cheyenne and Arapaho Ordeal*, 41. Thus he would not be listed on the 1879 census because it was taken several months after the group's arrival.

22. U.S. Senate, Report on the Removal of the Northern Cheyennes, vi.

23. Svingen, *Northern Cheyenne Indian Reservation*, 21; United States, Annual Report of the Commissioner of Indian Affairs (1879), xviii.

24. Berthrong, *Cheyenne and Arapaho Ordeal*, 38.

25. Miles to Commissioner of Indian Affairs, April 1881.

26. Miles to Commissioner of Indian Affairs, March 19, 1881.

27. Miles to Commissioner of Indian Affairs, April 1881.

28. Ibid.

29. Department of Arkansas Headquarters to the A.A.A. General, April 22, 1881.

30. Hill, "General Miles Put Us Here."

31. Miles to Commissioner of Indian Affairs, June 6, 1881.

32. Commissioner of Indian Affairs to the Secretary of the Interior, June 22, 1881.

33. Miles to Commissioner of Indian Affairs, June 27, 1881.

34. War Department to the Secretary of the Interior, July 7, 1881.

35. Secretary of the Interior to Little Chief, June 27, 1881.

36. Commissioner of Indian Affairs to Secretary of the Interior, August 28, 1881.

37. Ibid.; Lieutenant General to Adjutant General, September 21, 1881.

38. Svingen, *Northern Cheyenne Indian Reservation*, 21.

39. Miles to Price, July 26, 1881. According to this letter, when the letter arrived inviting Little Chief to Washington, he had been absent attending a Kiowa medicine man 150 miles from the agency. A courier went and got him and told him what was going on. Clearly, Cheyenne people continued to

maintain and establish intertribal relationships, even during the reservation era.

40. United States, Annual Report of the Commissioner of Indian Affairs (1881), li.

41. Ibid., lxii.

42. Starita, *Dull Knifes*, 74–75.

43. McGillycuddy to the Commissioner of Indian Affairs, December 31, 1881.

44. Miles to the Commissioner of Indian Affairs, January 3, 1882.

45. McGillycuddy to the Commissioner of Indian Affairs, December 31, 1881.

46. Little Chief used this same argument. It played on the American fears of an "Indian outbreak."

47. Miles to Price, April 22, 1882.

48. United States, Annual Report of the Commissioner of Indian Affairs (1882), lxii.

49. Svingen, *Northern Cheyenne Indian Reservation*, 22.

50. McGillycuddy to Price, December 6, 1881; Price to McGillycuddy, December 1881 (response filed with McGillycuddy's December 6 letter).

51. McGillycuddy to Price, June 23, 1882.

52. Yoakam to Arthur, August 18, 1882; Yoakam to Arthur, September 7, 1882.

53. Commissioner of Indian Affairs to Yoakam, September 9, 1882.

54. Ewers to McGillycuddy, August 23, 1882.

55. McGillycuddy to the Commissioner of Indian Affairs, October 5, 1882.

56. United States, Annual Report of the Commissioner of Indian Affairs (1881), 45, 34.

57. Sherman to the Headquarters of the Army, November 28, 1882.

58. Wilkins to Adjutant General, November 22, 1882.

59. Secretary of the Interior to Secretary of War, November 28, 1882.

60. Yoakam to the Commissioner of Indian Affairs, December 12, 1882.

61. Little Chief to the Commissioner of Indian Affairs, March 17, 1886.

62. Little Chief to the Commissioner of Indian Affairs, May 13, 1886.

63. The Carlisle School has a record of an Elkanah C. Dawson. In a letter from Pratt to Dryer, the agent at the Cheyenne and Arapaho Agency in 1885, Pratt stated that Dawson was entitled to return home. He continued that although Dawson arrived at the school from Indian Territory, he would be sent back to Pine Ridge because that was where his father had come to reside. Pratt to Dryer, June 13, 1885.

64. Little Chief to the Commissioner of Indian Affairs, September 28, 1886.

65. Little Chief to Cleveland, July 12, 1887.

66. Little Chief to Gallagher, August 13, 1888.

67. Little Chief to the Commissioner of Indian Affairs, March 31, 1890.

68. Weist, "Ned Casey," 36.

69. Marquis, *Cheyennes of Montana*, 99. This was a common reason to scout; see Hill, "General Miles Put Us Here."

70. To learn more see DeMallie, "Lakota Ghost Dance," 385–405; Greene, *American Carnage*; Grua, *Surviving Wounded Knee*; Kehoe, *Ghost Dance*; Mooney, *Ghost Dance Religion*; Thornton, *We Shall Live Again*.

71. Gitlin, *Wounded Knee Massacre*, 95–97.

72. Svingen, *Northern Cheyenne Indian Reservation*, 90.

73. Ibid., 92; Mooney, *Ghost Dance Religion*, 862; Marquis, *Wooden Leg*. Wooden Leg states that some of these Cheyennes had fled the southern agency with Dull Knife and Little Wolf.

74. The Office of the Adjutant General to the Department of the Interior, July 22, 1891.

75. Grant to Noble, September 18, 1891.

76. Tully to Morgan, November 2, 1891.

77. Lyons, *X-Marks*.

Chapter 7

1. Hill, "General Miles Put Us Here."

2. Hoxie, *Final Promise*, 3.

3. For a detailed explanation of the tragedies of 1879 and the loss of faith in the peace policy, see Hoxie, *Final Promise*. See also Mathes and Lowitt, *Standing Bear Controversy*.

4. Hoxie, *Final Promise*, 15.

5. Ibid., 34, 19.

6. Mr. BC, interview by the author, Lame Deer, Northern Cheyenne Indian Reservation, August 17, 2005. Mr. BC related that this was a common practice and people would leave the community for at least four years. Some sources claim the dispute between Little Wolf and Starving Elk was over domestic matters, while others believe it began as a political disagreement. For a description of Cheyenne law regarding murder, see Llewellyn and Hoebel, *Cheyenne Way*, 165–68. For a description of Little Wolf's actions against Starving Elk, see Grinnell, *Cheyenne Indians*, 1:356–57; Marquis, *Wooden Leg*, 330–33; Llewellyn and Hoebel, *Cheyenne Way*, 82–86; Stands In Timber and Liberty, *Cheyenne Memories*, 239–41.

7. Dusenberry, "All They Have Asked," 30.

8. Stands In Timber and Liberty, *Cheyenne Memories*, 239; Ms. DG, interview by the author, Lame Deer, Northern Cheyenne Indian Reservation, August 16, 2006.

9. Grinnell, "Mountain Sheep," 4.

10. Ms. DG, interview by the author, Lame Deer, Northern Cheyenne Indian Reservation, August 16, 2006.

11. Mr. BC, interview by the author, Lame Deer, Northern Cheyenne Indian Reservation, August 17, 2005.

12. Dusenberry, "All They Have Asked," 30.

13. Only five short years later, Congress would pass the Seven Major Crimes Act, inspired by the murder of Spotted Tail at Pine Ridge and horrified by what they believed to be too gentle of a punishment. But when Little Wolf killed another Cheyenne man, Native nations still doled out their own punishments for murder.

14. Elva Stands In Timber, interview by the author, Lame Deer, Northern Cheyenne Indian Reservation, August 21, 2005.

15. "Proceedings of a Council," April 15, 1890.

16. Stands In Timber and Liberty, *Cheyenne Memories*, 240, 239.

17. In Cheyenne oral histories, many people remember William Rowland, not Yoakam, as the one who helped them build homesteads and learn to farm. This is perhaps because Rowland was seen as a member of the community and Yoakam was seen as a government agent. Ms. DG, interview by the author, Lame Deer, Northern Cheyenne Indian Reservation, August 16, 2006.

18. Yoakam to the Secretary of the Interior, December 24, 1880.

19. Mr. BC, interview by the author, Lame Deer, Northern Cheyenne Indian Reservation, July 23, 2005.

20. McLaughlin, *Proposed Removal*, 4.

21. Mr. BC, interview by the author, Lame Deer, Northern Cheyenne Indian Reservation, August 17, 2005.

22. War Department to Secretary of the Interior, October 20, 1881.

23. Kappler, "Acts of Forty-Third Congress, Second Session, 1875," *Indian Affairs*, 1:23.

24. Hill, "General Miles Put Us Here."

25. Ewers to Miles, October 29, 1890. Ewers was the man who assigned Yoakam to assist the Cheyennes and teach them to build houses and farm.

26. Ibid.

27. Milburn to Price, February 13, 1883.

28. Ewers to the Assistant Adjutant General, October 20, 1881.

29. Milburn to Price, February 13, 1883.

30. Ibid.

31. Ibid.

32. Millen to the Commanding Officer, August 27, 1883. This is the same Black Wolf who had left from Pine Ridge after he arrived there with Little Chief's people.

33. Milburn to Price, February 13, 1883.

34. Millen to the Commanding Officer, August 27, 1883.

35. Banner, *How the Indians Lost Their Land*; Genetin-Pilawa, *Crooked Paths*; Tonkovich, *Allotment Plot*.

36. Ewers to Miles, October 29, 1890.

37. Svingen, *Northern Cheyenne Indian Reservation*, 31.

38. Milburn to Price, February 13, 1883.

39. Svingen, *Northern Cheyenne Indian Reservation*, 43, 42.

40. Ibid.

41. Ewers to the Commissioner of Indian Affairs, August 14, 1884.

42. Milburn to the Commissioner of Indian Affairs, October 28, 1884.

43. Kappler, "Executive Orders Relating to Reserves: Northern Cheyenne Reserve, 1884," *Indian Affairs*, 1:860.

44. Ewers to Miles, October 29, 1890.

45. Council for Citizens to the Secretary of the Interior, "Citizens Memorial," April 25, 1885.

46. Ibid.

47. Svingen, *Northern Cheyenne Indian Reservation*, 43.

48. Hoxie, *Final Promise*, 44, 26.

49. Harjo, *Nation to Nation*.

50. For a detailed discussion of the transformation of the reservation as a space of forced containment to a homeland, see Hoxie, "From Prison to Homeland," 55–75.

51. Ms. DG, interview by the author, Lame Deer, Northern Cheyenne Indian Reservation, July 13, 2005.

52. Ms. DG, interview by the author, Lame Deer, Northern Cheyenne Indian Reservation, August 27, 2005.

53. Ms. DG, interview by the author, Lame Deer, Northern Cheyenne Indian Reservation, July 13, 2005.

54. Ms. DG, interview by the author, Lame Deer, Northern Cheyenne Indian Reservation, August 27, 2005.

55. Ibid.

56. In his report on the condition of Northern Cheyenne homesteaders, Millen stated that Little Wolf had done this in 1883. See Millen to the Commanding Officer at Fort Keogh, August 27, 1883. Several Northern Cheyennes have also reported in interviews that their families used to get rations at Pine Ridge.

CHAPTER 8

1. I have found that only Orlan Svingen has written about the expansion of the reservation. Svingen, *Northern Cheyenne Indian Reservation*.

2. The federal government planned to move the Northern Cheyennes onto the eastern side of the Crow Indian Reservation. This land includes the Powder River and the site of the Battle of the Little Bighorn. The Northern Cheyennes in conjunction with the Northern Arapahos and the Lakotas still saw it as their own territory. Even today some people argue that the

Little Bighorn battlefield belongs to the Cheyennes because they emerged victorious from this battle.

3. Many American Indian nations in the United States were moved from place to place as multiple reservations were established for them over a period of decades at the whims of the federal government. Although reservation boundaries were meant to contain Native people and to be impermeable to them, these boundaries were often not fixed or permanent in the eyes of the United States. Accordingly, the federal government frequently changed reservation boundaries or even locations altogether.

4. Svingen, *Northern Cheyenne Indian Reservation*, 145.

5. Yoakam to Arthur, December 25, 1882.

6. Yoakam to Arthur, December 24, 1884.

7. Atkins to Banister, June 11, 1885.

8. "Agreement to Remove," June 24–25, 1885.

9. Banister to Atkins, July 16, 1885.

10. Ibid.

11. Atkins to Banister, June 11, 1885.

12. Atkins to Larson, October 5, 1885.

13. Ibid.

14. Don Hollow Breast, *Cheyenne News*, January 21, 1999.

15. Upshaw to Atkins, February 15, 1886.

16. Upshaw to Oberly, May 23, 1889.

17. Yoakam to Larson, May 24, 1886.

18. This mission was established in 1883 by a group of Catholic nuns and is still operating on the eastern bank of the Tongue River today, as St. Labre Catholic Mission.

19. Yoakam to Larson, May 24, 1886.

20. Upshaw to Oberly, May 23, 1889.

21. "Proceedings of a Council," April 15, 1890.

22. Ibid.

23. Tully to Morgan, December 26, 1891.

24. For detailed descriptions of McLaughlin's role in the massacre see Mooney, *Ghost Dance Religion*, 843–86; Ostler, *Plains Sioux*, 289–337.

25. McLaughlin, *Proposed Removal*, 3.

26. Ibid., 4.

27. Ibid.

28. Ibid.

29. William Rowland and James Rowland sat as interpreters for both councils. They were fluent in Cheyenne as well as English and had been acting as interpreters for many years. They were well trusted by both sides.

30. McLaughlin, *Proposed Removal*, 86.

31. Ibid., 87.

32. Ibid., 89, 88.

33. Ibid., 11.

34. Ibid., 15–16, 11.

35. Svingen, *Northern Cheyenne Indian Reservation*, 139.

36. McLaughlin, *Proposed Removal*, 11.

37. Ibid., 89.

38. Kappler, "Executive Orders Relating to Reserves: Northern Cheyenne Reserve, 1884," *Indian Affairs*, 1:860.

39. Mr. BC, interview by the author, Lame Deer, Northern Cheyenne Indian Reservation, August 25, 2005.

40. McLaughlin, *Proposed Removal*, 85. Although he understood the Cheyenne language well, it is hard to know William Rowland's motives as the interpreter. He may have been trying to talk these Northern Cheyennes into this move, believing it was the best thing for them.

41. Mr. BC, interview by the author, Lame Deer, Northern Cheyenne Indian Reservation, August 17, 2005; multiple interviews by the author, Lame Deer, Northern Cheyenne Indian Reservation, summer 2006.

42. Hoxie, *Final Promise*, 44.

43. Harjo, *Nation to Nation*.

CONCLUSION

1. Howe, "Above the Trees," esp. 164.

2. Mr. SD and Ms. DG, interviews by the author, Lame Deer, Northern Cheyenne Indian Reservation, summers 2005 and 2006. Ms. DG declared that the Northern Cheyennes think beyond seven generations. When they think about their future, they think about all those yet to come.

3. Ms. DG, interview by the author, Lame Deer, Northern Cheyenne Indian Reservation, July 22, 2006.

4. Ms. DG, interview by the author, Lame Deer, Northern Cheyenne Indian Reservation, July 13, 2005; Mr. BC, interview by the author, Lame Deer, Northern Cheyenne Indian Reservation, July 23, 2005.

5. Ms. DG, interview by the author, Lame Deer, Northern Cheyenne Indian Reservation, July 13, 2005.

6. Kappler, "The Extent or Character of Title Acquired by Indians in Lands Withdrawn for Their Benefit by Executive Order," *Indian Affairs*, 4:1061–63.

7. American Indian Tribal Histories Project, "Separation and Migration."

8. Ms. DG, interview by the author, Lame Deer, Northern Cheyenne Indian Reservation, July 22, 2006.

9. Superintendent to Commissioner of Indian Affairs, October 5, 1923.

10. Assistant Commissioner of Indian Affairs to Superintendent, October 20, 1923.

11. Superintendent to Commissioner of Indian Affairs, November 24, 1923.

12. Kappler, "An Act to Provide for Allotting in Severalty Lands within the Northern Cheyenne Indian Reservation in Montana, and For Other Purposes," *Indian Affairs*, 4:556–57.

13. "Resist Sale of Lands," 1.

14. Woodenlegs, "War Ponies," 3, 4.

15. Northern Cheyenne Tribal Council, "Land Program."

16. Woodenlegs, "War Ponies," 3.

17. Woodenlegs, "Northern Cheyenne Goal," 1.

18. Northern Cheyenne Tribe, "Official Site of the Tsistsistas and So'taa'eo'o People," www.cheyennenation.com (accessed June 15, 2016).

19. Multiple interviews by the author, Lame Deer, Northern Cheyenne Indian Reservation, summers of 2005 and 2006.

20. See especially Sandoz, *Cheyenne Autumn*; Monnett, *Tell Them*; Maddux and Maddux, *Dull Knife's Wake*.

21. Many Northern Cheyennes also point to the breakout as the bellwether event in the establishment of the reservation. Nevertheless, they do not talk about the reservation as "given to them" by the United States, nor do they emphasize that this event led to any action on the part of the federal government. This event is used to illustrate the people's struggle to return to their homeland and thereby emphasizes the sacrifices the people made to live on their own land.

22. Svingen, *Northern Cheyenne Indian Reservation*, 151.

23. Schlesier, *Wolves of Heaven*, 76–83.

24. Rand, "Primary Sources," 137.

BIBLIOGRAPHY

PUBLISHED MATERIALS

Agamben, Giorgio. *Homo Sacer: Sovereign Power and Bare Life.* Translated by Daniel Heller-Roazen. Stanford, Calif.: Stanford University Press, 1998.

Agonito, Rosemary, and Joseph Agonito. *Buffalo Calf Road Woman: The Story of a Warrior of the Little Bighorn.* Thorndike, Maine: Center Point, 2007.

Aikau, Hokulani K. "Indigeneity in the Diaspora: The Case of Native Hawaiians at Iosepa, Utah." *American Quarterly* 62, no. 3 (2010): 477–500.

Albers, Patricia C. "Changing Patterns of Ethnicity in the Northeastern Plains, 1780–1870." In *History, Power, and Identity.* Edited by Jonathan Hill. Iowa City: University of Iowa Press, 1996. 90–188.

———. *The Home of the Bison: An Ethnographic and Ethnohistorical Study of Traditional Cultural Affiliations to Wind Cave National Park.* 2 vols. A special report prepared at the request of the U.S. National Park Service. September 2003.

———. "Sioux Kinship in a Colonial Setting." *Dialectical Anthropology* 6, no. 3 (March 1982): 253–69.

———. "Symbiosis, Merger, and War: Contrasting Forms of Intertribal Relationship among Historic Plains Indians." In *Political Economy of North American Indians.* Edited by John Moore. Norman: University of Oklahoma Press, 1993. 94–132.

Albers, Patricia, and William R. James. "On the Dialectics of Ethnicity: To Be or Not to Be Santee (Sioux)." *Journal of Ethnic Studies* 14, no. 1 (1986): 1–27.

Albers, Patricia, and Jeanne Kay. "Sharing the Land: A Study in American Indian Territoriality." In *A Cultural Geography of North American Indians.* Edited by Thomas Ross and Tyrel G. Moore. Boulder, Colo.: Westview, 1987. 47–92.

Aleiss, Angela. *Making the White Man's Indian: Native Americans and Hollywood Movies.* Westport, Conn.: Greenwood, 2005.

Alfred, Taiaiake. "Sovereignty." In *Sovereignty Matters: Locations of Contes-
tation and Possibility in Indigenous Struggles for Self-Determination.* Edited
by Joanne Barker. Lincoln: University of Nebraska Press, 2005. 33–50.
———. *Peace, Power, Righteousness: An Indigenous Manifesto.* New York: Oxford
University Press, 1999.
———. *Wasáse: Indigenous Pathways of Action and Freedom.* Peterborough, Ont.:
Broadview, 2005.
Alfred, Taiaiake, and Jeff Corntassel. "Being Indigenous: Resurgences against
Contemporary Colonialism." *Government and Opposition* 40, no. 4 (2005):
597–614.
Alonso, Ana María. "The Politics of Space, Time and Substance: State Forma-
tion, Nationalism and Ethnicity." *Annual Review of Anthropology* 23 (1994):
379–405.
American Indian Tribal Histories Project. *Northern Cheyenne Educational DVD
Set.* Billings, Mont.: Western Heritage Center, 2007.
Anderson, Benedict. *Imagined Communities: Reflections on the Origin and Spread
of Nationalism.* New York: Verso, 1983.
Anderson, Gary Clayton. *Kinsmen of Another Kind: Dakota-White Relations in
the Upper Mississippi Valley, 1650–1862.* Lincoln: University of Nebraska
Press, 1984.
Anderson, Jeffrey D. *The Four Hills of Life: Northern Arapaho Knowledge and Life
Movement.* Lincoln: University of Nebraska Press, 2008.
Banner, Stuart. *How the Indians Lost Their Land: Law and Power on the Frontier.*
Cambridge, Mass.: Harvard University Press, 2005.
Barker, Joanne, ed. *Sovereignty Matters: Locations of Contestation and Possibility
in Indigenous Struggles for Self-Determination.* Lincoln: University of
Nebraska Press, 2005.
Barr, Juliana. *Peace Came in the Form of a Woman: Indians and Spaniards in the
Texas Borderlands.* Chapel Hill: University of North Carolina Press, 2007.
Barth, Fredrick. *Ethnic Groups and Boundaries: The Social Organization of Cul-
ture Difference.* London: George Allen and Unwin, 1969.
Basso, Keith H. *Wisdom Sits in Places: Landscape and Language among the
Western Apache.* Albuquerque: University of New Mexico Press, 1996.
Bauerkemper, Joseph. "Narrating Nationhood: Indian Time and Ideologies of
Progress." *Studies in American Indian Literatures* 19, no. 4 (2007): 27–53.
Bell, David Avrom. *The Cult of the Nation in France: Inventing Nationalism, 1680–
1800.* Cambridge, Mass.: Harvard University Press, 2009.
Bergland, Renée L. *The National Uncanny: Indian Ghosts and American Subjects.*
Lebanon, N.H.: University Press of New England, 2000.
Berkhofer, Robert F. *The White Man's Indian: Images of the American Indian from
Columbus to the Present.* New York: Vintage, 2011.
Berndt, Christina Gish. "Kinship as Strategic Political Action: The Northern
Cheyenne Response to the Imposition of the Nation-State." PhD
diss., University of Minnesota, 2008.

Berthrong, Donald J. *The Cheyenne and Arapaho Ordeal: Reservation Life in the Indian Territory, 1875–1907.* Norman: University of Oklahoma Press, 1976.
———. *The Southern Cheyennes.* Norman: University of Oklahoma Press, 1963, 1972.
Biolsi, Thomas, and Larry J. Zimmerman, eds. *Indians and Anthropologists: Vine Deloria, Jr., and the Critique of Anthropology.* Tucson: University of Arizona Press, 1997.
Blackhawk, Ned. *Violence over the Land: Indians and Empires in the Early American West.* Cambridge, Mass.: Harvard University Press, 2006.
Blu, Karen I. *The Lumbee Problem: The Making of an American Indian People.* Cambridge: Cambridge University Press, 1980.
Bourke, John G. *On the Border with Crook.* New York: Charles Scribner's Sons, 1891; New York: Time Life Books, 1980.
Boye, Alan. *Holding Stone Hands: On the Trail of the Cheyenne Exodus.* Lincoln: University of Nebraska Press, 1999.
Braun, Sebastian Felix. "Against Procedural Landscapes: Community, Kinship, and History." In *Transforming Ethnohistories: Narrative, Meaning, and Community.* Edited by Sebastian Felix Braun. Norman: University of Oklahoma Press, 2013.
Brooks, James. *Captives and Cousins: Slavery, Kinship, and Community in the Southwest Borderlands.* Chapel Hill: University of North Carolina Press, 2002.
Brooks, Lisa Tanya. *The Common Pot: The Recovery of Native Space in the Northeast.* Minneapolis: University of Minnesota Press, 2008.
Brown, Jennifer S. H. *Strangers in Blood: Fur Trade Company Families in Indian Country.* Vancouver: University of British Columbia Press, 1980.
Buecker, Thomas R., and R. Eli Paul, eds. *The Crazy Horse Surrender Ledger.* Lincoln: Nebraska State Historical Society, 1994.
Byrd, Jodi A. *The Transit of Empire: Indigenous Critiques of Colonialism.* Minneapolis: University of Minnesota Press, 2011.
Calloway, Colin G. *New Worlds for All: Indians, Europeans, and the Remaking of Early America.* Baltimore: Johns Hopkins University Press, 1997.
———. *One Vast Winter Count: The Native American West before Lewis and Clark.* Lincoln: University of Nebraska Press, 2003.
Chang, David A. "Enclosures of Land and Sovereignty: The Allotment of American Indian Lands." *Radical History Review* 109 (Winter 2011): 108–19.
Clifford, James. *The Predicament of Culture.* Cambridge, Mass.: Harvard University Press, 1988.
Clifford, James, and George E. Marcus. *Writing Culture: The Poetics and Politics of Ethnography: A School of American Research Advanced Seminar.* Berkeley: University of California Press, 1986.
Deloria, Ella Cara. *Speaking of Indians.* New York: Friendship Press, 1944; Lincoln: University of Nebraska Press, 1998.

Deloria, Philip J. *Indians in Unexpected Places.* Lawrence: University Press of Kansas, 2004.

———. *Playing Indian.* New Haven, Conn.: Yale University Press, 1998.

Deloria, Vine, Jr. *Custer Died for Your Sins: An Indian Manifesto.* New York: Macmillan, 1969.

———. "Kinship with the World." In *Spirit and Reason: The Vine Deloria, Jr. Reader.* Edited by Barbara Deloria, Kristen Foehner, and Sam Scinta. Golden, Colo.: Fulcrum, 1999. 223–29.

Deloria, Vine, and Clifford M. Lytle. *The Nations Within: The Past and Future of American Indian Sovereignty.* Austin: University of Texas Press, 1984.

Deloria, Vine, and David E. Wilkins. *Tribes, Treaties, and Constitutional Tribulations.* Austin: University of Texas Press, 1999.

DeMallie, Raymond. "Kinship and Biology in Sioux Culture." In *North American Indian Anthropology: Essays on Society and Culture.* Edited by Raymond DeMallie and Alfonso Ortiz. Norman: University of Oklahoma Press, 1994. 125–46.

———. "The Lakota Ghost Dance: An Ethnohistorical Account." *Pacific Historical Review* 51, no. 4 (November 1982): 385–405.

———. "'These Have No Ears': Narrative and the Ethnohistorical Method." *Ethnohistory* 40, no. 4 (Fall 1993): 515–38.

Dorsey, George A. "The Cheyenne." Chicago: Field Columbian Museum, 1905.

Dunlay, Thomas W. *Wolves for the Blue Soldiers: Indian Scouts and Auxiliaries with the United States Army, 1860–90.* Lincoln: University of Nebraska Press, 1987.

Dusenberry, Verne. "The Northern Cheyenne, All They Have Asked Is to Live in Montana." *Montana: The Magazine of Western History* 15 (Winter 1955): 23–40.

DuVal, Kathleen. "Indian Intermarriage and Métissage in Colonial Louisiana." *William and Mary Quarterly* 65, no. 2 (2008): 267–304.

———. *The Native Ground: Indians and Colonists in the Heart of the Continent.* Philadelphia: University of Pennsylvania Press, 2006.

Eastman, Charles. *Indian Heroes and Great Chieftains.* New York: Dover, 1997.

Eggan, Fred. *The American Indian: Perspectives for the Study of Social Change.* Chicago: Aldine, 1966.

———. "The Cheyenne and Arapaho Kinship System." In *Social Anthropology of North American Indian Tribes: Essays in Social Organization, Law, and Religion.* Edited by Fred Eggan. Chicago: University of Chicago Press, 1937. 35–95.

Ekberg, Carl J. *Stealing Indian Women: Native Slavery in the Illinois Country.* Urbana: University of Illinois Press, 2007.

Fabian, Johannes. *Time and the Other: How Anthropology Makes Its Object.* New York: Columbia University Press, 1983.

Fisher, Andrew H. *Shadow Tribe: The Making of Columbia River Indian Identity.* Seattle: University of Washington Press, 2010.

Fixico, Donald. *The American Indian Mind in a Linear World: American Indian Studies and Traditional Knowledge.* New York: Routledge, 2013.

———. *Indian Resilience and Rebuilding: Indigenous Nations in the Modern American West.* Tucson: University of Arizona Press, 2013.

Fogelson, Raymond. "The Ethnohistory of Events and Non-Events." *Ethnohistory* 36, no. 2 (1989): 133–47.

Forest, Ohki Siminé. "Return of the Ancient Council Ways: Indigenous Survival in Chiapas." In *Original Instructions: Indigenous Teachings for a Sustainable Future.* Edited by Melissa K. Nelson. Rochester, Vt.: Bear, 2008. 229–38.

Foucault, Michel. *"Society Must Be Defended": Lectures at the College de France, 1975–1976.* Translated by David Macey. New York: Picador, 2003.

Fowler, Loretta. *Shared Symbols and Contested Meanings: Gros Ventre Culture and History, 1778–1984.* Ithaca, N.Y.: Cornell University Press, 1987.

———. *Tribal Sovereignty and the Historical Imagination: Cheyenne-Arapaho Politics.* Lincoln: University of Nebraska Press, 2002.

———. *Wives and Husbands: Gender and Age in Southern Arapaho History.* Norman: University of Oklahoma Press, 2012.

Fredlund, Glen, Rebecca Armstrong, and Linea Sundstrom. "Crazy Mule's Maps of the Upper Missouri, 1877–1880." *Plains Anthropologist* 41, no. 155 (February 1996): 5–27.

Fried, Morton H. "On the Concept of 'Tribe' and 'Tribal Society.'" In *Essays on the Problem of Tribe: Proceedings of the American Ethnological Society, 1967.* Edited by June Helm. Seattle: University of Washington Press, 1968. 3–20.

Gallay, Alan. *The Indian Slave Trade: The Rise of the English Empire in the American South, 1670–1717.* New Haven, Conn.: Yale University Press, 2002.

Gearing, Fred. *Priests and Warriors: Social Structures for Cherokee Politics in the 18th Century.* Menasha, Wis.: American Anthropological Association, 1962.

Genetin-Pilawa, C. Joseph. *Crooked Paths to Allotment: The Fight over Federal Indian Policy after the Civil War.* Chapel Hill: University of North Carolina Press, 2012.

Gitlin, Marty. *Wounded Knee Massacre.* Oxford: Greenwood, 2011.

Greene, Jerome. *American Carnage: Wounded Knee 1890.* Norman: University of Oklahoma Press, 2015.

———. *Washita: The U.S. Army and the Southern Cheyennes, 1867–1869.* Norman: University of Oklahoma Press, 2004.

Greene, Jerome, and Douglas D. Scott. *Finding Sand Creek: History, Archeology, and the 1864 Massacre Site.* Norman: University of Oklahoma Press, 2004.

Greenwald, Emily. *Reconfiguring the Reservation: The Nez Perces, Jicarilla Apaches, and the Dawes Act.* Albuquerque: University of New Mexico Press, 2002.

Grinnell, George Bird. *By Cheyenne Campfires.* 1926. Reprint, New Haven, Conn.: Yale University Press, 1962.

———. *The Cheyenne Indians*. 2 vols. New Haven, Conn.: Yale University Press, 1923; Lincoln: University of Nebraska Press, 1972.

———. *The Fighting Cheyennes*. New York: Charles Scribner's Sons, 1915; Norman: University of Oklahoma Press, 1956.

———. "Mountain Sheep." *Journal of Mammalogy* 9, no. 1 (February 1928): 1–9.

———. "Social Organization of the Cheyennes." In *Proceedings of the International Congress of Americanists*. New York, 1902; Nendeln, Liechtenstein: Kraus, 1968.

———. "Tenure of Land among the Indians." *American Anthropologist* 9, no. 1 (January-March 1907): 1–11.

Grua, David W. *Surviving Wounded Knee: The Lakotas and the Politics of Memory*. Oxford: Oxford University Press, 2016.

Gupta, Akhil, and James Ferguson. "Beyond 'Culture': Space, Identity, and the Politics of Difference." *Cultural Anthropology* 7, no. 1 (February 1992): 6–23.

Gussow, Zachary. "Cheyenne and Arapaho Aboriginal Occupation." In *Arapaho-Cheyenne Indians*. Edited by David Horr. New York: Garland, 1974. 31–95.

Hämäläinen, Pekka. *The Comanche Empire*. New Haven, Conn.: Yale University Press, 2008.

Hardorff, Richard G. *Cheyenne Memories of the Custer Fight: A Source Book*. Spokane: Arthur H. Clark, 1995.

———. *Hokahey! A Good Day to Die!: The Indian Casualties of the Custer Fight*. Spokane: Arthur H. Clark, 1993.

Hardt, Michael, and Antonio Negri. *Empire*. Cambridge, Mass.: Harvard University Press, 2000.

Harjo, Suzan Shown, ed. *Nation to Nation: Treaties between the United States and American Indian Nations*. Washington, D.C.: Smithsonian Institution, 2014.

Harmon, Alexandra. *Indians in the Making: Ethnic Relations and Indian Identities around Puget Sound*. Berkeley: University of California Press, 1998.

Hill, Christina Gish. "'General Miles Put Us Here': Northern Cheyenne Military Alliance and Sovereign Territorial Rights." *American Indian Quarterly* 37, no. 4 (2013): 340–69.

Hobbes, Thomas. *Leviathan*. Edited by Edwin Curley. Indianapolis: Hackett, 1994.

———. *On the Citizen*. Edited by Richard Tuck and Michael Silverthorne. New York: Cambridge University Press, 1998.

Hoebel, E. Adamson. *The Cheyennes: Indians of the Great Plains*. Minneapolis: University of Minnesota Press, 1978.

Hoig, Stan. *Peace Chiefs of the Cheyennes*. 1980. Reprint, Norman: University of Oklahoma Press, 1990.

———. *Perilous Pursuit: The U.S. Cavalry and the Northern Cheyennes*. Boulder: University Press of Colorado, 2002.

————. *The Sand Creek Massacre*. Norman: University of Oklahoma Press, 1961.

Holm, Tom, J. Diane Pearson, and Ben Chavis. "Peoplehood: A Model for the Extension of Sovereignty in American Indian Studies." *Wicazo Sa Review* 18, no. 1 (Spring 2003): 7–24.

Howe, Craig. "Keep Your Thoughts Above the Trees." In *Clearing a Path: Theorizing the Past in Native American Studies*. Edited by Nancy Shoemaker. New York: Routledge, 2002. 161–79.

Howe, LeAnne. "The Story of America: A Tribalography." In *Clearing a Path: Theorizing the Past in Native American Studies*. Edited by Nancy Shoemaker. New York: Routledge, 2002. 29–48.

Hoxie, Frederick E. *A Final Promise: The Campaign to Assimilate the Indians, 1880–1920*. Lincoln: University of Nebraska Press, 2001.

————. "From Prison to Homeland: The Cheyenne River Reservation before World War I." In *The Plains Indians of the Twentieth Century*. Edited by Peter Iverson. Norman: University of Oklahoma Press, 1985. 55–76.

————. "Retrieving the Red Continent: Settler Colonialism and the History of American Indians in the US." *Ethnic and Racial Studies* 31, no. 6 (2008): 1153–67.

Hurt, Wesley. *Sioux Indians II*. New York: Garland, 1974.

Hyde, Anne F. *Empires, Nations, and Families: A History of the North American West, 1800–1860*. Lincoln: University of Nebraska Press, 2011.

Hyde, George E. *Life of George Bent Written from His Letters*. Edited by Savoie Lottinville. Norman: University of Oklahoma Press, 1968.

Igler, David. "Captive-Taking and Conventions of Encounters on the Northwest Coast, 1789–1810." *Southern California Quarterly* 91, no. 1 (Spring 2009): 3–25.

Innes, Robert Alexander. *Elder Brother and the Law of the People: Contemporary Kinship and Cowessess First Nation*. Winnipeg: University of Manitoba Press, 2013.

Jablow, Joseph. *The Cheyenne in Plains Indian Trade Relations, 1795–1840*. Lincoln: University of Nebraska Press, 1994.

Jacobs, Sue-Ellen, Wesley Thomas, and Sabine Lang, eds. *Two-Spirit People: Native American Gender Identity, Sexuality, and Spirituality*. Urbana: University of Illinois Press, 1997.

Josephy, Alvin, Jr. *500 Nations: An Illustrated History of North American Indians*. New York: Knopf, 1994.

Justice, Daniel Heath. *Our Fire Survives the Storm: A Cherokee Literary History*. Minneapolis: University of Minnesota Press, 2006.

Kan, Sergei. *Strangers to Relatives: The Adoption and Naming of Anthropologists in Native North America*. Lincoln: University of Nebraska Press, 2001.

Kappler, Charles. *Indian Affairs: Laws and Treaties*. 5 vols. Washington, D.C.: GPO, 1904.

Kauanui, J. Kēhaulani. *Hawaiian Blood: Colonialism and the Politics of Sovereignty and Indigeneity*. Durham, N.C.: Duke University Press, 2008.

Kehoe, Alice Beck. *The Ghost Dance: Ethnohistory and Revitalization.* Long Grove, Ill.: Waveland, 2006.

Kelman, Ari. *A Misplaced Massacre: Struggling over the Memory of Sand Creek.* Cambridge, Mass.: Harvard University Press, 2013.

Kidwell, Clara Sue. "Indian Women as Cultural Mediators." *Ethnohistory* 39, no. 2 (Spring 1992): 97–107.

———. "Native American Systems of Knowledge." In *A Companion to American Indian History.* Edited by Philip J. Deloria and Neal Salisbury. New York: John Wiley, 2008. 87–102.

Kilpatrick, Jacquelyn. *Celluloid Indians: Native Americans and Film.* Lincoln: University of Nebraska Press, 1999.

King, Thomas. *The Truth about Stories: A Native Narrative.* Toronto: House of Anansi, 2003.

Klopotek, Brian. *Recognition Odysseys: Indigeneity, Race, and Federal Tribal Recognition Policy in Three Louisiana Indian Communities.* Durham, N.C.: Duke University Press, 2011.

Lakomäki, Sami. *Gathering Together: The Shawnee People through Diaspora and Nationhood, 1600–1870.* New Haven, Conn.: Yale University Press, 2014.

Lazarus, Edward. *Black Hills, White Justice: The Sioux Nation versus the United States, to the Present.* New York: Harper Collins, 1991.

Leiker, James, and Ramon Powers. *The Northern Cheyenne Exodus in History and Memory.* Norman: University of Oklahoma Press, 2011.

Leman, Wayne, ed. "Black Hills Claim." In *Náévâhóo'ohtséme / We Are Going Back Home: Cheyenne History and Stories Told by James Shoulderblade and Others.* Winnipeg: Algonquin and Iroquoian Linguistics, 1987.

Liberty, Margot. "Cheyenne Primacy: The Tribes' Perspective as Opposed to That of the United States Army; A Possible Alternative to 'The Great Sioux War of 1876.'" Friends of the Little Bighorn Battlefield, November 2006. http://www.friendslittlebighorn.com/cheyenneprimacy.htm. Accessed May 26, 2016.

Liu, Shaunda A. K. "Native Hawaiian Homestead Water Reservation Rights: Providing Good Living Conditions for Native Hawaiian Homesteaders." *University of Hawaii Law Review* 25 (2002): 85.

Llewellyn, Karl N., and E. Adamson Hoebel. *The Cheyenne Way: Conflict and Case Law in Primitive Jurisprudence.* Norman: University of Oklahoma Press, 1941.

Lomawaima, K. Tsianina. "The Mutuality of Citizenship and Sovereignty: The Society of American Indians and the Battle to Inherit America." *Studies in American Indian Literatures* 25, no. 2 (2013): 331–51.

Long, Stephen H. *Account of an Expedition from Pittsburgh to the Rocky Mountains.* Philadelphia: H. C. Carey and I. Lea, 1823.

Lyons, Scott Richard. *X-Marks: Native Signatures of Assent.* Minnesota: University of Minnesota Press, 2010.

Maddux, Vernon R., and Albert Glenn Maddux. *In Dull Knife's Wake: The True Story of the Northern Cheyenne Exodus of 1878.* Norman, Okla.: Horse Creek, 2003.

Marquis, Thomas. *The Cheyennes of Montana.* Algonac, Mich.: Reference Publications, 1978.

———. *Wooden Leg: A Warrior Who Fought Custer.* Minneapolis: Midwest Company, 1931; Lincoln: University of Nebraska Press, 1967.

Mathes, Valerie Sherer, and Richard Lowitt. *The Standing Bear Controversy: Prelude to Indian Reform.* Urbana: University of Illinois Press, 2003.

McLaughlin, James. Letter from the Secretary of the Interior Transmitting a Report Relating to the Proposed Removal of the Northern Cheyenne Indians. 55th Cong., 3rd Sess., 1899. H. Doc. 153.

Medicine, Beatrice. "Warrior Women: Sex Role Alternatives for Plains Indian Women." In *Learning to be an Anthropologist and Remaining "Native."* Edited with Sue-Ellen Jacobs. Urbana: University of Illinois Press, 2001. 128–36.

Merrell, James H. *The Indians' New World: Catawbas and Their Neighbors from European Contact to the Era of Removal.* Chapel Hill: University of North Carolina Press, 1992.

Message from the President of the United States, Transmitting a Letter of the Secretary of the Interior and Documents Related to the Condition of the Northern Cheyenne Indians. 51st Cong., 1st sess., 1890. S. Ex. Doc. 121.

Miles, Nelson A. "The Indian Problem." *North American Review* 128 (1879): 304–14.

———. *Personal Recollections and Observations of General Nelson A. Miles.* Chicago: Werner, 1896.

Miles, Tiya. *Ties That Bind: The Story of an Afro-Cherokee Family in Slavery and Freedom.* Berkeley: University of California Press, 2015.

Miller, Jay. "Kinship, Family Kindreds, and Community." In *A Companion to American Indian History.* Edited by Philip J. Deloria and Neal Salisbury. Malden, Mass.: Blackwell, 2002. 139–53.

Miller, Robert J. *Native America, Discovered and Conquered: Thomas Jefferson, Lewis and Clark, and Manifest Destiny.* Westport, Conn.: Praeger, 2006.

Monnett, John H. *Tell Them We Are Going Home: The Odyssey of the Northern Cheyennes.* Norman: University of Oklahoma Press, 2001.

Mooney, James. *The Ghost Dance Religion and Wounded Knee.* Smithsonian Institution, Fourteenth Annual Report of the Bureau of Ethnology, 1892–93, part 2. Washington, D.C.: GPO, 1896. Reprint, New York: Dover, 1973.

Moore, John H. *The Cheyenne.* Malden, Mass.: Blackwell, 1999.

———. *The Cheyenne Nation: A Social and Demographic History.* Lincoln: University of Nebraska Press, 1987.

———. "Cheyenne Political History, 1820–1894." *Ethnohistory* 21, no. 4 (Autumn 1974): 329–59.

————. "The Developmental Cycle of Cheyenne Polygyny." *American Indian Quarterly* 15, no. 3 (Summer 1991): 311–28.

————. "Evolution and Historical Reductionism." *Plains Anthropologist* 26, no. 94, part 1 (November 1981): 261–69.

Moore, John H., and Gregory R. Campbell. "An Ethnohistorical Perspective on Cheyenne Demography." *Journal of Family History* 14, no. 1 (March 1989): 17–42.

Morgan, Louis Henry. *Ancient Society*. London: Macmillan, 1877.

————. *Systems of Consanguinity and Affinity of the Human Family*. Washington, D.C.: Smithsonian Institution, 1870. Reprint, Lincoln: University of Nebraska Press, 1997.

Nabokov, Peter. *A Forest of Time: American Indian Ways of History*. Cambridge: Cambridge University Press, 2002.

————. *Where the Lightening Strikes: The Lives of American Indian Sacred Places*. New York: Viking, 2006.

Nelson, Melissa K., ed. *Original instructions: Indigenous Teachings for a Sustainable Future*. Rochester, Vt.: Bear, 2008.

Noble, David W. *Death of a Nation: American Culture and the End of Exceptionalism*. Minneapolis: University of Minnesota Press, 2002.

Nugent, David. "Property Relations, Production Relations, and Inequality: Anthropology, Political Economy, and the Blackfeet." *American Ethnologist* 20, no. 2 (1993): 336–62.

O'Brien, Jean M. *Dispossession by Degrees: Indian Land and Identity in Natick, Massachusetts, 1650–1790*. Cambridge: Cambridge University Press, 1997.

Ortiz, Simon J. *From Sand Creek: Rising in This Heart Which Is Our America*. New York: Thunder's Mouth Press, 1981.

Ostler, Jeffrey. *The Plains Sioux and U.S. Colonialism from Lewis and Clark to Wounded Knee*. Cambridge: Cambridge University Press, 2004.

Otis, Delos Sacket. *The Dawes Act and the Allotment of Indian Lands*. Edited by Francis Paul Prucha. 1934; Norman: University of Oklahoma Press, 1973.

Peattie, Roderick, ed. *The Black Hills*. New York: Vanguard, 1952.

Perdue, Theda. *Cherokee Women: Gender and Culture Change, 1700–1835*. Lincoln: University of Nebraska Press, 1998.

Peters, Virginia Bergman. *Women of the Earth Lodges: Tribal Life on the Plains*. North Haven, Conn.: Archon, 1995.

Powell, Peter J. *The Cheyennes, Ma?heo?o's People: A Critical Bibliography*. Bloomington: Indiana University Press, 1980.

————. *People of the Sacred Mountain: A History of Northern Cheyenne Chiefs and Warrior Societies, 1830–1879*. San Francisco: Harper and Row, 1981.

————. *Sweet Medicine: The Continuing Role of the Sacred Arrows, the Sun Dance, and the Sacred Buffalo Hat in Northern Cheyenne History*. Norman: University of Oklahoma Press, 1998.

Powers, Ramon. "The Northern Cheyenne Trek through Western Kansas in 1878: Frontiersmen, Indians, and Cultural Conflict." *Trail Guide* 17 (September 1972): 2–33.

Prucha, Francis Paul. *American Indian Treaties: The History of a Political Anomaly.* Berkeley: University of California Press, 1994.

Raibmon, Paige. *Authentic Indians: Episodes of Encounter from the Late-Nineteenth-Century Northwest Coast.* Durham, N.C.: Duke University Press, 2005.

Rand, Jacki Thompson. *Kiowa Humanity and the Invasion of the State.* Lincoln: University of Nebraska Press, 2008.

———. "Primary Sources: Indian Goods and the History of American Colonialism and the 19th Century Reservation." In *Clearing a Path: Theorizing the Past in Native American Studies.* Edited by Nancy Shoemaker. New York: Routledge, 2002. 137–57.

Reyes, Alvaro, and Mara Kaufman. "Sovereignty, Indigeneity, Territory: Zapatista Autonomy and the New Practices of Decolonization." *South Atlantic Quarterly* 110, no. 2 (2011): 505–25.

Richter, Daniel K. *Facing East from Indian Country: A Native History of Early America.* Cambridge, Mass.: Harvard University Press, 2001.

Ricker, Eli. *Voices of the American West: Indian Interviews of Eli S. Ricker, 1903–1919.* Edited by Richard E. Jensen. Lincoln: University of Nebraska Press, 2005.

———. *Voices of the American West: The Settler and Soldier Interviews of Eli S. Ricker, 1903–1919.* Edited by Richard E. Jensen. Lincoln: University of Nebraska Press, 2005.

Rifkin, Mark. *Manifesting America: The Imperial Construction of U.S. National Space.* New York: Oxford University Press, 2009.

———. "Romancing Kinship: A Queer Reading of Indian Education and Zitkala-Sa's American Indian Stories." *GLQ: A Journal of Lesbian and Gay Studies* 12, no. 1 (2006): 27–59.

———. *When Did Indians Become Straight? Kinship, the History of Sexuality, and Native Sovereignty.* Oxford: Oxford University Press, 2010.

Robertson, Lindsay G. *Conquest by Law: How the Discovery of America Dispossessed Indigenous Peoples of Their Lands.* New York: Oxford University Press, 2005.

Rollins, Peter, ed. *Hollywood's Indian: The Portrayal of the Native American in Film.* Lexington: University Press of Kentucky, 2011.

Rosaldo, Renato. *Ilongot Headhunting, 1883–1974: A Study in Society and History.* Stanford, Calif.: Stanford University Press, 1980.

Roscoe, Will. *Changing Ones: Third and Fourth Genders in Native North America.* New York: St. Martin's, 1998.

Rowe, John Carlos. *Post-Nationalist American Studies.* Berkeley: University of California Press, 2000.

Rushforth, Brett. *Bonds of Alliance: Indigenous and Atlantic Slaveries in New France.* Chapel Hill: University of North Carolina Press, 2012.

———. "'A Little Flesh We Offer You': The Origins of Indian Slavery in New France." *William and Mary Quarterly*, 3rd series, vol. 60, no. 4 (October 2003): 777–808.

Rzeczkowski, Frank. *Uniting the Tribes: The Rise and Fall of Pan-Indian Community on the Crow Reservation*. Lawrence: University Press of Kansas, 2012.

Sandoz, Mari. *Cheyenne Autumn*. New York: McIntosh and Otis, 1953.

Santina, Adrianne. "Recreating the World: Tipi Ornaments by Cheyenne and Arapaho Women." *Women's Studies* 33, no. 7 (2004): 933–60.

Schaaf, Gregory. "From the Great Law of Peace to the Constitution of the United States: A Revision of America's Democratic Roots." *American Indian Law Review* 14, no. 2 (1988–1989): 323–31.

Schlesier, Karl H. *The Wolves of Heaven: Cheyenne Shamanism, Ceremonies, and Prehistoric Origins*. 1987; Norman: University of Oklahoma Press, 1993.

Schneider, Mary Jane. "Women's Work: An Examination of Women's Roles in Plains Indian Arts and Crafts." In *The Hidden Half: Studies of Plains Indian Women*. Edited by Patricia Albers and Beatrice Medicine. Lanham, Md.: University Press of America, 1983. 101–21.

Schoolcraft, Henry Rowe, and Seth Eastman. *Historical and Statistical Information Respecting the History, Condition, and Prospects of the Indian Tribes of the United States*. Philadelphia: Lippincott, Grambo, 1851.

Scott, James. *Seeing Like a State: How Certain Schemes to Improve the Human Condition Have Failed*. New Haven, Conn.: Yale University Press, 1998.

Shain, Yossi, and Martin Sherman. "Dynamics of Disintegration: Diaspora, Secession and the Paradox of Nation-States." *Nations and Nationalism* 4, no. 3 (July 1998): 321–46.

Sharrock, Susan R. "Crees, Cree-Assiniboines, and Assiniboines: Interethnic Social Organization on the Far Northern Plains." *Ethnohistory* 21, no. 2 (Spring 1974): 95–122.

Shoemaker, Nancy, ed. *Clearing a Path: Theorizing the Past in Native American Studies*. New York: Routledge, 2002.

———, ed. *Negotiators of Change: Historical Perspectives on Native American Women*. New York: Routledge, 1995.

———. *A Strange Likeness: Becoming Red and White in Eighteenth-Century North America*. New York: Oxford University Press, 2004.

Silko, Leslie Marmon. *Ceremony*. Penguin, 1977.

———. "Language and Literature from a Pueblo Indian Perspective." In *English Literature, Selected Papers from the English Institute, 1979*. Edited by Leslie A. Fiedler and Houston A. Baker Jr. Baltimore: Johns Hopkins University Press, 1981. 54–72.

Simpson, Audra. *Mohawk Interruptus: Political Life across the Borders of Settler States*. Durham, N.C.: Duke University Press, 2014.

Simpson, Audra, and Andrea Smith, eds. *Theorizing Native Studies*. Durham, N.C.: Duke University Press, 2014.

Slapin, Beverly, and Doris Seale. *Through Indian Eyes: The Native Experience in Books for Children.* Philadelphia: New Society, 1992.

Sleeper-Smith, Susan. *Indian Women and French Men: Rethinking Cultural Encounter in the Western Great Lakes.* Amherst: University of Massachusetts Press, 2001.

———. "Women, Kin, and Catholicism: New Perspectives on the Fur Trade." *Ethnohistory* 47, no. 2 (2000): 423–52.

Smith, Andrea. "Indigeneity, Settler Colonialism, White Supremacy." In *Racial Formation in the Twenty-First Century.* Edited by Daniel Martinez HoSang, Oneka LaBennett, and Laura Pulido. Berkeley: University of California Press, 2012. 65–79.

Smith, Linda Tuhiwai. *Decolonizing Methodologies.* London: Zed, 1999.

Smoak, Gregory E. *Ghost Dances and Identity: Prophetic Religion and American Indian Ethnogenesis in the Nineteenth Century.* Berkeley: University of California Press, 2006.

Snyder, Christina. *Slavery in Indian Country: The Changing Face of Captivity in Early America.* Cambridge, Mass.: Harvard University Press, 2010.

Spivak, Gayatri Chakravorty. "Nationalism and the Imagination." *Critical Studies* 37, no. 1 (2014): 31–55.

St. Germain, Jill. *Indian Treaty-Making Policy in the United States and Canada, 1867–1877.* Lincoln: University of Nebraska Press, 2001.

Stands In Timber, John, and Margot Liberty. *Cheyenne Memories.* New Haven, Conn.: Yale University Press, 1967.

———. *A Cheyenne Voice.* Norman: University of Oklahoma Press, 2013.

Starita, Joe. *The Dull Knifes of Pine Ridge: A Lakota Odyssey.* Lincoln: University of Nebraska Press, 2002.

Stark, Heidi Kiiwetinepinesiik. "Marked by Fire: Anishinaabe Articulations of Nationhood in Treaty Making with the United States and Canada." *American Indian Quarterly* 36, no. 2 (2012): 119–49.

———. "Nenabozho's Smart Berries: Rethinking Tribal Sovereignty and Accountability." *Michigan State Law Review* (2013): 339–53.

Stekler, Paul Jeffrey, James Welch, and David G. McCullough. *Last Stand at Little Big Horn.* Videocassette (VHS). Boston: WGBH Boston Video, 2004.

Straus, Anne S. "Northern Cheyenne Ethnopsychology." *Ethos* 5, no. 3 (Autumn 1977): 326–57.

———. "Tell Your Sister Come to Eat." In *Strangers to Relatives: The Adoption and Naming of Anthropologists in Native North America.* Edited by Sergei Kan. Lincoln: University of Nebraska Press, 2001. 175–84.

Sundstrom, Linea. "Mirror of Heaven: Cross-Cultural Transference of the Sacred Geography of the Black Hills." *World Archaeology* 28, no. 2 (1996): 177–89.

Svingen, Orlan J. *The Northern Cheyenne Indian Reservation, 1877–1900.* Boulder: University Press of Colorado, 1993.

Taylor, Alan. *American Colonies: The Settlement of North America.* New York: Viking, 2001.

Thorne, Tanis C. *The Many Hands of My Relations: French and Indians on the Lower Missouri.* Columbia: University of Missouri Press, 1996.

Thornton, Russell. *We Shall Live Again: The 1870 and 1890 Ghost Dance Movements as Demographic Revitalization.* Cambridge: Cambridge University Press, 2006.

Tölölyan, Khachig. "The Contemporary Discourse of Diaspora Studies." *Comparative Studies of South Asia, Africa and the Middle East* 27, no. 3 (2007): 647–55.

Tonkovich, Nicole. *The Allotment Plot: Alice C. Fletcher, E. Jane Gay, and Nez Perce Survivance.* Lincoln: University of Nebraska Press, 2012.

Tooker, Elisabeth. "The United States Constitution and the Iroquois League." *Ethnohistory* 35, no. 4 (Autumn 1988): 305–36.

Turner, Dale Antony. *This Is Not a Peace Pipe: Towards a Critical Indigenous Philosophy.* Toronto: University of Toronto Press, 2006.

Twitchell, Philip G. "Camp Robinson Letters of Angeline Johnson, 1876–1879." *Nebraska History* 77, no. 2 (Summer 1996): 89–95.

United States. Annual Report of the Commissioner of Indian Affairs. Washington, D.C.: G.P.O., 1873–1886.

U.S. Senate. Report on the Removal of the Northern Cheyennes. 46th Cong., 2nd sess., 1880. S. Ex. Doc. 708.

Utley, Robert Marshall. *The Last Days of the Sioux Nation.* New Haven, Conn.: Yale University Press, 1963.

Van Kirk, Sylvia. *Many Tender Ties: Women in Fur Trade Society, 1670–1870.* Norman: University of Oklahoma Press, 1980.

Vizenor, Gerald Robert. *Fugitive Poses: Native American Indian Scenes of Absence and Presence.* Lincoln: University of Nebraska Press, 2000.

———, ed. *Survivance: Narratives of Native Presence.* Lincoln: University of Nebraska Press, 2008.

Walker, James. *Lakota Society.* Edited by Raymond J. DeMallie. 1982; Lincoln: University of Nebraska Press, 1992.

Warren, Stephen. "'To Show the Public That We Were Good Indians': Origins and Meanings of the Meskwaki Powwow." *American Indian Culture and Research Journal* 33, no. 4 (2009): 1–28.

Weaver, Jace. "Indigenousness and Indigeneity." In *A Companion to Postcolonial Studies.* Edited by Henry Schwarz and Sangeeta Ray. Oxford: Blackwell, 2000. 221–35.

Weist, Katherine. "Ned Casey and His Cheyenne Scouts: A Noble Experiment in an Atmosphere of Tension." *Montana, the Magazine of Western History* 27 (1977): 26–39.

Weist, Tom. *A History of the Cheyenne People.* Billings: Montana Council for Indian Education, 1977.

West, Elliott. *The Contested Plains: Indians, Goldseekers, and the Rush to Colorado.* Lawrence: University Press of Kansas, 1998.

White, Geoffrey. "Epilogue: Memory Moments." *Ethos* 34, no. 2 (2006): 325–41.

White, Richard. *The Middle Ground: Indians, Empires, and Republics in the Great Lakes Region, 1650–1815.* Cambridge: Cambridge University Press, 1991.

———. "The Winning of the West: The Expansion of the Western Sioux in the Eighteenth and Nineteenth Centuries." *Journal of American History* 65, no. 2 (September 1978): 319–43.

Wightman, Abigail S. *Honoring Kin: Gender, Kinship, and the Economy of Plains Apache Identity.* Norman: University of Oklahoma Press, 2009.

Wilkins, David E. *American Indian Sovereignty and the U.S. Supreme Court: The Masking of Justice.* Austin: University of Texas Press, 1997.

Wilkins, David E., and K. Tsianina Lomawaima. *Uneven Ground: American Indian Sovereignty and Federal Law.* Norman: University of Oklahoma Press, 2001.

Williams, Robert A., Jr. *Like a Loaded Weapon: The Rehnquist Court, Indian Rights, and the Legal History of Racism in America.* Minneapolis: University of Minnesota Press, 2005.

Willinsky, John. *Learning to Divide the World: Education at Empire's End.* Minneapolis: University of Minnesota Press, 1998.

Witgen, Michael. *An Infinity of Nations: How the Native New World Shaped Early North America.* Philadelphia: University of Pennsylvania Press, 2011.

———. "The Rituals of Possession: Native Identity and the Invention of Empire in Seventeenth-Century Western North America." *Ethnohistory* 54, no. 4 (2007): 639–68.

Wolf, Eric. *Europe and the People without History.* Berkeley: University of California Press, 1982.

Worcester, Donald E. *Forked Tongues and Broken Treaties.* Caldwell, Idaho: Caxton, 1975.

Wright, James Leitch. *Creeks and Seminoles: The Destruction and Regeneration of the Muscogulge People.* Lincoln: University of Nebraska Press, 1986.

Zaum, Dominik. *The Sovereignty Paradox: The Norms and Politics of International Statebuilding.* Oxford: Oxford University Press, 2007.

Archival Materials

National Archives.

Letters Received. Bureau of Indian Affairs. RG 75. Washington, D.C.

Commissioner of Indian Affairs to the Secretary of the Interior, June 22, 1881.

Commissioner of Indian Affairs to George Yoakam, September 9, 1882.

Department of Arkansas Headquarters to the A.A.A. General, April 22, 1881.

E. P. Ewers to the Assistant Adjutant General, October 20, 1881.

E. P. Ewers to Agent McGillicuddy, August 23, 1882.

L. A. Grant, Acting Secretary of War to the Secretary of the Interior, John W. Noble, September 18, 1891.

Little Chief to H. D. Gallagher, Pine Ridge Indian Agent, August 13, 1888.

Little Chief to President Grover Cleveland, July 12, 1887.

Little Chief to the Commissioner of Indian Affairs, March 17, 1886.

Little Chief to the Commissioner of Indian Affairs, May 13, 1886.

Little Chief to the Commissioner of Indian Affairs, September 28, 1886.

Little Chief to the Commissioner of Indian Affairs, March 31, 1890.

Office of the Adjutant General to the Department of the Interior, July 22, 1891.

V. T. McGillycuddy to H. Price the Commissioner of Indian Affairs, December 6, 1881.

V. T. McGillycuddy to H. Price the Commissioner of Indian Affairs, June 23, 1882.

V. T. McGillycuddy to the Commissioner of Indian Affairs, October 5, 1882.

John D. Miles to Commissioner of Indian Affairs, March 19, 1881.

John D. Miles to Commissioner of Indian Affairs, April 1881.

John D. Miles to Commissioner of Indian Affairs, June 6, 1881.

John D. Miles to Commissioner of Indian Affairs, June 27, 1881.

John D. Miles to H. Price the Commissioner of Indian Affairs, July 26, 1881.

John D. Miles to H. Price the Commissioner of Indian Affairs, April 22, 1882.

"Proceedings of a Council between Major Henry Carroll and Certain Cheyenne Chiefs," April 15, 1890.

P. H. Sheridan to Townsend, September 19, 1878.

William Tecumseh Sherman to the Headquarters of the Army, November 28, 1882.

Agent Tully to the Commissioner of Indian Affairs, T. J. Morgan, November 2, 1891.

War Department to the Secretary of the Interior National Archives, July 7, 1881.

War Department to the Secretary of the Interior, October 20, 1881.

George Yoakam to the Secretary of the Interior, December 24, 1880.

George Yoakam to President Garfield, June 4, 1881.

George Yoakam to President Chester A. Arthur, August 18, 1882.

George Yoakam to President Chester A. Arthur, September 7, 1882.

George Yoakam to the Commissioner of Indian Affairs, December 12, 1882.

George Yoakam to President Chester A. Arthur, December 25, 1882.

George Yoakam to President Chester A. Arthur, December 24, 1884.

Special Case File 137. Letters Received. Bureau of Indian Affairs. RG 75.
Washington, D.C.

"Agreement to Remove," June 24–25, 1885.

James Atkins, the Commissioner of Indian Affairs to E. D. Banister, June 11, 1885.

James Atkins, the Commissioner of Indian Affairs to L. C. Larson, the Secretary of the Interior, October 5, 1885.

E. D. Banister to James Atkins, the Commissioner of Indian Affairs, July 16, 1885.

Council for Citizens to the Secretary of the Interior, "The Case of the Citizens Memorial to the President, Begging the Revocation of an Executive Order Which November 26, 1884 Burdened the Citizens of Montana with a New Indian Reservation," April 25, 1885.

Captain E. P. Ewers to the Commissioner of Indian Affairs, August 14, 1884.

George Milburn to Commissioner H. Price, the Office of Indian Affairs, February 13, 1883.

S. W. Millen to the Commanding Officer at Fort Keogh, Montana, August 27, 1883.

R. L. Upshaw to the Commissioner of Indian Affairs, James Atkins, February 15, 1886.

George Yoakam to L. C. Larson, the Secretary of the Interior, May 24, 1886.

Letters Received. White River Agency. Bureau of Indian Affairs. RG 75.
Washington, D.C.

P. H. Sheridan to W. T. Sherman, March 23, 1877.

Outbreak Rolls. Letters Received. Office of the Adjutant General (AGO).
Washington, D.C.

Fort Robinson to Commissioner of Indian Affairs, Telegram, January 15, 1879.

Commissioner of Indian Affairs to the Secretary of the Interior, January 16, 1879.

Henry W. Wessels to Quartermaster, Department of the Platte, Omaha, Telegram, January 6, 1879.

Letters Received. Bureau of Indian Affairs. Finance Division. RG 75.
Washington, D.C.

"Little Chief's Band," Annuity Payment Rolls 1841–1949, Northern Cheyenne, 1879.

Letters Received. Red Cloud Agency. Bureau of Indian Affairs. RG 75. Kansas City, Missouri.

> J. J. Saville, "Treaty with Northern Cheyenne and Arapaho Indians: Red Cloud Agency, DT," November 17, 1874.

Little Chief Rolls. Letters Received. Office of the Adjutant General. Washington, D.C.

> Commissioner of Indian Affairs to Secretary of the Interior, August 28, 1881.
> Lieutenant General to Adjutant General, September 21, 1881.
> V. T. McGillycuddy to the Commissioner of Indian Affairs, December 31, 1881.
> John D. Miles to the Commissioner of Indian Affairs, January 3, 1882.
> Secretary of the Interior to Little Chief, June 27, 1881.
> Secretary of the Interior to the Secretary of War, November 28, 1882.
> John Wilkins, Commanding Officer of Fort Keogh, to Adjutant General, Department of Dakota Territory, November 22, 1882.

The National Anthropology Archives, Suitland, Maryland

> Ben Clark to James Mooney, January 16, 1907, Fort Reno, Oklahoma, Letters Received, James Mooney Collection.
> General Hugh L. Scott, Notes on Sign Language and Miscellaneous Ethnographic Notes on Plains Indians, 1934, Cheyenne Folder 1, MS 2932.

Fort Robinson Archive, Fort Robinson State Park, Nebraska

> J. B. Johnson to Lt. Gen. P. H. Sheridan, October 25, 1878, Fort Robinson Archive, Fort Robinson State Park, Nebraska.
> Terry L. Steinacher and Gayle F. Carlson, "The Cheyenne Outbreak Barracks," 1999. Nebraska State Historical Society, Lincoln, Nebraska.

Breakout Newspaper Article Collection.

> "Another View of the Cheyenne Affair by an Inhabitant of Fort Robinson," *New York Herald,* January 31, 1879.
> "Gone for Good," *Sidney Plaindealer,* October 24, 1878.
> "Indians," *Army and Navy Journal,* February 8, 1879.
> "Indian Affairs," *Army and Navy Journal,* September 19, 1878.
> "Little Chief States the Desires and Wishes of His People," *Sidney (Nebraska) Telegraph,* September 28, 1878.
> "The Northern Cheyenne: They Pass by Dodge City," *Dodge City Times,* November 23, 1878, 1.
> "The Cheyenne Indians: Preparation at Sidney for Taking Care of the Warriors Who Have Lost Their Reservation," *Sidney (Nebraska) Telegraph,* September 21, 1878.

Montana State Historical Society. Helena, Montana

Fort Keogh Post Commissary Records. MS 15

Assistant Adjutant General to Commanding Officer, Fort Keogh, July 17, 1879.

Vertical Files. Cheyenne Indians: Economic Conditions

"Great Plains Tribes Resist Sale of Their Lands," *Indian Affairs* 25 (March 1958): 1.

Northern Cheyenne Tribal Council, "Land Program," *Plan for the Social and Economic Development of the Northern Cheyenne Tribe,* February 15, 1960.

John Woodenlegs, "Back on the War Ponies," *Indian Affairs* 37 (June 1960): 3.

John Woodenlegs, "Northern Cheyenne Goal—All Land in Tribal Ownership," *Indian Affairs* 34 (June 1959): 1.

Homesteading File. Montana Governor's Office Papers

R. L. Upshaw to the Commissioner of Indian Affairs, John H. Oberly, May 23, 1889.

John Tully to T. J. Morgan, the Commissioner of Indian Affairs, December 26, 1891.

Montana Indian Reservations Historical Jurisdiction Study File.
Montana Governor's Office Papers

Assistant Commissioner of Indian Affairs to Superintendent, October 20, 1923.

Superintendent to Commissioner of Indian Affairs, October 5, 1923.

Superintendent to Commissioner of Indian Affairs, November 24, 1923.

Carlisle School

Capt. R. H. Pratt to D. B. Dryer, June 13, 1885. Sie/Berthrong Cheyenne Collections, Boarding School Files, C&A Carlisle School File, Carlisle, Pennsylvania.

Newberry Library, Chicago, Illinois

E. P. Ewers to General Nelson A. Miles, October 29, 1890. Elmo Scott Watson Papers.

John S. Gray Collection. Ayer Manuscripts.

"Report of Produce." Fort Keogh. Elmo Scott Watson Papers.

Index

Page references in italics indicate illustrations.

Adoption Pipe ceremony, 70
adoptions, 77; Cheyenne identity, 66, 67; intertribal, 69–70
agencies, 103, 107, 122, 172; containment at, 131, 161–62; Northern Cheyennes at, 108, 130, 138–42, 149–50
Aikau, Hokulani K., 89
alliances, 102, 120, 160; establishing, 68–69; with Lakotas, 74, 105, 106; maintaining, 76, 110; multiethnic, 170–71; with Nelson Miles, 116–17, 145, 147–48, 151, 153–54, 226, 227, 243–44, 270, 275–77, 281–82, 301
Allison, William, 124
allotments, 265, 271, 324n148; sales of, 294–95, 296–97
American Horse (Cheyenne), 139, 168, 176, 281, 283
American Horse (Ogallala), 194
American Indian Tribal Histories Project, 62, 63, 293
ancestors, 18; in landscape, 91–93
animals: kinship with, 93–94; reciprocal relationships with, 91, 159, 241
Aorta band, 88

Arapahos, 32, 67, 99, 100, 101, 102, 139, 167, 321n109, 328n56; alliances with, 68, 69, 77; northern and southern bands, 74–75; relationships with, 71–72, 76, 106
Arikaras, 71, 99; alliances with, 68, 69, 73
Arthur, Chester A., 223, 257, 269
Ashland district, Northern Cheyenne reservation, 236
assimilation, 26, 28, 103, 108, 132, 149, 158, 258–59, 260–61; forced, 33, 127; as goal, 117–18, 239–40; homesteading and, 241, 250, 252–53
Assiniboines, 99
Atkins, John D. C., 272
Atsinas, 75, 76
authority: personal, 30; political, 42–43
autonomy: land and, 295–96; Northern Cheyenne, 261–62, 263–64; political, 13, 30–31, 41–42, 43–44, 162, 224–25, 234–35, 301; political power, 40–41

bands, 52, 62, 71, 142, 317n46; and camps, 58–59, 64; northern and southern, 74–75

369

Banister, E. D., 271–72

Barr, M. R., 254–55, 256–57, 259

Battle at Punished Woman's Fork, 178

Battle of the Little Bighorn, 17, 122, 162, 270, 345–46n2; aftermath, 108, 114, 124–25, 130

Battle Where the Girl Saved Her Brother (Battle of the Rosebud), 123, 270, 330n18

Bear Butte, S.Dak., 72, 96; origins of, 91–92; religious power from, 54, 55

Bear's Lariat, 215

Bear Woman, 141

Beaver Claw, 140

behavior: dualities of, 64–65; learning proper, 16–17

Bent, Charles, 70

Bent, George, 53, 68, 70, 75, 89

Bent, William, 70–71, 100, 323n127

Bent's Fort, 70, 71, 75

Big Horse, 133, 331n51, 333n81

Big Left Hand, Silas, 88–89

Big Nose, 141

Big Wolf, 106, 209

Birney district, Northern Cheyenne reservation, 237

Black Bear, 137, 140, 212

Black Coal, 119, 141

Black Coyote, 52, 141

Black Eagle, 140

Black Hairy Dog, 140

Black Hills, S.Dak., 10, 74; Cheyennes in, 104, 105, 106, 321n109, 210, 211, 322–23n125; Great Race, 88, 326n29; interethnic relationships in, 71–72; knowledge of, 57–58; negotiations over, 124–25; Sweet Medicine in, 54, 72–73; violations of 1868 treaty, 121–22

Black Kettle, 100, 101

Black Moccasin (Limber Lance), 141

Black Wolf, 140, 144, 223, *245*, 252, 258; hunting trip, 213–14; on land tenure, 226–27; leadership of, 224–25; in Tongue River valley, 225–26, 235, 254

Black Wolf's people, 251

Bobtail Horse, *196*, 281, 283

boundaries, 26, 111, 346n3; ethnic, 304–5; geopolitical, 267–68; nation-state, 298–99; reservation, 5, 257, 259, 270–71, 273–74, 283–84, 346n3

Bourke, John G., 209

Bow Strings, 60, 317n48

Box Elder, 141

Boye, Alan, 21, 178

Brave Bear, 140

Brave Wolf, 137, 141, 144, 275–77, 333n81

breakout, from Fort Robinson, 190–93, 195–97, 298–99, 348n21

Broken Dish. *See* Yellow Calfskin Shirt (Broken Dish)

Broken Jaw, 140

brothers, 65; in Cheyenne kinship network, 49, 174

Broughier, John, 134, 136, 137, 332n55

buffalo, in Great Race, 88, 91

Buffalo Calf Road Woman, 123, 330n17

Buffalo Hump, 192, 195

buffalo hunts, 59, 71, 175

Buffalo Paunch, 141

Bull Hump, 189; wife of, 186–87

bundles, sacred medicine, 54–55, 57, 140

Busby district, Northern Cheyenne reservation, 236

camp circle, summer, 63–64, 84

camps: Cheyenne, 58–59; choosing sites, 83–84; and military societies, 62, 63–64; Powder River, 130–31; winter, 128, 133

Camp Sheridan, 139
Cantonment Reno, 128
Cantonment Tongue River, 128. *See
    also* Fort Keogh, Mont.
captives, 66, 69, 324n148; kin ties
    of, 76–77; of Nelson Miles,
    133–37; and peace negotiations,
    77–78
Casey, Edward W., 231, *276*
ceremonies, 73, 92; to make plants
    and animals kin, 93–94; landscape
    and, 85, 109
Charcoal Bear, 139–40
Cheyennes, 72, 87, 313n56,
    321–22n114, 322–23n125; camps,
    58–59; containment of, 204–5;
    division into northern and
    southern bands, 74–75; ethnic
    definition of, 304–5; identity as,
    27, 51–52, 54, 55–58, 142; kinship
    networks of, 48–49; leaders of,
    145–46; membership, 65–67, 78;
    multiethnic alliances of, 170–71;
    national narrative of, 17–18;
    political organization of, 31, 35;
    treaties with, 99, 100, 101–2,
    104–5, 110–11. *See also* Northern
    Cheyennes; Southern Cheyennes
Chief Bear, 141
Chief Going Up Hill, 141
Chief Joseph, 148, 149, 205, 279
chiefs, 64, 140, 317–18n52, 318n62;
    and Council of Forty-Four, 60,
    62–63, 72, 106; families of, 50–51;
    social roles of, 145–46
children: kinship network, 48–49;
    separation from family, 173, 174;
    as war captives, 76–77
Children and the Bear, 55
Christianity, conversion to, 33, 103
citizenship: American, 252;
    Cheyenne, 66; contracts of, 25
civilizing process, 132–33

Clark, Ben, 87, 208, 209, 211, 218
Clark, William P., 160, 181–82, 198
Cleveland, Grover, 229
colonialism, 23, 36, 127; justification
    of, 24–25; kinship and, 37–38;
    and Native nations, 28–29
Colorado, 10, 101–2
Comanches, 71, 74, 76, 102
conquest, European, 23–24, 312n45
consensus, management of, 41–42
containment, 212; as Crook's goal,
    158–59, 161–62; as U.S. goal,
    117–18, 131, 176–77, 199–200,
    204–5, 219, 222, 224, 229, 235
Council of Forty-Four, 60, 62–64,
    72, 106. *See also* chiefs
Cox, Chris C., 161
Crazy Dogs, 60, 317n48. *See also*
    Dog Men, Dog Soldier bands
    (Cheyenne/Lakota)
Crazy Head, 137, 138, 141
Crazy Horse, 9, 129, 167, 336n10
Crazy Mule, 137, 141, 209, 212,
    215, 341n21
Creator, 86, 87
Cree, 53
Crook, George, 115, 123, 127, 128,
    132, 176, 194, 270, 336n11; agenda
    of, 160–62, 198–99; negotiations
    with, 138–39, 157, 158, 159–60,
    163–65, 209–10
Crooked Nose, 133
Crow (person), 189
Crow Agency, 107
Crow reservation, 267, 271–72, 274,
    278, 345–46n2
Crows, 71, 74, 75–76, 99, 102
Custer, George Armstrong,
    121, 124

Dakotas, 53, 69
Dakota Territory, 54
Daniels, J. W., 119

Darlington Agency, Indian Territory, 166, 168; Little Chief's people at, 212–14
Dawson, E. C., 228, 342n63
decolonizing, 21–22
Deloria, Ella, 48
Deloria, Philip, 126, 127, 177
Deloria, Vine, 31, 39–40, 43
depression of 1873, 121
Devil's Tower, 91, 92
diaspora, Northern Cheyenne, 108–9, 157
diplomacy, 115, 160; by captive women, 135–36; and kinship rules, 36–37, 78–79
Dog Growing Up, 141
Dog Men, Dog Soldier bands (Cheyenne/Lakota), 71, 80, 100, 101, 112, 317n48, 320n104
duality, 319n75; between chiefs and military societies, 64–65
Dull Knife (Morning Star), 9, 10, 12, 106, 118, 128, 157, 158, 174, 193, 195, *196*, 201, 209, 250, 296, 339n84; and Crook, 159–60; at Fort Robinson, 139, 182, 183–87, 188–89; and removal negotiations, 164–65; return to north, 179, 197–98
Dull Knife, George, 175, 219–20
Dull Knife, Guy, Jr., 193, 219
Dull Knife's people, 12–13, 20–21, 81, 115, 175, 214; at Fort Robinson, 182, 184–87, 188, 189–90; and Red Cloud Agency, 167, 183–84; as refugees, 128–29

earth, as grandmother, 85
education, 244
Eggan, Fred, 27
Elk River, Mont., 141
Elk Scrapers (Elk Horn Scrapers; Elks; Hoof Rattlers), 60, 317n48

enemies, enemy nations, trade relationships with, 77
enrollment, tribal, 81
Erect Horns, 54–55, 86
ethnicity, 51; Cheyenne, 304–5
Euro-Americans, 77; intermarriage with, 70–71; and land, 97–98; in Tongue River valley, 254–55
Ewers, E. P., 223–24, 247, 249, 253, 255–56, 257
executive orders: expanding reservation, 283–84; for Northern Cheyenne reservation, 257, 260, 266–67, 291

factionalism, 27, 42, 79–80
families, 5, 9, 65, 112, 157, 185, 227, 252; of chiefs, 50–51; and decision making, 8, 20; future of, 289–90; and historical actions, 11, 21; historical archives in, 17–18; individual place in, 47–48; of Little Chief's band, 222–23; as political units, 12–13; polygamous and extended, 56–57; separation of, 173–74; structure of, 59–60
farms, farmers, 103, 229, 270; at Fort Keogh, 148–49, 224; in Tongue River valley, 238, 240
Fast Whirlwind, 141
Fire Wolf, 141
Fixico, Donald, 90, 95
Fletcher, Alice, 260
Fleury, George, 181
Fort Casper, Wyo., 167
Fort Keogh, Mont., 114, 128, 136, 155, 183, 340n1; captives at, 134, 135; Dull Knife's band at, 195, 198; Little Chief's relatives at, 222–23; Northern Cheyennes at, 139, 145, 146–49, 154, 180–81, 198, 204, 207, 224, 243, 263, 279–80,

334n89, 334–35n99, 341n21; Two
Moons's people at, 116–17, 140,
141, 142–43
Fort Laramie Treaty (1851),
territories defined by, 99–100
Fort Laramie Treaty (1868), 102–3,
106, 330n34; Cheyennes under,
110–11; Native perceptions of,
122–23; violation of, 121–22
Fort Lincoln, N.Dak., Northern
Cheyenne removal to, 206, 208
Fort Peck reservation, 231
Fort Robinson, Neb., 9, 10, 138;
breakout from, 190–93, 195–97,
296, 298–99, 348n21; Dull Knife's
band at, 182, 184–87, 188–90;
massacre at, 155, 156–57, 239;
surrenders at, 139–40
Fort Robinson State Park, Neb., 155–56
Fort Wise Treaty (1861), 100
Franklin, Benjamin, 30
French fur trade, 54

Gallagher, H. D., 230
gender, flexible categories of, 57
General Allotment Act (Dawes
Act), 293, 309–11n3
generosity, 47, 62
Ghost Dance movement, 131,
231, 232
gifting, 69–70; negotiations and,
134, 136, 145, 160
Ginés de Sepúlveda, Juan, 34
gold rush, Black Hills, 121–22
Grant, Ulysses S., 121, 239
Gray Head, 209
Great Lakes, 53; as early
homeland, 88–89
Great Race, 55, 88, 91, 326n29
Great Sioux Reservation, Dakota
Territory, 9, 102, 103, 104, 123;
and Black Hills gold rush, 121–22;
Cheyennes and Arapahos, 105–6,

107; Northern Cheyennes on,
111, 199
Great Sioux Wars, 122
Grinnell, George Bird, 38, 53, 59, 75,
87, 88, 164, 331n51; on escape from
Fort Robinson, 191–92; and
Northern Cheyenne return,
185, 188–89
Gros Ventres, 99

Hairy Hand, 281
Hanging Woman Creek, Mont.,
250, 252, 269
Hastings, J. S., 126
hat keepers, 50
Hayes, Rutherford B., 213, 239
Hevhaitaneo band (Hair Rope
People), 70
Hidatsa, 68, 70
Hinman, Samuel D., 119, 120–21
histories, 39; family-based, 17–18;
hierarchical, 22–23; origin, 86–88
Hoebel, E. Adamson, 27, 38
homeland, 20; Northern Cheyenne,
105, 172; reciprocal relationships
with, 96–97
homesickness, 172–73
homesteading, homesteads, 5, 148,
246–47, 255–56, 257–58, 260, 268,
274–75, 277, 297–98, 344n17;
assimilation through, 240, 241;
flexibility of, 253–54; Tongue
River valley, 236, 248–52,
282–83, 284
Horse Road, 138, 141
horses, 71
hostiles, U.S. government definition of, 122, 126
houses, built by Northern
Cheyennes, 224, 227, 249, 251
Howling Wolf, 141, 275; on Nelson
Miles, 243–44
humans, creation of, 87, 88

Hump, 137, 138
hunting grounds, 99, 112

identity, 26, 29, 301, 319n80; band
    and society, 59–60; Cheyenne,
    51–52, 54, 55–58, 142; collective,
    65–66, 111; group, 31–33, 252;
    individual, 58–59; Native
    national, 18–19; tribal, 27, 81
Indian Homestead Act, 247, 248–49,
    258, 271
Indian Territory, 96, 101, 107, 302;
    Little Chief's people in, 203–4,
    205, 207, 212–16; Northern
    Cheyennes in, 108, 168–70, 171,
    218–19, 221–22; removal to, 159,
    162–63, 164–65, 166–67, 301;
    Southern Cheyennes in, 140–41
Indigenous peoples: as natural
    subjects, 23–24; as proto-nations,
    26; sovereignty and, 34, 40
individualism, 253
individuals, 52, 61; historical focus
    on, 8, 23; identity of, 58–59
interethnic relationships, 71–73
intermarriage, 58, 67, 79, 317–18n52;
    Cheyenne-Lakota, 74, 218; trade
    relationships, 69, 70–71
intertribal relations, 75–76
interviews, 5–6
Iron Shirt, 137, 141, 212
Iron Teeth, 130, 186, 187; on Fort
    Laramie Treaty, 122–23; on
    Northern Cheyenne journey, 178–79
Iroquois Confederacy, 30
Irwin, James, 167

Johnson, Angeline, 190
Johnson, Carter P., 183, 185, 187–88
Johnson, J. B., 183–85, 188

Kansas, 10, 101, 177–78, 337n59
kinship, 9, 19, 20, 24, 46–47, 92, 142,
    159, 263, 329n81; centrality of,
    44–45; and Cheyenne identity,

55–56; and colonial hegemony,
    37–38; diplomacy and, 36–37;
    flexibility of, 56–57, 81–82; future
    and, 289–90; and group identity,
    252; and landscape, 84–85, 286–87,
    297, 302–3; and market economy,
    52–53; narrative of, 300–301;
    networks, 37, 48–51, 57–59, 62,
    75, 109–10, 252, 304; peace
    negotiations and, 77–78; with
    plants and animals, 93–94; and
    political action, 12–13; and
    political authority, 41–43, 300,
    301–2; and political autonomy,
    234–35; and return to north, 197–98;
    social support and, 80–81; South-
    ern and Northern Cheyenne,
    168–69; and trade relationships,
    69–70; warfare and, 76–77
kinship systems, 12; cultural
    negotiation, 67–68; flexibility
    of, 79–80
Kiowa-Apaches, 32, 72
Kiowas, 32, 71, 72, 73, 76, 102,
    321n109, 322n119, 322–23n125;
    alliances, 68, 69, 74
Kirkwood, S. J., 217
Kit Foxes (Swift Fox society), 60,
    317n48
knowledge, family-based, 17–18
known geographic universe, 92

Lakotas, 10, 32, 53, 55, 67, 69, 80, 81,
    101, 104, 112, 183, 199, 326n29,
    340n1; as army scouts, 186–87;
    and Black Hills, 73, 124–25;
    Cheyenne relationships with,
    73–74, 105–6; Great Sioux War,
    123–24; negotiations with Nelson
    Miles, 138, 144–45; and Northern
    Cheyenne plight, 187–88; Northern
    Cheyennes with, 141, 167–68; at
    Pine Ridge, 193–94, 218, 219, 231,
    232, 301; at Red Cloud Agency,
    120, 167; treaties, 99, 102

Lame Deer, 141, 149, 279, 334n99;
   scouting against, 146, 147, 151
Lame Deer, Mont., 243, 292
Lame Deer Creek, Mont., 247
Lame Deer district, Northern
   Cheyenne reservation, 236, 293
land, 14, 20, 110, 152, 249; autonomy
   and, 295–96; Euro-American views
   of, 85–86, 97–98; relationships
   with, 84, 94–95; reservation as
   protected, 260–61, 293–94; sales
   of, 294–95, 296–97; survey of,
   272, 275, 277–78; treaties and,
   101–3; values of, 283
landscape, 103, 109, 258, 285; and
   kinship, 84–85, 286–87, 290, 297,
   302–3; and mobility, 89–90;
   multiple ethnic use of, 94–95;
   relationships with, 12, 55,
   89–94, 96–97, 241; and territory,
   95–96, 327n37
land tenure, ownership, 293;
   Cheyenne, 226–27; homesteading,
   246–47, 248–49; in Tongue River
   valley, 265–66
language, 32
Larson, L. C., 272–73
Last Bull, 141
leaders, leadership, 8; Cheyenne,
   145–46, 224–25, 230
Le Borgne, 69
Left Hand, 100
Left Handed Shooter, 141
letter-writing campaign, Little
   Chief, 202–3, 205, 227–31
Lightning Woman, 68
listening, 5–6, 22, 86–87
Little Bighorn River, Mont., 123–24
Little Chief, 137, 138, 139, 144, 172,
   259, 281, 283; in Indian Territory,
   168, 203–4; as leader, 224–25, 230;
   letter-writing campaign of, 202–3,
   205, 227–31; negotiations by,

208–11, 212–13, 214, 215–17,
   218–19, 233–35, 341–42n39; and
   Nelson Miles, 206–7; relocation
   to Pine Ridge, 217–18, 219–20;
   relocation to Tongue River
   valley, 231–32
Little Chief's people, 12–13, 250,
   340–41n20; Nelson Miles
   on, 206–7; removal, 203–4;
   resettlement of, 205, 214, 212–18,
   219–21, 231–32; in Sidney, 209,
   211–12, 341n21; and Tongue
   River valley, 222–23
Little Creek, 137, 141
Little Horse, 141
Little Raven, 141
Little Shield, 141
Little Wolf, 9, 10, 12, 105, 106, 139,
   157, 158, 174, 201, 243, 250, 296,
   340n73, 343n6; and Crook, 159–60;
   and removal negotiations,
   164–65; return to north, 175, 178,
   180–82, 197–98; self-banishment
   of, 241–42; U.S. negotiations
   with, 118, 119
Little Wolf's people, 12–13, 176;
   return north, 180–82, 214
Living Bear (Leaving Bear), 140,
   164–65, 168
Llewellyn, Karl N., 27
Lytle, Clifford, 31, 39–40

Mackenzie, Ranald S., 9, 17, 115,
   164, 165; attack on Dull Knife's
   village, 128, 167, 270
magpie, and Great Race, 91, 326n29
Ma'heo'o, 88
Mandans, 68, 71, 73, 99
Mann, Henrietta, 87, 88
Many Colored Braids, 141
Manypenny Commission, 125, 127
maps, 98
markers, territorial, 94

market economy, and Plains kinship
     system, 52–53
Marquis, Thomas, 138, 141, 231
marriages, 58, 68; polygamous, 56–57
Masikotas band, 71
massacres: Fort Robinson, 155,
     156–57, 191–93, 194, 195–96, 239;
     Sand Creek, 100–101; Wounded
     Knee, 232, 234
McGillicuddy, Valentine T., 195,
     220, 221, 222, 229; on Black Wolf,
     223, 224, 225
McKinley, William, 267, 284
McLaughlin, James, 278–79, 280–81,
     286; on expansion of reservation,
     282–83; and reservation
     boundaries, 283–84
Meat, 141
Medicine Bear, 140
medicine bundles, 54–55
Medicine Lodge Treaty, 102
Medicine Wolf, 141
migrations, Cheyenne, 53, 54, 68,
     322–23n125, 325nn6–7
Milburn, George, 254, 256, 271; on
     homesteads, 250–52, 255
Miles, John D., 168, 170, 171, 176,
     221–22; and control of Little
     Chief's band, 213–14, 215–16,
     218, 219, 220, 340–41n20; and
     Little Wolf's speech, 175
Miles, Nelson A., 114, 124, 128, 232,
     245–46, 275; alliances with, 226,
     227, 270, 275–77, 281–82, 301; on
     Cheyenne land rights, 238–39; on
     Cheyennes at Fort Keogh, 142–44,
     149, 195, 203, 205–6; negotiations
     with, 133–38, 144–45; relationships
     with, 146–48, 151, 152, 153–54,
     159, 233, 242–44, 263, 279–80,
     332n67, 340n73; on removal
     policy, 207–8, 211; on removed
     Cheyennes, 168–69; on "surrenders"
     at agencies, 139–40; and Two
     Moons's people, 116–17; winter
     campaign of, 131, 132
Miles City, Mont., 254, 255–56, 277–78
military model, of behavior, 64–65
military societies, 65, 80; structure
     and purpose of, 60–62; and
     summer camp circle, 63–64
Millen, S. W., on homesteaders,
     251–52, 255
Minneconjoux Lakotas (Sioux),
     141, 146
Minnesota, 53, 86, 89, 96
Missouri River, 73, 92, 96; peoples
     on, 67, 68–69; trade relationships
     on, 69–70
Mizner, John K., 214, 215
mobility: Cheyenne, 72, 263–64;
     and ties to landscape, 89–90
Montana, Cheyennes in, 152–53
Moore, John, 60, 64, 68, 72; on
     Cheyenne nation, 78–79; on
     Cheyenne origins, 53, 88; on
     flexible kin systems, 79–80
Morgan, Lewis Henry, 24, 132
Morgan, Thomas J., 279, 232
Morning Star. See Dull Knife
     (Morning Star)
Muddy Creek, Mont., 242, 243, 247,
     249, 257
Muddy district, Northern Chey-
     enne reservation, 236–37
murders, 52, 324n143, 343n6, 344n13;
     banishment for, 80, 241–42

nationalism, 25–26, 28; Cheyenne,
     39, 156–57
nationhood, versus self-govern-
     ment, 39–40
nation-state, 23, 25, 39, 51, 101,
     311n29, 312n36; boundaries
     of, 298–99; as means of
     recognition, 34–35

Native ground, 35–36
Native Hawaiians, 89
Native nations, 12, 27, 44, 51;
    identity and, 18–19; political
    autonomy of, 28–29, 41–42;
    sovereignty of, 30–31; use of
    term, 38–39
nature, reciprocity with, 84
Nebraska, 10, 180
negotiations: George Crook's,
    138–39, 159–60, 161, 163–65; kin
    relationships and, 234–35; Little
    Chief's, 208–9, 212–13, 214,
    216–17, 218–19, 228–29; Nelson
    Miles's, 133–38, 144–45, 146
Nez Perces, 148, 340n1
nisson, 49, 59
Northern Arapahos, 10, 101, 125,
    262; Great Sioux Wars, 123–24; at
    Red Cloud Agency, 119–20;
    treaties, 102, 103, 105; U.S.
    negotiations with, 118–19
Northern Cheyenne and Northern
    Arapaho Treaty, 105
Northern Cheyenne Fifty-Year
    Unallotment Program, 295
Northern Cheyenne reservation, 11,
    101, 244, 267; boundaries of, 5,
    227, 246, 257, 268, 270–71, 273–74,
    283–86; establishment of, 291,
    298–99; expansion of, 5, 269–70;
    formation of, 4, 196–97; land
    sales, 294–95, 296–97; military
    societies, 60–61; obtaining,
    152–53; as protected land base,
    260–62, 293–94
Northern Cheyennes, 37, 46, 54, 55,
    104, 213, 214; at agencies, 149–50;
    as army scouts, 143–44, 146–47,
    150–52, 153, 231–32, 238–39, 261,
    279; autonomy, 261–62; breakout
    from Fort Robinson, 190–93,
    195–97, 296, 298–99; diaspora,
108–9; as farmers and ranchers,
    148–49, 240; flight of, 11–12; at
    Fort Keogh, 116–17, 142–43, 204;
    at Fort Robinson, 188–90; and
    George Crook, 160–62; Great Sioux
    Wars, 123–24; homesickness,
    172–73; homesteading, 247–52,
    253–54; in Indian Territory,
    168–70, 218–19, 221–22; at Little
    Bighorn, 123–24; mobility of,
    225–26, 263–64; at Pine Ridge,
    193–94; and Red Cloud, 187–88;
    at Red Cloud Agency, 157–58,
    167–68; relationships with
    Nelson Miles, 134–38, 147–48,
    242–43; and removal policy,
    119–21, 125–27, 162–67, 198–200,
    203–8, 211; resistance by,
    108–9, 200–201; return to north,
    174–86, 197–98; separation of
    families, 173–74; "surrenders"
    of, 114–15, 129–30, 138–42,
    144–45; territory, 9–10; and
    Tongue River country, 280–82,
    303; treaties with, 102, 103,
    105, 106–7, 110–11; U.S. policy
    toward, 118–20

Oberly, John H., 275
obligations, 48, 65, 79, 230, 239
Ogallala, 103, 193, 194
Oivimana (Scabby) band, 70
Old Bear, 140
Old Crow, 173
Old Wolf (Cut Foot), 137, 138, 141
Omisis, 74
oral histories, 5, 18–19, 20, 87, 326n16
origin narratives, 87–88
Otter Creek, Mont., 224, 269;
    homesteads on, 248, 252, 256
outbreak, Northern Cheyenne
    journey as, 177, 296
Owl Woman, 70–71

Pawnee Killer, 101
Pawnees, 74, 102
Pawnee Woman, 159
peace, 76, 102; negotiations for, 77–78, 112
peace chiefs, behavior of, 64–65
peace policy, 239
People, the, Native group identity, 31–32
peoplehood, 32, 33
personal relationships, 4–5, 9, 19
Pine Ridge Agency, S.Dak., 81, 183, 231, 302; assistance from Lakotas at, 188, 301; life at, 229–30; Northern Cheyennes at, 186, 193–94, 195, 198, 217–18, 219–21, 234
Pipestone Quarry (Red Pipestone Quarry), Minn., 89, 326n20
Plains Apaches, 68, 102; in Black Hills, 71, 74; conflicts with, 74, 76
Plains peoples, 32, 51, 52, 67
plants, kinship with, 93–94, 241
Platte River, 96
Plenty Bears, 140
political action, kinship and, 12–13
political organizations, 29–30, 31, 35; duality in, 64–65; kinship networks and, 42–43, 300
political power, 106, 162; autonomous, 40–41; of kin-based groups, 41–42, 106
political units, kinship groups as, 12–13
polygamy, 56–57
Porcupine Bear, 80
Powder River, 99, 101, 123; as Northern Cheyenne territory, 9, 10, 54, 105, 127, 130–31, 182
Price, Hiram, 216, 220, 250, 256
prisoners of war: Northern Cheyennes as, 116, 161–62, 204, 242, 334n89; official designations as, 142–43

Public Land Leasing Act, 291, 293
public opinion, on Fort Robinson massacre, 194–95

quill workers' society, 60

raiding, 52, 76; in Kansas, 177–78, 337n59
ranches, ranchers: Euro-American, 254–55, 258; Northern Cheyenne, 228, 240
rations, 162, 221; Southern Cheyenne and Arapaho Reservation, 171, 174–75
reciprocity, 41, 43, 84; with landscape, 90–93; with plants and animals, 93–94; in social relationships, 305–6
Red Cloud, 103, 160, 183, 339n84; and Northern Cheyennes, 186, 187–88, 194, 198, 218, 219
Red Cloud Agency, 119, 123, 179, 183, 333nn80–81; Black Hills negotiations at, 124, 125; Northern Cheyennes at, 126, 130, 139, 140, 141, 157–58, 160, 161–62, 167–68, 200; removal from, 162–65, 166–67
Red Hat, 209
Red Owl, 140
Red Robe, 52
Red Shield society, 60, 317n48
Red War Bonnet, 181
Red Wolf, 228
Ree district, Northern Cheyenne reservation, 236
religion, 32, 54
removal, 158; to Indian Territory, 159, 166–67, 209–11; of Northern Cheyennes, 119–21, 125–27, 198–99, 203–4, 206–7, 271; treaty on, 307–8; U.S. policy of, 162–63, 194
research, 4–6
researchers, behavior of, 16–17

reservations, 81, 104, 106, 108–9,
130, 152; assimilation and, 239–40;
boundaries, 257, 346n3;
containment on, 127, 131; 1860s
treaties, 100, 101–3, 111;
petitioning for, 244, 245–46;
U.S. views toward, 117–18
resistance, 108, 200–201, 220–21
resources, access to, 94, 95
Rickers, Eli S., 138
Ridge Bear, 141, 209, 212
Rosebud district, Northern
Cheyenne reservation, 236
Rosebud River, Mont., 223, 243,
257; homesteads on, 224, 246,
247, 250, 251, 252, 256
Rowland, James, 191, 346n29
Rowland, William, 193, 215, 242;
and homesteads, 284, 344n17;
as interpreter, 165, 250,
346n29, 347n40

Sacred Arrows bundle, 54, 57, 58,
101, 140, 321n113
Sacred Buffalo Hat bundle, 50,
54–55, 57, 58, 101; keeper of,
139–40, 157–58
Sacred Hat Tipi, 73, 136
sacred history, 32, 54
sacred places, 55
Sand Creek massacre, 100–101,
155, 156
Saville, J. J., 161–62
Schofield, John M., 232
Schuyier, Lieutenant, 209
scouts: homesteading by, 246–48;
and Nelson Miles, 238–39; U.S.
army, 143–44, 146–47, 148, 150–52,
153, 183, 186–87, 198, 206, 208,
231–32, 261, 263, 279
Select Committee on the Removal
of the Northern Cheyenne, 132,
142–43, 163

self-determination, petitioning
for, 244–45
self-government, 39–40
settlers, Euro-American, 254–55, 268–69
settler society, 10, 36
Seven Major Crimes Act, 30, 344n13
Sheridan, P. H., 137, 138, 139, 176;
and Little Chief, 208, 209
Sherman, William Tecumseh, 137,
149, 217, 225
Short Hair, 106
Shoshone and Bannock
reservation, 216
Shoshones, 262
Sicangus, 103
Sidney, Neb., Little Chief's band at,
209, 211–12, 341n21
Silko, Leslie Marmon, 41
Siouan speakers, 53
Sioux Commission, 120
sisters, 61; in Cheyenne kin
networks, 49–50, 59
Sits Beside His Medicine, 141
Sits In the Night, 141
Sitting Bull, 148, 149, 151
Sleeping Rabbit, 137
Slow Woman, 192
smallpox epidemic, on Missouri
River, 73
Snow (White) Bird, 140, 141
social disorder, 52
social organization, 26, 197, 200;
and warfare decisions, 151–52
social relations, 80–81, 95, 285;
reciprocal, 305–6. See also kinship
social status, 140
societies, 60, 317n48. See also
military societies
Sooktis, Butch, 62
Sooktis, Rubie, 63, 293
Southern Arapahos, 101, 262
Southern Cheyenne agency, Indian
Territory, 9

Southern Cheyenne and Arapaho
    Reservation, Indian Territory,
    103, 107, 111, 140–41, 162, 313n56;
    Northern Cheyennes and, 118,
    119, 170, 171, 222
Southern Cheyennes, 10, 54, 112,
    139, 142, 165, 262, 323n127; 1865
    treaty, 101–2; in Indian Territory,
    140–41; and Northern Cheyennes,
    118, 168–70, 222
sovereignty, 29, 32; of Indigenous
    communities, 30–31, 34, 40; U.S.
    views of, 98–99
Spotted Elk, 139, 165
Spotted Tail, 101, 103, 138, 160, 163,
    336n10, 344n13
Spotted Tail Agency, Dakota
    Territory, 139, 161
Spotted Wolf, 141
squatters, on Northern Cheyenne
    homesteads, 283
Standing Elk, 119, 139, 152, 164–65,
    168, 199
Standing Elk, George, 283
Stands Different, 141
Stands In Timber, Elva, 83, 91, 106,
    113–14, 115, 137, 147, 273, 333n78;
    on Cheyenne origins, 87–88, 89;
    on homesickness, 172–73; on
    "surrender," 152–53; on Sweet
    Woman, 134–35
Stands In Timber, John, 56, 60,
    243, 152; on agency surrenders,
    140, 141; on Nelson Miles's
    negotiations, 135, 136, 137
Starving Elk, 241, 343n6
stories, storytelling, 13–15, 22,
    326n16; origin, 86–88
Straus, Anne, 78
Strong Left Hand (Arm), 140, 189
St. Vrain, Ceran, 70
Suhtaios, 50, 53, 57, 58, 65, 71, 74,
    86, 87, 89, 313n56, 316n37,

321n113, 325n8, 326n20; and
    Erect Horns, 54–55
Sun Dance, 50, 54, 59, 62, 64
surrenders, 114–15, 129–30; at agen-
    cies, 139–40, 161–62; perceptions
    of, 279, 280; reasons for, 144–45,
    152–53; U.S. push for, 126–27
surveillance, at Red Cloud Agency,
    161–62
surveys, land, 249, 254, 272, 275,
    277–78
survivance, 157
Svingen, Orlan J., 283, 299
Sweet Medicine, 31, 54, 86, 88,
    321nn112–13; societies organized
    by, 60, 63; Cheyenne unification
    of, 72–73
Sweet Woman, 275; and Nelson
    Miles's negotiation, 133–37
Swift Fox (Kit Fox) society, 60,
    317n48
Sword, George, 138

Tall Bull, 196–97
Tall White Man, 140
Tangle Hair (Big Head), 139, 140
Tangled Yellow Hair, James, 231
territory, 25, 238; defining, 95–96;
    marking, 94, 327n37; Native rela-
    tionships with, 89–90; Northern
    Cheyenne, 9–10; treaty assign-
    ment of, 99–100, 101–3, 111–12;
    U.S. views of, 98–99
Terry, Alfred, 123
Teton Sioux/Lakota, 71, 74
Thomas, Captain, 220
tobacco, gifting with, 160
Tongue River Cantonment, 128
Tongue River country, Mont., 273;
    Black Wolf's people on, 227,
    239–40; Euro-Americans in, 254;
    homesteading in, 240, 248–52,

255–56, 282–83, 284; land tenure in, 238–39, 265–66; Little Chief's people and, 208–9, 222–23, 231–32, 233; Northern Cheyennes in, 223–24, 228, 241, 243–44, 264, 267, 274, 279–82, 301, 303

trade relationships, 68, 72, 76, 77, 79, 112; adoption and intermarriage and, 69–71

transmotion, 89–90

treaties, 30, 98, 101, 302, 329n76; Fort Laramie (1851), 99–100; Fort Wise, 100; Medicine Lodge, 102; Native understanding of, 104–5; Northern Cheyennes and, 10, 106–7, 119; removal, 307–8. *See also* Fort Laramie Treaty (1868)

tribal nations, 27–28

tribal relations, and Indian Homestead Act, 247, 251

tribes, 33, 81; definition of, 26–27

Tsistsistas, 50, 53, 54, 55, 57, 65, 74, 86, 87, 89, 313n56, 316n37, 321n113, 325n8, 326n20

Tully, John, 277

Turkey Legs, 140, 168

Twin Woman, 68, 133

Two Moons, 12, 140, 250, 261, *276;* and Nelson Miles, 116–17, 134, 137–38, 145, 153–54, 159, 243, 246; and Northern Cheyenne reservation, 152–53; and Tongue River country, 254–55, 280–81

Two Moons's people, 12–13, 183, 214; at Fort Keogh, 139, 140, 142–43; and Nelson Miles, 137–38, 153–54

United States, 30; as benefactor, 10–11; military campaigns, 114–16; relationships with, 105–6, 108–9, 110–11; reservation program, 117–18; territorial sovereignty, 98–99

Upshaw, R. L., 273–75

U.S. Army, 176; and Black Hills gold rush, 121–22; after Little Bighorn, 124–25; Plains campaign, 114–16; scouts for, 143–44, 146–47, 148, 150–52, 153, 183, 186–87, 198, 206, 208, 231–32, 261, 263, 279; winter campaign, 127–29, 131–32

U.S. Bureau of Indian Affairs, 294, 295, 319n80

U.S. Indian Office (Office of Indian Affairs), 102, 153, 223, 224, 270, 271, 291; and Little Chief's band, 215, 217–18

U.S. Peace Commission, 102

U.S. Senate, Miles statements to, 207–8

U.S. War Department, 217

Utes, 102

violence, colonial, 36, 37

Vizenor, Gerald: on survivance, 157; on transmotion, 89–90

Vroom, P. D., 194

Walks On Crutches, 141

warfare, 74; interethnic kin ties and, 76–77; military societies, 60–61; and Northern Cheyenne removal, 125–27; Plains groups–U.S., 114–16, 122, 123–24; strategic positioning during, 151–52; after Sand Creek Massacre, 101–2

water, ancestors and, 92

water birds, 88

Weasel Bear, 141

Wessels, Henry W., 189–90

Whirlwind, 118

White Bear, 144

White Buffalo, 141

White Bull (Ice), 137–38, 147, 206, 224, 251, 252, 277

White Bull Hump, 144
White Bull's people, 139
White Dirt (Clay), 140
White Elk, 141, 281
White Hawk, 141, 334–35n99
White Necklace, 87
White River agencies, 139, 141. *See
    also* Red Cloud Agency; Spotted
    Tail Agency, Dakota Territory
White Thunder, 71, 137
White Wolf, 137, 141
Wild Hog, 139, 164, 169, 172, 183,
    189; on Indian Territory, 174–75
Wind River Agency, Wyo., 141
Wolf, Eric, 26; on kin-based
    groups, 41–42
Wolf Medicine, 140
Woman's Dress, 193
women, 59, 60; intermarriage by,
    70–71; and military societies,
    61–62; as war captives, 76–77
Wooden Leg, 128–29, 136, 138–39,
    141; on removal, 163–64, 166, 174
Woodenlegs, John, 294, 295, 296–97

Wooden Thigh, Teddy, 78
Wotapios band (Cheyenne/Kiowa),
    70, 71, 76; conflicts with
    Lakotas, 73–74
Wounded Knee, S.Dak., 183;
    massacre at, 232, 234
Wrapped Hair, 141

Yellow Calfskin Shirt (Broken
    Dish), 140, 165, 168
Yellow Eagle, 141
Yellow Hair, 141
Yellow Haired Woman, 87
Yellow Horse, 141
Yellow Nose, 140
Yellow Wolf, 70
Yoakam, George, 223, 227, 274;
    homesteading, 251, 252; petition-
    ing for reservation,
    244–45, 246–47, 259, 269–70;
    protection of Northern
    Cheyennes, 268–69

Zapatista communities, 40